D1531450

DATE DUE

Animal Variety

Fourth Edition
Animal Variety
An Evolutionary Account

Lawrence S. Dillon
Texas A & M University

ＵＣＢ
Wm. C. Brown Company Publishers
Dubuque, Iowa

Contents

Preface

Ten million species—think of it—ten *million* species of animals have been estimated to be alive on earth today. Such an amazing amount of animal variety is almost inconceivable. Were descriptions of all these extant forms published together in book form, with only one page devoted to a species, the resulting 10,000-volume set of 1,000-page tomes would require nearly a half mile of shelving to hold it!

Hence, no single textbook can hope to do more than to provide a glimpse into the vast array of diversification, let alone this one which is more compact than the others. To achieve adequate coverage and yet maintain economical proportions, included material has been carefully selected as to its relevance to an understanding of the nature of the differentiation that has occurred in the animal world. To provide that insight, differences between the numerous taxa must be pointed out, not of structure alone, but of functions, habits, relations to the environment, and those frequent special adaptations that make systematic zoology the fascinating science it is. To achieve the necessary conciseness, the long, tedious descriptions of morphology and taxonomy that characterize too many books on the subject have been reduced to a minimum. Insofar as possible the data of classification are presented in tabular form and the morphological details are shown in figures specifically designed for clarity at the introductory level of the subject. Together, then, the text, tables, and illustrations can be found to provide a firm foundation for full semester courses in either systematic or invertebrate zoology.

The presentation of the various factual aspects, then, is the goal of this expanded new edition, but not only of those facets. It also seeks, wherever possible, to suggest the paths along which the particular peculiarities of each major taxon may have been acquired. Or rather, it usually presents two or three conflicting interpretations of the data, not only to provide a choice for the students, but to enable them better to perceive the nature of the problems involved in making phylogenetic decisions. Such evolutionary histories lead to a fuller appreciation of the nature of the respective adaptations, but they also facilitate an understanding of the processes of change which have brought them into being. Thus the basic principles of evolution interweave the pages of the entire text to present the representative forms as vital, active organisms, responding day by day to short-term stimuli and to changing environments over the long periods of geologic time.

To provide greater depth as well as breadth, the suggested readings at the close of each chapter attempt to list readily available recent books and articles written from a diversity of approaches. Functional and behavioral, molecular and structural, evolutionary and ecological topics alike are included insofar as possible. Here again careful sampling has been necessary, for the literature rivals the animal world in quantity of diversification. However, page numbers and the resulting economic impact on the student also must receive full consideration, with brevity an essential consequence.

True mastery of a subject involves both a thorough knowledge of the factual matter and an understanding of that information, especially an appreciation of the interrelations involved. To assist the student in achieving such a goal, questions have now been included at the end of each chapter, which are of two principal types. The first includes more or less straightforward queries or statements that are designed to draw out the main points or to organize and condense the subject matter. In contrast, the second type, often closely interwoven with the first, helps in making comparisons of one group of organisms with another, in judging the relative strengths and weaknesses of two opposing schools of thought, and in perceiving possible evolutionary relationships. The evolutionary summaries have been added to each of the metazoan chapters to achieve the same end. It is hoped that in thus stimulating inquiring minds, perhaps a few students will be challenged into investigating the numerous unsolved problems of relationships that still persist in zoological systematics, which is what the subject of animal variety is all about.

Many persons have assisted in the preparation of this fourth edition through helpful suggestions and discussions. To all these colleagues I am deeply grateful and regret that each cannot be mentioned by name. Special thanks are due to several individuals, including Dr. William G. Degenhardt, University of New Mexico, and Ken Nemouras, both of whom generously supplied a number of their personal photographs of reptiles and amphibians. Finally, to my wife, who has typed the manuscript and has collaborated throughout the completion of this revision, I am more grateful than can possibly be stated here.

Lawrence S. Dillon

The Prelude to Animal Variety

1

Throughout most of mankind's history, living things were believed endowed with a mysterious force, the life principle, whose nature and origin were forever beyond reach of human comprehension. In more recent centuries, however, as analyses of the chemical constitution of organisms were made, it became increasingly clear that animals and plants are composed of the very same elements found in other physical objects and that the ordinary principles of chemistry apply equally to animals as to inanimate things. Only the specific compounds that compose living matter were found distinct from those of the inorganic world. Then, for many decades, such organic chemicals were believed incapable of being produced artificially—until Wöhler prepared urea in the test tube! The subsequent history of organic synthetic products is much too familiar to need repeating here.

Nevertheless, making such carbon-based compounds in laboratories and chemical plants is one thing and understanding how living creatures themselves arose on an inorganic earth is quite another. Before any inkling of understanding could be gained, it was necessary to learn of the complex interlocking chemical reactions which supply cells with their energy, new protoplasm, and other requirements. These metabolic processes themselves are not the concern here, however, only the current concepts of how the necessary biochemical ingredients may have arisen spontaneously billions of years ago and thereby set the stage for the eventual development of animal variety. The early products obviously simply did not mix together and result immediately in living organisms—at least four long major stages and innumerable lesser ones must have intervened. Some of the chief events that may have occurred in this interval are suggested in table 1.1.

THE ORIGIN OF LIFE'S MATERIALS

In concepts of life's origins, it is consistently agreed that life as it is known today could not arise under present earth conditions. First, any biochemical molecules usable by living things would be quickly consumed by bacteria, protozoans, or other forms of life. Thus *sterile conditions* are deemed essential for the creation of life by spontaneous means. Second, the earth's atmosphere now not only lacks certain of the necessary ingredients, but its abundant proportions of oxygen also would oxidize and quickly destroy any organic compound that might arise.

Table 1.1 Possible Major Stages in the Early Evolution of Life

Stage	Name	Chief Events	Example of Products
I.	Molecular	Creation of organic molecules	Amino acids, sugars, purines
II.	Polymeric	Polymerization of molecules	Proteins, nucleic acids, starches
III.	Semibiotic (interacting systems) or	Interaction of polymers	Coacervates, microspheres (protobionts)
	Precellular	Evolution of genetic apparatus	Viruses
IV.	Cellular	Formation of simple cells	Cell membrane, internal cell organization

Generally it is conceded that the primitive earth had a *reducing atmosphere,* more like the atmosphere of Uranus and Neptune than the oxidizing one that now exists here. Hence, hydrogen must have been an important constituent along with nitrogen, while uncombined oxygen was nearly absent. In addition, helium, argon, methane, and ammonia were probably abundant, and generous proportions of carbon dioxide, carbon monoxide, water vapor, and hydrogen sulfide possibly also were present.

The Molecular Stage

By use of various mixtures of gases to simulate the type of atmosphere conjectured to exist on the primeval earth, it has been found to be amazingly easy to create most of the basic ingredients of life, including amino acids, purines and pyrimidines, and simple sugars. To produce any of these classes of biochemicals, the basic principles are the same—a gas mixture including methane (or ethane), water, various other ingredients, and a suitable outside energy source.

A wide variety of energy sources has been employed successfully by experimenters. In the first ones of recent years, those by S.L. Miller, electric sparks were used with a gas mixture containing H_2, NH_3, CH_4, and H_2O. Upon analysis of the product, four amino acids (glycine, alanine, and aspartic and glutamic acids) were found, along with several other important biochemicals, such as formic and acetic acids. Following this example, electric discharge, which simulated lightning in the atmosphere, was widely used in conducting studies employing a great variety of primitive atmospheres and experiencing varying degrees of success.

Another energy source that proved popular in experimental investigations of prebiotic syntheses was ultraviolet light. Even today, in the presence of an ozone layer in the atmosphere, ultraviolet rays from the sun provide nearly 150 times as many calories annually as lightning. Since oxygen was probably nearly absent from the primitive atmosphere, ozone would have been too, so in early earth history even more energy from this source could have been available. Results with ultraviolet radiation at first were negative until favorable short wavelengths eventually were found; then several teams of investigators were able to produce a diversity of amino acids. A later modification used the longer wavelengths by adding a light receiving substance such as hydrogen sulfide, thereby avoiding exposing the products to the deleterious effects of short ultraviolet rays.

High energy (or ionizing) radiation usually is considered to break down amino and nucleic acids, but, surprisingly, it was found capable also of producing these substances. For example, glycine and aspartic acid were synthesized by exposing solutions of ammonium acetate to an electron beam. Heat also has proved effective in such syntheses, and one unexpected source of heat—shockwaves, such as thunder—has been demonstrated to be highly efficient as a synthesizer. It was found that shockwaves could convert gas mixtures to amino acids at an efficiency of up to 36 percent. Purine and pyrimidine bases also have been produced by similar methods.

The Polymeric Stage

Living things, however, do not consist of simple molecules like amino acids and nitrogenous bases, but of such great macromolecular polymers as proteins and nucleic acids. Hence, after the simpler products of prebiotic syntheses had eventually reached the seas either directly or by way of rain and rivers, further processing was necessary in the resulting "primitive soup."

Since this primitive soup undoubtedly was relatively dilute and because the polymerizing processes involved the removal of water from the constituents, a thermodynamic problem arose. The difficulty is best illustrated by means of an imagined synthesis of a small protein with a molecular weight of only 12,000. If all the amino acids necessary were present in molar concentrations, that is between 15 and 30 percent by weight, it would require a volume 10^{50} times the size of the earth to produce a single molecule of the protein by spontaneous means!

One way of avoiding the problem is by eliminating the water, and accordingly anhydrous methods have been widely explored by investigations of the polymeric stage. For example, one line of research used two amino acids (aspartic and glutamic acids) which melt without serious decomposition; when melted, these substances served as solvents for mixtures of other amino acids that interacted with one another and the solvents while in solution. Upon cooling, the products were found to consist of *proteinoids*—polymers of amino acids which resembled true proteins in many ways. Other workers have substituted complex phosphorus compounds for the molten aspartic and glutamic acids in anhydrous experiments and have had similar success.

In contrast, a number of investigators have found ways of producing polymers directly in primitive souplike suspensions, in spite of the presence of water. Such energy sources as light and X rays have been able to synthesize short peptides from aqueous solutions of amino acids, but only in small quantities. Various condensing agents have been much more successful, for they are capable of removing water from amino acids or nucleotides and inducing polymerization even when these substances are in aqueous solutions.

Among the first of the condensing agents to be tried was hydrogen cyanide, a by-product of many prebiotic syntheses; other prebiotic compounds related to cyanide, however, have proven more efficacious. Included among the outstanding types are cyanamide and dicyanamide, whose molecular structure is illustrated (fig. 1.1); with these, peptides of some complexity have been produced.

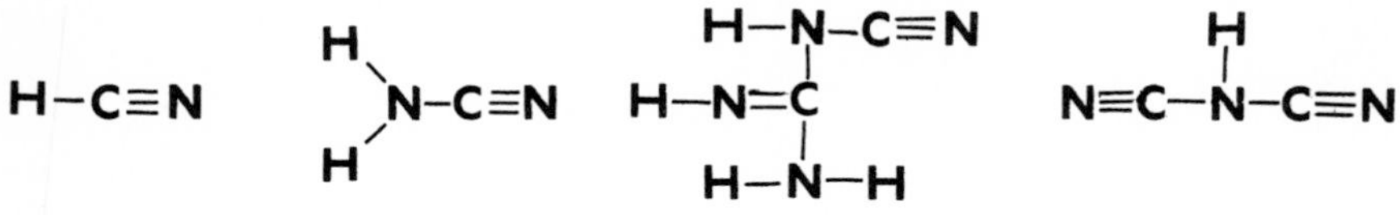

H—C≡N   H\N—C≡N (with H above and below)   H—N—C≡N / H—N=C / H—N—H   H / N≡C—N—C≡N

A. HYDROGEN CYANIDE   B. CYANAMIDE   C. DICYANDIAMIDE   D. DICYANAMIDE

Figure 1.1 *Molecular structure of some condensing agents.* The triple-bonded carbon-nitrogen combination is an essential feature of each agent.

Clay minerals, especially kaolinite and montmorillonite, also are effective in this same capacity through their ability to adsorb water and many types of amino acids.

As a whole, the experiments producing and polymerizing amino acids have been more successful than those with nucleotides. One reason for this is that nucleotide molecules have many more sites available at which they can be joined in chains during polymerization than do the amino acids, so many more atypical bonds are formed in experimental syntheses. Thus, to date many "polynucleotides" have been synthesized experimentally by use of condensing agents or related techniques, but no true nucleic acids have been.

DEVELOPMENT OF LIVING THINGS

Between the primitive soup that filled the primeval seas and the first living cell, a variety of intermediate forms must have existed, for even the simplest organism is infinitely more complex than the richest broth. In attempts to discover what some of the earlier precursor stages, or *protobionts,* may have been like, several different avenues of investigation have been followed.

Coacervates

The earliest major line of research was begun by A.I. Oparin, who showed that peculiar colloidal droplets have certain lifelike properties. These droplets, called *coacervates* (fig. 1.2), are formed when a dilute solution of a simple protein such as gelatin is mixed with one of a complex sugar like gum arabic at moderate temperatures. Under suitable conditions, the two substances interact, causing the solution to become turbid. This turbidity has been found to result from the formation of coacervates, which are simply clusters of the interacting molecules that range between 2 and 670 μ in diameter. One of their most outstanding traits is the ability to remove colloidal material from the surrounding medium and concentrate it within themselves. In so doing, the droplets increase in size and thus grow much as living things do. But unlike organisms, the concentration of organic matter within the coacervates decreases as the droplets themselves grow. Thus large ones are so dilute as to be scarcely differentiated from the medium in which they are suspended.

They have been made, however, to carry out a number of lifelike processes. For instance, they can absorb certain materials such as dyes and amino acids, but

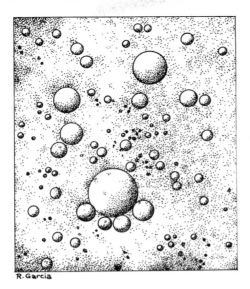

Figure 1.2 *Coacervates.* These colloidal droplets are quite minute, as they are less than 1 micron in diameter. (From Dillon, Lawrence S.; *Evolution,* 2nd ed., St. Louis, 1978, The C. V. Mosby Co.)

R. Garcia

not sugars, from the surrounding medium. In some tests they were found capable of breaking down sugars when a suitable enzyme was added and these droplets have even carried out some of the steps in cell respiration. In still other experiments, when chlorophyll, ascorbic acid, and a hydrogen-accepting dye were incorporated into the system, the droplets proved capable of carrying out photosynthesis in the presence of light. Unfortunately, coacervates are usually ephemeral and rarely last more than 30 minutes.

Proteinoid Microspheres

A second approach to the problem has been by way of another type of colloidal droplet formed by entirely different procedures. In the preceding pages a method of forming proteinoids was described in which molten aspartic or glutamic acids served as the solvent for mixtures of other amino acids. If, after such a mixture has interacted, it is plunged into boiling water and the suspension is permitted to cool, the presence of minute droplets may be detected by microscopic examination. These *proteinoid microspheres,* as their discoverers called them, also display a few characteristics of living things. They do not grow to the same extent as coacervates do, but they have been observed to engage in simple binary fission, largely as a consequence of surface tension. Budding, such as yeast cells do, is an even more outstanding characteristic (fig. 1.3). If the suspension containing such budding microspheres is heated or jolted mechanically, the buds are released; after release these may increase in size to the parental dimensions and in turn may be induced to bud. Moreover, a number of microspheres have been found to be capable of performing enzymatic activities, including transaminations, removal of carboxyl radicals, and other processes characteristic of cells. Their greatest flaw is their extreme sensitivity to acidity, for they disrupt under the slightest changes in pH.

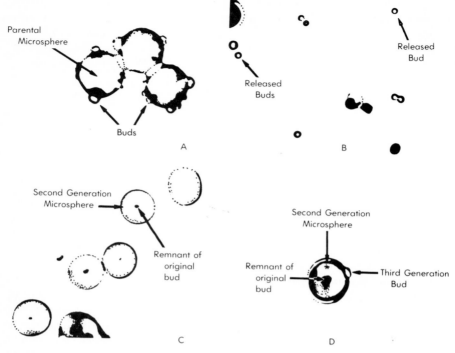

Figure 1.3 *Budding in proteinoid microspheres*. Among the peculiar properties of these colloidal droplets is their ability to bud, much in the manner of yeast cells as shown in this series of photomicrographs. (A) The original microspheres have produced buds that are released by mechanical shock (B). In turn these buds grow into microspheres (C), which then can produce a third generation by budding (D). (Courtesy of Professor Sidney W. Fox.)

A Biological Approach

Although the two experimental models presented above and others created by comparable means provide information as to how the earliest forebears of living things *may* have arisen, they fail to indicate how they *actually* did. Hence a number of biologists are persuaded that it would be advantageous to examine the only known objects which possess properties of both living and nonliving matter, the viruses. Because the viruses cannot multiply except in living cells, they were formerly believed to be degenerate bacteria of sorts, but later they were more widely considered fragments of cells or liberated genes from advanced types of organisms. Now it is becoming increasingly evident that they are actually very primitive organisms. The point of view presented by adherents of this theory is that if the early seas ultimately became sufficiently enriched in organic matter that cellular organisms could evolve from the contents, then viruslike particles certainly should have been able to live and reproduce in it before the cell arose. Nevertheless, the following brief account should be viewed as entirely conjectural.

The starting place for the account, in the form of a model of the earliest protobiont, is one of the simplest and very smallest viruses known, the causative agent of a disease of sheep known as scrapie. As this virus has now been demonstrated to contain neither nucleic acids nor lipids, it consists entirely of proteins, yet these proteins are capable of being replicated within the sheep cells by methods that still have not been deciphered. On the basis of this evidence and for theoretical reasons, the very earliest protobionts may be considered to have been extremely minute and consisted of simple proteins that were capable of replicating themselves, using amino acids drawn from the primitive soup. Since thus there is no cell membrane to contain the protein molecules—one does not come into existence until late in this account—all the reactions of reproduction and the like took place directly in the enriched seas.

From this point, the remainder of the account suggests, from evidence drawn from viruses or cellular processes, how the genetic mechanism as we know it today was gradually developed. The simplest stage of protobiontic life after the one described above apparently is represented by processes recently found in mammalian cells. As in these processes the proteins are built enzymatically without ribosomes, messenger RNA, or DNA, only transfer RNAs are involved along with the enzymes. Hence, it appears that transfer RNAs were the first nucleic acid to be employed in building proteins; then, as now, they expedite those processes by carrying amino acids to the scene of action (fig. 1.4).

To judge from some other very simple viruses, the next type of nucleic acid added to the protein-building processes in the protobionts was messenger RNA. It should be noted here that these protein-synthesizing steps, even the simplest

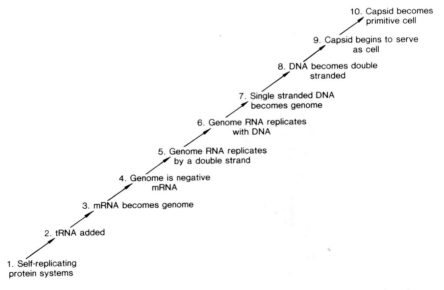

Figure 1.4 *Apparent stages in the early development of life.* Stages 1 and 3 to 9 are represented by extant viruses; stage 2 occurs as the "soluble system" in animal cells; and stage 10 is found among chlamyids, such as the ornithosis agent.

ones, actually represent the genetic mechanism of the organism, for the sole function of the genetical apparatus is that of producing proteins and the nucleic acids used in their production. A number of viruses, especially those like tobacco mosaic virus that attack plants, are very small, and possess no DNA; only messenger and transfer RNAs and but two or three kinds of proteins are present. However, there is a whole series of viral types, including many pathogens of man and other animals, that seem to represent a progression leading from these simpler forms to viruses which are quite large, contain a number of proteins, and eventually acquire a lipid coat around the latter substances. At the lower end of the series, the messenger RNA that served as the genetic material, or *genome*, was translated directly into proteins; later, copies of the genome were first transcribed to make active messenger. Still later a template of DNA was transcribed from the genomic RNA but was temporary, only serving in the replication of the RNA, which substance still served as the means of inheritance. This higher level of viral evolution provides the basis for "reverse transcription" that still is carried out in human and other complex cellular organisms.

A second series of steps of increasing complexity leads from this point. Whereas the earlier RNA viruses had only a single chain of RNA that is replicated and passed to later generations, the more advanced kinds developed a double molecule of RNA, the most complex ones of which used DNA during replication as shown above. At the next subsequent evolutionary level the RNA genome is replaced by a single-stranded molecule of DNA which has the advantage of being even more inert than RNA. This molecule is replicated by the formation of a second molecule in complementary sequence, and at the very most advanced levels, a permanent double-stranded DNA molecule finally came into service as the genome. At the latter levels, too, the viruses developed the third major variety of RNA (ribosomal) that provides a basis on which numerous proteins serve in reading messenger RNAs and building proteins.

While the proteins and nucleic acids of viruses are active only when free within the cells of their hosts, like the ancestral protobiont that used materials directly from the primitive broth, an inactive stage called the *virion* exists in almost all viruses. In a sense, this virion corresponds to a spore, for it is inert and serves principally in dissemination of the species from one host to another. As a rule, the virion is formed of a number of proteins arranged as a coat or capsid surrounding the genome and other proteins; frequently, too, it is coated with lipids as mentioned before. In those forms that have complex genomes, the capsid becomes double, and consists of two separated layers of proteins. At the very most advanced levels, the proteins within the capsid no longer remain completely inactive but start the processes of translating the DNA before emergence occurs, as in the pox virus. Thus the capsid and its contents begin to correspond to the cell; the steps ending its conversion into the cell appear to be marked by such chlamyids as the ornithosis agent, while the first actual cell seems to be represented by the smaller types of rickettsias.

No matter how fallacious the above conjectural account may ultimately prove to be, one thing is evident—even before life in a strict sense had arisen, its predecessors of necessity exhibited the ability to diversify. In the absence of this capacity, the stepwise transition from the brothlike seas into true organisms never could have been accomplished. It is this early acquired attribute, adaptation by evolutionary change, which eventually led to the wide variety of animal life which provides the theme for the following pages.

QUESTIONS FOR REVIEW AND THOUGHT

1. What features of the primordial earth were different from those of today and in what ways? Why might it have been essential for the formation of life that the primitive atmosphere was reducing (H_2) or oxidized (CO_2, H_2O, CO) rather than strongly oxidizing (O_2) as at present?

2. What two types of biochemicals are necessary in order for life to begin to form? What chemical and physical ingredients are necessary for the formation of each type?

3. What types of energy sources have been found capable of synthesizing amino acids from primitive atmospheres?

4. After the basic molecules have been formed, what else is needed for life's origin? What specific macromolecules are necessary and how can each be formed?

5. Define coacervates and proteinoid microspheres. What features does each type possess that makes it favorable as a model of a protobiont? What are the principal weaknesses of each?

6. What weakness is inherent to all synthetic models of primitive living things?

7. What might some sort of genetic apparatus be requisite for any primitive organism to undergo evolutionary development?

8. Describe the biological concept for precellular life. What are the principal steps in life's origin that the viruses seem to represent? What are the chief strong points and weaknesses of this concept?

SUGGESTIONS FOR FURTHER READING

Abel, E.L. 1973. *Ancient views on the origins of life*. Rutherford, N.J., Fairleigh Dickinson University Press.

Argyle, E. 1978. Chance and the origin of life. *Orig. Life*, 8:287–298.

Brooke, S., and S.W. Fox. 1977. Compartmentalization in proteinoid microspheres. *Bio Systems*, 9:1–22.

Cavalier-Smith, T. 1975. The origin of nuclei and of eukaryotic cells. *Nature*, 256:463–468.

Dickerson, R.E. 1978. Chemical evolution and the origin of life. *Scient. Amer.*, 239(3):70–80.

Dillon, L.S. 1978. *The genetic mechanism and the origin of life*. New York, Plenum Press. (Chapters 1, 2, and 10 are especially pertinent).

Farley, J. 1977. *The spontaneous generation controversy from Descartes to Oparin.* Baltimore, Md., Johns Hopkins University Press.

Murray, B., S. Gulkis, and R.E. Edelson. 1978. Extraterrestrial intelligence: An observational approach. *Science,* 199:485–492.

Sagan, C. 1974, *The cosmic connection: An extra-terrestrial perspective.* Garden City, N.Y., Anchor Press.

Animal Variety and Relationships 2

Back in the days of the early Greek philosophers, it was quite a simple matter to become familiar with all the diversification that existed among what were then considered to be animals. In the first place, the life of but a relatively small part of the globe was known in those times. Secondly, microscopic forms, such as protozoans and bacteria, were of course unknown; and thirdly, only such actively moving creatures as worms, insects, crabs, spiders, fish, birds, and mammals were classed as animals. Corals, sponges, and other sessile organisms were placed in a distinct category called the Zoophyta by Aristotle; this group, whose name means "animal-plants," was separated from both animals and plants, being viewed as intermediate between those two types.

This simple arrangement persisted throughout most of the Middle Ages, until two series of events suddenly upset the world of biologists. The first of these consisted of the extensive explorations into previously unknown corners of the world, bringing to light many living things completely unknown to the Greek fathers of biology. But the second, the advent and development of the microscope, had an even more profound effect, for this instrument opened a whole new world of life, disclosing a seemingly endless variety of new organisms, whose existence previously never had been so much as suspected.

EARLY SCHEMES OF CLASSIFICATION

By the end of the eighteenth century, even after more than 200 years of world and microscopic explorations, relatively little of the extent of variation among animals had become apparent. When Carl Linné, the father of the modern system of classification, first published his outline of animal nomenclature in 1758, he included names and descriptions of all the animals then known; yet only about 4,000 species were described in the 700 pages of his volume. Because the extent of variation was both unknown and unappreciated, he grouped all of the animals he listed into six *classes*—not phyla, it should be noted, as the latter category did not come into use until a considerable number of years later. It is interesting to observe that in his scheme he continued the early superficiality of his forerunners, for his six major subdivisions consisted of the Mammalia, Aves, Amphibia, Pisces, Insecta, and Vermes—four for the vertebrates and only two for all the invertebrates, including the unicellular forms.

But one must bear in mind that in those days, the early concepts of *abiogenesis*[1] were still prevalent to some extent. Hence the attitude existed, that, if worms and microscopic life could arise from muck or fermenting broths, their form and structure certainly could hold very little of real significance.

However, a somewhat better appreciation of the invertebrates came even before Pasteur's studies in 1862 forever ended the notions of spontaneous generation. These advances were provided by the then new science of paleontology, the study of fossil organisms, because in the rocky strata of the earth invertebrates occur in far greater variety than do the vertebrates. The first advances were provided by two French paleontologists and zoologists, J.B. Lamarck in 1809 and 1815 and G. Cuvier in 1816 and 1829. In Cuvier's scheme of classification, the invertebrates were separated from the vertebrates and then subdivided into three classes. To accomplish this, the annelids and almost all the arthropods were united under the name Articulata, the brachiopods and barnacles were placed in the Mollusca, and the remaining invertebrates were classed as the Radiata, including many that were not radiate. Lamarck's scheme went even further and established many more invertebrate classes—ten in his earlier version and twelve in his later versions. His classes included the Mollusca, Cirripedia (barnacles), Annelida, Crustacea, Arachnida, Insecta, Infusoria (rotifers and some protozoans), Polypes (sponges, polypoid coelenterates, and certain protozoans), Radiata (jellyfish, ctenophores, and echinoderms), Vermes (flukes, tapeworms, roundworms, and a few earthworms), Tunicata, and Conchifera (ostracods, brachiopods, and certain mollusks). In spite of Lamarck's scheme being vastly superior, that of Cuvier was more widely accepted and dominated zoological thinking until about 1850.

Since the latter date, studies on the embryology and life history of the many forms, as well as on their cytology and habits, have gradually contributed to a better understanding of the relationships of the great variety of animal life now known. While the concept of evolution has contributed to an appreciation of how diversification originated, more detailed researches on morphology and new fossil discoveries have added to our comprehension of its nature, as have additions to the list of described species—the list, it might be pointed out, currently includes no fewer than a million forms. Obviously, this weight of numbers alone makes the study of animal life far more complicated for the modern zoologist than it was for the Greeks. Yet the knowledge of existing creatures enables us to wander through the densest forest without fear of being attacked by a griffin, nor do travelers need to pause to answer riddles posed by a sphinx, for the extensive information available about what does exist has also, to a large extent, established what does not.

MODERN SCHEMES OF CLASSIFICATION

Although much thus is now well in hand about the extensiveness of variety among animals, all is not cut and dried by any means so far as the extent and significance of the diversification is concerned. For instance, though the figure

1. The theory that living things arise spontaneously from mud, offal, slime, decaying flesh, and the like.

of one million species cited above may appear quite impressive—and admittedly it is a large number—biologists generally believe that this represents perhaps only a tenth of the total actually extant on earth today.

Nor are the implications of kinships always clear and universally agreed upon. At the present time there is considerable disagreement in the literature over even the number of principal subdivisions into which living things appear to be arranged. Although most systematists still adhere to the concept that there are two kingdoms,[2] one of plants, the other of animals, some suggest three or four, or even ten or more, and still others try to show that all life is one and that it is, therefore, not divisible into separate kingdoms. A brief review of these major concepts may be pertinent.

The Two-Kingdom System

Although this scheme of classification is often called the classical one in the sense that it has been employed during most of biology's existence as a formal science, from a stricter standpoint this is a misnomer. As was seen above, certain Greek scholars, including Aristotle, added a third kingdom for sponges, corals, and other sessile life, and it was this scheme that persisted through much of classical and medieval times. Hence the two-kingdom scheme might be more appropriately referred to as the ''neoclassical.''

In any event, the content, not the name, of the system is the principal concern here. Since the major features are doubtless already quite familiar, the discussion need be detailed only enough to call to mind the particulars for later comparisons. First, two kingdoms are set up, one for plants, the second for animals (fig. 2.1). In the Plantae are placed those forms which as a rule are immotile, usually have walls about their cells, and either manufacture their food by photosynthesis or are saprophytic. This kingdom is divided into the *Embryophyta*, which have an embryo during their development, and the *Thallophyta* that lack such a developmental stage. The latter is then subdivided into photosynthetic *Algae* and saprophytic *Fungi* and further arranged into divisions as shown in table 2.1. Usually bacteria and yeasts are included in the latter category.

As a rule the Animal Kingdom is divided into two subkingdoms, one for the unicellular *Protozoa*, the other for the multicellular *Metazoa*. Occasionally the sponges are removed from the latter as a separate subkingdom called the *Parazoa*, but this is exceptional to the more general treatment of the group as the most primitive phylum among the metazoans. The Protozoa formerly were divided into five classes, but this number is more frequently reduced to four. These four are the *Flagellata* or *Mastigophora*, flagellated throughout much of their life histories; the *Sarcodina*, amoeboid forms that move by pseudopods; the *Sporozoa*, parasitic species with no means of locomotion as adults; and the *Ciliophora*, with bristles, or cilia, over their surfaces, at least in the juvenile

2. The hierarchy of categories commonly used in classifying animals has the *kingdom* as the largest unit, which is usually broken into a number of *subkingdoms*. Typically the latter are divided into *phyla*, these into *classes*, which in turn are broken into *orders*, and the latter into *families*. A family consists of a number of *genera*, each of which contains anywhere from one to hundreds of *species*. Species alone are viewed as existing in nature; the rest are manmade devices to express relationships.

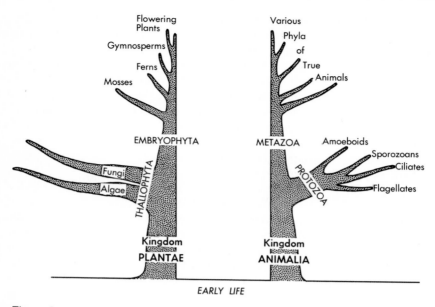

Figure 2.1 *The two-kingdom, or classical, scheme.* This familiar system of classification proposes separate kingdoms for "plants" and "animals," thus suggesting that each of these types of organisms arose independently from primitive life.

stages. Although some deviation in the terminology applied to these larger units is occasionally encountered within the animal section, many more changes have been proposed for plant subdivisions, with considerable improvement as a consequence.

The Multiple-Kingdom Approaches

So long as one does not delve too deeply or broadly into the unicellular forms, the foregoing scheme is quite satisfactory. Admittedly there are occasional difficulties, as, for instance, with *Euglena*, the familiar flagellated form that contains chloroplasts. Because of its active habits, zoologists class this genus as an animal among the protozoans and explain the presence of chloroplasts as indicative of its relatively primitive position close to its plant forebears. To support their concept, they point to a number of other genera, including *Peranema* and *Copromonas*, which are quite similar to *Euglena* except that they are completely animal-like in lacking chloroplasts. At the same time, botanists support their inclusion of these forms among the Algae by citing such creatures as *Colacium*. The members of this genus are, like the other genera cited, also structurally close to *Euglena*, but possess chloroplasts; they are, however, usually both devoid of flagella and produce growths which are decidedly plantlike in all respects. Were these the only instances of ambiguity, the explanation offered by the zoologists might be acceptable, but such is far from the case. Comparable dual treatment in classification, that is, inclusion in both the Algae and the Protozoa, is encountered among many diverse types of organisms. (See table 2.1).

To show the interrelationships more clearly among the unicellular groups, it was proposed by John Hogg in 1860 that all these organisms represent a distinct kingdom, variously called the *Protista* or *Protoctista* (fig. 2.2). The kingdom *Plantae* thereby was reduced to an equivalent of the classical Embryophyta, while the kingdom *Animalia* became equivalent to the Metazoa, including the sponges. Somewhat later, because of the blue-green algae and bacteria do not possess a nucleus like that of the other protists and hence do not undergo mitosis during cell division, it was suggested by E.H. Haeckel in 1866 that these two groups be removed into still another kingdom, the *Monera* (fig. 2.2). Such organisms that lack a true nucleus are often classed as prokaryotes, in contrast to eukaryotes whose cells are nucleated.

Still greater multiplicity in kingdoms has been suggested by Smith. Briefly stated, his system combines the *Embryophyta* and green algae as one kingdom, the euglenoids and the dinoflagellates as a second, called the *Euglenophyta,* and so on through all the algal groups. Consequently, a total of ten kingdoms is outlined. However, because this botanist was concerned solely with algae, his scheme makes no disposition for the bacteria, fungi, protozoans, and metazoans, so that, thus incomplete, it has never come into widespread use.

One multiple-kingdom approach to the origin of variety among living things has attracted much attention in recent years, one known as the *endosymbiontic theory.* Included in its novel features is the proposal that prebiotic events in the primeval soup ultimately gave rise to a diversity of primitive cellular types. One of these was chloroplastlike in being specialized for photosynthetic purposes and accordingly contained a series of membranes on which chlorophyll was imbed-

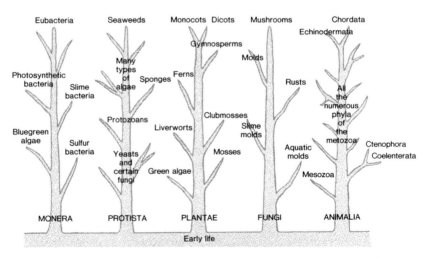

Figure 2.2 *The five kingdom concept.* In addition to separate kingdoms for multi-cellular plants and animals, a third kingdom, the Protista, is erected for most algae and protozoa, while blue-green algae and bacteria are placed in the Monera. In addition a separate kingdom is created for fungi. Each thus represents a separate tree that arose independently from primitive life.

Table 2.1 Comparison of Various Schemes of Classification

Two-Kingdom	Three-Kingdom
I. PLANTAE	I. PROTISTA
A. Thallophyta	A. Green algae
1. Algae	B. Yellow-green algae
a. Green algae	C. Golden-yellow algae
b. Yellow-green algae	D. Diatoms
c. Golden-yellow algae	E. Cryptomonads
d. Diatoms	F. Dinoflagellates
e. Cryptomonads	G. Chloromonads
f. Dinoflagellates	H. Euglenoids
g. Chloromonads	I. Blue-green algae
h. Euglenoids	J. Red algae
i. Blue-green algae	K. Brown algae
j. Red algae	L. Ciliates
k. Brown algae	M. Amoeboids not contained
2. Fungi	elsewhere
a. Bacteria	N. Flagellates not included elsewhere
b. Slime molds	O. Sporozoa
c. True fungi and yeast	P. Bacteria
B. Embryophyta	Q. True fungi and yeasts
Mosses, ferns, seed plants, etc.	II. PLANTAE
II. ANIMALIA	Mosses, ferns, seed plants, etc.
A. Protozoa	III. ANIMALIA
B. Metazoa	Sponges and all multicellular animals
Sponges and all multicellular animals	

ded. Another resembled a mitochondrion and contained cristae, which bore enzyme systems capable of carrying out cell respiration. Still another had a centriolelike body and a flagellum, with which it actively swam about (fig. 2.3). Many others perhaps existed too, but these have long since disappeared without leaving any trace.

In addition to the above, another major type had evolved, one which was relatively simple and unspecialized in that it lacked all cell organelles except that of prime importance—a true nucleus containing chromosomes. This so-called preprotozoan stock is viewed in the concept as being the ultimate ancestor of all advanced forms of life. Its increases in cell complexity are explained as having arisen by a series of invasions by the other primitive forms. During the earliest stages, the various invaders were probably parasitic, and thus harmed the host species. Over the millenia, however, some of the parasites gradually became further adapted to the host and accordingly were modified in turn to harmless commensals and, ultimately, to helpful mutualistic forms. Through these processes, the mitochondrionlike organism became a permanent feature of the preprotozoan cell and supplied energy through its respiratory properties and received protection and food in return. After a second mutualist in the form of the cen-

Five-Kingdom	Single-Kingdom

I. MONERA (MYCHOTA)
    Bacteria and blue-green algae
II. PROTISTA (PROTOCTISTA)
    A. Red algae
    B. Brown and yellow-green algae;
       diatoms
    C. Euglenoids and dinoflagellates
    D. Amoeboids and many flagellates
    E. Sporozoa
    F. Ciliates
III. FUNGI
    Mushrooms, molds, yeasts, rusts, etc.
IV. PLANTAE
    Green algae, mosses, ferns, seed
    plants, etc.
V. ANIMALIA
    Sponges and all multicellular animals
	PLANTAE
	    A. Colorless sulfur bacteria
	    B. Blue-green algae
	    C. Sulfur purple bacteria
	    D. Slime bacteria
	    E. True bacteria
	    F. Yeasts
	    G. Euglenoids and dinoflagellates
	    H. Thecate and soil amoeboids
	    I. True amoeboids
	    J. Parasitic amoeboids
	    K. Protociliates
	    L. Green algae and higher green plants
	    M. Yellow, red, and brown algae, fungi,
	       ciliates, sponges, and metazoans

triolelike type had been acquired by comparable steps, the preprotozoan became converted to what is today considered a flagellated protozoan from which all animal types ultimately arose. In the meantime, some of these simple flagellates became infected by the chloroplastlike forms and, after the latter had acquired mutualist habits through similar processes, eventually developed into the early algae. These in turn gave rise to the higher algae and the seed plants. As a result of these processes, five kingdoms are believed to have arisen.

The Single-Kingdom Concept

Although the provision for more major categories avoids many of the difficulties encountered in the classical system, no relationships between the different kingdoms can be perceived when they are thus segregated from one another (fig. 2.2). And it should be remembered that systematists, in their schemes, attempt to reflect the real kinships of organisms as closely as possible. Moreover, while the larger problems are avoided, many of the lesser ones are not; for example, the probable relationships of the chlorophyll-bearing amoeboids, the flagellated amoeboids, the ciliates, and others formerly placed in the Protozoa still remain unsolved.

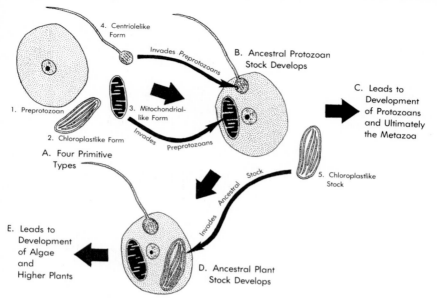

Figure 2.3 *The endosymbiontic concept.* This concept of the origin of complex (eukaryotic) cells suggests that (A) several primitive types arose first. Thereafter (B) a centriolar and a mitochondrial type invaded the preprotozoan stock originally as parasites, but then as mutualistic symbionts. This combination led to the protozoa and higher animal types of today (C). Later in primitive times, the chloroplastlike stock invaded certain of the protozoans (D), resulting in the ancestral type from which algae and plants eventually were derived (E).

In an effort to overcome these shortcomings and to show relationships more clearly, one approach known as the *progressive evolutionary* concept utilizes the internal structure of the cell and its organelles, especially as revealed by the electron microscope. To begin with, it makes two basic assumptions, the first being that if life arose through biochemical means as generally believed, the cell probably first arose in an extremely simple condition and from that point gradually became more complex. Secondly, it suggests that some of the stages in the evolution of the cell from the simple to the advanced state are represented among the organisms living today.

In attempting to trace what appeared to be the evolutionary history of the cell, one organelle at a time was studied throughout all the major types of organisms extant today, regardless of whether they were protozoans or metazoans, seed plants or fungi, algae or bacteria. Because the nucleus has been more thoroughly studied than the other cell organelles, its possible phylogeny was worked out first and the results later used to provide clues to the events in the remaining, less well known structures. For example, in certain primitive sulfur bacteria the nuclear material consists solely of short strands of DNA arranged in vesicles scattered throughout the cytoplasm; in blue-green algae the DNA is similar, but is more

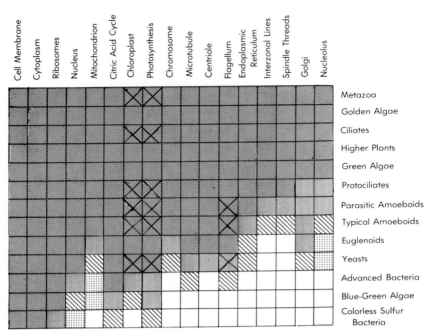

Figure 2.4 *The cellular basis for the single-kingdom concept.* If the various structural and certain major biochemical characteristics are plotted as above, it becomes evident that a gradient of increasing complexity exists among all principal groups of living things. Thus there appears to be no broad structural basis for dividing the biotic world into several kingdoms. White blocks indicate absence of the trait, whereas the darkest shaded ones indicate the most advanced state. Intermediate intensities suggest relative degrees of development; secondary loss is indicated by an X.

concentrated in irregular central masses; and in true bacteria the DNA consists of long, circular molecules arranged in a compact body. In all these forms, the DNA molecules, being devoid of membranous coverings, lie in direct contact with the cytoplasm. At more advanced levels, a nuclear membrane and nucleoplasm are added around the DNA, but chromosomes are completely or virtually absent, as in the yeasts. Then one by one the other nuclear structures are added—the chromosomes, spindle threads, interzonal lines, and the rest—first in simple condition, then increasingly complex, until the definitive nucleus of the higher plants and animals has finally emerged. As may be seen in the chart (fig. 2.4), the remaining cell organelles, including the flagellum, mitochrondrion, and chloroplast, are found to have similar evolutionary histories when the fine structural details revealed by the electron microscope are utilized.

When the various developmental histories thus derived were correlated with one another, a sequence of organisms was found, progressing from the simplest known types existing today to the most complex. Expressed in typical tree form (fig. 2.5), the sequence is seen to be a continuum, without clear-cut divisions

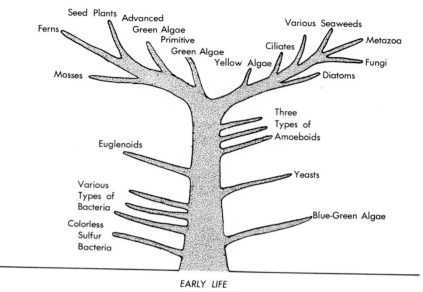

EARLY LIFE

Figure 2.5 *The single-kingdom concept.* Because of the absence of clear cellular differences between major types of organisms, this scheme of classification proposes that all living things represent one kingdom. The branches of the tree trunk are considered as subkingdoms.

suggestive of the existence of separate kingdoms. Consequently, it was concluded that since all extant organisms represent a single tree of life, all belong to one kingdom. Due to the limitations of choice and technical requirements, the single kingdom was designated as the Plant Kingdom, but it could with equal logic be referred to as the Biotic Kingdom. Each of the tree's thirteen major branches was regarded as a subkingdom, secondary ones were viewed as phyla, and so on (table 2.1).

QUESTIONS FOR REVIEW AND THOUGHT

1. What are the three major schools of thought regarding the basic interrelationships of organisms? Compare the usage of the important groupings known as Plantae and Animalia, protozoa and algae.

2. How do you suppose fungi differ from algae? From protozoa?

3. On what assumptions and distinctive characteristics are the chief groupings in the Classical (dual-kingdom) concept based? The three- and five-kingdom concepts? The single-kingdom concept?

4. What are some of the strong and weak points of the two-kingdom view of life? Of the multiple-kingdom concepts? Of the single-kingdom concept?

5. Outline the endosymbiontic theory of the origins and evolution of cellular life. What are its basic assumptions? Which are more primitive according to this theory, plant or animal cells? On what is your answer based? If Fungi are considered a separate kingdom, how does this concept provide for that group's origins?

6. Outline the progressive evolutionary account of the origins and evolution of cellular life. What are its basic assumptions? Which are more primitive according to this concept, plant or animal cells? Why do you think so?

7. Compare the endosymbiontic and progressive evolutionary theories as to their principal strong points and weaknesses. Which one provides for the origin of mitosis and other features of the nucleus?

SUGGESTIONS FOR FURTHER READING

Cohen, S.S. 1970. Are/were mitochondria and chloroplasts microorganisms? *Amer. Sci.*, 58:281–289.

Dillon, L.S. 1962. Comparative cytology and the evolution of life. *Evolution*, 16:102–117.

Kubai, D.F. 1975. The evolution of the mitotic spindle. *International Review of Cytology*, 43:167–228.

Mahler, J.R., and R.A. Raff. 1975. The evolutionary origin of the mitochondrion: A nonsymbiotic model. *International Review of Cytology*, 43:2–123.

Margulis, L. 1970. *Origin of eukaryotic cells*. New Haven, Conn., Yale University Press.

Mayr, E. 1978. Evolution. *Scient. Amer.*, 239(3):46–55.

McQuade, A.B. 1977. Origins of the nucleate organisms. *Quart. Rev. Biol.*, 52:249–262.

Milner, J. 1976. The functional development of mammalian mitochandria. *Biol. Rev.*, 51:181–209.

Regan, M.A., and D.J. Chapman. 1978. *A biochemical phylogeny of the protists*. New York, Academic Press, Inc.

Schopf, J.W. 1978. The evolution of the earliest cells. *Scient. Amer.*, 239(3):110–138.

Schwartz, R.M., and M.O. Dayhoff. 1978. Origins of prokaryotes, eukaryotes, mitochondria, and chloroplasts. *Science*, 199:395–403.

Sokal, R.R. 1974. Classification: Purposes, progress, prospects. *Science*, 185:1115–1123.

Valentine, J.W. 1978. The evolution of multicellular plants and animals. *Scient. Amer.*, 239(3):140–158.

Whittaker, R. H., and L. Margulis. 1978. Protist classification and the kingdoms of organisms. *Bio Systems* 10:3–18.

The Early Evolution of Variety among Animals

The foregoing discussion makes it clear that the light microscope and, more recently, the electron microscope, have disclosed much greater diversification among living things than was ever conceived previously and that these instruments have added to the complexity of the problems confronting biologists, rather than simplifying them. This is particularly illustrated by the unsettled conditions pertaining to the number of kingdoms and similar broad aspects of kinships. As it is not our purpose to support any single point of view, the groups containing animal-like members will be treated here one by one, without any real regard for conjectured relationships. Instead, outlines of classification will be provided to indicate the several more important treatments of the groups to facilitate comparisons.

Before the principal types are discussed, some attention should be given to the term *protozoa*. While in the two-kingdom concept, this is, of course, employed as the name of the subkingdom that includes all unicellular animal-like forms, both the multiple-kingdom and the single-kingdom approaches alike discard it. This term, however, is both convenient and too deeply ingrained in zoological literature to be cast aside entirely. For those using a nonclassical concept, it may refer in a nonsystematic sense to those unicellular or essentially unicellular organisms that are actively motile during much of their life histories or that parasitize any of the Metazoa. Although this definition does not distinguish these organisms from the bacteria and yeasts, it still carries approximately the same implications that it has in the dual-kingdom scheme (table 2.1).

Several terms also having systematic status in the latter system may similarly be of value in the other schemes, especially those that describe the *body type* of the unicellular organisms. The name *flagellate,* for example, can refer to organisms that possess one or more whiplike appendages, or *flagella,* by means of which they move about in the water. Usually these organelles are located at the anterior end so that their movements pull the protozoans through the liquid medium, but sometimes they are situated toward or upon one side, and, in rare instances, they are attached at the posterior end. In contrast, *amoeboid* organisms usually lack permanent locomotive organelles but send out and retract projections of the cytoplasm to provide movement and to assist in feeding. Typically such *pseudopods* are ephemeral, persisting for only a few minutes, but in some groups they are semipermanent, being retracted only under exceptional circumstances. *Ciliates* are protozoans which possess bristlelike organelles; often the *cilia* cover the greater part of the cell's surface, but in certain groups they are confined to specialized areas. In actuality, cilia are shortened flagella, as shown in their ultrastructural details revealed by electron microscopy. *Coccoid* forms are entirely devoid of a means of locomotion and very frequently are enclosed in a wall-like covering. Quite often these organisms are spherical in shape, but they may be small crescents, elongate rods, discs, or one of many other geometric designs.

Although agreeing with this latter variety of body form in being motionless, *palmella* colonies differ in having several cells enclosed in a common wall or envelope; hence, they may be viewed as being colonial coccoids. In a similar sense, a *plasmodium* (or syncytium) may be considered a colonial amoeboid type, from the usual forms of which it is distinguished in having numerous nuclei that share a common cytoplasmic mass. This simple colony is capable of sending out pseudopods as an ordinary uninucleate amoeba does. *Filamentous* colonies consist of long chains of threads of coccoid forms but are rarely found among animal-like groups; and, finally, *dendroid* colonies are branched filaments which are quite as scarce among protozoans as the unbranched type just mentioned.

THE EUGLENOIDS

Among both botanists and zoologists it is customary to consider the flagellated body condition the most primitive, and, in turn, *Euglena* and its relatives are often suggested to be the simplest type of flagellate. Consequently, the Euglenoids comprise the lowermost branch of the protozoans. Many different names have been given to the members of this group, but these are best enumerated in the form of a chart (table 3.1).

Although a number of forms are strictly marine and others live in mud banks, the home of these organisms is predominantly in the fresh waters of the earth. In this habitat the euglenoids frequently play a role of considerable importance, especially in ponds containing large aquatic plants or in those rich in organic matter. Sometimes they occur in such abundance that their bodies impart a characteristic color to the water. Usually green results from the presence of most species of *Euglena* (fig. 3.1) or other chlorophyll-bearing types, but a brown coloration is produced by the species of *Trachelomonas* and red by *Euglena sanguinea*.

Nutrition

As a whole, the chlorophyll-bearing members of the group obviously are holphytic,[1] but even though they can synthesize their own carbohydrates, they are not entirely independent of the chemical contents of the waters in which they occur. All draw upon the dissolved minerals, and, as far as is presently known, every species of *Euglena* requires the presence of certain amino acids in the

---

1. Some biologists prefer either the term "autotrophic" or "phototrophic" to designate forms that manufacture food by photosynthesis. The term "holozoic" is applied to cases in which particulate matter is ingested and "saprophytic" or "saprozoic" when dissolved matter is employed as food.

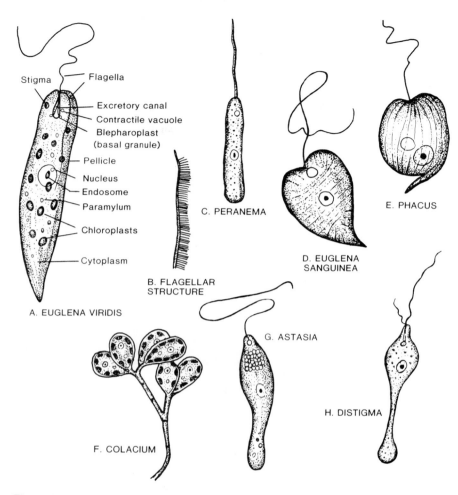

Figure 3.1 *Typical structure and representative genera of the euglenoids.*

medium. Most forms seem also to need short chains of amino acids referred to as peptones. To this extent all are saprozoic. In the continued absence of light, free-living *Euglena* and other normally holophytic species lose their chloroplasts and live quite well if supplied organic nutrients. Similarly, treatment with the familiar antibiotic streptomycin permanently destroys the chloroplasts whether illumination is present or not; individuals treated in this fashion can nevertheless grow and multiply freely as long as the proper organic substances are in the culture medium. Colorless individuals of such normally chlorophyll-bearing species as *Euglena gracilis, Phacus pleuronectes,* and *Colacium vesiculosum* can satisfy their needs for both proteins and energy sources solely from amino acids, but most forms need acetic or formic acid or simple carbohydrates in addition to a nitrogen source.

Table 3.1 Names Applied to the Unicellular Groups Discussed in the Text

	Two-Kingdom Scheme	
Group	Kingdom Plantae	Kingdom Animalia
	Algae Divisions	Protozoa Class and Order
Euglenoids	Euglenophyta	Flagellata : Euglenoidina
Dinoflagellates	Pyrrhophyta	Flagellata : Dinoflagellata
Amoeboids	—	Sarcodina : Amoebina
Yellow-green protozoans	Xanthophyta	Flagellata : Chrysomonadina
Golden-yellow protozoans	Chrysophyta	Flagellata : Chrysomonadina
Green protozoans	Chlorophyta	Flagellata : Phytomonadina
Trypanosomes	—	Flagellata : Protomonadina
Multiflagellated protozoans	—	Flagellata : Polymastigina, Hypermastigina
True ciliates	—	Ciliophora : several orders
Sporozoans	—	Sporozoa : several orders

In this connection it is of interest to note that chlorophyll-less individuals sometimes develop in rapidly growing cultures of species which normally possess chloroplasts. Particularly has this condition been observed in *Euglena gracilis* and *Phacus pleuronectes*. The German algologist, C. Ternetz, has suggested that such oddities arise when by accident the chloroplasts of a cell fail to divide during fission, for chloroplasts are self-reproductive bodies to a large degree. Consequently, repeated failure of this sort results in a gradual diminution in numbers of these organelles and, finally, a total absence in some of the descendants.

A number of euglenoids, including the species of *Astasia* and *Distigma,* are normally colorless saprophytes, occurring in abundance in stagnant or polluted waters rich in organic matter. Other species of *Astasia* frequently are found in the intestines of vertebrates, probably as harmless commensals. Indeed, this habit is not confined to colorless forms. Robert W. Hegner, the noted American protozoologist, described the occurrence of several distinct chlorophyll-bearing species of the genus *Euglena* in the cloaca of tadpoles from eastern United States. By means of a series of experiments, he demonstrated that these forms cannot be cultured by ordinary means, that they will not grow in such related vertebrates as salamanders, for example, and that they are accidentally passed from one individual frog to another. In other words, these species of *Euglena,* in spite of the presence of chlorophyll, can survive only within the confines of the tadpole's digestive tract, where they absorb nutrients saprozoically.

Multiple-Kingdom Scheme		Single-Kingdom Scheme
Kingdom Protista		Kingdom Plantae
Phylum	Class	Subkingdom
Pyrrhophyta	: Mastigophora	Euglenophytaria
Pyrrhophyta	: Mastigophora	Euglenophytaria
Protoplasta	: Sarcodina	Arcellophytaria, Amoebophytaria, Enterophytaria
Phaeophyta	: Heterokontae	Chrysophytaria
Phaeophyta	: Heterokontae	Chrysophytaria
Chlorophyta	: several classes	Chlorophytaria
Fungilli	: Sporozoa	Chrysophytaria
Protoplasta	: Zoomastigoda	Chrysophytaria
Ciliophora	: Infusoria	Chrysophytaria
Fungilli	: Sporozoa	Chrysophytaria

By and large the colorless forms are holozoic, feeding on bacteria, small algae, and protozoans. In some of these species, including members of the genera *Peranema, Entosiphon,* and *Urceolus,* a special tube or siphon is embedded within the cytoplasm toward the anterior end. This sort of structure, while movable forward and backward as well as from side to side, is really protrusible only in *Peranema* and *Entosiphon.* But, as even here its protrusibility is highly restricted, its function is not entirely clear. Among the possibilities is that movement of the siphon induces a streaming action in the substrate, causing suspended particles or minute organisms to flow toward the opening called the *cytostome,* which serves as a mouth.

Regardless of the type of nutrition, all known euglenoids store excess carbohydrates in the form of paramylum (or paramylon), a substance similar to both starch and glycogen in being a complex sugar. Unlike either of these, it fails to stain with iodine and is insoluble in boiling water; on the other hand it is similar to both in being soluble in potassium hydroxide and concentrated sulfuric acid. As a rule paramylum is deposited directly in the cytoplasm, not in the chloroplast as starch is in the seed plants. Deposition may be in the form of rings, rods, disks, spheres, or irregular blocks, the particular shape being constant for each species. In chlorophyll-bearing types, the size and number of paramylum grains increase rapidly during active photosynthesis and decrease during starvation, so the employment of these particles as food reserves appears evident.

Cell Characteristics

Although here, as elsewhere throughout this book, structural details are presented mainly in the illustrations, certain features of the cell among the euglenoids are so unique that they require at least a brief discussion in addition to the figure (fig. 3.1).

Structural Details

It has not always been realized that *Euglena* and others which appear to bear but a single flagellum actually have two; the second one in these forms, being embedded in the cell covering (the *pellicle*), is not visible unless special techniques are used. Under the electron microscope each flagellum can be seen to bear hairlike structures called *flimmer*. In the present protozoans, the flimmer are confined to a single row on one side of the flagellum, whereas in other groups which possess them, they are arranged in two rows (except in the dinoflagellates).

The short canal at the anterior end of *Euglena* has often been labeled the gullet, pharynx, or similar term suggestive of an ingestive function. But it has been shown by Hall and other workers that in those forms which engulf prey, a special opening (the *cytostome*) is present, which is in no way associated with this canal. Since the contractile vacuoles empty their contents into the canal, its only likely function is that of carrying off excreted water and other waste products. Hence, the less commonly employed name *excretory canal* seems more appropriate for this organelle.

Some of the most characteristic features of euglenoid cytology become evident only during cell division. Within the centrally placed nucleus is a body of chromatin called the *endosome*. When the nucleus undergoes mitosis, the endosome elongates until it finally splits into two approximately equal parts. In the meantime chromosomes appear and behave quite normally; however, no spindle fibers or interzonal lines can be noted during the mitotic processes. It is because of the relative simplicity of the nucleus that the euglenoids are frequently treated as the most primitive of the animal-like unicellular organisms.

Behavior

Because behavior is basically comparable in all flagellates, that of the euglenoids can serve as the example for the rest, no matter what their relationships. Consequently, detailed attention to this aspect can be given here.

Behavior patterns in the euglenoids, as in other flagellates, are based primarily upon changes in the method of swimming under the influence of various stimuli. Normally, the path followed in swimming is in the form of a narrow spiral. Because the cell rotates on its long axis once with each complete spiral twist, a certain side of the organism always faces the spiral's outside. As a matter of convenience, this special side is referred to as the *dorsal surface*.

Reaction to Contact and Chemicals

When a freely swimming euglenoid encounters a solid object, it reverses its movement for a short distance, then resumes a forward motion. However, the spiral course is now widened so that the anterior end points successively in many directions, in any one of which the organism may finally swim forward. If the obstacle is again encountered, the protozoan repeats the whole performance, reversing its direction, swerving widely in a broad spiral, and then swimming forward again. When large obstructions are involved, this *avoidance behavior* pattern may be repeated many times before a clear path is found.

In the case of a mild chemical stimulus, such as the presence of a dilute acid in the medium, the reaction is similar, but with a few slight differences. Upon initial contact with the chemical, the organism, instead of abruptly reversing, first retards its forward movement and then momentarily stops swimming. Frequently no reversal may occur before a wide spiral path is assumed. This broadened pattern may be continued for some distance until a more favorable region is reached, when normal swimming begins once more. If a more intense chemical stimulus is encountered, the euglenoid may contract into a sphere, retract its flagella, and secrete a protective coat about itself and thus *encyst*.

Many of the euglenoids, including *Peranema,* show an entirely different type of behavior upon encountering a solid object. Although quite capable of swimming, the members of the genus mentioned frequently react to contact with solid surfaces by creeping upon them. In creeping, the cell is repeatedly looped and straightened in a strikingly wormlike fashion. Most species of *Euglena* can also progress in like manner—in fact this type of locomotion was first observed in this genus and is named "euglenoid" movement accordingly. Some genera carry this habit even further. For instance, *Jenningsia,* a diatom-eating euglenoid, has not been observed to swim in spite of its well-developed flagellum, but creeps along the substrate in a peculiar fashion.

Reaction to Light

As might be anticipated, the pigmented euglenoids react differently to light than the so-called colorless members of the group, but as the distinction is merely one of direction, only the former type needs to be described in detail. If several drops of medium containing *Euglena* are placed on a microscope slide and observed under a stereoscopic microscope near a window, most of the organisms may soon be seen swimming toward the light. If the light now is screened off, the flagellates immediately display the avoidance reaction, reversing their direction of movement, or, at least, ceasing to swim. This initial response is then followed in turn by the wide spiral pattern described above and a resumption of forward progress in a new direction.

The first reaction to diminished light intensity is a very striking one, for all the organisms respond nearly simultaneously, even those individuals that may have by chance been swimming away from the window when the culture was shaded. Hence it is clear that the response is produced by the change in intensity, not by a change in direction of the light. This interpretation is further substantiated by the euglenoids' resuming their original direction even when the illumination is maintained in the decreased state for several moments.

By throwing shadows on individual portions of the organism, Engelmann established in 1882 that shading only the extreme anterior tip was just as effective as decreasing the light on the entire organism. Through use of similar procedures, it has been shown in *Euglena* that the base of the flagellum is the actual light-receptor organ, not the eye-spot, or stigma, which merely acts as a shield. Orientation toward a light source results from a series of avoidance reactions, during each set of which the swerving sequence occurs when the shadow of the stigma falls across the flagellar base (fig. 3.2). Only after the anterior end of the organism has become approximately aligned with the direction of the light rays so that the flagellar base is constantly illuminated does the spiral course of swimming narrow to its normal condition. It is pertinent to note that the eyes of lower metazoans are dependent upon the presence of flagellar bases for their light receptive powers and that similar bases are characteristic features of cells throughout the brains of vertebrates including man.

While chlorophyll-bearing forms are thus *positively phototropic*—that is, they react to light by moving toward the source—if the light becomes too intense their reaction is in the opposite direction. Those forms that do not contain chlorophyll are likewise negatively phototropic, no matter how dim the light. In many of the colorless species, the stigma, being no longer of value, may be absent.

THE DINOFLAGELLATES

Unlike the euglenoids, the dinoflagellates are largely marine, with relatively few freshwater members. Also in contrast to that group, in which conformity to a single structural pattern is the rule, the present organisms have evolved along many lines, especially among saltwater representatives. Aside from the morphological diversity described below, different temperature adaptations have also been developed, some taxa being confined to warm waters, others to cool. Depth specializations also are found, with those organisms having a heavy cell wall, or "armor," inhabiting the shallower regions closer to shore and the unarmored ones frequenting the open waters beyond the continental shelf. Indeed, certain forms have even invaded the beaches, several species of *Amphidinium* and *Gymnodinium* at times being so abundant as to color the sand greenish brown.

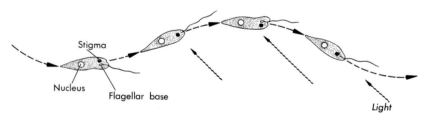

Figure 3.2 *Movement of Euglena in response to light.* The stigma of *Euglena,* which is insensitive to light, serves partly to shield the light-sensitive organ, the flagellar base. Orientation toward a light source is achieved by a series of avoidance reactions.

Characteristic Features

Because of the extensive evolutionary developments mentioned above, the dinoflagellates resist clear definition insofar as their gross external traits are concerned; however, several finer details of structure are shared by all the members. First a close relationship to the euglenoids is suggested, for, as in that group, the nucleus during cell division lacks interzonal lines and spindle threads, the chloroplast has thick lamellae, and the mitochondrion is relatively simple in having few cristae. Secondly, although one flagellum is bare, the other, which usually encircles the cell, possesses the single row of flimmer that characterizes the euglenoids. The chief distinctive traits are found in the chromosomes, which are extremely numerous and appear like so many short strings of beads. In addition, vacuoles are present in this group, and a peculiar starch, rather than paramylum, is deposited as the food reserve.

Evolutionary History

The history of the dinoflagellates, as we can interpret it today, seems to have begun in a stock similar to modern dinoflagellates known as *desmomonads*. The representatives of this group are scarcely distinguishable from the euglenoids in general structure, for the body is naked and the two flagella are located at the tip of the anterior end. However, one flagellum shows the early stage of a peculiarity that marks later forms, as it projects transversely and beats in a circular fashion rather than in the typical whiplike style (fig. 3.3, A).

Although forming what appears to be a later stage in evolutionary development, the *prorocentrads* show few changes from the above (fig. 3.3, B). In fact, only one real advancement seems to have been achieved in the direction of greater specialization, the acquisition of a *theca*. This is merely a thin coat, or cell wall, perforated by numerous pores and composed of two pieces with joints that run longitudinally. A special pore at the anterior end is provided for the flagella.

More marked advancement is shown by the *dinophysids* (fig. 3.3, C). Although the theca is similar to the above in being thin and in consisting of halves joined along longitudinal sutures, the pore through which the flagella emerge has migrated toward one side to about the apical third. Because of this lateral location, the coil of the transverse flagellum now encircles the organism and is largely enclosed within a deep groove in the theca. A similar groove is provided also for the second flagellum that now is directed posteriorly, rather than forwards as in more primitive types.

Among the most highly evolved members, the *armored dinoflagellates,* these traits have been developed to their greatest extent (fig. 3.3, D–F). As suggested by the common name, the theca in these forms has been so greatly increased in thickness as to be referred to as armor; instead of just two parts, it is subdivided into several plates and is frequently equipped with long spines. A second advancement can be noted in the relocation of the transverse flagellum and its groove toward the middle of the cell, as shown in *Ceratium* (fig. 3.3, D). Since this group of dinoflagellates appears to have been unusually successful, many branches of specialization exist. One, marked by the development of col-

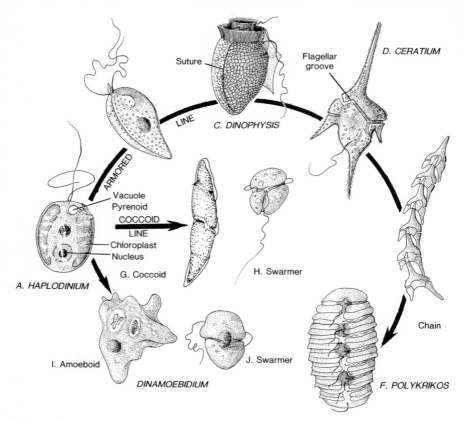

Figure 3.3 *Evolutionary paths among the dinoflagellates.* In the upper series (A–F) an armor is first gained and then colonial types are developed (E,F). A second line (A,G) leads to the loss of flagella and the formation of the coccoid body type, except in swarmers (H). A third line (A,I) develops the amoeboid body type, except in swarmers (J).

onialism, possibly begins with species resembling *Ceratium tripos* (fig. 3.3, E), in which newly formed cells remain attached instead of separating, so that long filaments develop. Toward the end of this branch, represented by *Polykrikos* (fig. 3.3, F), colonial organization is quite complex, for the theca of newly formed cells remains completely continuous to that of the older region. Moreover, the cytoplasm does not undergo division, the organism being a plasmodium with a number of nuclei but no separate cells.

Other lines of diversification extant among these higher dinoflagellates include that in which the flagella have been lost in mature forms. In such coccoid types, which, like *Blastodinium,* are often parasites of various crustaceans or segmented worms, only the so-called *swarmers* or *zoospores* are flagellated (fig. 3.3, G, H). Another particularly interesting line of evolution leads to *Dinamoebidium* (fig 3.3, I), a large amoeboid organism that lost armor and chloroplasts, as well as the flagella; normally it lives on the sea bottom, where it creeps about by means of short pseudopods. Under proper conditions it encysts and divides into four to eight swarmers. Only because these reproductive cells show the characteristic theca, grooves, and flagella (fig. 3.3, J) can these amoebalike forms be recognized as members of the dinoflagellates.

THE AMOEBOIDS

Among the various groups whose members typically bear flagella are isolated representatives that lack such organelles and move by means of pseudopods instead. Although therefore "amoeboids" in every sense of the term, in each case these amobae possess other cellular features that very clearly indicate their relationships to the flagellated forms. One such instance, *Dinamoebidium*, has already been described, and others will be encountered later. However, there are numerous colorless species which do not share cellular characteristics with any flagellated group, but have in common many distinctive traits in addition to an amoeboid type of movement. It is these organisms that will receive attention at this time. Because these amoeboids can serve as the illustration for the other unicellular types which move by the same means, locomotion and behavior patterns can be described in more detail than might otherwise be warranted.

Locomotion

Although several varieties of pseudopodal locomotion occur among amoeboids, all can be arranged into three principal categories. First is the common pseudopodal type in which one or more variously shaped pseudopods are projected outward. This action is followed by a flowing movement on the part of the remaining cytoplasm, accompanied by marked changes in cell shape. To the contrary, both the second and the third types are characterized by a high degree of stability in cell form. The second is called the *limax* type after a species of *Vahlkampfia* by that name. The cell, usually a more or less oblong, elongated mass (fig. 3.4), moves as a unit, without discrete pseudopods. Because of the relatively rapid movement and the transparent, seemingly fluid cytoplasm, a limax amoeba closely resembles a flowing droplet of water or, perhaps better, a moving garden slug. The third and final type moves more deliberately than the last, the cytoplasm appears much less fluid, and the surface of the cell is greatly wrinkled. Probably the most familiar representative is *Thecamoeba verrucosa*.

Regardless of type, the forward progress of an amoeba can best be likened to the tread of a military tank or so-called caterpillar tractor. In other words, in side view the upper surface of a moving amoeba is seen to flow forward, descend upon attaining the anteriormost point, and then remain stationary when it contacts the surface of the substrate (fig. 3.4, B). Only after the remainder of the cell has progressed completely over a given point does that part ascend to the upper surface to flow forward once more. In profile, too, the front edge of an actively moving amoeboid appears thin and rather flat, while the posterior portion is high and rounded. Moreover, the entire lower portion may be observed to be free of the substrate, supported by several short vertically placed pseudopods (fig. 3.4, B).

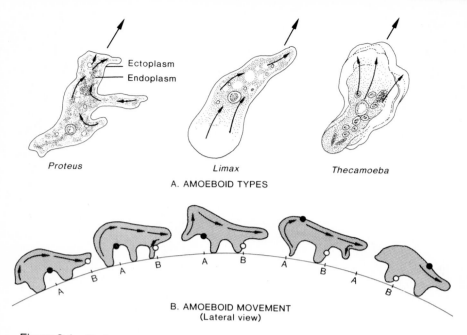

Figure 3.4 *Various types of amoebae and their means of locomotion.*

Many theories of pseudopod formation have been advanced, none of which is completely satisfactory. The earliest concept, that surface tension changes induced pseudopodal growth, was disproved early in the twentieth century, when it was largely replaced by the ''sol-gel'' hypothesis advocated by Pantin and Mast in the 1920s. This latter concept was widely accepted, and still is promulgated by many textbooks, years after it was disproven, largely because it was partially based on an easily observable phenomenon involving the endoplasm. In actively moving amoebae the endoplasm can be observed to become a semifluid sol at the tail end, following which it flows forward into the growing pseudopod, a movement made evident by the granules it contains. Close observation discloses that, on reaching the growing tip of the pseudopod, the cytoplasmic granules move toward the sides, where, beneath the enclosing ectoplasmic tube, they seem to be held by the surrounding endoplasm forming a gel. That much is factual, but the concept proposed that the endoplasmic sol is moved forward by the ectoplasmic tube contracting at the tail end of the amoeba. Disproof of this idea eventually came through the discovery that the endoplasm continued to stream even after being removed from the cell and from the ectoplastic tube. Furthermore, the pressure gradients that would have resulted from the ectoplasmic contractions were demonstrated to be lacking.

In the meantime, the endoplasm of amoebae has been found to contain several features which are believed to be important in muscle contraction, namely microtubules and actin- and myosinlike proteins. Thus recent studies of pseudopodal formation are conducted at the molecular, rather than structural, level and center on the interactions between those two proteins and ATP (or GTP in some cases). Hence, while amoebae and muscle cells appear on the surface to have almost nothing in common, their cytoplasmic movements may prove to be functionally related. This kinship may exist wherever cytoplasmic movement is found, for actin- and myosinlike proteins and microtubules have also been isolated from cilia, flagella, and almost every organism in which they have been sought. It would appear that, when the knotty problem of pseudopod formation is solved in amoebae, the solution will provide an understanding, not only of how these interesting creatures move, but of similar cytoplasmic processes in all of life.

Behavior

Reaction to Stimuli

When an amoeba encounters a broad solid object, forward movement ceases; then after a pause, a new pseudopod is sent out near the posterior end. Complete reversal of direction is not usually attained, however, as the new pseudopod develops slightly to one side of the tail region; consequently, the new course that is pursued lies at an obtuse angle to the original one.

While accordingly amoeboids appear to react negatively to contact, there is another aspect that needs consideration. When an amoeba becomes suspended in water, the organism, being entirely free of contact with anything solid, is as completely unstimulated by mecahnical stimuli as is possible. Because it cannot then move from place to place or feed, this situation is not a favorable one for the amoeba, and it reacts by sending out long pseudopods in all directions, reducing the cell proper to a small central axis of the projections. Thus outstretched, these organelles have a much greater opportunity of encountering a solid object. As soon as one pseudopod happens to do so, it spreads out and clings to the surface. Then by means of streaming activities throughout the cytoplasm, the other pseudopods shorten and the organism eventually flows onto the surface of the contacted object to resume normal behavior.

Reaction to Food

One of the common foods of amoebae consists of the spherical cysts of *Euglena,* but having a smooth surface, these objects roll readily and frequently present considerable difficulty to an amoeba attempting to engulf them. Upon encountering a cyst that rolls away when contacted, the amoeba approaches it again. To ensure success in this second attempt, upon regaining a position close to the encysted euglenoid, the amoeba halts the forward movement of that portion of its cell directly in line with the cyst. Then a pseudopod is formed on each side of the food, while simultaneously a thin sheet of cytoplasm is sent over the top. After passing the cyst's middle, the two pseudopodal tips approach one another and finally fuse, along with the overlying cytoplasmic sheet. In this manner the cyst is successfully engulfed.

QUESTIONS FOR REVIEW AND THOUGHT

1. Name and briefly characterize the four body types of unicellular organisms. Distinguish the several major types of colonies that occur among protozoans. Do you know which of these types occur also in certain metazoan tissues?

2. What types of feeding behavior are found among the euglenoids? Compare holozoic and holophytic types; holozoic and saprozoic. What, if anything, serves as a mouth in holozoic euglenoids? In what form are excess foodstuffs stored?

3. Give the chief distinguishing cellular characteristics of the euglenoids. In what ways are dinoflagellates similar? In what ways do they differ from the euglenoids?

4. The flagellum and its base have been shown in the literature to have served as the basis for the evolutionary origins of eyes, including those of vertebrates. What other organs or system may have had a similar origin? Give the basis for your answer.

5. Compare the behavioral reactions of euglenoids and amoeboids to contact and chemicals, including food. How do euglenoids react to light?

6. Outline a possible evolutionary history of the dinoflagellates.

7. What precisely is meant by an amoeboid? Are all amoebae members of just one group? Give the basis for your answer. How does amoeboid movement occur? Does this explanation apply equally to all three types of pseudopod formation?

SUGGESTIONS FOR FURTHER READING

Allen, R.D., and N.S. Allen. 1978. Cytoplasmic streaming in amoeboid movement. *Annual Review of Biophysics and Bioengineering.* 7:469–495.

Ayala, F.J. 1978. The mechanisms of evolution. *Scient. Amer.,* 239(3):56–69.

Bovee, E.V., and T.L. Jahn. 1973. Taxonomy and phylogeny. In *The Biology of Amoeba,* ed. K.W. Jeon, p. 38–82. New York, Academic Press.

Corning, W.C., and R. Von Burg. 1973. Protozoa. In *Invertebrate Learning,* ed. W.C. Corning, J.A. Dyal, and A.O.D. Willows, Vol. 1, p. 49–121. New York, Plenum Press.

Daniels, E.W. 1973. Ultrastructure. In *The Biology of Amoeba,* ed. K.W. Jeon, p. 125–169. New York, Academic Press.

Goldberger, R.F., R.G. Deeley, and K.P. Mullinix. 1976. Regulation of gene expression in prokaryotic organisms. *Advances in Gentics,* 18:1–68.

Lenci, F., and G. Colombetti. 1978. Photobehavior of micro-organisms: A biophysical approach. *Annual Review of Biophysics and Bioengineering,* 7:341–361.

Loeblich, A.R. 1976. Dinoflagellate evolution: Speculation and evidence. *J. Protozool.*, 23:13–28.

Schweiger, H.G., and M. Schweiger. 1977. Circadian rhythms in unicellular organisms; an endeavor to explain the molecular mechanisms. *Int. Rev. Cytol.*, 51:315–342.

Scott, G.H. 1974. Biometry of the foraminiferal shell. In *Foraminifera,* ed. R.H. Hedley and C.G. Adams, Vol. 1, p. 55–151. New York, Academic Press, Inc.

Tangen, K. 1977. Blooms of *Gyrodinium aureolum* (Dinophyceae) in north European waters accompanied by mortality in marine organisms. *Sarsia,* 63:123–133.

Evolution among Advanced Protozoans

4

As the three taxa discussed in the preceding chapter illustrate the basic structural patterns and behavior found among the protozoans, the remaining unicellular organisms do not need such detailed attention. Although thus treated relatively briefly, by no means should the present taxa be considered of lesser importance; on the contrary, several groups presented here are of outstanding biological significance. Moreover, collectively they demonstrate the higher degree of diversification that can evolve as better cellular organization is achieved. For their technical names and various proposals that have been made regarding their relationships, reference should be made to table 3.1 (p. 26).

THE YELLOW FLAGELLATES AND THEIR RELATIVES

As a rule the yellow flagellates and their kin receive little attention in zoology textbooks and consequently they have remained relatively unfamiliar to biologists in general. Yet they so clearly illustrate the principle of parallel evolution that an effort to bring them further to the forefront seems in order.

Included under the general term yellow flagellates are actually two separate taxa which have so many traits in common that a combined approach provides considerable simplification to their study. Shared characteristics are found in the flagella, pigmentation, and the stored products of metabolism. The two flagella, instead of being at the extreme anterior end of the cell, are located slightly to one side; one of them always extends forward and is provided with two rows of flimmer, whereas the other is recurved posteriorly and is completely bare. On each, the tip narrows abruptly to form a slender "whiplash" (fig. 4.1). Instead of the starch that characterizes many photosynthetic organisms, these yellow flagellates produce and store oil or fat. Although the chloroplasts contain chlorophylls a and c, the green color of those compounds is at least partially obscured by the greater abundance of yellow pigments, called xanthophylls. It is from these compounds, then, that the name of this group actually is derived. The two taxa included here differ largely in relative proportions of xanthophylls. In the yellow-green protozoans, a lesser concentration is present, so that the chlorophylls are only partially concealed, whereas in the golden-yellow forms, the density is so high the green is completely masked.

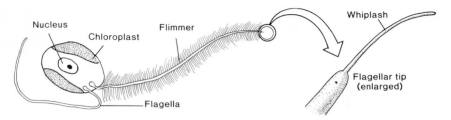

Figure 4.1 *Cellular characteristics of yellow flagellates.* Included in the distinctive traits are three associated with the pair of flagella—their lateral location, one being bare, the other flimmered, the tips being strongly narrowed into "whiplashes." Other distinctions include the storage of lipids, rather than starches, the presence of chlorophylls *a* and *c,* and an abundance of yellow pigments.

Evolution of the Yellow-Green Protozoans

Among the yellow-green protozoans, a relatively scarce group, the simplest type extant today is represented by *Chlorochromonas* (fig. 4.2, A) and other naked biflagellated genera. Aside from the features characteristic of the entire taxon, such forms show few traits that distinguish them from the primitive euglenoids and dinoflagellates. Probably beginning with some similar ancestral stock, two major branches of evolution apparently have been followed by these organisms; each of these lines shows a gradual reduction in the importance of the flagella. Both also illustrate some of the problems inherent to the classical approach to classification.

The first line of descent underscores the occasional difficulty of deciding whether a particular form should be considered a flagellate or an amoeboid. The species of *Chloramoeba,* for instance, generally swim by the usual two flagella (fig. 4.2, B), but under certain conditions they lose these organs and creep by means of pseudopods. Representatives of *Heterochloris* behave in comparable fashion, but show some advancement in that the pseudopods are long and filamentous (fig. 4.2, C). In another genus, *Stipitococcus,* additional evolutionary progress is shown by two features—the acquisition of a theca and further suppression of the flagellated stage (fig. 4.2, D). In their vaselike, sessile theca, the organisms are continuously amoeboid; however, when cell division occurs, one daughter cell acquires flagella and becomes free living for a brief period. But upon finding a new suitable location, the protozoan attaches itself to the substrate by a fine filament, secretes a theca, and resumes the amoeboid condition after losing the flagella.

The second evolutionary line, in which the coccoid condition replaces the flagellated, illustrates the problems involved in distinguishing algae and protozoans with any degree of objectivity. As a consequence of the immobility of this type of cell organization, many species are considered algae; a few, nevertheless, are placed among the Protozoa, including one whose members secrete a stalked theca not unlike that formed by *Stipitococcus.* These organisms, belonging to the genus *Peroniella,* have rather thick organs of attachment and protective coats that

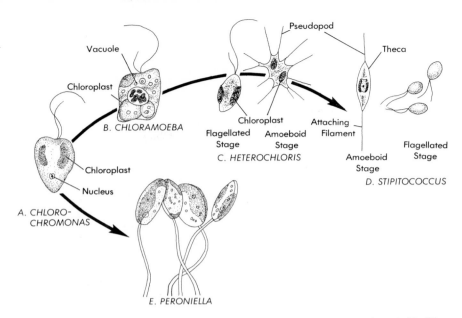

Figure 4.2 *Evolution among yellow-green protozoans*. Along the upper branch (B–D), an amoeboid condition gradually becomes predominant, whereas along the lower one, a coccoid body type (E) is developed.

are entirely closed (fig. 4.2, E). Most of these, algae and protozoans alike, develop flagellated swarmers for dissemination after cell division. One of the end products of this line, a rather common species, consists of long filamentous colonies in which the individual cells are variously coccoid or amoeboid. Although usually considered an alga, its flagellated swarmers show all the characteristic features of the yellow-green protozoans.

Golden-Yellow Protozoans and Parallel Evolution

Except for the generic names, the paths suggested for the yellow-green protozoans can be traced in nearly identical fashion among the golden-yellow protozoans, evolution having evidently proceeded in parallel fashion in the two taxa. Again the most elementary types are naked biflagellated species, possibly the most familiar examples being the members of the genera *Ochromonas* (fig. 4.3, A) and *Chromulina*. Early steps in evolutionary development appear to be represented by forms with a covering of thick scales, for example *Mallomonas* (fig. 4.3, B; 4.4), followed later by the appearance of a vaselike theca, as in *Derepyxis* (fig. 4.3, C).

Although the flagellum-bearing sorts are the most common, amoeboid forms are far from scarce. In fact Dr. Libbie Hyman formerly one of the foremost specialists in invertebrates, has stated: "The whole order exhibits strong amoeboid tendencies and shows affinities in many directions. Thus they may

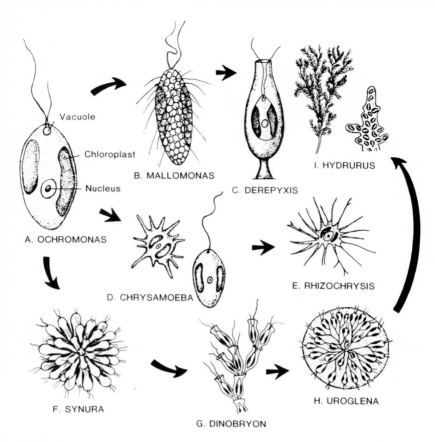

Figure 4.3 *Evolutionary trends among the golden-yellow protozoans.*

pass into the palmella stage and resemble algae; or lose the chloroplasts and appear as protomonads [a simple group of animal-like flagellates]; or by loss of both flagella and chloroplasts become indistinguishable from typical rhizopods [amoeboids]." At least one genus, *Chrysamoeba* (fig. 4.3, D), is transitional in being either flagellated or amoeboid with equal facility, while the extremity of the amoeboid condition is represented by *Rhizochrysis* (fig. 4.3, E), which contains chloroplasts but is not known to form flagella at any time, even its reproductive bodies being amoeboid.

Colonial representatives also are highly diversified and include one type that has not been encountered among any of the groups described above. This variety consists of a number of flagellated cells arranged as a sphere that floats about in the water. Although not infrequently the spheres are made entirely of naked flagellates, as in *Synura* (fig. 4.3, F) and *Skadovskiella,* many genera like *Syncrypta* are enclosed in a gelatinous envelope. Occasional members of the latter variety are equipped with long rods or needles, which, as in *Chrysosphaerella,* may be freely movable.

Another colonial type of common occurrence within this group is the dendroid. Most of the representatives, including *Pedinella* and *Dendromonas,* are quite simple in consisting of only three or four flagellated individuals; the cells are pigmented in the first-named genus and without chlorophyll in the second. Other colonies are formed of series of flagellates enveloped separately in open capsules, frequently with that of one individual attached directly to another, as shown in *Stylobryon* and *Dinobryon* (fig. 4.3, G). Perhaps the most striking dendroid variety is *Uroglena* (fig. 4.3, H). While this colony is constructed like *Chrysodendron,* it is entirely embedded in a gelatinous coat and floats in the water, so that it bears a close resemblance to the spherical colonies related to *Synura* described above.

Palmelloid colonies are also highly developed, in some genera (e.g., *Phaeosphaera* and *Hydrurus*) consisting of branched growths up to 15 inches in height. In these, hundreds of coccoid individuals are loosely arranged in a gelatinous matrix. *Hydrurus* (fig. 4.3, I) forms especially complex colonies in cold freshwater streams that are indistinguishable, insofar as construction is concerned, from forms uniformly considered to be algae. Yet most protozoologists list this genus among the protozoans.

GREEN FLAGELLATES AND RELATED FORMS

Probably the most sharply defined of the chlorophyll-bearing protozoan groups is that containing the green flagellates and their kin. Among its distinctive features is the formation of true starch as the storage product of metabolism, a substance formed even in those which lack chloroplastids. Where present, the latter organelle usually is a single large, cup-shaped body, filling much of the posterior half of the organism and enclosing the nucleus. Besides the chlorophyll *a* found in almost all pigmented, single-celled organisms, a second type, chlorophyll *b,* is also present; this combination of chlorophylls is also found among the flowering plants, ferns, mosses, and the like. Since the chlorophylls are more abundant than the xanthophylls, the chloroplastids are bright green in color.

Another characteristic feature is a cellulose cell wall; although often well developed, in the simpler representatives it is sometimes completely absent or is replaced by one made of pectin. The flagella also are distinctive. With the exception of a few of the most primitive flagellated members, these organelles are devoid of flimmer; their tips are simply rounded, as they lack the prolonged whiplash characteristic of the yellow flagellates. Also, except in the lower members, centrioles are either absent or degenerate.

These and other distinctions are shown diagrammatically in figure 4.5. Because this highly unique combination of traits is shared with the mosses, ferns and their allies, and seed plants, the green unicellular forms are generally considered ancestral to those higher plants, even to the point of being included within the same taxon in some outlines of classification.

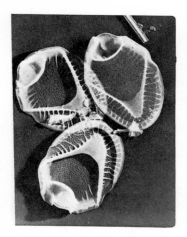

Figure 4.4 *Scales from Mallomonas.* This scanning electronmicrograph reveals the intricate nature of these scales. Magnified 4,200 X. (Courtesy of Jørgan Kristiansen.)

The Colonial Forms

Probably the principal contribution of the group is provided by the body types showing a high degree of parallelism with the two taxa of yellow flagellates just described. As in those protozoans, the series commences with solitary flagellates, *Chlamydomonas* (fig. 4.5, A) being the most noted representative. Coccoid species also are abundant, and these in turn lead to loose colonies of four to eight cells held together in open circles by delicate strands of cytoplasm (see *Dangeradinella,* fig. 4.5, C).

Following this circular type are numbers of spherical floating colonies. The sequence begins as a flat cluster of flagellated individuals embedded in a gelatinous matrix, as shown by *Gonium* (fig. 4.5, D), while in slightly more advanced genera, the cells are scattered around the matrix's periphery to form more or less perfect spheres as in *Eudorina* (fig. 4.5, E). At a still higher level, represented by *Pleodorina* (fig. 4.5, F), the cells are both more numerous and more evenly spaced, while at the height of development, exemplified by *Volvox* (fig. 4.5, G), the colonies may consist of more than 20,000 cells, all interconnected by cytoplasmic threads.

All the present spherical colonies are considered to be *polarized,* for they always swim with one region forward. This region, the so-called anterior end, in *Volvox* and *Pleodorina* is further specialized for strictly vegetative functions. The cells of the anterior region are smaller in size, have larger stigmata, and are incapable of reproduction. In contrast, the components at the posterior end are specialized primarily for propagative activities. Among these posterior cells asexual processes continue more or less constantly throughout life, the daughter cells either remaining to increase the size of the parent colony or breaking off in clusters to form miniature colonies of their own. The latter usually develop within the cavity of the larger sphere; when mature they escape to the exterior through ruptures in the wall of the parent. At certain times sexual reproduction also occurs. In these processes some of the posterior cells enlarge to form eggs while others undergo multiple fission to establish clusters of flagellated sperm.

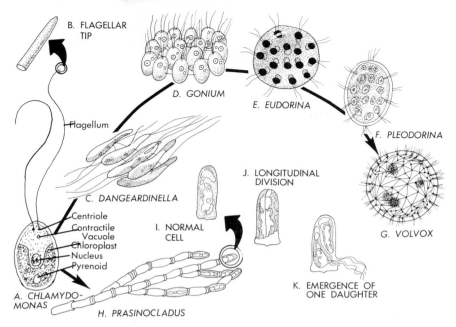

Figure 4.5 *Cell structure and evolution in the green protozoans.* In contrast to the yellow flagellates, the paired flagella (A) are situated at the anterior end of the cell and (B) the tip lacks a whiplash. Chlorophylls *a* and *b* are present, and starch, not lipids, is stored, even in colorless species. The upper sequence (C–G) leads to complex colonies, one (H) ends in filamentous types.

Although most species of *Volvox* have bisexual colonies, in a few the male and female gametes are produced in separate ones.

Palmelloid colonies very similar in morphology to those of such yellow flagellates as *Hydrurus* and *Phaerosphaera* are both well developed and of frequent occurrence; however, these, as well as filamentous colonial species, are in the present group usually considered to be algae. Hence consideration will be given to only one of these, a genus named *Prasinocladus,* which makes particularly clear the difficulties involved in even distinguishing sharply between such seemingly distinct types as flagellates and filamentous colonies. In this marine organism the cells are held in chainlike series largely by means of the cell wall as in most filamentous algae, but cell division occurs longitudinally, not transversely. After division the daughter cells move so as to occupy upper and lower positions; the lower one thereafter remains in the parental chamber, while the upper one secretes new cell walls and thus extends the filament. Periodically the apical cell may add to the filament without undergoing division. On such occasions the cell develops four flagella and uses these to assist in migrating upward as it secretes a new set of walls. In similar fashion any cell in the filament may also develop flagella, break free, and eventually establish a new colony (fig. 4.5, H–K).

OTHER ANIMAL-LIKE FORMS

While it becomes apparent from the foregoing discussion that certain pigmented flagellates and amoeboids have added greatly to the zoologist's problem of discerning marked differences between protozoans and algae and, hence, between animals and plants, the remaining groups offer no such difficulty. All those that follow are obviously animal-like in habit and appear to have no close relatives among plant-like groups.

The Trypanosomes

The important assemblage known as the trypanosomes contains a large number of forms which are parasitic in vertebrates, including man and his domestic animals. Within the cell of these organisms is a large granule called the basal body or blepharoplast, which is closely associated with the base of the flagellum. As only one or two other unicellular types are known to possess a similar organelle, this structure provides a ready means for identifying the members of the present taxon.

Principal Types

Among the trypanosomes four principal types occur, distinguished primarily by flagellar characteristics. The first, *Leishmania,* is normally coccoid, with the blepharoplast placed some distance anterior to the nucleus (fig. 4.6, A). The second representative genus, *Leptomonas,* is similar except that a single flagellum is present at the anterior end. In the third variety, the basal body is located close to the nucleus, as the flagellum arises near the middle of one side. From that point the organelle extends anteriorly, embedded in the plasma membrane in such a fashion that a thin flap is produced. This extension, known as the undulating membrane, is employed in swimming. In the fourth variety, *Trypanosoma,* the basal body and the flagellum's point of origin have migrated to the posterior portion of the organism, so that the undulating membrane now occupies one entire side of the cell.

As indicated before, many of these forms are important parasites, living largely in the blood of vertebrates. One example, *Leishmania donovani,* is the causative agent of *Kala-azar,* a disease of mankind found in the northern half of Africa and in southern Asia. Within the host the parasite invades the white blood cells and the organs that form such cells, including the spleen, bone marrow, and lymph glands, as well as the liver. It appears to be transmitted from one person to another by biting flies of the genus *Phlebotamus,* in which it lives in a *Leptomonas*-like stage.

The principal parasitic species, however, belong to the genus *Trypanosoma,* and, as a whole, live free in the blood stream. Like all pathogenic members of the genus, the two in Africa that affect man are strictly tropical in distribution. These two, *T. gambiense* and *T. rhodesiense,* are the causative organisms of African sleeping sickness and are transmitted by tsetse flies of the genus *Glossina.* After spending a period in the human blood stream, the pathogens enter the nervous system, first producing a lethargic condition and, later, death.

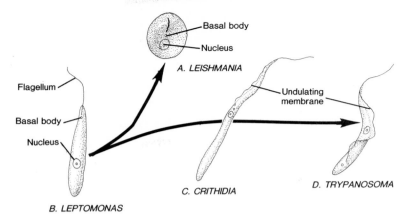

Figure 4.6 Diversification among the trypanosomes. Evolutionary advancement in these protozoans is marked by the development of an undulating membrane as the flagellum and basal body progress posteriorly (C,D) from the primitive anterior location (B). In *Leishmania* (A) the flagellum is absent when the organism is mature.

Multiflagellated Types

Among certain protozoans usually considered to constitute two orders, multiplicity of flagella is a conspicuous feature. Although several forms have as few as four of these organelles, others possess six, eight, or upwards to several hundred. In *Trichomonas* and its kin, two distinctive organelles are found at the flagellar base, including a large parabasal body. In addition there is an elongate rodlike organelle called the *axostyle,* the function of which is unknown. The majority of the species appear to feed on bacteria and yeasts within the intestines of vertebrates; however, a few occur in the internal organs of termites and leeches.

The greatest number of flagella characterizes those protozoans that inhabit the intestines of termites and wood roaches (fig. 4.7). Although these insects feed solely on wood, the enzymes necessary to digest that material appear to be absent; consequently, if treated with an antibiotic that kills their normal protozoan inhabitants, the insects, despite their continuing to feed upon wood as usual, soon die of starvation. In turn, the protozoans are unable to survive outside the digestive tract of their hosts. Such intimate interrelationships between members of different species represent one example of *symbiosis,* a term from Greek words meaning "living together." Where the close associations are mutually beneficial, as in this case, the symbiosis is of the type referred to as *mutualism.* In those instances in which one species is benefitted and the second one (the *host*) is harmed or even killed, the type of symbiosis is known as *parasitism;* when one species is benefitted and the other is neither harmed nor especially benefitted, the term *commensalism* is applied. Sharks carrying remoras might represent an illustration of the latter variety of symbiosis.

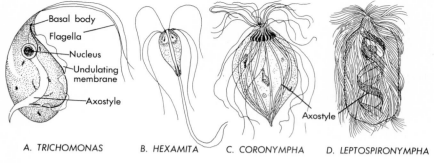

Figure 4.7 *A few multiflagellated protozoans from termites.*

A. TRICHOMONAS   B. HEXAMITA   C. CORONYMPHA   D. LEPTOSPIRONYMPHA

The True Ciliates

A highly adaptive group, the ciliates occupy a large variety of habitats, including fresh and marine waters as well as the internal organs of multicellular animals. Most of them swim actively by means of shortened flagella called *cilia* (figs. 4.8, A; 4.9), that coat much of their body surface; others, however, possess fused tufts of cilia, known as *cirri,* by means of which they creep about pond and sea bottoms (fig. 4.8, B).

All true ciliates are at once distinguished by having two types of nuclei. Of these, one is single and large and is referred to as the *macronucleus,* while the second type, known as the *micronucleus* because of its small size, may be single or quite numerous—as many as eight micronuclei are present in several species.

Evolution of Food Habits

In the majority of the ciliates, prey is taken directly into the cell through an opening, the *cytostome.* From this structure it passes through a short tube into a *food vacuole;* after it has become full, the latter breaks free to circulate through the cytoplasm and receives enzymes that digest its contents. Most members are active swimmers, ingesting such things as bacteria, yeasts, and small protozoans as they move about. In a few sessile types, including some dendroid colonial varieties, a specialized mode of feeding has evolved. By beating movements of the cilia, currents are set up that carry any suspended matter toward the cytostome. In some forms, including *Stentor* and *Folliculina* (fig. 4.8, D, E), the processes of thus filtering organic matter from the medium are augmented by the funnel shape of the body.

A second modification of the food habits, perhaps best illustrated by *Didinium* (fig. 4.8, C), occurs in a type sometimes referred to as the "hunter ciliates." These actively swimming organisms feed upon species that are nearly as large as themselves, taking in their prey whole through a cytostome placed at the tip of the proboscis. To accomplish this feat, the cytostome, equipped with a number of strong ribs, is capable of being distended to the full diameter of the cell. While swimming about by means of its two encircling rows of cilia, *Di-*

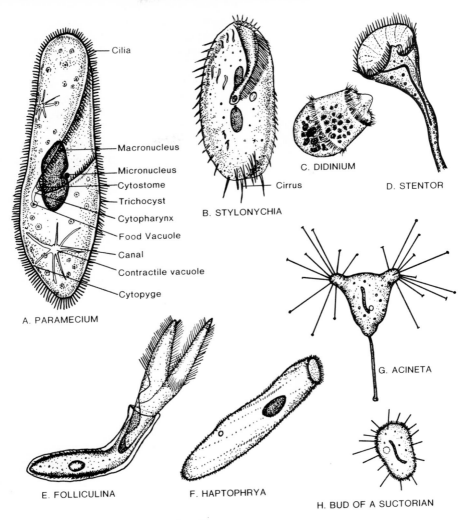

Figure 4.8 *Diversity among the ciliates.*

dinium changes direction frequently, until a solid object of any sort is contacted by accident. Then it presses its proboscis against the object and, spinning rapidly around on its long axis, seemingly attempts to bore through the substance, using the cytostome's ribs as a drill. If the contacted subject chances to be a bit of glass or wood, or perhaps an organism with a thick protecting covering, the *Didinium* goes through these boring processes several times, but eventually swims away. On the other hand, if it is a soft-bodied protozoan, such as a *Paramecium*, the ribs soon pierce the prey's body and then hold it fast. Once the victim has been secured, it is quickly engulfed through the full distended cytostome directly into the cytoplasm, as no special organelle is present internally for the reception of the food. If, as sometimes happens, the ingested *Paramecium* exceeds the *Didinium* in size, the latter becomes so distended that it appears as a mere sac of cytoplasm around the other protozoan.

A third evolutionary development in food habits is represented by a group called the *astomate* ciliates, in which the cytostome is lacking as in *Haptophrya* (fig. 4.8, F). As these forms inhabit the intestines or other internal organs of aquatic invertebrates, the food is absorbed directly into the cell.

Still another adaptation for feeding, and probably the most outstanding of all, is that found in the *suctorians*. These organisms are looked upon as ciliates which have secondarily lost their cilia because of their sessile habits; only the young are actually ciliated and capable of swimming (fig. 4.8, G, H). After a juvenile is budded off by asexual means, it leaves the parent and swims actively for a few hours. Then, upon encountering a favorable location, it attaches itself by secreting a short stalk, loses the cilia, and gradually assumes the parental form. As a rule, both juvenile and mature individuals are provided with long, rather rigid projections called *tentacles*. Although most of these structures are armed with a knob at the tip, occasionally a second type of tentacle may be present. This type has sticky ends instead of terminal knobs and serves solely in the capture of prey. In most suctorians the food, typically other protozoans or rotifers, is caught by means of toxic substance secreted by the knobbed tentacles. The knobs then penetrate the victim and the contents are drawn into the cell through the hollow stems. Just how the sucking action is produced is not clear.

The Evolution of Macronuclei

Since the presence of two distinct types of nuclei is one of the most outstanding characteristics of the true ciliates, the question naturally arises as to how this condition may have evolved. According to a recent study, some of the stages in the evolution of nuclear diversity seem to be represented among certain ciliate groups, so a tenative outline can now be suggested. But in order to understand the changes fully, it is first necessary to examine the nature of the two types of nuclei.

Macronuclear characteristics are best shown in certain of the more primitive ciliates, such as *Loxodes* (fig. 4.10, A) and *Tracheloraphis*. In these and related genera, the macronucleus never undergoes division, although it has the diploid number of chromosomes.[1] In these early forms, this failure to divide results from an inability to make DNA; since all chromosomes consist of DNA to an extent of nearly 50 percent, those of the macronucleus are therefore unable to be replicated. In contrast, the micronucleus is the generative nucleus and undergoes mitosis, for, since it can produce DNA, its chromosomes are replicated in normal fashion. Consequently, new macronuclei must be suspected to arise by modification of micronuclei, and such has proven to be the case.

---

1. The *diploid* number (2*n*) is the usual complement of chromosomes in sexually reproducing animals and is the product of two *haploid* (*n*) sets of chromosomes, one from the egg, the other from the sperm.

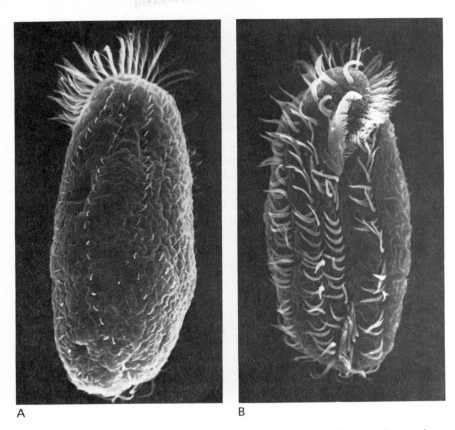

A   B

Figure 4.9 *Paraurostyla*, an advanced ciliate. These scanning electron micrographs show the dorsal (A) and ventral (B) surfaces of the protozoan magnified 600 X. The four types of ciliary structures should be especially noted. (Reprinted from the *Journal of Protozoology*, vol. 25, pp. 65–74, by permission of the Society of Protozoologists, G.W. Grimes and S.W. L'Hernault.)

  While the micronucleus is able to undergo division and thus produce new nuclei of both types, it can do very little else, so that ciliates from which the macronucleus has been removed soon perish. This is because the micronucleus lacks an important structure, the nucleolus. As the student is aware, the cell uses DNA as the template from which messenger, ribosomal, and other classes of RNA are transcribed. Even in metazoans, these substances are not sent directly to the cytoplasm, but must undergo enzymatic treatment in the nucleolus. Because in ciliates this structure is wanting, the micronucleus is unable to produce RNA and therefore cannot direct the formation of proteins or other aspects of metabolism. Consequently, when a micronucleus in *Loxodes* is being transformed into a macronucleus, it begins to develop nucleoli one at a time, as it gradually increases in size. Thus there is a period when these ciliates contain nuclei that are intermediate in size and structure to the normal two types. Although the nucleoli disappear as discrete bodies as these precursors mature, they remain functionally present, so that the definitive macronucleus is highly active in synthesizing RNA and thus directing the metabolism of the cell.

On the basis of these observations, it might be conjectured that the original stock of the ciliates was uninucleate like most protozoans. Then over long periods of time, these progenitors slowly gained mutations that in sequence induced the formation of dinucleate, trinucleate, and, finally, multinucleate conditions. In the latter of these states, all the nuclei, although numerous, were of one type, much as in those protociliates that are symbionts in frog intestinal tracts. Gradually, with the passing of additional millenia, some of these nuclei became more and more specialized for somatic functions, increasing in size and losing the powers of reproducing themselves. Concurrently, the remaining nuclei became smaller and slowly lost the ability to develop the nucleolus, thus losing metabolic function and becoming strictly generative. Up to this point, all the nuclei, large and small, were diploid, as in *Loxodes* and *Tracheloraphis;* but when the final stage was attained, the macronucleus became polyploid. That is, at this most advanced level, represented by *Paramecium* and the others shown in the illustration (fig. 4.8), the number of macronuclei is reduced to one, but the number of genes present is greatly increased through the union of a number of chromosome sets in a single nucleus (fig. 4.10, B). With this acquisition, the macronucleus somehow regained the ability to divide, although it now does so in the primitive, nearly amitotic fashion found also among a number of soil-dwelling flagellated amoeboids.

Conjugation

One of the characteristic activities carried out by the true ciliates is a type of mating called *conjugation,* which is often viewed as an unusual kind of sexual process. However, no sperm or eggs are involved. In conjugation, two individuals come into contact as shown in the scanning electron micrograph (fig. 4.11), after which the cell membrane breaks down between them at one point. The cytoplasm of the two cells thus is in contact, forming a *cytoplasmic bridge.* At the same time, the macronucleus degenerates and the micronuclei divide several times, but only two micronuclei remain at the end of these processes in each ciliate. After micronuclear division is completed, one of the remaining two pronuclei thus formed of one conjugant is exchanged with one from the other, the nuclei travelling across the cytoplasmic bridge. The ciliates then separate, the pronuclei in each individual fuse and then the cells undergo a complex series of divisions, both nuclear and cellular, until the original numbers of macro- and micronuclei have been restored. The details of the preliminary nuclear divisions and post-conjugation events vary from one species to another.

The Sporozoans

One last major type of protozoan will be used to illustrate the abundant variety achieved by unicellular organisms. This group, the Sporozoa, are parasites in a large number of vertebrates and higher invertebrates. Among them are included

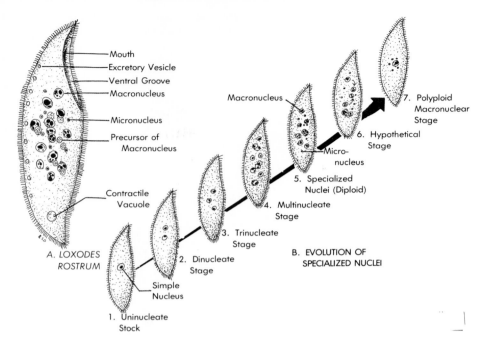

Figure 4.10 *Evolutionary development of two types of nuclei in ciliates.* It is proposed that a multinucleated stage led from the ancestral uninucleated condition to the differentiation of macro- and micronuclei.

some of the largest protozoans, *Porospora gigantea,* a parasite of the lobster, attaining a length up to 10 mm. On the other hand, some important pathogens, like *Babesia bovis,* which attacks European cattle, are as small as many bacteria, not exceeding 1 to 1.5 μ in length.

Adaptation for a parasitic life is the most striking evolutionary adaptation found among these organisms, a specialization that is best illustrated by members of the genus *Plasmodium,* the causative agents of malaria. In man four species produce this disease, all of which have become adapted for their particular mode of living through the development of a highly complex life cycle. The cycle may arbitrarily be considered to begin when an infected mosquito, in feeding upon a human being, introduces a number of the protozoans into the puncture. During this period, the organisms are elongate, slender *sporozoites* capable of gliding movements (fig. 4.12). These forms migrate to and penetrate into the cells of the liver, where they assume a rounded amoeboid condition. Within these cells, the pathogens undergo fission at a rapid rate, bursting out of exhausted cells period-ically and entering new ones, so that in a week's time a large population of *mero-zoites* has been built up. This second type of individual leaves the liver cells and penetrates the erythrocytes, where they behave much as they did before, dividing rapidly until the blood cells containing them rupture and thereupon they enter fresh erythrocytes. During these steps, which are many times repeated, a so-

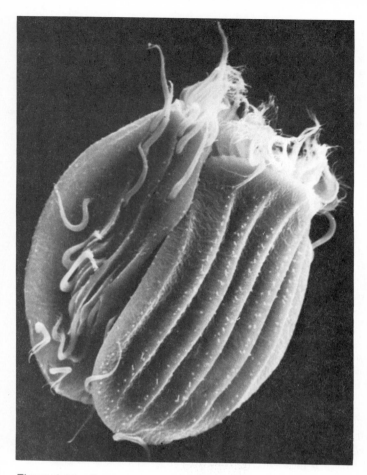

Figure 4.11 *Conjugation in Euplotes.* This unusual scanning electron micrograph shows two individuals united during conjugation, a complex reproductive act that involves an exchange of special micronuclei, called pronuclei. The thick cirri, comprised of many cilia fused together, are also a prominent feature. (Courtesy of John A. Kloetzel, UMBC, Catonsville, MD. Reprinted from *The Journal of Protozoology,* Volume 22, pages 385–392, by permission of the Society of Protozoologists.)

called ring stage is developed, the form of which is characteristic for each species (fig. 4.12). A series of asexual reproductive processes such as the one described above that is carried out directly within the host's cells is usually referred to as *schizogony.* Through the employment of these numerous steps, the organisms are capable of building up a large number of individuals from the relatively few that were originally introduced into the host.

After a latent period of three to five days (that is, a toal of ten to twelve days after infection), the first symptoms of malaria induced by these organisms appear

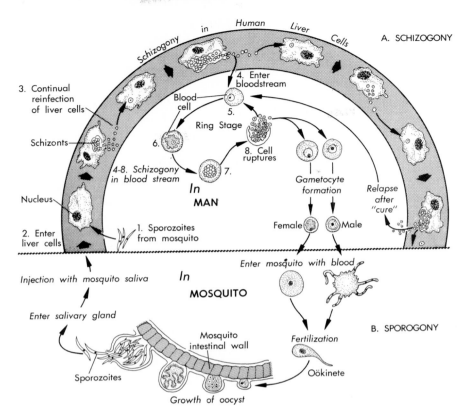

Figure 4.12 *The life cycle of Plasmodium.*

in the form of a series of chills and high fever. The attacks occur at intervals of forty-eight or seventy-two hours, depending on the species of *Plasmodium,* and correspond to the length of the schizogony cycle. As the growth cycle is rhythmic, innumerable infected erythrocytes rupture simultaneously; thus large numbers of merozoites and the toxins produced by them are released together into the blood, resulting in the periodic symptoms.

Although schizogony can continue indefinitely within the host, after five or eight days a new type of individual, the *gamont,* is produced; this stage in turn requires an additional three to six days before it is fully mature. After that period, if a gamont is taken into a mosquito's stomach during feeding, it develops into either an egg or a sperm. Still within the stomach cavity, the gametes unite to form an actively motile stage called the *oökinete.* Without aid of such locomotive organelles, as flagella or pseudopods, the oökinete penetrates *between,* not into, the cells of the stomach wall; it then rounds up and secretes a covering to form a cyst. Here within this *oocyst,* cell division takes place hundreds of times, resulting in the production of as many as 10,000 *sporozoites.* When mature, these rupture the wall of the oocyst and enter the body cavity of the mosquito, in which they move about until they encounter the salivary gland. After penetrating into this organ, they are ready to infect the next person the insect feeds upon. The reproductive processes within the mosquito, termed *sporogony,* differ from those of schizogony both in being initiated by sexual means and in proceeding within a sac (the oocyst) formed by the pathogen. Depending upon the temperature, between ten and twenty days are required for completion of the cycle.

QUESTIONS FOR REVIEW AND THOUGHT

1. Compare the yellow-green and golden-yellow protozoans as to their distinctive charcteristics, including likenesses and differences. How do these two groups differ from the euglenoids? Compare the chloroplasts of the present groups with those of euglenoids; state which seems to be more advanced and why you think so. Now compare the green flagellates and their chloroplasts in the same fashion.

2. Describe how the golden-yellow protozoans show evolution parallel to that demonstrated by the yellow-green forms. In what ways do the dinoflagellates show any comparable parallel evolution? To what extent do the green protozoans exhibit similar parallel development?

3. Name as many types of colonies found among the protozoans as you can and cite a specific example of each. Which group in your opinion shows the most complete series of forms illustrating the evolutionary development of spherical colonies? Be prepared to support your decision with facts and examples.

4. Prepare a full list of instances where it is difficult objectively to distinguish whether the organism is an alga or a protozoan. If green protozoans and algae are considered to be related to the mosses and other higher plants, and accordingly placed in the Plantae, on what basis is it valid to place all the other unicellular forms together as the kingdom Protista or Protoctista?

5. Define symbiosis and each of its three types. How many cases of mutualism have been encountered among the protozoans? How many of parasitism? Among the euglenoids a photosynthetic type was listed (p. 26) that cannot live outside the frog's intestine; how would you classify this case of symbiosis?

6. Give the life cycle of *Plasmodium.*

SUGGESTIONS FOR FURTHER READING

Berger, J.D., and H.J. Schmidt. 1978. Regulation of macronuclear DNA content in *Paramecium tetraurelia*. *J. Cell Biol.*, 76:116–126.

Corliss, J.O. 1973. History, taxonomy, ecology, and evolution of species of *Tetrahymena*. In *Biology of Tetrahymena*, ed. A.M. Elliott, p. 1–55. Stroudsburg, Penna, Dowden, Hutchinson and Ross, Inc.

Dutta, G.P. 1974. Recent advances in cytochemistry and ultrastructure of cytoplasmic inclusions in Ciliophora (Protozoa). *International Review of Cytology*, 39:285–343.

Elliott, A.M. 1973. Life cycle and distribution in *Tetrahymena*. In *Biology of Tetrahymena*, ed. A.M. Elliott, p. 259–287. Stroudsburg, Penna, Dowden, Hutchinson, and Ross, Inc.

Hausmann, K. 1978. Extrusive organelles in protists. *Inter. Rev. Cytol.*, 52:197–276.

May, R.M. 1978. The evolution of ecological systems. *Scient. Amer.*, 239(3):160–175.

Raikov, I.B. 1976. Evolution of macronuclear organization. *Annual Review of Genetics*, 10:413–440.

Sleigh, M.A., and J.R. Blake. 1977. Methods of ciliary propulsion and their size limitations. In *Scale effects in animal locomotion*, T.J. Pedley, ed. New York, Academic Press, p. 243–256.

Schweiger, H.G., and M. Schweiger. 1977. Circadian rhythms in unicellular organisms: An endeavor to explain the molecular mechanism. *Inter. Rev. Cytol.*, 51:315–342.

Introduction to Metazoan Variety

5

Although many doubts may exist about the true relationships of the various unicellular organisms, there is rarely question about the metazoans proper constituting a natural close-knit group, in spite of the wide variety of forms that exists. Jellyfish bear no resemblance to beetles, for instance, and lobsters look not at all like kangaroos, but in between such extremes of morphology are found so many intermediate forms that all are readily discerned to be interrelated. Only the inclusion of the sponges in the Metazoa is ever questioned, for reasons that become apparent when that group is described in the next chapter.

DISTINGUISHING TRAITS

Even where species transitional in general morphology or appearance are absent, other traits are found within the bodies of all metazoans that indicate relationship. As nearly all these multicellular animals feed on living things, whether of plant or animal origin, most possess a *digestive tract.* Moreover, *muscle cells* that provide movement are present in nearly every animal, and *neural cells,* with only minor exceptions, coordinate the muscle cells and the other body parts. These three traits, it must be remembered, are not only shared by the majority of metazoans but are universally absent in every other group— including the unicellular types and green plants.

Within their cells are other unusual traits which further distinguish the typical Metazoa. When undergoing normal division, the cells display astral rays, organelles found elsewhere in identical condition solely in the brown seaweeds and in a modified state only among the primitive fungi and termite symbionts. In addition, the spermatozoa have a posterior flagellum that is devoid of flimmer, a feature shared only by dinoflagellates and the sperm of certain aquatic molds.

DIVERSIFICATION IN STRUCTURE

Since so many kinds of Metazoa exist, wide diversity in internal organization might be anticipated. In fact, variation in structure of every body organ conceivable is to be found among the representatives. In different combinations, the principal variable traits are viewed as indicative of basic relationships; consequently they are used in arranging the members of this subkingdom into a number of phyla.

Overall Plan, or Symmetry

Metazoan variety begins with the general body plan, or *symmetry*, of the numerous types. Usually the kind of organization displayed is determined by means of a simple test, that of actually or, more frequently, visually, dividing the organisms into halves—mirror-image halves, to be more specific. If a knife or imaginary plane would cut the specimen into corresponding halves almost anywhere as long as it passes through a central point, the animal must be *spherically symmetrical*, for only a globe can form mirror-image halves in this manner. Similarly, if mirror-image halves can be produced by any plane passing through a central line, the form in question must be constructed like a cylinder, cone, or other geometric figure based on the circle; hence, it shows *radial* symmetry (fig. 5.1, A). Most animals, however, can be divided into two corresponding portions by only a single plane, one extending along the central axis from front to back. Since the forms are thus divided into two sides (right and left), they are said to display the *bilateral* (two-sided) variety of symmetry (fig. 5.1, B). Sometimes as in the snails or others with spirally built bodies, there is no possible way of dividing the organisms into mirror-image parts; consequently, in spite of a well-marked body plan, these animals are said to be *asymmetrical*.

Because the type of symmetry produces considerable differences in the general organization of the animals, distinctive sets of terminology are employed for each. For instance, bilateral animals have one end that consistently goes foremost; this is referred to as the *anterior* region while the opposite end is the *posterior*. In contrast, radially symmetrical animals are either sessile or can move in any direction, with no single region going foremost to a greater degree than any other; therefore these terms are inapplicable. For these organisms, the mouth is used as a point of reference. Accordingly the *oral* side is that surface on which the mouth is located and the *aboral*, that which lacks it. The remaining comparable terms used in describing shape and location are made sufficiently clear by the diagram (fig. 5.1).

Development of the Embryo

There are several ways in which a fertilized egg may develop into an embryo and then into a fully developed young. Since the patterns of forming the embryo are constant within a given type of organism, zoologists make use of this trait to assist in uncovering the often obscure relationships of the various phyla and other taxa. Although the details thus vary from group to group, the major features are constant—only the means by which these basic traits are attained are distinctive. For clarity, the pattern followed by the developing starfish and mammalian egg is described before the more important variants are briefly discussed.

A Basic Pattern

As in all animals, development is considered to commence in starfish and mammals, including man, when the sperm penetrates the egg. Once *fertilization* has thus been accomplished, the resulting fertilized egg, or *zygote*, divides (cleaves) first into two embryonic cells, then into four, eight, sixteen, and so on.

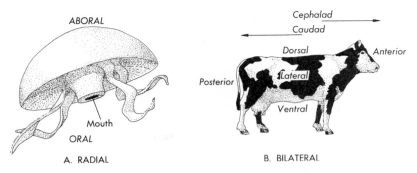

ABORAL

Mouth

ORAL

A. RADIAL

Cephalad

Caudad

Dorsal   Anterior

Posterior   Lateral

Ventral

B. BILATERAL

Figure 5.1   *Types of symmetry.*

Eventually these processes of *cleavage,* as they are called (fig. 5.2, A–C), produce an embryonic stage known as the *morula,* that consists of a solid ball of cells. In section the cells of the morula are seen to be large so that they reach the center of the cellular mass (fig. 5.2, D). As further development occurs and division continues, the cells, of course, become smaller and smaller, so that the ball of cells now becomes hollow, representing the embryonic stage called the *blastula* (fig. 5.2, E). The cavity within this embryo is known as the *blastocoel,* a term that enters into the discussion of body cavities that follows.

In the development of starfish and others with a scanty supply of yolk, a peculiar development leads to the next stage of the embryo. One side of the ball-like blastula becomes first flattened and then folded within itself. As the infolded part, or *invagination,* deepens, the result is a two-layered embryo called the *early gastrula,* now having two cavities (fig. 5.2, F). One of the cavities is the remnants of the blastocoel, while the new one is the cavity of the *primitive gut* (archenteron), which opens to the outside by the *blastopore.* Two layers of cells, known as *germ layers,* are now present; that one forming the wall of the whole gastrula is referred to as the *ectoderm,* while the one that makes up the wall of the gut is the *entoderm,* often also spelled *endoderm.* The third layer is formed in many ways. In the starfish and vertebrates, the walls of the primitive gut begin to bulge outward on each side and eventually form two pockets (fig. 5.2, G). In other groups, certain cells grow or migrate inward to produce a similar result (fig. 5.2, H). However it may be produced, a third germ layer arises, called the *mesoderm* from its location between the ectoderm and entoderm. After this *late gastrula* has thus been brought into existence, further development into a young animal involves differentiation of each of these three germ layers. While the full processes are fascinating to study, the details are beyond the scope of this book; however, a summary of the structures of the adult produced by each germ layer is presented in table 5.1.

Other Major Patterns

A great many characteristic patterns of embryonic development occur as a result of the presence in the egg of large quantities of yolk as already intimated.

These, however, are more pertinent to the study of the embryo as a specialized science, rather than as an aid to discerning relationships between animals, which is the concern here. Hence, it is necessary to view only two further sets of distinctions at the present point.

One set involves the number of germ layers that develop within the embryo. In a few organisms, among them the jellyfishes, no mesoderm ever is established, so that only two layers are present, even in the adult. Such groups are said to be *diploblastic,* and if the derivatives of the mesoderm are viewed in table 5.1, it is immediately clear why such animals which lack that middle germ layer are necessarily relatively simple in structure. In contrast, those groups that develop the usual three layers are said to be *triploblastic,* a condition that typifies the vast majority of metazoans.

The second set concerns the direction in which cell division takes place during early cleavage, best seen when the 4-celled stage becomes 8-celled. In vertebrates, the two poles of each dividing nucleus lie vertically to the plane of the 4-celled embryo, so that division of the cells occurs squarely across each component (fig. 5.2, I). Thus, in this *radial* type of cleavage, the cells become arranged in vertical stacks. Among earthworms, mollusks, and many other phyla, on the other hand, the poles of the dividing nuclei are arranged diagonally to the plane of the embryo, with cell division consequently taking place obliquely. Hence, the resulting new cells are placed between, rather than upon, the others, so that a *spiral* arrangement of cells ensues (fig. 5.2, J). Another detail of some importance is that the blastula in a few taxa is not hollow but is filled with cells. This solid form is known as a *stereoblastula* in contrast to the hollow *coeloblastula;* similarly solid gastrulas, called stereogastrula, also occur in some phyla.

In at least a few species in the majority of the metazoan phyla, the developing embryo breaks free of the egg coverings at an early stage, maybe even as early as the blastula or gastrula, and thereby becomes an active *larva,* quite different in

Table 5.1 Principal Derivatives of the Three Germ Layers

Ectoderm	Mesoderm	Entoderm
Epidermis of skin; sweat glands, etc.; feathers, hair, reptilian scales	Dermis of skin; scales, of fish, sharks, etc.	Liver and pancreas
Lining of mouth and nostrils; enamel of teeth	Dentine of teeth	Thyroid and thymus glands
Lining of anus	Involuntary muscles of digestive tract, etc.	Epithelium of digestive tract except mouth and anus
Nervous system and sense organs	Skeletal system, blood and circulatory system	Pharynx
	Excretory and reproductive systems	Middle ear
	Lining and mesenteries of body cavity	Lining of lungs and bladder
	Voluntary muscles	

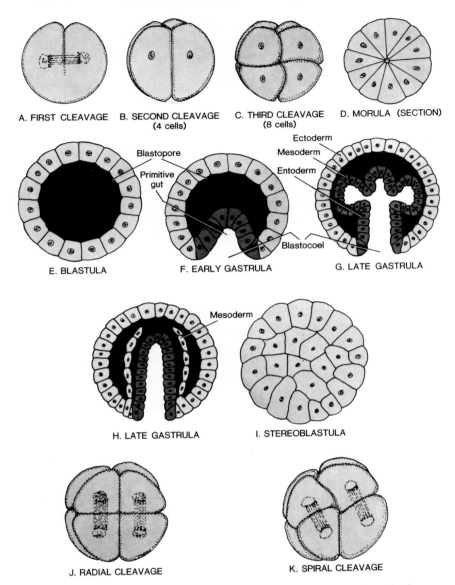

A. FIRST CLEAVAGE B. SECOND CLEAVAGE   C. THIRD CLEAVAGE   D. MORULA (SECTION)
(4 cells)   (8 cells)

Blastopore
Ectoderm
Mesoderm
Primitive
gut
Entoderm
Blastocoel

E. BLASTULA   F. EARLY GASTRULA   G. LATE GASTRULA

Mesoderm

H. LATE GASTRULA   I. STEREOBLASTULA

J. RADIAL CLEAVAGE   K. SPIRAL CLEAVAGE

Figure 5.2 *Principal steps in the development of an embryo.* A–G. Steps in the development of starfishes and certain vertebrates. G,H. Two of the numerous ways are shown by which mesoderm arises in the late gastrula. I. Not uncommonly, the blastula may be solid as here, when it is referred to as a stereoblastula in contrast to the more typical, hollow coeloblastula (E). Similarly gastrulas may be either solid or hollow, with corresponding prefixes used to distinguish the two types. J. In many animal groups, cells divide vertically and horizontally to the plane of the embryo to yield a radial type of cleavage; in others, cell division occurs obliquely to the plane and cleavage is referred to as the spiral type (K).

form from the adult. These larvae are often considered to represent models of the ancestral forms which ultimately gave rise to their respective phyla. Since they thus provide evidence suggesting how the extensive variety that now exists among the metazoans may have come into being, they find particular use in the brief phylogenetic discussions which summarize the principal points in each chapter or group of chapters that follows.

Body Cavities

One of the principal criteria used in classifying animals to phylum is a body part that does not seem like a structure at all—the *body cavity*. What the function of this feature may be has been the subject of much speculation, but no clear-cut conclusions have been forthcoming. Nevertheless, since the body cavity comes in several different types, it often offers clues to the proper relationships of a given organism where all other structures may be contradictory. Several instances of this sort are encountered in the chapters that follow immediately.

The Major Types

The most primitive type of body cavity is none at all (fig. 5.3, A, B). Such *acoelomate* groups are met with in the next succeeding chapters, where jellyfish, man-of-wars, and combjellies are described. In these forms, the space between the digestive tract and body wall (consisting of the epidermis, dermis, and body muscles) is filled with a loose cellular material called *mesenchyme*, derived from the mesoderm of the embryo. The digestive tract itself consists only of entodermal derivatives, largely lacking musculature and having no covering such as a sheath or lining.

The second type of body cavity, the *pseudocoel*, may be readily derived from the acoelomate type merely by eliminating the mesenchymatous filling (fig. 5.3, C). Hence there is merely a cavity, usually filled with fluid, between the body wall and the digestive tract; consequently the body wall has musculature underlying the epidermis and dermis, but the digestive tract typically lacks a membranous covering and has few muscles except in the pharynx. Thus phyla like those containing the parasitic worms known as nematodes and their relatives are considered to have this unlined type of body cavity. During development of the embryo, the pseudocoel forms between the mesoderm and entoderm and therefore corresponds to the blastocoel. One could say that the acoelomates have the blastocoel filled with mesenchyme and that the pseudocoelomates have it fluid filled. Unfortunately, because of the large amount of animal variety that exists, as cited in the preface, the differences are often clearer in the definition than in the actual organism! Later, forms which have mesenchyme filling a cavity that is nevertheless classed as a pseudocoel are encountered that require consideration by the student.

The third and final major type is the coelom (fig. 5.3, D). This kind, present in all (or most all) coelomate animals, is characterized by forming in the midst of the mesoderm of the embryo. Hence, it is entirely surrounded by mesodermal derivatives—musculature and a *peritoneal lining* (peritoneum) being found both

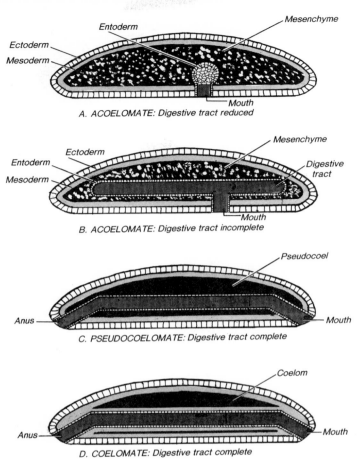

Entoderm
Mesenchyme
Ectoderm
Mesoderm
Mouth

A. ACOELOMATE: Digestive tract reduced

Mesenchyme
Ectoderm
Entoderm
Mesoderm
Digestive tract
Mouth

B. ACOELOMATE: Digestive tract incomplete

Pseudocoel
Anus
Mouth

C. PSEUDOCOELOMATE: Digestive tract complete

Coelom
Anus
Mouth

D. COELOMATE: Digestive tract complete

Figure 5.3 *Types of body cavities and digestive tracts.* Among the metazoans, three major types of body cavities are found and two types of digestive tracts. A. Among certain acoelomate worms (those lacking a body cavity), the digestive tract is virtually absent; hence they are called the acoels. B. Other acoelomates usually have the digestive tract incomplete, the anus being absent. C,D. Pseudocoelomates and coelomates typically have a complete digestive tract.

on the body wall and the digestive tract. Since during development the digestive tract receives supplemental derivatives from the mesoderm in the form of muscles, glands, and lining, that system is typically much more complex in organization than is the case in acoelomates and pseudocoelomates. Development of the coelom is bilateral, as pockets form within the mesoderm on each side of the digestive tract (fig. 5.4). As these increase in size to make the body cavity, the two growing pockets eventually contact at top and bottom, where they fuse to form the mesenteries that support the digestive tract and other internal organs. Because of the manner in which the coelomic sacs form, it is clear that the coelom is a new cavity, not merely a modified blastocoel.

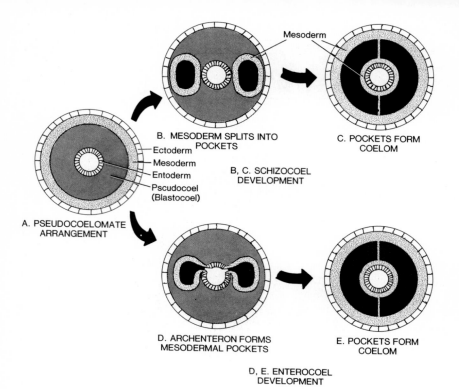

Mesoderm

B. MESODERM SPLITS INTO
POCKETS

C. POCKETS FORM
COELOM

Ectoderm
Mesoderm
Entoderm
Pseudocoel
(Blastocoel)

B, C. SCHIZOCOEL
DEVELOPMENT

A. PSEUDOCOELOMATE
ARRANGEMENT

D. ARCHENTERON FORMS
MESODERMAL POCKETS

E. POCKETS FORM
COELOM

D, E. ENTEROCOEL
DEVELOPMENT

Figure 5.4 *Formation of the two types of coeloms.* A–C. Schizocoel formation involves a split within the mass of mesoderm, while enterocoel formation is from pockets of mesoderm that grow out of the entoderm (A,D,E).

Types of Coeloms

Two varieties of coeloms are recognized, based on the way in which the pockets that give rise to them develop within the mesoderm. In earthworms and many related taxa, the pocket begins as a split in the mesodermal masses located on each side of the growing digestive tract (fig. 5.4, B, C). These pockets then grow until they fill much of the interior, as just described. Since the body cavity thus is formed by a split, or schism, in the mesoderm, the resulting coelom is referred to as a *schizocoel*. In the second type, found in starfish and in the vertebrates, including man, the pockets form as saclike outgrowths of the primitive gut as seen in the preceding section. Several pairs of such saccules appear, the number depending on the type of organism (fig. 5.4, D, E). These then increase in size until, like the foregoing, they each fill one side of the interior until the two unite along the top and bottom of the digestive tract. Because of their derivation from the archenteron, this variety of body cavity is termed an *enterocoel*.

Homology, Homoplasy, and Analogy

When different types of metazoans are compared, three major categories of structural resemblances may be encountered. On one hand, correspondingly located parts, such as a bird wing and a human arm, may on the surface appear quite different, yet upon close comparison the two structures are found to have much in common. Within each a calcareous skeleton is present that begins with a single large bone; that is followed by two long, rather slender bones, then a series of short flattened ones, and finally several rows of small rodlike elements (fig. 5.5). Whatever other anatomical feature is compared, whether musculature, blood vessels, nerves, or integument, comparable resemblances are revealed. Such close correspondences of construction reflect common origin, both embryological and ancestral, and organs displaying them are said to be *homologous* (fig. 5.5).

On the other hand, while totally dissimilar outwardly from a human arm, the bird wing does bear some resemblance to the wing of a bat (fig. 5.5), but, because primitive and most other mammals do not possess wings, the flying appendage of the bat is not derived from that of a bird. So although all three structures mentioned are homologous as *fore appendages* because of their common ancestry from a reptilian stock, as *wings* the bird and bat appendages have been developed separately. Such independently derived structures that are similar in appearance are said to display *homoplasy* (fig. 5.5).

In contrast, if the wing of either creature discussed is compared to that of a butterfly, very little in common in structure or appearance can be perceived that would reflect either homology or homoplasy. Nevertheless, the insect wing serves the same function, that of providing flight, as do the other two. Corresponding parts which thus lack common origin and structural similarity but have like functions are said to be *analogous* to one another (fig. 5.5).

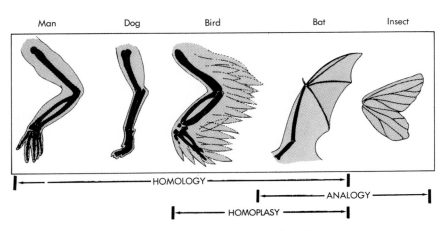

Figure 5.5   *Comparison of homology, homoplasy, and analogy.*

Segmentation

The bodies of many metazoans are composed of longitudinal series of more or less similar parts, variously called *segments, somites,* or *metameres.* In some cases, while no serial arrangement is visible externally, the internal organs may nevertheless be built of repetitious series, as in the vertebral column of a fish or cat; consequently these organisms, too, are considered to be segmented.

Many variations on the general theme of segmentation exist, including its complete absence, as in snails. On the other hand, earthworms and many others are segmentally constructed both externally and internally. In contrast, insects, although distinctly segmented externally, have become so highly modified that much of the repetitiousness of structure has been lost in their internal organs. And finally, the vertebrates are distinct in lacking external segmentation but show it clearly internally in the vertebrae, ribs, nerves, and, among fishes especially, in body musculature.

The Organism

As the various types of animals are described in the following pages, several distinctive features of these advanced forms of life in general should be noted. Because all consist of cells and cell products, in a sense they may be considered to be colonies. But they are much more than merely well-organized colonies. In the first place, the cells themselves are, as a rule, diversified for specialized functions, whole series of each chief type being joined together to form *tissues,* as nervous tissue for conducting impulses or as muscle tissue for producing movement. Typically, tissues of several varieties are united to form *organs,* such as muscles, bones, and blood vessels, and these in turn function together in series called *systems,* whether reproductive, digestive, or circulatory.

But the whole animal, or *organism,* is not just a group of separate systems bound together by its integument. Far from being a mere accumulation of so many digestive, neural, reproductive, muscular, and other organs, each animal, it will frequently be seen, is greater than the sum of its parts.

QUESTIONS FOR REVIEW AND THOUGHT

1. Enumerate and define the distinguishing traits of the metazoans and their cells.

2. What is the test for symmetry in the basic body plan of organisms? Compare the three types. Which seems to provide the basis for the greatest amount of animal variety? Are asymmetrical forms always haphazard in body plan? Cite examples.

3. Name in sequence five steps in the embryological development of a metazoan.

4. In what stage does a blastopore appear? the blastocoel? What is a primitive gut? In what stage or stages are three different layers of cells found? Which have two? Which have only one? How does a morula differ from a typical blastula?

5. What is meant by a stereoblastula? How does it differ from a morula? How does spiral cleavage differ from radial?

6. Define the several types of body cavities that occur among metazoans. How is a coelom formed? Compare schizocoel formation with that of an enterocoel.

7. Define the terms: mesenchyme; mesoderm; peritoneum; somite; tissue; organ. Can a body cavity be considered to be an organ? Why or why not?

8. Compare homologous, analogous, and homoplastic organs.

9. Distinguish between acoel and acoelomate.

SUGGESTIONS FOR FURTHER READING

Alexander, R.M. 1975. Evolution of integrated design. *American Zool.,* 15:419–425.

Anderson, S. 1974. Patterns of faunal evolution. *Quart. Rev. Biol.,* 49:311–332.

Braitenberg, V. 1977. The concept of symmetry in neuroanatomy. *Ann N.Y. Acad. Sci.,* 299:186–196.

Clark, R.B. 1964. *Dynamics in metazoan evolution: Origin of the coelom and segments.* Oxford, Claredon Press.

Cohen, J. 1967. *Living embryos.* New York, Pergamon Press.

Costeau, J.Y. 1973. *The art of motion.* New York, World Publishing Co.

Costello, D.P., and C. Henley. 1976. Spiralian development: A perspective. *American Zool.,* 16:277–292.

Dyal, J.A., and W.C. Corning. 1973. Invertebrate learning and behavior taxonomies. In *Invertebrate learning,* ed. W.C. Corning, J.A. Dyal, and A.O.D. Willows, Vol. I, p. 1–45. New York, Plenum Press.

Gould, S.J. 1977. *Ontogeny and phylogeny.* Cambridge, Mass., Harvard University Press.

Oppenheimer, J.M. 1977. Studies of brain asymmetry: Historical perspective. *Annals of the New York Academy of Sciences,* 299:4–17.

Tait, J. 1928. Homology, analogy, and plasy. *Quart. Rev. Biol.,* 3:151–173.

Wilkie, D.R. 1977. Metabolism and body size. In *Scale effects in animal locomotion,* T.J. Pedley, ed. New York, Academic press, p. 23–36.

The Sponges: An Evolutionary Enigma

6

The members of the sponge group have become so highly diversified that their proper position relative to other forms of life has been the subject of debate for several centuries. As will be recalled, the Greek fathers of biology avoided the controversy by placing these organisms in a kingdom separate from both plants and animals. But when the two-kingdom scheme of classification was formalized in Linné's time, their relationships became an issue that remained active for at least a century, with many biologists advocating their inclusion among the plants and an equal number favoring them as animals. Though the "animal" school of thought finally prevailed, differences of opinion concerning their relationships still persist. Present contention centers around the respective merits of considering the organisms variously as an independent subkingdom, as a mere phylum among the metazoans, or as close relatives of a peculiar group of protozoans. Since no single point of view shows signs of immediately becoming universally accepted, attention is confined here to indicating the basis for the diversity of opinion. As the description of the main features of structure, reproduction, and behavior unfolds, the student undoubtedly will agree that the wonder of the matter is not the three conflicting concepts, but the absence of even more.

DISTINCTIVE TRAITS

For the greater part, sponges are irregular in shape and thus asymmetrical; however, a small number of species are vase- or cup-shaped, and therefore *radially symmetrical*. A few forms live as separate individuals, that is, they are *solitary;* but the vast majority occur as closely united *colonies*. While solitary forms are rarely more than several inches in height or breadth, the colonial varieties occasionally assume fairly immense proportions, perhaps a meter or more in diameter. Even the largest of such colonies lack the ability to react visibly to stimuli of any sort. Their inability to respond animal-like even to violent blows was one reason for their being considered plants by earlier biologists.

Body Organization

The relative inertness of the sponges arises through the absence of both nerve cells and properly arranged muscle cells. Contractile cells are present nonetheless, but neither encircle nor ascend the body wall; instead they merely regulate the size of the openings that lead into the numerous canals found penetrating the

71

body on all sides. Beyond doubt, the canals themselves are the most striking feature of the group, their openings providing the basis for the scientific name *Porifera*, that is, pore-bearers. During the processes of diversification, the canals have become organized into three distinct types of systems called *asconoid*, *syconoid*, and *leuconoid*, the major likenesses and differences between which are shown in the illustration (fig. 6.1, A–C). Often the outer surface of the body wall is covered with a layer of cells known as the *epidermis*, but the inner cavity, variously referred to as the *spongocoel* or *paragaster*, has no special lining (fig. 6.1, A, D). As will be noted below, all bodily functions are carried out at a cellular or tissue level of organization, for no organs, let alone systems, are present.

Choanocytes

Within the canals proper or in enlargements of the canals, depending upon the type of system, occurs another striking feature of the sponges—the *collar cells*, or *choanocytes* (fig. 6.2, A). It was the presence of these peculiar cells equipped with a collar and a long flagellum that first convinced biologists of the sponges' animal-like character, for the beating of the flagella induces water to flow through the canal system—in short, these cells provide active movement of a kind not usually found in plants. However, the current they set up behaves in a most unusual fashion, for the flow is *inward* through the sides and *outward* through the spongocoel's mouthlike opening, the *osculum*—quite the opposite direction from that found in fish or other aquatic creatures which are clearly metazoan in every sense of that word. The flow of water produced by these cells is of the utmost importance to the life processes of sponges, for the exchange of gases, ingestion and egestion of food, and the elimination of wastes are all dependent upon it.

The "collars" or "funnels" which supply the basis for both the English and the Latin version of the cell's name appear to be food-collecting devices. Formerly it was assumed from their appearance that they might function much as funnels do. That is to say, food particles carried in the current produced by the beating flagella were thought to fall into the interior of the funnel and then possibly to be taken into the cell by pseudopodal action. Recent investigations have disclosed that this preliminary concept is only partially correct. Instead of dropping into the interior as supposed, food particles actually adhere to the *outside* surface of the collar. After a particle has become attached, contraction of the collar is initiated, while the cell membrane in that region moves first upward toward the free end of the collar, and then over the upper edge, and down inside the collar toward the cell's surface, carrying the particle with it to be engulfed by pseudopodal activity.

Other Features

After capturing food in the manner described above, the choanocyte does not seem to digest the substance itself but instead passes the particle to an amoeboid cell. Such *amoebocytes*, situated in the jellylike matrix (*mesenchyme*) which sur-

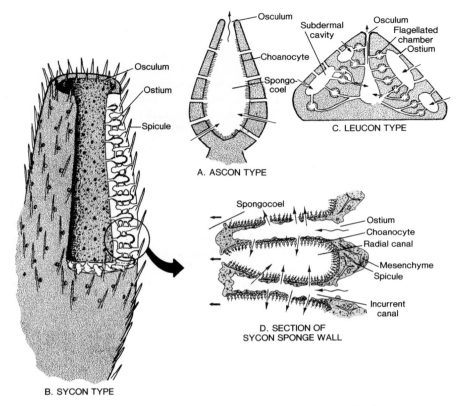

Figure 6.1 *Sponge structure and diversity.* The structure and diversification of sponges is centered around the movement of water, a process essential to ingestion, respiration, reproduction, and elimination of wastes. A. The simplest of three general patterns of structures is the ascon type, in which the flagellated cells are within the spongocoel. In the other two (B,C), it should be noted that in these, too, the flagellated cells pump water outwards, not into the sponge.

rounds all or most of the cells of the body, engage in many of the sponge's activities. They digest food and may either pass digested materials not needed by themselves to other cells or store it in the form of fat for later consumption. Furthermore, they can become transformed into any other type of cell as required. Should a wound occur in the surface of the sponge, for example, a number of amoebocytes migrate to the area and develop into epidermal cells, sporocysts, choanocytes, or any other cell type that may be needed to repair the injury. Finally, in addition to a function to be discussed later, that of reproduction, they may become specialized as *sclerocytes,* cells that produce the characteristic skeletal elements called *spicules.*

Spicules

Since sponges are so comparatively simple in structure, it is fortunate for systematists who are interested in classifying them that their skeletal elements are highly diversified; otherwise there would be little to distinguish the species or to establish relationships at the various levels represented by genera, families, and the like. As can be seen in the table (table 6.1), even the classes are based primarily on these structures, for they are undoubtedly the most distinctive feature of these organisms.

Because spicules are both extensively varied and so unusual in construction, it has been necessary to establish whole sets of terms to describe them. Subdivision based on size is first employed with two categories, one for large and the other for small components. The larger type, called *megascleres,* form the principal skeletal framework of the organisms, while the smaller spicules, the *microscleres,* are scattered throughout the body. Because much intergradation is found between the two subdivisions, the distinctions are in no way absolute ones. Nor can any such size differences be found among the skeletal elements in the Calcarea and in certain other sponges.

All spicules can be further classified according to the number of axes along which they are built. On this basis there are five chief types, most of which

Table 6.1 A Frequently Used Scheme of Sponge Classes

| Characteristic | Classes | | |
	Calcarea	Hexactinellida	Demospongiae
Spicules			
Composition	Calcareous	Siliceous	Siliceous, spongin, or both; sometimes absent
Size types	Not differentiated	Megascleres and microscleres	Megascleres and microscleres often present
Principal types	Monaxons, triradiates	Triaxon	Tetraxon
Epidermis	Present	Absent	Present
Canal systems	Asconoid, syconoid, and leuconoid	Syconoid and leuconoid	Syconoid and leuconoid
Habitat	Shallow marine waters, particularly cooler ones	Usually deep seas, especially tropical	Shallow or deep seas and fresh waters
Common name	Calcareous sponges	Glass sponges	Siliceous sponges; horny sponges

include varieties bearing spines at the ends. *Monaxons,* as the name implies, are built along a single axis, which may be either straight or curved; an especially frequent variety found in this category includes C-shaped ones called *sigmas* (fig. 6.2, C). *Tetraxon* spicules, the second class, frequently have one axis elongate and three others grouped at one end of the long one, where they radiate outward in different planes. However, in a modification of the tetraxon called the *triradiate,* the commonest spicule of calcareous sponges, the usual long axis is nearly or entirely absent, leaving only the three lesser ones to form the same number of rays, arranged nearly on one plane.

Whereas in the tetraxon type the four axes simply meet at a central point, in the third major variety, the *triaxon,* only three axes exist, but cross through one another so that six rays are formed. This type is found only among members of the class Hexactinellida. The fourth type, the *polyaxon,* consists of a large number of equal rays arranged around a central point. Usually they occur most commonly as microscleres and may be known as *asters.* The fifth type, *spheres,* is well described by the name; it includes rounded bodies surrounding a central point.

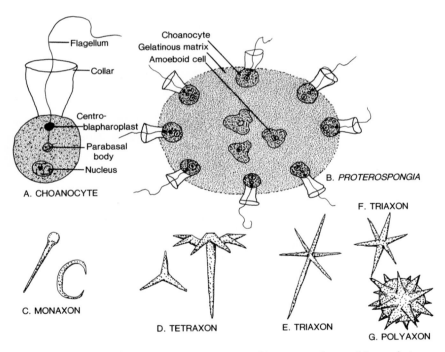

Figure 6.2 *Fine structural features of sponges.* The structural resemblances between the choanocyte (A) and the flagellated protozoan *Proterospongia* (B) provide a basis for the belief that sponges are derived from a stock similar to the latter type of colonial protozoan.

Development of Spicules

Among the several types of amoebocytes found in the mesenchyme of sponges is the sclerocyte, whose specialty is that of forming spicules in a most unusual manner. Uniqueness is evident from the very onset of the processes, as shown in calcareous sponges by the steps involved in forming the monaxon variety of spicules. When beginning to secrete a monaxon, a sclerocyte undergoes nuclear division, but its cytoplasm fails to follow suit. Having thus achieved a binucleated condition, the cell becomes quite elongate (fig. 6.3, A), while its two nuclei move apart. As the latter do so, a minute limey thread appears between them, which the cell gradually thickens and lengthens with deposits of lime. This thread continues to receive deposits until it has become of such a size that the sclerocyte no longer can encompass it, and at that point cell division finally occurs. The two resulting daughter cells then remain on their respective halves of the growing spicule, travelling back and forth and depositing calcium on the surface and tips until it is ready for emplacement. How the cells determine that the spicule is finished has not been established.

The development of triradiates is similar, but the processes are initiated by three sclerocytes which gather together in a group. After the nucleus of each cell has divided by mitosis, the three fuse together to form a single six-nucleate cell (fig. 6.4). Between each pair of nuclei, a minute calcareous ray is formed, all of which the cell slowly increases in thickness and length by calcareous depositions. Eventually the bases of this trio of separate elements make contact and fuse to form a three-armed precursor (fig. 6.3, B). Later, after further depositions have enlarged this triradiate precursor to sufficient size, multiple cell division takes place, and the resulting six cells thereafter work in pairs on individual rays. While one member of each team secretes material only on the tip, thereby lengthening the arm, the other one adds material to thicken it, especially near the base. Consequently each ray tapers to a sharp point.

Spongin

In place of spicules some sponges have spongin fibers, arranged in a treelike, branching fashion or in a network of sorts. Among those so constructed are the sponges sold on the market for washing windows, automobiles, or other articles. The actual sponges of commerce consist of only the skeleton; the living material is removed by the sponges' being deposited in very shallow water until the soft parts have become thoroughly decayed. In some other groups a small amount of spongin may be present that serves principally in binding the spicules together. Unlike spicules, which contain large amounts of inorganic matter, spongin consists almost exclusively of a special type of protein.

REPRODUCTION

In reproductive habits sponges are highly varied, for they exhibit asexual and sexual methods of propagation, as well as extensive powers of regeneration.

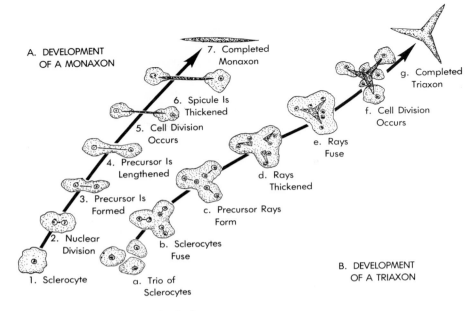

A. DEVELOPMENT OF A MONAXON

7. Completed Monaxon

6. Spicule Is Thickened

5. Cell Division Occurs

4. Precursor Is Lengthened

3. Precursor Is Formed

2. Nuclear Division

1. Sclerocyte

a. Trio of Sclerocytes

b. Sclerocytes Fuse

c. Precursor Rays Form

d. Rays Thickened

e. Rays Fuse

f. Cell Division Occurs

g. Completed Triaxon

B. DEVELOPMENT OF A TRIAXON

Figure 6.3 *Development of spicules.*

Regeneration

Since sponges are relatively simply organized, it is not too surprising to find that they possess great abilities in regenerating lost parts. In fact, even small pieces are capable of growing into complete individuals; the processes are so slow, however, that many months or even years may be required for growth to be completed. But several groups of true animals to be studied later, such as the flatworms and starfishes, are similarly able to regenerate whole individuals from small parts. The extent of the sponges' powers is best shown by an experiment first reported by H.V. Wilson in 1907. By forcing live specimens through silk cloth, this biologist broke the organisms into isolated cells and fragments containing several cells. Under the microscope he then observed these particles as they moved about by means of the amoebocyte's pseudopodal activities. Whenever a cell or tiny clump encountered another, fusion occurred, so that larger and larger aggregates resulted, consisting of various combinations of amoebocytes and collarless choanocytes. Formation of such clusters has recently been established as involving a special substance known as an *aggregation factor*. This has been found to be a very large macromolecule consisting of a protein combined with a polysaccharide. As the aggregates gradually became still larger, some of the amoebocytes arranged themselves in the form of an epidermis; concurrently the choanocytes gathered into hollows and developed collars and thus began to establish typical flagellated chambers. Over a considerable period, these processes, accompanied by ordinary growth, slowly restored the originally minute fragments into a complete, functional sponge.

Asexual Reproduction

Among the asexual means of reproduction found in sponges are several which differ only slightly from regenerative processes. So similar are the two types of activities that the most important distinction probably lies in their origin, regeneration occurring after accidents or human experimentation, whereas the other is induced by climatic influences. For example, under adverse conditions, many adult poriferans may disintegrate or collapse, leaving small remnants called *reduction bodies*. Basically consisting of amoebocytic masses covered with an epidermal layer, the reduction bodies redevelop into adult sponges when favorable conditions return.

A more typical reproductive process, however, is found among all freshwater and certain marine species, in which special bodies known as *gemmules* are formed. In the freshwater sponges, gemmule formation is initiated early in the fall by amoebocytes gathering into clusters here and there throughout the body of the organism. Initiation of the processes is known to be stimulated by decreasing day length and is totally inhibited by continuous light, effects known collectively as *photoperiod* influences. To these clustered cells, other specialized amoebocytes called nurse cells, or *trophocytes*, carry food until the former have become filled with food reserves (fig. 6.4, A). After fattening has proceeded sufficiently, still other amoebocytes surround the original cluster and assume a columnar shape to form a cellular wall. When completed, this living wall secretes a hard membrane over the inner and outer surfaces. In the meantime, spicules have been carried to the developing gemmule and inserted between the columnar cells; distribution of the spicules is made in such a fashion that an area of the sphere is left free where a closed pore, the *micropyle*, eventually develops (fig. 6.4, C). Soon after the gemmule has thus been completed, cold weather generally sets in and the adult sponge dies. As the old sponge disintegrates, the enclosed gemmules are set free into the water, and, being resistant to freezing, survive the winter. In spring, after the micropyle has opened, the amoebocytes emerge and, by processes not unlike those of regeneration, slowly develop into a mature sponge.

Sexual Reproduction

Although all types of sponges are capable of reproducing sexually, the complete details of the processes have not been clearly established. Doubt centers especially around the origin of the egg and sperm. The sperm, for example, has been described by some biologists as being derived from an amoebocyte, but others claim it arises from a modified choanocyte. It is evident, however, that the fertilization of the egg involves a distinctive feature. At least in many species, after entering a sponge by way of the canal system, the sperm penetrates either a choanocyte or an amoebocyte, depending on the species. The latter acts as a nurse cell and actually carries the sperm to the egg, where it assists in uniting the two gametes. After fertilization is completed in this peculiar fashion, the zygote develops into a larva bearing numerous flagella; this swims about perhaps for as long as a day before attaching itself to the substrate. Once attachment is com-

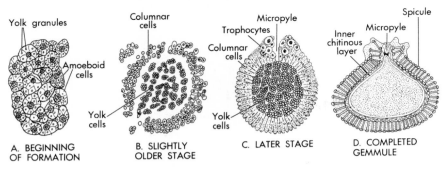

Figure 6.4 *Formation of a gemmule.*

pleted, the entire ciliated region of the larva infolds and thus comes to occupy the body's interior, where the ciliated cells develop into choanocytes. At the same time, the remaining portion gradually forms the epidermis, mesenchyme, spicules, and other parts of the adult sponge.

CELLULAR TRAITS AND RELATIONSHIPS

Although, as has been seen, the sponges are amply different from the more typical metazoans in structure and even in the reproductive processes, still other distinctions are to be found within the cells. These unusual features of cytology are frequently employed by biologists in suggesting possible relatives of the group.

Cellular Characteristics

Although the illustration (fig. 6.2, A) makes clear the structureal features of the most characteristic sponge cell, the choanocyte, a few of the organelles present may not be familiar to the reader. The *centroblepharoplast* (fig. 6.2, A), lying at the extreme base of the flagellum, corresponds to a combination of the centriole and basal body; a second unique structure, the *parabasal body,* lies between this organelle and the nucleus. It may be recalled that a body similar in structure and name to the present one is found also in the trypanosomes. In addition to these traits, the flagellum bears two rows of flimmer.

During cell division no trace appears of the astral rays, which are so characteristic of typical metazoan mitotic processes; instead there is an entirely distinct set of events (fig. 6.5). As the parabasal body disintegrates, the centriole separates from the blepharoplast, undergoes division, and descends to the nucleus. There each centriole secretes a new parabasal body and, at the same time, is active during the separation of the chromosomes in providing spindle threads (fig. 6.4, C). After division is completed, the centriole ascends to, and reunites with, the blepharoplast, where it secretes a new flagellum as the old one disintegrates.

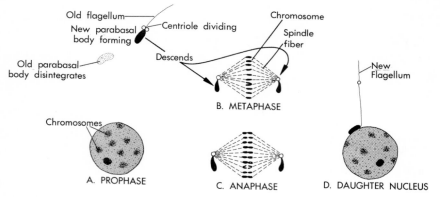

Figure 6.5 *Cellular features of sponges.*

Possible Relatives

Among those unicellular forms classified as both protozoans and algae is a group of colorless flagellates variously called the *craspedomonads* and *choanoflagellates*. These organisms are frequently regarded by biologists as possibly having a common ancestry with the Porifera, a suggestion based on the many unusual features shared by the cells of both groups. For instance, in these choanoflagellates is also found the distinctive cytoplasmic collar of the sponge choanocyte; this structure encircles a single flagellum (fig. 6.2, B), which has been shown by electron microscopy to be similarly double-flimmered. Moreover, the collar has recently been observed by J.B. Lackey to behave during food-catching in exactly the same manner described above for the Porifera. Resemblances are further accentuated by the cells' internal construction, for a centroblepharoplast and a parabasal body are present, arranged in a corresponding relationship with the nucleus. And finally, cell division has been shown to proceed without astral rays and along lines similar to those figured for the sponges.

Although most of the choanoflagellates are solitary, a few simple colonial types are also known. One of these, *Proterospongia,* is often regarded as intermediate between the two groups, though it certainly appears closer to the protozoans than to the sponges. These colonies consist of a gelatinous mass bearing scattered collared individuals embedded around the surface, while in its interior are found a number of amoeboid cells (fig. 6.2, B).

QUESTIONS FOR REVIEW AND THOUGHT

1. For how long have sponges been generally accepted to be animals? How else have they been classified?

2. State the characteristic features of the Porifera. Which ones seem to be especially distinctive? How do the cells undergo mitotic division?

3. Describe a choanocyte and tell how it serves in feeding. What other organisms have a similar cell type? What other kind of cell is essential in providing nourishment to the sponge?

4. Define the various types of spicules. By what methods are these produced within a sponge? What may replace spicules in certain members of the phylum?

5. Distinguish between reproduction and regeneration. Describe the extent of regeneration that has been documented in sponges. What organism, if any, demonstrates greater powers of regeneration?

6. Describe the two types of reproductive processes found among poriferans.

SUGGESTIONS FOR FURTHER READING

Berquist, P.R., M.E. Sinclair, and J.J. Hogg. 1970. Adaptation to intertidal existence: Reproductive cycles and larval behavior in Demospongiae. *Symposia Zool. Soc. London,* 25:247–271.

de Ceccaty, M. P. 1974. Coordination in sponges: the foundations of integration. *Amer. Zool.,* 14:895–904.

Frost, T.M. 1976. Sponge feeding: A review with a discussion of some continuing research. In *Aspects of sponge biology,* F.W. Harrison and R.R. Cowden, eds., New York, Academic Press, p. 283–298.

Hartman, W.D., and H.M. Reiswig. 1973. The individuality of sponges. In *Animal colonies,* R.S. Boardman, A.H. Cheltham, and W.A. Oliver, eds., Stroudsburg, Pa., Dowden, Hutchinson and Ross, Inc. p. 567–584.

Humphreys, T. 1970. Biochemical analysis of sponge cell aggregation. *Symposia Zool. Soc. London,* 25:325–334.

Korotkova, G.P. 1970. Regeneration and somatic embryogenesis in sponges. *Symposia Zool. Soc. London,* 25:423–436.

Lackey, J.B. 1959. Morphology and biology of a species of *Protospongia. Trans. Amer. Micro. Soc.,* 78:202–206.

Reed, C., M.J. Greenberg, and S.K. Pierce. 1976. The effects of cytochalasins on sponge cell reaggregation: New insights through the scanning microscope. In *Aspects of Sponge Biology,* F.W. Harrison and R.R. Cowden, eds., New York, Academic Press, p. 153–169.

Simpson, T.L. 1973. Coloniality among the Porifera. In *Animal colonies,* R.S. Boardman, A.H. Cheltham, and W.A. Oliver, eds., Dowden, Hutchinson, and Ross, Inc., p. 549–565.

Wilson, H.V., and J.T. Penney. 1930. The regeneration of sponges (*Microsciona*) from regenerating cells. *J. Exper. Zool.,* 56:73–147.

Variety among Elementary Metazoans

7

Above the sponges, but at the most primitive levels of the typical Metazoa, animal variety has evolved along lines entirely different from those encountered among the more advanced forms. These early specializations may be viewed as results of experiments on Nature's part, as it were, in attempts at finding an efficient manner of organization. At any rate, whether the result of experiment or mere accident, these primitive metazoans must certainly be considered aside from the main line of ascent for reasons that will quickly become apparent.

THE MESOZOA

Among the remnants of one of the earliest side branches that developed is a group of organisms highly specialized for a parasitic mode of living. So simple are they and so distinct from the more familiar animals that they might readily pass for protozoans were their cells not provided with that identifying mark of all metazoans, the astral rays formed during cell division. Their name is suggestive of unicellular trends, for the term Mesozoa may be translated "mid-animals," that is, between the Protozoa and the Metazoa proper.

For many years, zoologists believed that these creatures might have been much more complex at one time and became degenerate as a consequence of their parasitism. Indeed, it was frequently suggested that the mesozoans were degenerate flatworms of the type called trematodes, to be discussed in the next chapter. But because no evidence supporting this concept has been found as the group has become better known, the trend now is toward accepting the animals for what they appear to be—extremely simple metazoans.

Morphology

Among the better-known mesozoans are the dicyemids, a group of parasites common in the kidneys of the squids and octopi. As a whole, they are wormlike animals up to seven or eight millimeters long, whose bodies are densely covered with cilia. Each individual consists of a definite number of cells constant for each species, but usually not exceeding twenty-five. Of these, one, an elongate *axial cell,* is centrally located and surrounded by the remainder, the ciliated *somatic cells* (fig. 7.1). Often the anterior somatic cells are somewhat differentiated into a *head,* the remainder of the body then being referred to as the *trunk.*

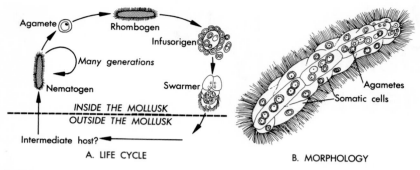

Figure 7.1 *The life cycle and structure of a dicyemid mesozoan.*

Reproduction

Whereas the somatic cells are concerned with such vegetative activities as absorbing dissolved foodstuffs from the environment, the axial cell is primarily devoted to reproduction. Although the several accounts that describe propagation disagree in some details, the following appear to comprise the main events: the processes begin with the axial cell nucleus undergoing mitosis. While one of these products remains unchanged to provide the axial nucleus for future generations, the second daughter nucleus undergoes numerous divisions. Large numbers of nuclei result from these mitoses, but, as cell division does not occur, the nuclei remain within a common cytoplasmic mass. Furthermore, because they are produced by simple mitosis, not meiosis, the nuclei are not looked upon as eggs, but as *agametes*. After cell maturity has been attained, each agamete nevertheless behaves much as a normal egg, for further development is by growth and ordinary cell division repeated numerous times. The first division in each case is somewhat unequal, so that a larger and a smaller cell result. The larger one does not undergo further mitotic division but eventually froms the elongate axial cell of the juvenile. On the other hand, the lesser cell divides into smaller and smaller parts that gradually arrange themselves as the ciliated layer of somatic cells. After cellular differentiation has been completed, the young leave the adult's body and enter directly into the host's kidney.

Life Cycle

As long as the host itself is sexually immature, the parasites continue to produce generation after generation of the typical form described above, called the *nematogen* (fig. 7.1, A). However, once the squid or octopus has become fully mature, the nematogen is replaced by a second type, known as the rhombogen. *Rhombogens* (fig. 7.1, A) are produced either by modificatioin of the nematogens existing at the period of change or directly from agametes. Basically nematogens and rhombogens are identical in structure, but differ in the type of offspring they produce. Among rhombogens the agametes do not develop into new adult forms; instead they remain within the adult's body to establish a cluster of cells. These cellular balls, referred to as *infusorigens,* are themselves reproductive bodies and repeatedly give off single cells from the surface; each single cell after release in turn undergoes multiple cleavage to form a free-swimming, ciliated *infusoriform* larva, or *swarmer* (fig. 7.1, A). The short, oval body of this larva consists of several central cells overlaid by a series of large outer ones, all but the two anteriormost of which bear long cilia. After completing development, the larva leaves the parental rhombogen, escapes from the host, and enters the sea. Beyond this point the cycle remains unknown; generally it is assumed that the larva infects another kind of host, where it probably matures and undergoes sexual reproduction. Then after this conjectured intermediate host has been eaten by a squid or octopus, the life cycle described above apparently begins once more.

THE CNIDARIA (COELENTERATA)

How far the present phylum has become diversified from other animals is perhaps suggested by the disagreement that existed in bygone years over their relationships. During the formative stages of modern biology, its members were classed along with sponges, starfishes, and an assortment of other animals in the Zoophyta. Then, after such "radiates" as starfishes had been separated into several distinct phyla, the present animals and the sponges were together designated as the Coelenterata by Leukart in 1847. It was not until 1888, however, that Hatschek finally separated the organisms into the groups usually accepted today.

Part of the difficulty over their relationships arises through the presence within this phylum of two entirely different-appearing body forms. One type, the *medusoid,* represented by the familiar jellyfish, is actively swimming and more or less bell-shaped, while the other, the *polypoid,* is sessile and cylindrical. In the corals, sea anemones, and hydra, the polypoid type alone is present and in certain jellyfish only the medusoid, but frequently both body forms are found during the course of the life cycle of a single species (fig. 7.2, B). A distinctive flat, ciliated larva, called the *planula* (fig. 7.3), is characteristic of the cnidarian life cycle. The name Cnidaria, which has largely replaced the former name Coelenterata for this phylum, is based on the Greek word *knide* (nettle) and refers to the stinging capabilities of the members.

Structural Characteristics

Until very recently only three major lines of development had been recognized, as was reflected by that number of classes. In the mid 1970s, however, Werner worked out the life cycle of an unusual type previously placed, for lack of complete information, in the class Scyphozoa (table 7.1). During the life cycle of one species of these cubomedusoids from the Caribbean Sea, strong resemblances to the Hydrozoa were also noted. This was especially true of the structure of the polypoid, whose gastrovascular cavity lacked the division found in the medusoid adults, quite like that of *Hydra.* In contrast, as may be noted in table 7.1, these organisms also share many characteristics with the Scyphozoa;

Table 7.1   The Classes of Cnidaria

	Classes		
Hydrozoa	**Cubozoa**	**Scyphozoa**	**Anthozoa**
Polypoids and/or medusoids	Polypoids and medusoids	Medusoids; polypoids reduced or absent	Polypoids only
Gastrovascular cavity not divided; contains neither tentacles nor nematocysts	Gastrovascular cavity divided into 4 sacs containing nematocysts	Gastrovascular cavity divided into 4 sacs containing nematocysts or tentacles	Gastrovascular cavity divided by 4 septa bearing nematocysts
Mesoglea without cells	Mesoglea containing muscle cells	Mesoglea containing muscle cells	Mesoglea containing connective tissue
Nerve ring present	Nerve ring present	Nerve ring absent	Nerve ring absent
Gonads ectodermal	Gonads entodermal	Gonads entodermal	Gonads entodermal
Fresh water or marine	Tropical seas	Marine	Marine
3,000 species	Perhaps 50 species	200 species	6,500 species
Hydras; hydromedusae; man-of-war	Sea-wasps	True jellyfish	Corals; sea anemones

accordingly it was necessary to erect a new class for these forms, which are known as "sea-wasps" because of the severity of their stings.

While cnidarian variety is thus relatively restricted to four major lines, great diversity occurs within each class, as shown later. Yet, in spite of the many outward modifications, a high degree of internal structural similarity is shared by all members of the phylum. The *gastrovascular cavity*, or coelenteron, which contains no other organs, is especially diagnostic. While the fundamental characteristics are best brought out by the diagram of *Hydra* morphology (fig. 7.2, A), one point that is not self-evident requires particular notice.

Cellular Organization

The point in question concerns the nature of the two cellular layers respectively derived from the ectoderm and entoderm in these diploblastic animals. Often these creatures are considered to reflect a tissue grade of organization. If by the term "tissue" any sheetlike arrangement of the cells is implied, it is entirely applicable here. If, however, the more specific usage of zoology as defined on page 68 is meant, its appropriateness is not so evident. Notice, for instance, the number of kinds of cells found in the outside layer (fig. 7.2, A), the epidermis. Here, intermixed with epithelial cells, are a number of glandular, sensory, nervous, and stinging varieties. As a whole, too, the several types are not grouped together but are randomly scattered throughout the layer. Within the

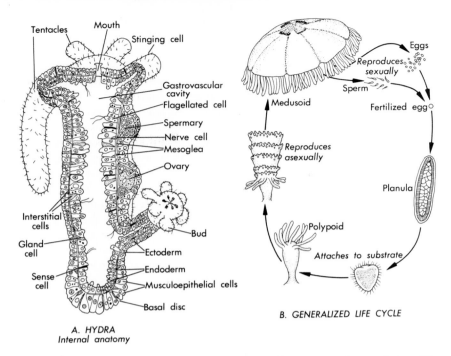

A. HYDRA
Internal anatomy

B. GENERALIZED LIFE CYCLE

Figure 7.2 *Characteristics of the Cnidaria.* Among the numerous characteristics of the phylum are its primary radial symmetry, the two layers of cells separated by mesoglea, a gastrovascular cavity, tentacles, and a stinging mechanism, including nematocysts.

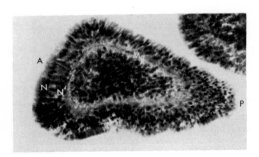

Figure 7.3 *A planula larva of Pennaria tiareli.* The letters A and P mark the anterior and posterior ends of the 24 hr-old larva, respectively. N indicates the nuclei of the epithelio-muscle cells and N′, those of the mucous cells. The mesoglea is lettered Mg. X 142. (From Martin, V.J., and M.B. Thomas, 1977: *Biol. Bull.,* 153:198–218.)

lining of the gastrovascular cavity, the *gastrodermis,* a similar situation is encountered. Consequently it is evident that the organization of these animals, even at the cellular level, is quite distinct from that of other metazoans. It is because of this and other peculiarities that the cnidarians are often considered to represent a side branch of the Metazoa, well off the main line of evolution. Be that as it may, many advances over the sponges in structure and function alike will be noted below, not to mention a much more typical animal pattern of behavior. No longer is dependency placed upon flowing currents of water for food, gas exchange, and other activities. Yet the tissue type of organization does impose a degree of restraint that is absent among more advanced phyla, as becomes evident later.

Nematocysts

The stinging cells mentioned above are not entire cells, but only specialized parts, and are therefore more correctly referred to by their technical name, *nematocysts.* Normally, each nematocyst is enclosed tightly within the specialized cell that secreted it. During use it is released through a trapdoorlike lid, the *operculum,* which is activated by a triggering mechanism, the *cnidocil.* After being discharged, typical nematocysts are seen to consist of a spherical or ovate *bulb,* from one end of which projects a long *thread.* Frequently at the base of the latter are several spines, but much variation in structure exists. In fact, through the detailed studies of the French invertebrate zoologist R. Weill, seventeen distinct types have been named and described. A few representatives of these are shown in the illustration (fig. 7.4).

Not all the types are present in any single species, of course; a few are common among most cnidarians, while others are confined to certain classes or orders. *Hydra,* for example, possesses four different kinds, two of which, the *volvents* and *penetrants,* are especially abundant. After discharge, the former is shaped like a corkscrew; its function seems to be that of entangling itself upon the prey and thus assisting in the capture of food. On the other hand, the tip of the penetrant's thread, slender and too weak for the task though it may appear to be, penetrates the epidermis (even the chitinous covering of arthropods!) and, releasing its poisonous contents, paralyzes, or perhaps kills, the victim.

Toxins of Nematocysts

Although human beings may handle most living coelenterates without being able so much as to detect the ''sting'' of the nematocysts, this is not always the case. Occasionally ocean beaches are closed to bathers when jellyfish become too abundant, for some species can produce unpleasant burns. Indeed, several scyphozoans inhabiting warmer seas can cause very serious illness or even death if accidentally brushed against. The sting of the Portuguese man-of-war (fig. 7.5) is similarly dangerous to human beings; contact with only a single tentacle may result in prostration, interference with breathing, or, with good fortune, only severe lesions that may leave permanent scars.

These effects arise from a combination of four different sets of toxic substances that can be distinguished by their solubility and other properties. A

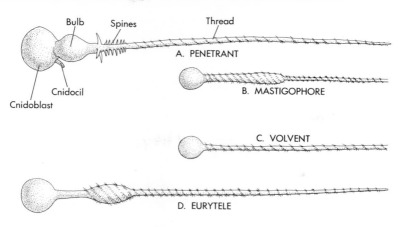

Figure 7.4 *Major types of nematocysts.*

water-soluble anaesthetic called *hypnotoxin* paralyzes the prey, whereas alcohol-soluble *thalassin* causes irritation and itching when applied to the skin of vertebrates. In larger doses, the latter induces severe gastric upsets, weakness, and death. A glycerine-soluble substance named *congestin* appears related to thalassin, for the effects of both are similar. In contrast to the first three toxins, which are proteins, the fourth is *tetramine,* that is, tetramethylammonium hydroxide. Its actions resemble those of curare in paralyzing the endings of motor nerves.

Some animals seem able to acquire an immunity against these toxins, either by heredity or by their food habits alone. The anemone, *Adamsia,* for instance, has been found to feed regularly upon various crabs, which it stings into inactivity with its nematocyst-bearing tentacles. However, it is frequently found attached to mollusk shells in which certain hermit crabs dwell. The crab actually places the anemone on its shell, in this way securing a degree of protection against predators, especially from other crabs. Moreover, the hermit crab is known to be immune to the anemone's poison; if some of its body fluid is injected into other crab species, the latter become immune to the anemone's stings, too.

The Evolution of Diversity

Although the cnidarians differ anatomically in many essentials from the remaining metazoan phyla, they nevertheless can serve to illustrate many features of animals in general. Not least among these is the clear-cut picture they provide of evolutionary changes within each of several classes. While diversification is equal in extent in all four classes, in three the developments can be made clear only by long discussions of morphological details. Consequently, attention will be confined here to the class Hydrozoa which can serve as the example for all.

Of the 3,000 species belonging to this class, both the majority and simplest occur among the *hydroids* that resemble *Hydra* in basic structure (fig. 7.6, A).

Figure 7.5 *The Portuguese man-of-war and a commensal fish.* The sting of the man-of-war (*Physalis physalis*) is so strong as to be dangerous to man; the fish (*Nomeus gronovii*), however, swims freely among the tentacles without harm and is thus protected against predators. (Courtesy of Dr. Charles E. Lane.)

Hydra itself is generally accepted as being among the most primitive members—it is difficult to conceive how any animal could be much simpler in structure than it is! While that genus and others are solitary and naked, one line of development leads to the establishment of colonies of a peculiar sort. These consist of two types of individuals; one type, the *hydranth,* bears tentacles and is concerned chiefly with feeding, while another, the *gonangium,* is without tentacles and is specialized for reproductive purposes (fig. 7.6, B, D). Along this branch, *Syncoryne* (fig. 7.6, B) is primitive in that its gonangia are borne upon the hydranth, not separately, and produce sperm or eggs, whereas more typically they reproduce only asexually by budding. In more advanced genera like *Obelia,* the budded-off forms are medusoids and are generally short-lived. Usually they

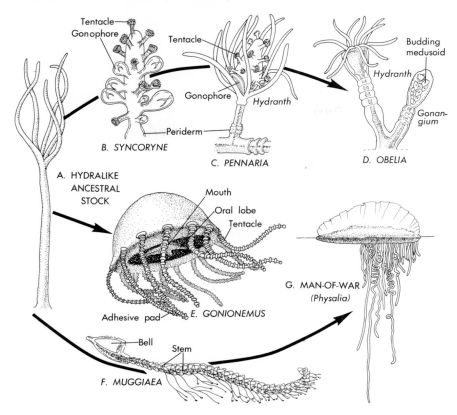

Figure 7.6 *Evolution within the class Hydrozoa.* Three major lines of evolution seem to exist within this class. The first leads to minute colonies (A–D), the second to actively swimming jellyfish (E), and the third to complex floating colonial forms (F,G).

do not feed and exist only long enough to shed gametes into the sea, where fertilization occurs. Since the fertilized egg grows into a new colony of polypoids, the medusoid stage appears to serve principally in disseminating the species.

As the above advancements are made, the beginnings of another set of events can be detected. The colonies, again as shown by the genus *Syncoryne,* originally are protected by a transparent sheath only along the basal growth; with further development, this jacket, or *periderm,* becomes extended into bell-like enclosures around the hydranths and gonangia, as in *Pennaria* (fig. 7.7) and *Obelia* (fig. 7.6, C, D). In some side branches of this line, instead of a chitinous covering, a calcareous deposit is secreted over the colony, forming a coral-like growth. This type, known as hydrocoral, grows in tropical marine waters together with true corals and makes important contributions to the growth of coral reefs.

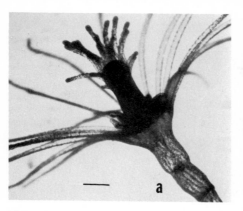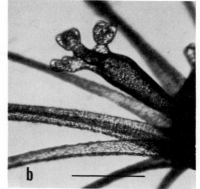

Figure 7.7 *A colonial hydrozoan budding.* These light micrographs of *Corymorpha* clearly show the hydranth (A) and the immature medusoid buds (B). (Reprinted by permission by Dr. Clay Sassaman and *Biol. Bull.,* 154:485–496.)

In a second line of evolution within the Hydrozoa, the medusoid stage of the life cycle becomes accentuated, with polypoid stages reduced or even entirely absent (figs. 7.6, E; 7.8). These *hydromedusae,* or *hydroid jellyfish,* differ from the true jellyfish of the class Scyphozoa in having the lower side of the bell-like body partially enclosed by an ingrowing membrane or *velum* (fig. 7.6, E). As jellyfish swim by spreading the bell, or umbrella, and then forcefully closing it to expel the enclosed water, the narrow opening formed by the velum provides a stronger jetlike action and, consequently, more efficient propulsion.

Probably the most remarkable branch of hydrozoan evolution is the final one, whose point of origin remains conjectural. In this line, colonialism is even more greatly developed than in the hydroids, and the colonies passively float or actively swim about the ocean. To assist in swimming, a specialized type of individual is present (fig. 7.6, F, G). The *bell* represents the most primitive specialization of this sort; from this individual the remainder of the chainlike colony is attached, often as in *Muggiaea* (fig. 7.6, F). With evolutionary advancement a float individual, or *pneumatophore,* is added above the bell or bells. In the simplest animals of this type, the float is small, but with increased advancement it becomes very large and the bell is lost, as in *Physalia,* the Portuguese man-of-war (fig. 7.5, 7.6, G). In these highly developed forms, each apparent tentacle is really a specialized individual called a *dactylozooid,* while other types of individuals (*gastrozooids*) are adapted especially for feeding. On the dactylozooids, the nematocysts are particularly potent and, as was pointed out earlier, are dangerous even to organisms as large as man.

Figure 7.8 *Cyanea capillata, one of the true jellyfish of the class Scyphozoa.* (Photo courtesy of the Virginia Institute of Marine Science.)

Distinctive Activities

Locomotion Among Polypoids

Although hydroids are sessile, not all are permanently fixed to the substrate. As an illustration, *Hydra* is known to move from one place to another using several different behavior patterns. If it needs to move only a short distance, it may do so by contracting and expanding the "foot," while the body remains upright. If a greater distance is involved, *Hydra* may creep wormlike along the substrate, but it has a more striking adaptation for travel—that of somersaulting. When movement of this kind is initiated, the body bends over until the tentacles touch the substrate. After the foot releases its hold from the surface, the body inverts and loops overhead until the foot again makes contact. By repetition of these processes over and over again, considerable distance may be covered.

Movement Among Anthozoans

An interesting discovery on cnidarian behavior has recently been made by M. Pavans de Ceccatty and B. Buisson, working with a bottom-dwelling form from the coast of France. This species, *Veretillum cynomorium,* is colonial and reaches a length of 2 to 3 inches. Basically the colony consists of a bare "peduncle," that anchors it in the sand, and a thick prostrate "rachis," from which dozens of individual polypoids extend. The French zoologists noted that the whole colony is often involved in slow rhythmical movements, in which periods of contraction alternate with expansion, especially in response to light. While these activities are not known to move the colony from one location to another, they do demonstrate that colonial forms, even when composed of numerous individuals each capable of independent responses, can react as a single unit to changes in the environment.

Perhaps more striking still is a swimming response found during recent years in an anemone (fig. 7.9). Working with specimens of *Stomphia coccinea* in aquaria, C.S. Yentsch and D.C. Pierce observed that when certain starfish contact that cnidarian a whole set of reactions within the latter is triggered. If a starfish contacts the oral disk of an anemone, the latter's body partially contracts and immediately reexpands. Then the entire upper portion of the animal begins a series of whirling movements, much as a human being might roll his head in a circle. Several complete rotations, each requiring about one second, may occur before the base becomes detached from the substrate. Then by undulating the body from side to side, the anemone swims tentacled-end foremost for distances up to 30 inches, after which it settles to the bottom and becomes reattached. While locomotion by this means is slow and awkward, it nonetheless provides an effective mechanism for escape from starfish.

Another recent study of movement in anemones by R.M. Ross and L. Sutton provides an insight, not into any remarkable mode of locomotion, but into the selectivity often displayed by even such primitive animals as these. The species studied, *Calliactis parasitica,* is a common inhabitant of the Atlantic Ocean off the coast of Europe, where it occurs most frequently upon shells of a whelk occupied by a hermit crab (*Pagurus bernhardus*). In earlier years it had been shown that in a different set of species, the crab (*Eupagurus prideauxi*) places the anemone (*Adamsia palliata*) upon the shell as a sort of defense, but such has not proven to be the case with the present species. The zoologists mentioned show that the present anemone actually seeks out a shell and moves onto it whether occupied by a crab or not. Whenever a shell, being moved by ocean currents or a crab inhabitant, contacts an anemone that is attached to the ocean floor, a series of reactions is initiated. The cnidarian's body bends until several tentacles reach the whelk shell and explore its surface. If the shell is of the proper species (*Buccinum undatum*), more tentacles extend until waves of tentacular movements flutter over it. Many of these organs attach, especially around the shell's margin, and such a firm hold is eventually secured that even a large crab occupant is prevented from moving its habitation farther. Once a secure hold has been established, series of contractions pass down the anemone's body, causing it to become shortened and often twisted, until eventually the pedal disk is loosened from the substrate. After the disk has been freed, the animal bends itself nearly double as it vaults the lower end of the body onto the shell. Once located upon the shell, the pedal disk attaches firmly by means of secretions, the tentacles relinquish their hold, and the anemone resumes normal activities. Only shells of the proper species elicit the response, during which no role of any sort is played by the crab.

Figure 7.9 *Mediterranean sea anemone (Cerianthus doheni).* (Courtesy of the New York Zoological Society.)

THE CTENOPHORA

So closely allied to the cnidarians are the Ctenophora that occasionally they are placed as a subphylum of that taxon. Among their similarities are radial symmetry, jellylike mesoglea, a coelenteron or gastrovascular cavity, and a two-layered pattern of organization. On the other hand, these *sea walnuts* or *comb-jellies*, as the animals are popularly called, are so distinct that full phylum status frequently is accorded them.

Probably the most striking differences from the cnidarians are the absence of nematocysts and the presence on the body surface of eight rows of *combs*. These structures are so characteristic that the phylum name refers to them, *cteno*, Greek for comb, and *phoros*, also Greek, bearing. The combs are really clusters of cilia fused together to form flat platelets (fig. 7.10, A), which, by moving back and forth, provide locomotion for the organism. The combs' movements are quite peculiar. While at rest all stand more or less upright, but in swimming, the combs beat downward, the hindmost moving first, then the next one, and so on to the anteriormost comb in waves—quite like a row of dominoes falling over, but in reverse sequence. All then return slowly to rest before another series of beats provides forward movement again.

Despite the radial symmetry characterizing these animals, the phrase "forward movement" can correctly be applied, because during swimming, one end, the oral, always goes foremost. Moreover, the symmetry is modified by the presence of a pair of tentacles, each located in a pouch on the side of the body. Consequently, while the body is built on a circular pattern, it can be divided into actual mirror-image halves by only a single plane. Thus modified, the animals are more strictly said to possess *biradial symmetry*.

The tentacles, often more than twice the length of the body, can be retracted into the pouches by means of muscles at their bases. Each is provided with a number of *glue cells,* or colloblasts, the secretion of which assists in capturing prey. By and large the food consists of small invertebrates, fish eggs, and plankton, but often the comb-jellies do extensive damage to oyster fisheries by consuming the larvae, thus preventing growth and replacement of the beds.

Fewer than 100 species of ctenophores are known, nearly all of which are found in the surface waters of the oceans. One of the most widely distributed forms, *Pleurobrachia pileus,* occurs in north temperate waters on both sides of the Atlantic and on the American side of the Pacific Ocean. About an inch in length and ovoid in shape (fig. 7.10, A), it is often of an attractive rose color. *Mnemiopsis leidyi,* a 5-inch long species of the west Atlantic, is transparent green; like many other comb-jellies, it is brilliantly luminescent at night. Probably the largest form is the so-called Venus' girdle (*Cestum veneris*), which, though only 2 inches wide, may reach a length of 3 feet. This Mediterranean oddity is often beautifully colored, being transparent green, violet, or blue; besides the usual locomotion provided by the comb rows, it swims by rhythmic movements of the ribbonlike body in water snake fashion.

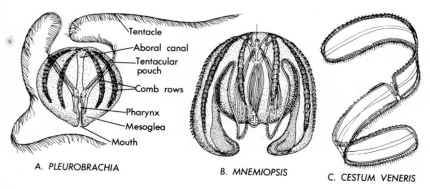

A. PLEUROBRACHIA   B. MNEMIOPSIS   C. CESTUM VENERIS

Figure 7.10 *Some characteristic ctenophores.* Among the distinctive features of the phylum are the biradial symmetry, two layers of cells, extensive mesoglea, and the rows of comblike swimming apparatus.

As a whole, ctenophores are hermaphroditic. All individuals produce both eggs and sperm in gonads located in the digestive tract just below the comb plates. When mature, the gametes leave the coelenteron by way of the mouth and enter the sea, where fertilization occurs. The fertilized eggs may develop either directly into the adult or indirectly by way of a peculiar larva called the cydippid. In the parasitic genus *Gastrodes,* however, a planula larva is found, providing strong additional evidence suggestive of close relationship with the Cnidaria.

EVOLUTIONARY SUMMARY

At the most primitive levels of metazoan organization represented collectively by the several phyla discussed in the present chapter, it is inevitable that relationships are often obscure and controversial. In the first place, the evolutionary events that led to the origins of these early organisms undoubtedly took place during Precambrian times, the fossils of which are notoriously poorly preserved and scantily represented. Secondly, kinships between groups have been dimmed by the diversification that has occurred in each taxon during the 650 million years that have followed the advent of the Cambrian. Thus, while contrasting views of phylogeny prevail for all groups of Metazoa, the routes followed during the development of Mesozoa, Cnidaria, and Ctenophora are particularly speculative. Hence, the following discussion is meant to be suggestive only.

Although it is commonly agreed that the Metazoa arose from some unicellular organism, the specific group is in doubt. Perhaps, as the single-kingdom system proposes, the ancestral stock was a biflagellated form not unlike the gamete of brown algae that is illustrated (fig. 7.11, A). After losing the chloroplasts and becoming holozoic in habit, a two-celled multiflagellated stage resembling

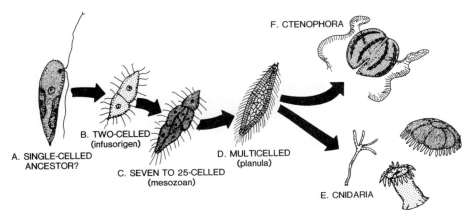

Figure 7.11 *Hypothetical steps in the evolutionary development of the primitive metazoans.*

the infusorigen of the Mesozoa may have arisen. With the passage of time, this seems to have led to the eventual formation of definitive mesozoans possessing 7 to 25 cells, depending on the species and sex. Later, but still probably during the Precambrian—perhaps 1.3 billion years ago—further evolutionary progress brought in a multicellular, ciliated, 2-layered worm, which today is referred to as the planular larva. From such a stock the Cnidaria later developed, beginning with such simple forms as hydras and adding cubozoans, scyphozoans, and anthozoans as the Cambrian period approached. The Ctenophora, too, developed from the planula, but did so along lines entirely apart from the cnidarian—at least, there is no evidence among modern combjellies of polypoid or medusoid stages in their life histories.

QUESTIONS FOR REVIEW AND THOUGHT

1. In what ways is the name Mesozoa (mid-animals) appropriate for the members of this phylum? Could these organisms be considered diploblastic like the Cnidaria are? By what processes do mesozoans reproduce? What are the principal steps in their life cycle?

2. It is difficult to imagine an animal much simpler than a *Hydra*. How does it actually compare at the cellular level with sponges? Be specific in your answer.

3. Compare the four classes of cnidarians as to their distinctive characteristics. State the principal steps in the life cycle.

4. Compare the phyla Cnidaria and Ctenophora, summarizing distinctive traits as well as similarities.

5. List the larval stages discussed in this chapter, including the phylum or phyla in which each occurs.

6. Name all the types of locomotion that have been described in this chapter.

SUGGESTIONS FOR FURTHER READING

Burnett, A.L., R. Lowell, and M.N. Cyrlin. 1973. Regeneration of a complete *Hydra* from a single, differentiated somatic cell type. In *Biology of Hydra,* ed. A.L. Burnett, p. 255–269. New York, Academic Press.
Horridge, G.A. 1974. Recent studies on the Ctenophora. In *Coelenterate biology,* ed. L. Muscatine and H.M. Lenhoff, p. 439–468. New York, Academic Press.
Lenhoff, H.M. 1968. Behavior, hormones and *Hydra. Science,* 161:434–442.
Lewis, J.B. 1977. Processes of organic production on coral reefs. *Biol. Rev.,* 52:305–347.
Loya, Y. 1976. Recolonization of Red Sea corals affected by natural catastrophies and man-made perturbations. *Ecology,* 57:278–289.
Morin, J.G. 1974. Coelenterate bioluminescence. In *Coelenterate biology,* ed. L. Muscatine and H.M. Lenhoff, p. 397–433. New York, Academic Press.

Otto, J.J., and R.D. Campbell. 1977. Budding in *Hydra attenuata*. Bud stages and fate map. *J. Exp. Zool.,* 200:417–428.

Phillips, P.J. 1973. Evolution of holopelagic Cnidaria: Colonial and noncolonial strategies. In *Animal colonies,* eds. R.S. Boardman, A.H. Cheetham, and W.A. Oliver, p. 107–118. Stroudsburg, Pa., Dowden, Hutchinson and Ross, Inc.

Reisa, J.J. 1973. Ecology. In *Biology of Hydra,* ed. A.L. Burnett, p. 60–107. New York, Academic Press.

Ross, D.M. 1974. Behavior patterns in associations and interactions with other animals. In *Coelenterate biology,* ed. L. Muscatine and H.M. Lenhoff, p. 281–311. New York, Academic Press.

Rushforth, N.B. 1973. Behavior. In *Biology of Hydra,* ed. A.L. Burnett, p. 3–41. New York, Academic Press.

Shostak, S. 1974. The complexity of *Hydra:* homestasis, morphogenesis, controls and integration. *Quart. Rev. Biol.,* 49:287–310.

Williams, R.B. 1975. Catch tentacles in sea anemones: occurrence in *Haliplanella luciae* (Verrell) and a review of current knowledge. *J. Nat. Hist.,* 9:241–248.

The Flat
Wormlike Phyla

8

Although the mesozoans and the others of unusual basic anatomy described in the foregoing chapter frequently are recognizable as metazoans only with considerable difficulty, no such problem is encountered with the animals discussed beyond this point. All hereafter are of triploblastic origin and bilaterally symmetrical, at least in the larva. Since appendages for locomotion are found only among the more advanced groups, numerous other actively motile types to be described in ensuing pages have acquired a body shape adapted for creeping movements—that is, they are of a long, slender, or wormlike form. "Worms," then, are abundant among the early phyla, but they come in many varieties.

THE PLATYHELMINTHES

Probably the simplest of the wormlike phyla is the Platyhelminthes, distinguished from nearly all other metazoans by the flat, unsegmented body. This trait is referred to by the phylum name, which is derived from two Greek words, *platys,* flat, and *helminth-,* worm. In combination with the absence of both a body cavity and a circulatory system, it at once sets the members apart from all others, but additional structural peculiarities, including flame bulbs[1] used in excretion (fig. 8.1, B), are also diagnostic.

The 13,000 species known to exist today are arranged in three classes (table 8.1). One of these, the Turbellaria (flatworms), consists largely of free-living forms, found primarily in fresh and marine waters. The other two, the Cestoda (tapeworms) and Trematoda (flukes), contain only parasites, many of which are of economic importance in attacking either man or his domestic animals. Since the three types are so distinct in structure as well as in habit, each must be discussed separately.

The Turbellaria

Morphology

Although the vast majority of Turbellaria are free-living in water, a few are terrestrial, and a number live upon or within other metazoans as either parasites or harmless commensals. Great diversity is exhibited even among the nonpara-

---

1. *Flame bulbs* should be noted here to contain a flamelike *tuft* of flagella, the beating of which propels the excreted substances into the tubule. Later a similar structure, called *solenocytes*, containing only a single flagellum or rarely two, is found in a number of phyla (fig. 8.1, C).

Table 8.1   The Classes of Platyhelminthes

	Classes		
Characteristic	Turbellaria	Trematoda	Cestoda
Digestive tract	At least a mouth present	Well developed	Absent
Intestines	Usually present, of various form	Present, bifurcate	Absent
Epidermis	Ciliated, at least in part	Absent	Absent
Body	Undivided	Undivided	Usually divided into segments
Holdfast organs	Usually absent	Present, frequently with hooks	Present, often with hooks
Rhabdoids	Present	Absent	Present
Life cycle	Simple	Usually complex	Usually complex
Habitat	Fresh or seawater, usually free living	External or internal parasites	Internal parasites
Common name	Turbellarians	Flukes	Tapeworms

sitic forms, particularly in the structure of the digestive tract. In one marine order, the Acoela (fig. 8.1, D), this system consists solely of a mouth or of a mouth and pharynx, a stomach and intestines being uniformly absent. In all others, intestines are present, but an anal opening is lacking; such digestive systems which do not possess an anus are said to be of the *incomplete* type.

The shape of the intestine is subject to extensive variation. It may be a simple straight sac, as in the rhabdocoels, or it may have a number of lateral out-pocketings called *diverticula* (fig. 8.1, A). Sometimes the organ is divided into three major parts, as in the group called the triclads, which includes the common laboratory genera *Dugesia* and *Planaria*. Perhaps the greatest development is to be found in the polyclads, in which a large number of branches extend throughout the body (fig. 8.1, G).

Probably the most striking feature of the turbellarians is the location of the mouth at the middle of the ventral surface, instead of anteriorly, as is normally expected. This opening leads into a chamber called the *pharyngeal cavity,* in which lies the long, tubular *pharynx.* When such triclads as *Dugesia* and *Planaria* feed, the pharynx protrudes through the mouth and pumps the food into the intestine.

Feeding Habits

Although a few acoels and rhabdocoels feed upon algae, the great majority of turbellarians eat either other small animals or bits of wounded or dead larger

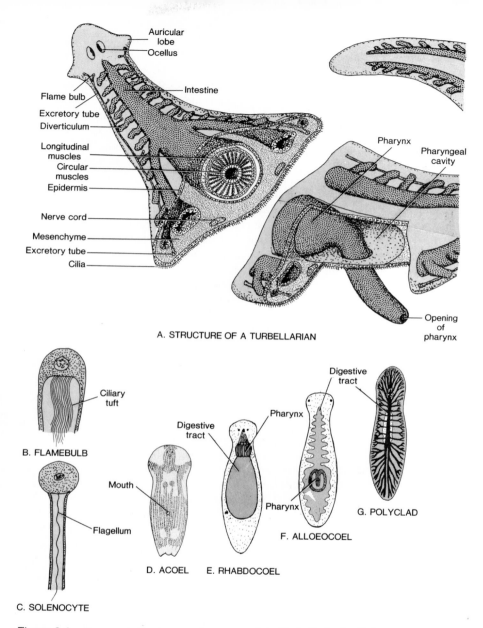

Figure 8.1 *Representative types and structure of the Turbellaria.* In all these worms, a body cavity, segmentation, and a circulatory system are absent; a cellular mass called mesenchyme (A) surrounds the internal organs. The flame bulb (B) functions in excretion; this compares to the solenocyte (C) that carries out that activity in certain more advanced phyla.

The Flat Wormlike Phyla 103

forms, such as fish and clams. Despite their lack of intestines, or in many cases both pharynx and intestine, the acoels ingest small worms and the like, too. Most turbellarians feed upon any kind of animal flesh, but a few are restricted to particular items. For example, a polyclad named *Stylochus* that occurs along the Atlantic coast of the southeastern United States lives solely on oysters, and some freshwater planarians consume only live water fleas.

Live prey appear to be detected by turbellarians mainly by direct contact or the disturbance in the water resulting from the prey's movements. Once the food has been located and approached, the turbellarian secures a hold by means of adhesive organs on its head and, after encircling the animal with its body, employs secretions from the epidermal glands to entangle and subdue the prey.

In running water, flatworms detect juices from dead or wounded animals at considerable distances. If a fish head or piece of raw meat is placed in a shallow stream, the planarians downstream can be observed emerging from beneath cover in large numbers and crawling toward the bait. Upon reaching the meat and testing it thoroughly with their chemical receptor organs, the planarians creep upon it and protrude the pharynx through the mouth. Only if the bait is large do the planarians crawl completely upon it; otherwise they keep at least a portion of their body attached to the substrate by means of secretions.

Ingestion varies with the type of planarian. In polyclads and certain others, the prey is swallowed whole by rhythmic muscular contractions in the pharynx, the latter becoming greatly distended during the process. But more typically the pharyngeal contractions merely provide suction so that the prey is taken in bit by bit.

Digestion

The processes of digestion in these worms may be indicative of their general level of development. Digestive activities probably are confined entirely to the intestine, where they proceed in a most unusual fashion. Instead of secreting digestive enzymes to break down ingested food as most animals do, the intestinal cells engulf the material themselves. If a series of planarians are fed some meat, for example, and specimens then prepared for microscopic study at intervals over several days, these cells are found to have become active as soon as the food contacted them. By intake of water which entered the tract along with the food, they are indicated to have increased in size because they bulge into the intestinal lumen (fig. 8.2). Here, they sent out pseudopods to engulf the food and form food vacuoles in amoeboid fashion. About eight hours are required to empty the intestine of food, and another period of similar duration is necessary to condense the vacuolar contents into homogenous masses. These masses are then gradually digested within each cell, the processes requiring perhaps five days for completion. As the proteins disappear, fat droplets accumulate in the outer portion of the cells for storage against future needs. Apparently the worms are incapable of digesting carbohydrates, but derive their energy from the fats formed from proteins. Nothing appears to be known of the processes by which digested and stored foods are conveyed to the other parts of the body.

The Trematoda

Morphology

In contrast to the turbellarians, the *flukes* comprising the class *Trematoda* vary not at all in the structure of the digestive tract. Perhaps this constancy stems from the worms' parasitic habits, as all species live either upon or within the bodies of other metazoans, particularly vertebrates. Probably associated with their mode of life, too, are their most striking external features, the disks, spines, and suckers by means of which they cling to the host. Even the name of the class is based on these holdfast structures, for its stem, the Greek word *trema,* means "hole" and refers to the pit of the suction disk.

Holdfast mechanisms of three major types (figs. 8.3, 8.5) provide the basis for systematists to classify these worms into orders. These differences, summarized in table 8.2, are associated with such distinctive traits as the method of parasitizing the host and the often highly specialized life cycle.

The Life Cycle of Monogenea

In the Monogenea, development is quite simple, especially among the common ectoparasitic species. The eggs after deposition become attached by means of threads to the fish's gills on which most of the worms feed; after hatching, the juveniles grow more or less directly into the adult form. This basic pattern, however, often shows specializations which have been acquired in adapting to the parasitic existence.

For one example, the endoparasitic genus *Polystoma,* which lives in the urinary bladder of frogs, may be cited. In spring, this fluke releases its eggs into the frog's bladder to exit with the excreta into the water. After about four weeks, the larvae hatch and attach to the gills of tadpoles that are approaching metamorphosis. At first the larva is quite distinct from the adult *Polystoma* (fig. 8.3, A). On the dorsal surface are four eyes, and the entire epidermis is covered with transverse bands of cilia. The attachment organ is especially distinct in bearing numerous hooks, but no trace exists of the six suckers that characterized the mature fluke. After the host tadpole has metamorphosed into a frog, the larva passes down the digestive tract and enters the bladder through the cloaca. It then

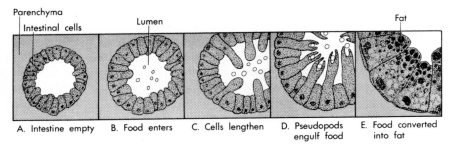

| Parenchyma / Intestinal cells | Lumen | | | Fat |

| A. Intestine empty | B. Food enters | C. Cells lengthen | D. Pseudopods engulf food | E. Food converted into fat |

Figure 8.2 *Digestion in a turbellarian.* The individual cells of the tissue, not the organ, carry out the digestive processes.

completes development by losing the eyes and ciliated epidermis and by gaining one pair of suction disks at a time upon the holdfast until the normal three pairs have been acquired. In the meantime the hooks disappear or become incorporated into the suckers.

Some of the gill-dwelling forms, too, show peculiarities of development. In *Gyrodactylus,* for instance, after the original embryo has developed to a certain point, a second embryo forms inside it. When the second has similarly reached a suitable stage, a third embryo may grow within the second, and, frequently, a fourth may appear within the third. Hence, a single egg may give rise to as many as four embryos. After completing its development, the first embryo hatches, still with its fellows enclosed, and attaches directly to the host. In turn the second, enclosing the later embryos, emerges from the first when ready and commences feeding, the third and fourth leaving their immediate predecessor in similar fashion. This adaptation, besides being striking, throws light on some developments found later among the Digenea.

But the most curious adaptation is that shown by members of the genus *Diplozoon.* After emerging from the egg and losing such larval features as eyes and cilia, the immature animal attaches to fish gills and begins to develop into a second larva, known as the *diporpa.* A suction disk forms centrally on the ventral surface while at a corresponding position dorsally a papilla appears. Two diporpa larvae then unite, one using its midventral sucker to grasp the middorsal papilla of the other. As the bodies of the pair do not lie completely superimposed, they cross over one another in the form of an X (fig. 8.3, B). Lying in this position, the bodies of the two flukes permanently fuse; even the reproductive systems become joined together so that the sperm formed in one individual flows directly into the other, insemination being reciprocal in these bisexual organisms.

The Life Cycle of the Digenea

Probably nowhere else in the animal world are adaptations for an endoparasitic mode of living so complex as in the life cycle of the Digenea. As a rule,

Table 8.2 The Orders of the Trematoda

Characteristic	Orders		
	Monogenea	Aspidobothria	Digenea
Oral sucker	Absent or weak	Absent	Well developed
Ventral sucker	Well developed, located posteriorly	Well developed, located medially	Usually present, varied in location
Hooks	Present	Absent	Absent
Excretory pores	Paired, anterior, dorsal	Single or double, posterior	Single, posterior
Mode of life	Ectoparasites	Endoparasites	Endoparasites
Alternation of hosts	None	None	Marked

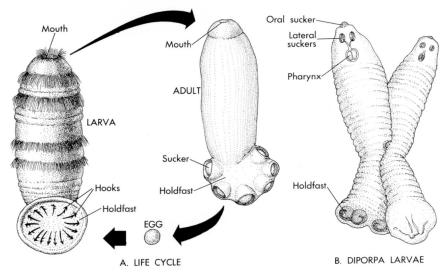

Figure 8.3 *Developmental stages in the Monogenea.* Much diversity is found, as partly exemplified by (A) *Polystoma* and (B) *Diplozoon.*

during development four distinct kinds of larvae occur in sequence, and these usually parasitize three, or sometimes even four, different species of animals. Most frequently the final host is a vertebrate, including freshwater, marine, and terrestrial species, while the first host typically is a mollusk, such as a clam or snail (fig. 8.4).

Some of the features of larval development recall certain of those found in the Monogenea, including the presence of eyes and ciliated epidermis on the first larva. As the eggs are usually deposited in water, this larva, the *miracidium,* swims actively after hatching until it encounters a suitable host. Often a snail of a particular genus or even species is parasitized, but sometimes bivalves serve as this first host. Being quite minute (0.2 mm in length), the miracidium is incapable of surviving longer than twenty-four hours as a free-living form. If fortunate in encountering a host soon enough, the larva enters that organism by dissolving a hole through the flesh by means of enzymatic secretions from special organs called *penetrating glands.* Either during passage into the host's body or shortly afterward, the miracidium sheds its entire epidermis, including the cilia and eyes, to develop into the second larval type, the sporocyst.

Sporocysts, which may attain an inch in length, vary extensively in shape, ranging from wormlike to rounded or highly branched. Unlike the miracidium the sporocyst's body is hollow. At this stage, still devoid of a digestive tract, the parasite moves freely through the host tissues and often does extensive damage. In the meantime, special bodies, called *propagative cells* or *germ balls,* show a resemblance to the monogenetic *Gyrodactylus* discussed earlier. These cells, located posteriorly in the cavity, produce other embryos, either daughter sporo-

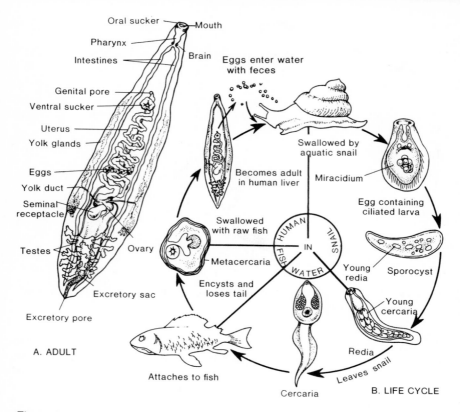

Figure 8.4 *Structure and life cycle of a digenetic trematode.* The Chinese liver fluke shown here is a standard example.

cysts or larvae of the next type, each of which in turn contains its own set of propagative cells within it.

The next larval stage, the wormlike *redia,* differs most strikingly from the preceding in having a collar near the anterior end and two projections on the ventral surface. Probably a more important distinction, however, is the presence of a digestive tract. This system is quite simple, consisting only of a mouth, a muscular pharynx, and a saclike intestine. Another new feature, the birthpore, leads from the interior and provides an exit for the products of the propagative cells.

The propagative cells give rise to either a second generation of redia or, more frequently, a very distinctive type of larva named the *cercaria.* After exiting through the birthpore, the cercariae penetrate the host's body wall and enter the surrounding water. With their broad, rounded bodies and thick tails, these worms resemble tadpoles on a minute scale, the body rarely exceeding 0.02 inch in length. Internally the anatomy is far more complex than that of any preceding stage. The digestive tract, like that of the adult, consists of a mouth surrounded by an oral sucker, a pharynx, an esophagus, and a bifurcated intestine. The excretory system, too, is similar to the adult's, but the bladder opens into a tubule which extends nearly to the tip of the tail. Just before the apex, however, it divides into two, to end in a pore on each side. Depending on the family, the tail is often highly specialized; in certain forms it may be forked much like that of a fish, and in others it is coated with long hairs.

A cercaria swims about for a period varying from a few minutes to as long as three days before encysting either upon or within a second intermediate host. This host may be one of many types of metazoan, including jellyfish, annelid worms, flatworms, crabs, lobsters, insects, and fish, but it is frequently specific for any stated fluke. Entrance into this host is effected by means of the penetration glands and a sharp rostrum; during entrance the tail is generally shed. Once inside, the cercaria secretes a thick wall around its body and remains inactive as this cystlike *metacercaria* until the host chances to be eaten. If the predator proves to be the definitive host of the trematode, the cyst ruptures, and the young gradually matures after reaching the host organs for which it is adapted.

Reexamination of the foregoing cycle discloses that great odds exist against a given egg producing a larva that will reach maturity. First, since the adults live internally and often in terrestrial organisms, the eggs depend upon favorable wind or rain to reach the water needed for successful hatching. Second, that water must contain healthy representatives of the first intermediate host, usually members of a particular genus or even species. Third, the minute miracidium needs to encounter one of these within the short span of its free life. Fourth, suitable examples of the second intermediate host need to be available for the cercaria when it emerges, and, finally that host must be eaten by the definitive host, often of a specific nature. And it should be remembered that these hazards are additional to all the others to which animals in general are subject, such as predation and disease. Consequently, the chief advantages to the species of the complex life cycle of these parasites lies in the abundance of end products which ultimately derive from any single successful miracidium. Although that first larva typically gives rise to only one sporocyst, the latter engenders numerous rediae, each of which in turn produces a profusion of cercariae by means of the propagative bodies. According to calculations made by Libbie Hyman, a single fertilized egg on the average may in indirect fashion result in as many as 10 to 50 thousand cercariae.

Respiration in Trematodes

The life of any parasite that occupies internal organs of the host is subjected to a number of hazards, not the least of which is survival in the oxygen-deficient (anaerobic) environment existing there. Thus endoparasites should be expected to exhibit adaptations for such conditions, a suspicion which has now been well confirmed for adult trematodes. The egg and such larval stages as the miracidium and even the cercaria, however, do not share in this adaptation for a parasitic life, as they tend to show a pronounced dependency on oxygen.

The degree of adaptation toward this parameter is best shown by the changes that occur during the life cycle of digenetic trematodes. In one species (*Gynae-*

cotyla adunca), the metacercaria has a body mass 60 times as great as that of the cercaria, but its relative respiratory rate is 40 percent less. After the metacercaria has been taken into the final host and the adult has emerged from it, the adult body mass is double that of the metacercaria, but the relative respiratory rate is an additional 40 percent less. Furthermore, during the next three days of its existence, an additional slight but steady decrease in oxygen consumption is noted. In some cases adaptation to anaerobiosis is so strong that adult human blood flukes (*Schistosoma mansoni*) have proven capable of surviving five days under completely oxygen-free conditions and adult sheep liver flukes (*Fasciola hepatica*) twenty days. Body temperature of the normal host also is involved in adaptation for survival under an anaerobic environment. For example, trematode endoparasites of cold-blooded vertebrates died from oxygen deficiency when transplanted into birds, which have relatively high body temperatures.

The Cestoda

Like the flukes, the *tapeworms* that comprise the present class are highly specialized for an endoparasitic existence, and similarly lack epidermis and cilia. Eyes, too, are absent, but in the cestodes they are never present, not even in the larvae. Moreover, parasitism is obligatory in tapeworms because a digestive tract is absent during the entire life history. Still further likenesses to the Trematoda exist, but these are usually looked upon as parallel developments acquired independently in the two classes as adaptations for the same kind of life. Included among these is a complex life cycle, involving as many as three different host species, and organs for attachment to the host body. That these are separate acquisitions is suggested by the evolutionary diversifications found within the present class, as will be seen below.

Morphology

As a whole the tapeworms are more extensively diversified in body morphology than the Trematoda and display a greater range in size, some being only a few millimeters long whereas others reach 18 meters. The flat body is either simple or divided into numerous segments called *proglottids* (fig. 8.7). When proglottids are present, an unsegmented *scolex* at the anterior end of the worm functions in attaching the organism to the host and forming new proglottids.

Since both a digestive tract and body cavity are absent, internally the scolex and proglottids consist of muscle and mesenchyme surrounding the nervous, reproductive, and excretory organs. These systems, shown diagrammatically in figure 8.7, need no further discussion here, except to indicate that the reproductive organs are confined to the proglottids. It is thus apparent that the scolex produces proglottids asexually by budding, while the latter are concerned largely with sexual propagation.

Holdfasts

Among the main specializations of the scolex are the external structures used for securing a hold onto the lining of the host's organs. The origins and development of such holdfast structures are represented by an evolutionary series that begins with their complete absence. In *Spathebothrium*, for one illustration, the head is differentiated from the remainder of the worm solely by the absence of reproductive organs, for it and the entire body are devoid of external features for anchorage (fig. 8.5, A). Probably the first holdfasts to evolve are represented by the simple grooves on the sides of the scolex as in *Diphyllobothrium*, one species of which is parasitic in man (fig. 8.5, B). *Bothria*, as such grooves are called, are in general provided with few muscles. Of the many varieties that are known, the most extremely diversified is probably the frilly folded organ found in *Duthiersia* (fig. 8.5, C), but another interesting group of genera has multiples of the folds side by side, as in *Glaridacris* (fig. 8.5, D).

Perhaps derived from the last variety is the second major type of holdfast, known as the *bothridium*. These leaflike extensions of the scolex wall are often arranged in groups of four around the anterior end. In its most elementary form, each extension bears a simple groove as in *Myzophyllobothrium*, but with advancement the groove becomes subdivided to form two or so chambers. Further subdivision culminates in the very elaborate organ found in *Echeneibothrium* (fig. 8.5, F).

True *suckers* (fig. 8.5, G), circular depressions in the scolex wall, are similarly arranged in groups of four. Equipped with several sets of muscles, suckers can create a strong vacuum to attach to the smoothest lining of a host organ.

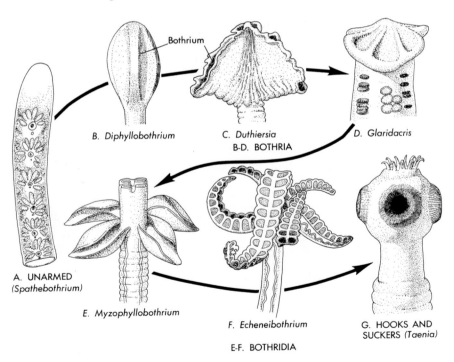

Bothrium

B. *Diphyllobothrium*

C. *Duthiersia*

D. *Glaridacris*

B-D. BOTHRIA

A. UNARMED
(*Spathebothrium*)

E. *Myzophyllobothrium*

F. *Echeneibothrium*

G. HOOKS AND
SUCKERS (*Taenia*)

E-F. BOTHRIDIA

Figure 8.5 *Possible evolutionary path of holdfasts in the Cestoda.*

Taenia solium, the pork tapeworm of man, for example, is quite capable of maintaining its position on the slippery mucosa of the human intestine and is dislodged only with considerable difficulty. It is perhaps assisted by the ringlet of *hooks*, the fourth and final type of holdfast found among tapeworms (figs. 8.5, G; 8.7).

Typical Life Cycle

So frequently, often as a matter of necessity, is the life cycle of *Taenia solium* given as the sole example in introductory biology courses that a beginning student is not aware of the specialized nature of that species. Actually the basic pattern is far better shown by another parasite of man, the broad tapeworm (*Diphyllobothrium latum*), which is illustrated in figure 8.6.

In this species, as in the majority of tapeworms, the eggs develop to maturity within the proglottids, from which they pass to the outside. By action of wind or rain, some eggs eventually reach water and the larva hatches. This larva, the *coracidium*, is ciliated and swims about for a time; to undergo development into the second larva, the *oncosphere* (fig. 8.7, B), it must be eaten by the first intermediate host (usually a crustacean). After entering the crustacean's body cavity, this stage develops into the *procercoid*, which remains inactive until its host is swallowed by a fish or other vertebrate. Within the second host, the procercoid becomes modified into the fourth larva, the *plerocercoid*, which in turn becomes quiescent until a third host, such as a larger fish, bird, or mammal, consumes the second one. In this final host species, the plerocercoid attaches to the intestinal lining, where it absorbs digested foodstuffs through its body wall, assumes the adult form, and produces many proglottids each day.

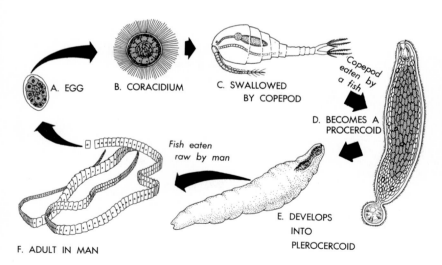

Figure 8.6 *Life cycle of the broad tapeworm of man.* The life cycle of such forms as this (*Diphyllobothrium lata*) is typical of the majority of cestodes.

A. STRUCTURE

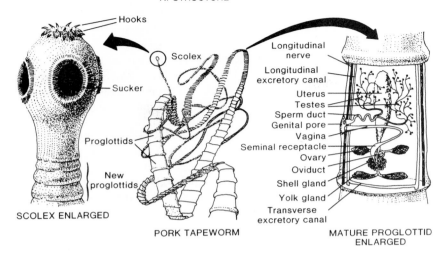

SCOLEX ENLARGED

PORK TAPEWORM

MATURE PROGLOTTID
ENLARGED

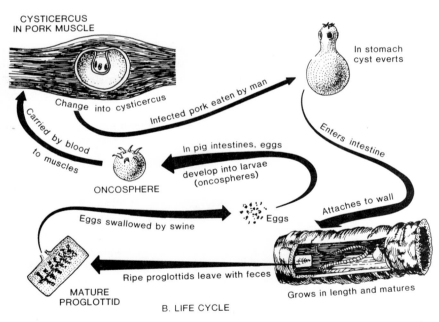

CYSTICERCUS
IN PORK MUSCLE

In stomach
cyst everts

Change into cysticercus

Infected pork eaten by man

Enters intestine

Carried by blood to muscles

ONCOSPHERE

In pig intestines, eggs
develop into larvae
(oncospheres)

Attaches to wall

Eggs swallowed by swine

Eggs

Ripe proglottids leave with feces

MATURE
PROGLOTTID

B. LIFE CYCLE

Grows in length and matures

Figure 8.7 *The life cycle of Taenia solium.* The pork tapeworm of man is representative of the highly advanced cestodes.

Among such specialized tapeworms as *Taenia,* the foregoing cycle has evolved to permit existence in terrestrial hosts, largely through elimination of certain stages and modification of others. For instance, the formerly free-swimming coracidium phase is now passed in the egg or as a membrane-covered embryo. Hence, the first actual larva is the *oncosphere,* which breaks free of its coverings after being swallowed by an intermediate host. Subsequent steps, including penetration through the host's intestine and entrance into other organs, are similar to the basic pattern; however, the procercoid and plerocercoid stages are combined and modified into a *cysticercus.* This larva first forms an oval, hollow cyst, one end of which folds inwardly. Inside this invagination the suckers and ring of hooks develop, which later characterize the scolex (fig. 8.7). When the intermediate host is eaten by man or another final host, the invagination turns inside out, the bladderlike portion is shed, and the resulting scolex, after attaching to the intestinal wall, commences production of proglottids.

THE NEMERTINEA

The 600 known species that constitute the phylum Nemertinea are not too unlike certain free-living Platyhelminthes in appearance, except that the body tends to be less flattened, and similarly lacks a distinct head, all trace of segmentation, and a body cavity. But there all resemblances cease. The name of the phylum is based on a type of sea nymph and has no structural basis.

Although most nemertineans are free living on the ocean bottom, a number occur in fresh water, and a very few are terrestrial. Their common name, *ribbonworm,* refers as much to their attractive colors as to their slender form. The dorsal surface of many species is green, patterned with contrasting stripes or bands, while others are variously pigmented with red, brown, or orange. The range in body length is truly exceptional, for the maximum for several species is just a few millimeters whereas *Lineus longissimus* from the North Sea attains a length up to 30 meters.

Morphology

Outstanding among the traits that distinguish the members of this phylum from the flatworms is the presence of a complete digestive tract (fig. 8.8, A). Aside from the addition of an anal pore, the tract is quite similar to that of the Platyhelminthes, the intestine often bearing sets of diverticula along the entire length. A circulatory system provides a second major distinction; this is of the closed type—that is, the blood remains within vessels throughout the body. Some of the longitudinal vessels are contractile and serve as hearts to pump the blood. Usually the blood is colorless, but may be red, yellow, green, or orange, depending on the species. The blood cells are of the white type, except in red-blooded species, where special corpuscles carry hemoglobin.

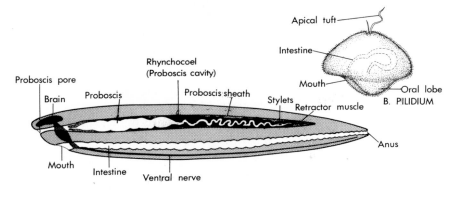

A. INTERNAL ANATOMY

Figure 8.8 *Characteristics of the Nemertinea.* The ribbonworms (A) resemble the platyhelminths in lacking segmentation and a body cavity, but differ in having a complete digestive tract and a long proboscis. The larva (B) is also distinctive.

The Proboscis Apparatus

While the other structural features are sufficiently clear in the illustration (fig. 8.8), one peculiarity, the *proboscis apparatus,* requires attention because nothing identical to it is found in any other phylum. Basically it consists of the *rhynchocoel,* a fluid-filled cavity that is lined with a *proboscis sheath* (fig. 8.8). Within the rhynchocoel lies the *proboscis;* essentially this organ is a muscular tube, closed at its innermost end and often twice the length of the body. Except for a slender muscle fastened to the closed end, it is attached only at the anterior pore, through which the cavity opens to the outside. In many species the proboscis is provided posteriorly with a set of sharp hooks or stylets.

This peculiar organ, employed principally in capturing food, also serves as an effective defense mechanism. When used for either purpose, it is shot out explosively through the pore by means of pressure exerted upon the rhynchocoel's fluid created by contractions of the sheath. The action can best be understood by comparison to a rubber glove. If such a glove is inflated lightly and one finger pushed back into the hand portion, the finger turned inward corresponds to the proboscis at rest. Now if strong pressure is placed upon the glove's hand, the finger is ejected quite forcibly as it resumes its usual position. The proboscis differs in that normally it lies within the cavity; hence, when it is expelled by muscle contraction, it actually becomes turned inside out. Any stylets present in the interior thus are pointed outward at the extreme tip after eversion, and can assist in capturing and holding prey. Afterwards, the proboscis is withdrawn into the rhynchocoel by means of the slender retractor muscle.

Reproduction

Although a few hermaphroditic species are known, the greatest majority have the sexes separate. Usually the eggs, enclosed in a gelatinous sheath, are deposited in the water for fertilization. In many ribbonworms the fertilized ovum develops directly into a juvenile that resembles the adult, but in others it gives rise to a larva called the *pilidium*. The pilidium, whose entire surface is covered with short cilia, bears an *apical tuft* of long cilia at its upper pole (fig. 8.8); this tuft and the thickened epidermis to which it is attached forms the *apical organ*, the larval nervous system. While basically bell-shaped, the larva possesses an oral lobe on each side of the mouth that gives it an appearance not unlike a soccer or football helmet. Internally the anatomy is extremely simple, the digestive tract being the most prominent feature. This system consists of three parts only: the mouth, foregut, and intestine. No anus is present. After swimming actively for a few days, the pilidium undergoes metamorphosis and becomes a juvenile ribbon-worm.

EVOLUTIONARY SUMMARY

In addition to providing origins for the Ctenophora and Cnidaria, the planula larva, or a form closely allied to it, appears to have served as the remote ancestral stock for certain more advanced metazoans. However, before giving rise to discrete side-branches, it seems first to have gained considerable complexity, especially in increasing in size and acquiring a number of systems (fig. 8.9). Among the organs gained were undoubtedly the flame cells used in excretion, muscles for locomotion, and a simple nervous system for coordination. As these parts developed, the complex, flat, ciliated worm was thus adapted for an existence on the ocean floor. There it became advantageous to take in particulate food, instead of feeding on dissolved substances as it probably had previously, for a simple cavity gradually invaginated into the ventral portion of the body. After this had developed into a sort of sac that opened by way of a mouth, the ancestral stock then differed little in general structure from modern acoels (fig. 8.9, B).

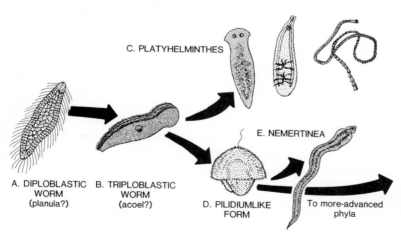

C. PLATYHELMINTHES

E. NEMERTINEA

A. DIPLOBLASTIC WORM (planula?)

B. TRIPLOBLASTIC WORM (acoel?)

D. PILIDIUMLIKE FORM

To more-advanced phyla

Figure 8.9 *Possible stages in the evolution of acoelomates.*

From this point, the acoels appear to have provided the basis for the evolution of the remainder of the Platyhelminthes; possibly the development of the Trematoda had to await the appearance of such advanced metazoans as mollusks and echinoderms, which they now parasitize. The equally parasitic cestodes which lack a digestive system entirely, are usually viewed as a similar late branch. In contrast, that class sometimes is suggested to represent a line that departed from the main path of ascent before the invaginated digestive tract had formed; however, evidence is too scanty to resolve the issue at the present time.

After the pre-acoel had eventually resumed a floating existence and the digestive tract had become complete through the development of an anus, it appears to have given rise to other lines of advancement. Possibly this floating form had acquired many of the characteristics of the pilidium, the larval type that serves as a model of the stock that gave rise to the phylum Nemertinea (fig. 8.9, D). This larva should be kept in mind, for it appears also to have led to the origins of more complex larvae that serve as models of the ancestors of certain more advanced phyla to be described in later chapters.

QUESTIONS FOR REVIEW AND THOUGHT

1. Name as many phyla as you can in which a true body cavity is lacking.

2. What structural features are distinctive of the Platyhelminthes? Is bilateral symmetry a *distinctive* characteristic? Why or why not?

3. Characterize the three classes of the Platyhelminthes and give the common names of the representatives of each.

4. On what characteristic are the five orders of Turbellaria based? Describe the major varieties of this structure. In which order is the mouth located at the middle of the undersurface?

5. Describe the feeding habits of turbellarians. How is the food digested?

6. In what ways do trematodes resemble turbellarians? What features distinguish them?

7. Compare the life cycles of monogenetic and digenetic flukes. In what ways is the digenetic life cycle either more or less complex than that of a typical tapeworm? Of a tapeworm like *Taenia*?

8. Should tapeworms be considered more or less adapted for a parasitic existence than a fluke? Why do you think so?

9. Why cannot all tapeworms be considered to be equally well adapted for a parasitic mode of life? Several reasons should be given.

10. What characteristics suggest that the Nemertinea are related to the Platyhelminthes? List as many traits as possible that distinguish the two phyla. Name and describe the larva of the nemertineans.

SUGGESTIONS FOR FURTHER READING

Benazzi, M. 1974. Fissioning in planarians from a genetic standpoint. In *Biology of the Turbellaria*, ed. N.W. Riser and M.P. Morse, p. 476–492. New York, McGraw-Hill Book Co.

Corning, W.C., and S. Kelly. 1973. Platyhelminthes: The Turbellarians. In *Invertebrate learning*, ed. W.C. Corning, J.A. Dyal, and A.O.D. Willows, vol. 1, p. 171–223. New York, Plenum Press.

Erasmus, D.A. 1972. *The biology of trematodes*. New York, Crane, Russak and Co.

Gibson, R. 1972. *Nemerteans*. London, Hutchinson University Library.

Hodgson, E.S. 1977. The evolutionary origin of the brain. *Annals of the New York Academy of Sciences*, 277:23–25.

Karling, T.G. 1974. On the anatomy and affinities of the turbellarian orders. In *Biology of the Turbellaria*, ed. N.W. Riser and M.P. Morse, p. 1–16. New York, McGraw-Hill Book Co.

Mitchell, R.W. 1974. The cave-adapted flatworms of Texas. In *Biology of the Turbellaria*, ed. N.W. Riser and M.P. Morse, p. 402–430. New York, McGraw-Hill Book Co.

Rothschild, M., and T. Clay. 1952. *Fleas, flukes, and cuckoos*. New York, Philosophical Library.

The Important Pseudocoelomates

9

The animals that have a body cavity of the variety known as the *pseudocoel* (p. 64) are a mixed lot, falling rather naturally into about seven clear-cut groups; formerly an eighth taxon, the Priapulida, was included here, too, but these animals now are known to have a true coelom and accordingly are treated in a later section. Several of the true pseudocoelomate types are so obviously different from the others that there is no question about their representing separate phyla and are described in the following chapter. The rest, however, are another matter. Some zoologists, including a number of highly-respected specialists in this area, consider each a separate phylum in its own right, while others, equally highly regarded, place them as classes of a single phylum called the Aschelminthes. More recently, it has been suggested that the latter term should really be elevated to superphylum rank, with its component taxa then recognized as phyla. Since this practice seems to be a reasonable, middle-of-the-road solution to the classification of these pseudocoelomates, it is followed here (table 9.1).

The characteristic pseudocoel will be recalled as being a body cavity that lacks a mesodermal covering on the digestive tract and represents the space between the mesodermal and entodermal germ layers. Thus it is a direct derivative of the blastocoel that first appears in the blastula stage of development. Other distinctive features found in most of the phyla are a tripartite construction of the pharynx as seen in cross-section (fig. 9.1) and growth in body size resulting from the increase in size of the cells rather than in number, because cell division ceases in most organs late in the embryonic period.

To keep the present chapter from becoming too unwieldy, it is confined to the two larger and more important phyla of the Aschelminthes. The remaining three components are microscopic animals which are superficially similar in form and habits. Thus they are reserved for discussion in the following chapter, along with the two distinct phyla of pseudocoelomates mentioned earlier.

THE PHYLUM NEMATODA

The phylum Nematoda, sometimes also termed the Nemathelminthes, includes more than 10,000 known species of worms called *nematodes*. The slender form that characterizes them is the basis of the name of the phylum, for it is derived from the Greek word, *nemo*, thread, that is threadlike. Aside from this there are few visible characters to note. All species have smooth, whitish or dull yellowish bodies, usually tapering at each end. No segmentation is visible, and

Table 9.1 The Phyla of the Superphylum Aschelminthes

Characteristic	Nematoda	Nematomorpha
Size	0.2 mm to 1 m	100 mm to 1 m
Cuticle	Simple	Simple, with areoles
Body	Undifferentiated	Undifferentiated
Cilia	Absent	Absent
Spines	Usually absent	Absent
Protonephridia	Absent	Absent
Pharynx	Tripartite	Absent
Pseudocoel	Fluid-filled, with a few pseudocoelomocytes	Filled with mesenchyme
Habitat	Aquatic, terrestrial and parasitic	Juveniles parasitic; adults freeliving
Number of species	10,000	300?

neither cilia nor proboscis are present, and only rarely do spines ornament the body. About half the species are parasitic, some of which may reach a meter in length, although most do not exceed 50 to 200 mm. As a whole, the free-living species are much smaller, averaging a few millimeters in length, but some marine forms may grow to 50 mm. The habits of these free-living species are quite diversified; many live in soil, others in fresh water, and still others in the seas. Several occur in the water contained in pitcher plants, and another group is found in the snow fields of high elevations and frigid regions. One form, the vinegar eel, inhabits vinegar, and one of its relatives has thus far been found only in the felt mats placed under beer mugs in Germany. The phylum is generally divided into two classes (table 9.2), the first of which is far larger and more important than the second.

Structure

Generally speaking, the structure of nematodes is amazingly simple, especially in view of the large size some members attain. The body is covered with a tough cuticle, made of as many as ten layers of complex proteins, which are secreted by the layer of cells that lies beneath it, called the hypodermis. Beneath this is a thin basement membrane, below which are the somatic muscles, all of which lie in single longitudinal layers. Since there are no circular muscles, the locomotion of nematodes involves bending the body into an S, first in one direc-

Phylum		
Rotifera	**Gastrotricha**	**Kinorhyncha**
0.04 to 2 mm	0.1 to 1.5 mm	0.1 to 1.0 mm
Simulate segments	Warty or scaled	Spiny
Trunk and foot	Undifferentiated, or with head & trunk	Head and trunk; 13 to 14 segments
In the form of a corona or funnel	On head and ventral surface	Absent
Present or absent	Often present	Present
1 pair of flame bulbs	1 pair solenocytes or absent	1 pair of solenocytes
A mastax	Simple; tripartite	Tripartite or cylindrical
Fluid-filled, with amoebocytes	Reduced; divided by membranes	Fluid-filled, with amoebocytes
Aquatic	Aquatic	Marine
2000	1500	100

tion, then the other. Although these motions are often rapid, sometimes to the point of being violent, only slow forward progress is achieved.

The *digestive tract* (fig. 9.1, A, B) basically is a long, straight tube. It may be cylindrical, triangular, or flattened, as is the case in *Ascaris,* the form usually dissected in the laboratory. At the extreme anterior end is a mouth, followed by a buccal cavity that varies considerably in shape. This leads into a muscular pharynx, usually referred to as the esophagus by nematologists (fig. 9.1, C); the arrangement of muscles and the tripartite central cavity of this structure should be especially noted, as similarities are found in two other phyla classed in the

Table 9.2 The Classes of the Nematoda

	Classes	
Characteristic	**Phasmidia**	**Aphasmidia**
Excretory canal	Present	Absent
Caudal Glands	Usually absent	Present
Pseudocoelomocytes	4–6	More than 6
Phasmids	Present	Absent

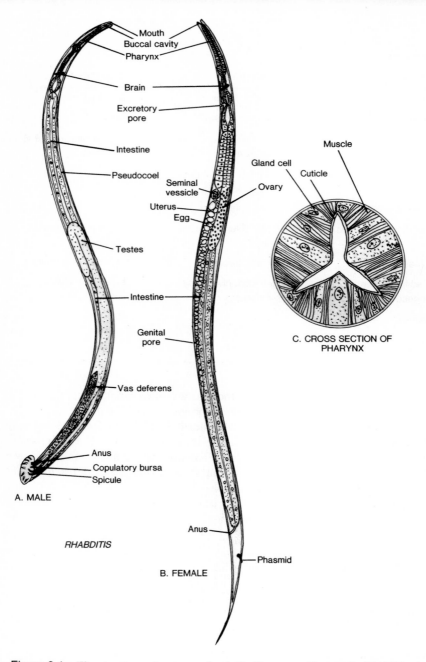

Figure 9.1 *The structure of a nematode.* A,B. The genus illustrated, *Rhabditis,* is representative of the very abundant free-living nematodes. In cross section the pharynx (C) shows the characteristic three-parted (tripartite) structural pattern.

Aschelminthes (Chapter 10). Behind the pharynx is the intestine, separated by means of a valve from the rectum that follows it. A cloaca, used also by the excretory system, terminates through the anus.

The *excretory system* is unique in consisting of a pair of tubules, which extend along the middle of each side in some forms but are confined to the anterior portion in the taxon containing *Rhabditis,* the genus illustrated (fig. 9.1, A, B). In both cases the tubes are embedded in the body wall and are most easily seen in prepared sections. Flame bulbs and nephridia, the characteristic excretory organs of other wormlike phyla, are entirely wanting; even the tubules are lacking in members of the class Aphasmidia.

Some of the features of the *body cavity* may raise questions in the student's mind as to its really being a pseucocoel. Although it develops as described in Chapter 5 and represents the modified blastocoel of the embryo, it is lined by a so-called pseudocoelomic membrane. This membrane, which originates from a single large cell (the mesenterial cell) located above the pharynx, covers the intestine, the reproductive organs, and muscles, and accordingly lines most of the cavity. In addition it forms mesenteries. The pseudocoel is filled with fluid, which is always under pressure, owing to the muscle tone of the body. This fluid thus is of great importance in locomotion, feeding, and excretion and serves also in respiration and circulation. Up to six specialized cells, called pseudocoelomocytes, are found on the sides of the pseudocoel, but their function remains unknown.

Another peculiarity involves the nearly complete absence of a structure that occurs widely among animals. For many years no *cilia* of any type had been detected in embryonic, juvenile, or adult nematodes—even the sperm cells were found to be devoid of cilia and to travel by amoeboid movement (fig. 9.2). Quite recently, however, modified cilia have been found in certain sensory organs of a species parasitic in the dog, and others have been reported in the intestine of nematodes belonging to the European genus *Eudorylaimus.*

The *nervous system* consists of four main longitudinal cords, each of which bears several ganglia. No brain is present, the longitudinal cords simply being interconnected by the circumenteric ring that encircles the pharynx (fig. 9.1, A, B). Eyes are lacking, but sense organs of various kinds are associated with the reproductive organs; others, including phasmids, are located in the cuticle (fig. 9.1, A). These are neurosecretory structures, usually consisting of a tiny gland internally and a papilla on the cuticle; usually they are confined to the caudal region of the body.

Reproduction and Development

The sexes are separate but similar in form, except that the male is usually smaller (fig. 9.1, A, B). In the female, the *reproductive system* consists of two identical sets of genital tracts. Each begins in an ovary (fig. 9.1, B) which becomes larger in diameter distally and grades into an oviduct; the latter in turn enlarges until it joins the thick-walled uterus. Posteriorly, the two uteri unite to form a common vulva, around the walls of which is an ovijector. As its name

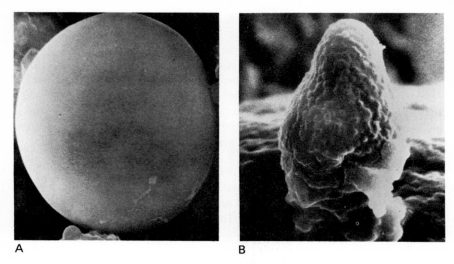

A   B

Figure 9.2 *The amoeboid sperm cells of Ascaris.* A. When inactive, the sperm of nematodes are spherical and smooth, but become amoeboid after being activated (B). (Courtesy of Drs. R.C. Burghardt and Foor; Copyright 1978 by *Journal of Ultrastructural Research,* 62:190–202.)

implies, the latter organ assists in expelling the eggs through the genital pore and has stout muscles to aid in those processes.

In the male, only a single genital tract is the rule (fig. 9.1, A), although two testes are sometimes present. Contrasting to the gonads of the female, the testes are rather stout, in diameter being quite equal to the rest of the tract. At the end of this is a seminal vesicle that serves in storing the ripe sperm, followed by a rather thick-walled vas deferens. This is usually a dual-compartmented structure, the first part of which is glandular and contributes fluid, while the latter half is ejaculatory and aids in moving the sperm into the cloaca to leave by way of the anus. Within the cloaca is a pair of hard rodlike structures, the spicules, which are made of cuticle; these are employed in dilating the vulva of the female during mating.

The fertilized egg develops through steps not unlike those of starfish and mammals. Cleavage is radial, although somewhat irregularly so (fig. 9.3, A–C), development quickly passing through the morula stage to form a hollow but somewhat flattened blastula. Invagination then takes place to produce the gastrula (fig. 9.3, D, E), which can readily be noted to be somewhat elongate. After some further development has occurred, a second invagination often occurs anteriorly to lay the foundation for the buccal cavity and pharynx (fig. 9.3, F, G). No true larval stages are to be found, for the embryonic worm soon takes on the basic features of the adult; however, four juvenile stages precede adulthood, each marked by molting of the old cuticle and the secretion of a new one. In spite of the lack of larval stages, parasitic species often have one or more intermediate hosts, as seen in a following section.

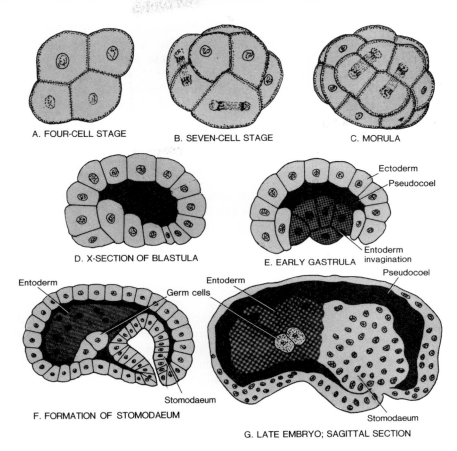

A. FOUR-CELL STAGE B. SEVEN-CELL STAGE C. MORULA

D. X-SECTION OF BLASTULA E. EARLY GASTRULA

Ectoderm
Pseudocoel
Entoderm
invagination

Entoderm Entoderm Pseudocoel
Germ cells

F. FORMATION OF STOMODAEUM
Stomodaeum

G. LATE EMBRYO; SAGITTAL SECTION
Stomodaeum

Figure 9.3 *Development in the Nematoda.* Embryos develop by spiral cleavage (A,B) through fairly typical stages until the late embryo. G. Then the cell membranes between cells break down, so that the entire embryo is a syncytium. (Based on Bovier, 1899, and Miller, 1908.)

Responses to Stimuli

Although it is obviously important to understand the mechanisms whereby plant or animal parasitic nematodes locate their hosts, relatively little progress toward that end has been made, despite an abundance of experimentation. This comparative deficiency of new general knowledge stems from two factors, the unresponsiveness of many forms and the frequent contradictory results obtained with different species. Some of the difficulties also are related to the relative simplicity of the nematode nervous system and the lack of well-developed receptor organs. As a whole, the most satisfactory progress has been made in connection with responses to two parameters—light and heat.

Photoreceptors, and accordingly light responses, are poorly developed in free-living and parasitic nematodes alike. Their presence or absence is in large measure associated with habitat preferences, as has been shown by a study of marine forms. In that investigation it was found that, among those nematodes which occurred in such brightly lighted situations as on exposed algae, 66 percent of the specimens possessed ocelli, while among those which lived under dimly illuminated conditions as on deeply submerged plants, only 30 percent had ocelli. Among the occupants of the interstices of sand particles on beaches or on the bottom stratum offshore, less than 1 percent possessed eyespots of any sort. Few studies on the nature of the visual pigment have been conducted, but in one species it was determined to be melanin and in another, surprisingly, it was found to be oxyhaemoglobin.

Eyes, however, are not essential for the detection of light, for a *dermal light sense* has been found to be widespread in the Protozoa and throughout much of the Metazoa, including man. Many of the responses among free-living types are positive (toward) to dim light but negative (away from) to either darkness or bright light. In the field, for example, many types of larvae were found to migrate upwards on grasses at dawn and dusk but reversed the direction of movement during sunlight hours and night. In contrast, nematodes that live on mushrooms, including the beds in mushroom houses, have been shown to react positively to bright illumination. The phototropic reaction sometimes varies in relation to the temperature. For instance, the infective larvae of the hookworm (*Ancylostoma duodenale*) failed to respond to light at ordinary temperatures but reacted negatively to it at temperatures above 31° C. The wavelength of the light also is effective in some cases. In general, reaction is negative to the longer wavelengths, such as red and yellow, and positive to the shorter ones from blue through ultraviolet.

The responses of nematodes to heat are less diversified. Many types, including most—but by no means all—free-living species, fail to react to thermal stimuli in any fashion. On the other hand, the majority of those larvae that actively penetrate the host, as well as a small percentage of free-living forms, respond positively to heat. No correlation between warm-bloodedness of the host and parasite behavior to heat exists here, however, because the list of species which react in this fashion includes a number of parasites of frogs, lizards, snakes, and other cold-blooded vertebrates. The nematodes appear unable to discriminate relative intensities of heat, so that they often respond positively to extreme thermal conditions, even those that are lethal to themselves. The only exception to this suicidal tendency that has been noted pertains to specimens of *Enchytraeus* which moved up a heat gradient to, but not beyond, a point where a temperature of 40° C existed, a temperature which approaches the limits of harmlessness to the organisms.

Plant Parasites

Basically the nematode parasites of seed plants are soil inhabitants which have become diversified to a greater or lesser extent for existence in or upon plants. The most elementary stage in the evolution of phytoparasitism is shown by those soil species whose juveniles merely attach externally to roots and feed on the juices. A greater advance toward development of the parasitic habit is found in species whose juveniles may either spend their entire lives free in the soil or else may penetrate into plant tissue and there develop into adults. The young from such adults escape into the soil and may or may not parasitize a plant, depending on circumstances, not heredity.

On the other hand, at the highest stage of specialization, parasitism is obligatory. This level is best exemplified by *Tylenchus tritici,* which infests wheat. The young of this species penetrate a growing wheat plant and ultimately reach the flowering head, where they grow to maturity and begin to reproduce. As each female produces several hundred juveniles, a thickening called a *gall* gradually forms where wheat grains normally would. With the approach of winter the adults die while the larvae remain in the gall. Since wheat plants usually become prostrate by spring, the larvae readily leave the gall then and penetrate the soil to infest young wheat plants as new growth is initiated. Should the gall, however, fail to reach the ground, the juveniles show a remarkable resistance to desiccation; wheat galls as old as twenty years have released living nematodes when opened.

Animal Parasites

Perhaps the commonest nematode parasite of man is the *pinworm* (*Enterobius vermicularis*). Unlike many other parasitic worms, the present one is more prevalent in the temperate zones than in the tropics. Surveys have shown that in the United States about 35% of the total population and 50% of the children are infected with this species, and in Germany, the Netherlands, and the USSR, nearly 100% of the children. Contrastingly, in such tropical lands as India and Malaya, the infection rate is only 10 to 15%. Female worms are only 13 mm in length, the males being half as long. The latter sex and young females live predominantly in the large intestine and lower end of the small intestine, while mature females occur in the rectum from which they emerge through the anus at night and deposit clusters of eggs containing well-developed embryos. After being deposited, the eggs usually fall off and may be found, not only in the clothing and bedding, but in the dust of the house. Since the egg-laying processes induce itching, persons become infected by swallowing eggs from food or the fingers and also by inhaling the household dust. After being swallowed the eggs hatch in the upper part of the small intestine of the host; from there the juveniles gradually move to the lower part of the digestive tract as they mature.

Another nematode of frequent occurrence in man is the *ascarid worm* (*Ascaris lumbricoides*), a parasite much more common in the tropics and subtropics than in temperate regions. The worms, which may grow to a length of 30 cm, live in the intestines, where huge number of eggs are deposited. Females may lay 200,000 eggs per day and thus may produce as many as 26 million eggs during a normal life span of about 5 months. After being deposited, the eggs leave the host's body with the feces, and only then begin developing, since they need oxygen for those processes. Consequently they do not become infective for about two weeks after deposition. Then if they are taken in with food, the eggs hatch in the intestines of the host, and as they grow, undergo one molt. They then drill through the intestinal wall, enter the lymph vessels, and migrate to the liver. Here they remain for a time before entering the blood vessels to pass through the heart into the lungs. After further development there for a few days, they pass up the trachea to the pharynx; here they are swallowed and enter the intestines once more. The chief damage these parasites do to the host is in inducing anemia and, in heavier infestations, abdominal pain and swelling, loss of weight, and even convulsions.

Among the most important nematode parasites of man are the hookworms of the genera *Ancylostoma* and *Necator,* the former being largely Old World and the latter New World. The life cycles of the two are nearly identical. The adults live attached to the intestinal walls of the host, sometimes in such numbers as to appear like the pile of a rug. Here they feed on the tissues of the intestine, frequently rupturing the walls of capillaries and causing such loss of blood that the host becomes anemic. The numerous eggs each female produces pass out of the body along with feces.[1] Should the latter be deposited on soil, the eggs hatch into minute "larvae" (actually juveniles), which feed on the organic matter. After two molts, they reach the infective stage, during which they remain on the surface of the ground, awaiting contact with the bare skin of a passing human being. After penetrating the skin, the young enter the lymphatic system and are carried through the vessels to the heart. Then migrating through the blood stream they enter the lungs, from which they move up the trachea and into the digestive tract by way of the epiglottis. In the intestines they grow rapidly to the adult stage after two additional molts. Adults are known to remain active for as long as twenty years.

Undoubtedly the worst offenders of the nematodes are the highly specialized forms that require an intermediate host. As a general rule, the latter is an insect or other arthropod that becomes infected by swallowing the early juvenile stage. Accordingly in most of these parasites, eggs develop within the female nematode body into tiny "larvae" (really juveniles) known as *microfilariae.*

Among these the most interesting is possibly the "fiery serpent" which receives mention in biblical accounts. The infective larvae live in copepods, a kind of minute crustacean that abounds in fresh water. If a copepod is accidentally swallowed by a human being in drinking water, the larvae leave their first host and penetrate through the intestinal tract of the second. After reaching the subcutaneous tissue, they mature and increase in length as they migrate from one body part to another. Here beneath the skin, fertilization may occur, after which the males perish while the females form a blister or abscess, most frequently on the host's legs or back. Within this blister the female lies with the vagina adjacent to a central opening, through which she pours out thousands of living young when the lesion becomes wet, as during bathing. These juveniles swim about until they are swallowed by a copepod in which they become semidormant.

---

1. Each female hookworm produces between 10,000 and 30,000 eggs per day, when infections are heavy. If relatively few adults are present in a given host, mature females may produce as many as 50,000 eggs per day.

Another all-too-common parasite of this type is almost entirely confined to tropical and subtropical parts of the world, especially in more humid regions. This nematode, *Wuchereria bancrofti*, is the causative agent of a condition called elephantiasis, the males of which are only about 20 to 40 mm long, while females attain lengths of 100 mm. Both sexes live in the lymph glands and vessels. Because of the resulting blockage of the lymphatic system by the adult worms, the body parts of the host, particularly the lower extremities, may become greatly distended (fig. 9.4). This enlargement, accompanied as it is by a thickening and wrinkling of the skin, is the basis of the common name of the infection. In the lymph glands, the females produce living young, each about 0.2 to 0.3 mm long and enclosed in a sheath. These microfilariae leave the lymphatic system at night, arriving in the peripheral blood vessels near the surface of the skin around 10:00 P.M. There they remain until around 2:00 A.M., when they migrate back to the lymph vessels. When a mosquito of the right species feeds on a person infected with these worms during those night-time hours, microfilariae may enter the insect's stomach with the blood. In this intermediate host, the juveniles first penetrate through the digestive tract into the body cavity, but remain only a few hours before passing into the mosquito's thoracic muscles, where they grow and undergo two molts. This growth requires a period of about

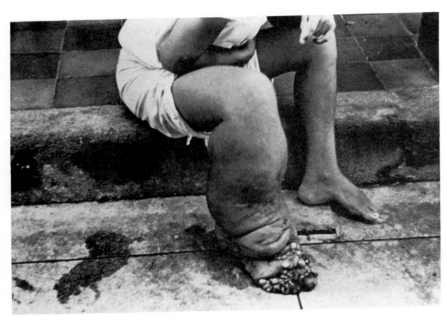

Figure 9.4 *A case of elephantiasis.* The swelling results, not only from physical blockage of the lymphatic vessels, but also from production of connective tissues induced by secretions of the nematode. (From "A Pictorial Presentation of Parasites," edited by N. Zaimon, M.D., Dept. of Radiology, Mercy Hospital, Valley City, N. Dakota.)

two weeks, the young then being between 1.5 and 2.0 mm in length. At this time they migrate to the mosquitoe's mouthparts and enter the body of a human host when the next feeding occurs.

Two other nematodes similarly having intermediate hosts are of interest, the first of which is parasitic in man, particularly in West Africa. The adults of this form, named *Loa loa* or the African eye worm, live in the connective tissues located beneath the dermis, especially in the back, thorax, scalp, and eye sockets. Males reach lengths of 35 mm and females, 70 mm; the young are born alive, and like those of *Wuchereria,* are ensheathed and show similar daily rhythmicity. However, the rhythm is in the opposite sense, for the microfilariae enter the superficial blood vessels during the daylight hours and return to the deeper ones during the night. The intermediate host is a deerfly of the genus *Chrysops,* a relative of the familiar horsefly. After being taken in when the fly has a blood meal, the young develop much as they do in *Wuchereria,* requiring a week or two to mature into the third stage infective juvenile. As there, too, they migrate to the mouth parts of the insect, where they can be transmitted to a human being when the fly feeds again. The adults may persist in the human host as long as 15 years.

The second species is a pest in dogs and related mammals throughout the world. This is *Dirofilaria immitis* and may be familiar to the student under the name *heart worm.* It is a moderately large form, males attaining a length of 200 mm and females 310 mm, that lives in the right ventricle of the heart. As in other related nematodes, the young are born alive and enter the blood stream; however, in this case there is no or little periodicity, so they may be found in the blood vessels throughout the body at any hour of the day. The intermediate host, any of a large number of mosquito species, becomes infected when feeding. In the insect the juveniles undergo development for between 10 to 14 days. If the mosquito is too heavily infected, it may die before the young worms have become sufficiently mature, but when lightly infected, it can introduce them into a dog when it feeds after they have reached the infective stage. First these juvenile nematodes enter the muscles of the dog and undergo two molts as they increase in size over a three-month period. After that they enter the right ventricle and begin to reproduce. The resulting partial blockage of circulation caused by their presence in the heart induces affected dogs to tire easily and gasp for breath when exercised; in heavy infections, collapse and even death may result.

THE NEMATOMORPHA

Sometimes the "horsehair snakes" that constitute the Nematomorpha are treated as the subclass Gordiacea[2] within the Nematoda, but more often they are ranked separately. However classified, these worms bear obvious relationships with the nematodes, for many structural similarities are shared by the two taxa. The elongate slender body, in shape not unlike that of the preceding group,

2. This name refers to the Gordian knot, which may have been little more difficult to untie than the body of a bottled horsehair snake sometimes is to untangle.

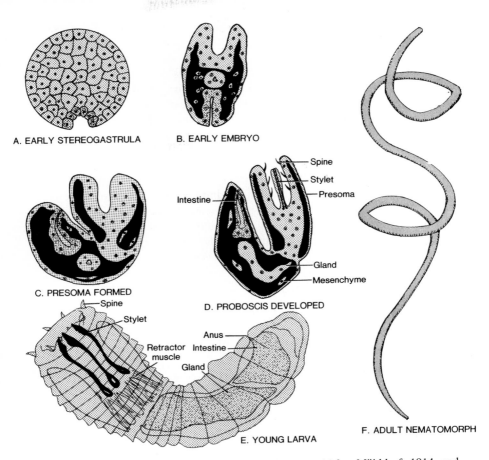

A. EARLY STEREOGASTRULA

B. EARLY EMBRYO

C. PRESOMA FORMED

D. PROBOSCIS DEVELOPED

Spine
Stylet
Presoma
Intestine
Gland
Mesenchyme

Spine
Stylet
Anus
Retractor Intestine
muscle
Gland

E. YOUNG LARVA

F. ADULT NEMATOMORPH

Figure 9.5   A typical nematomorph and its development. (After Mühldorf, 1914, and Montgomery, 1904.)

ranges from 100 to 1000 mm in length and from 0.3 to 2.5 mm in diameter (fig. 9.5, A). Frequently the cuticle is tan or brownish, but the color varies extensively even within species. Adults are free living in freshwater or marine habitats, but the larvae are parasitic in insects.

Among the major distinctions between the horsehair snakes and nematodes are the complete absence of an excretory system and the degeneracy of the digestive tract. Usually the tract is represented largely by a cloaca, to which is also attached the reproductive system that opens near the posterior end by way of an anus. Frequently even a mouth may be wanting and no trace of a tripartite pharynx is ever found; a reduced pharynx and a mouth, however, do exist in the genus *Nectonema* but the latter does not connect to the cloaca.

Life Cycle

In the larva the digestive tract is reduced to even a greater degree, for at most a short posterior intestine and anus are present (fig. 9.5, E). The absence of a mouth in the larva is more striking because the eversible proboscis on the anterior end appears designed for feeding. However, no opening exists through which ingestion could possibly occur, so the organ functions only in penetrating host tissues. The larvae hatch from eggs deposited in water and secrete mucus in which they encyst. Here they may lie for some time until swallowed by the proper host, usually a cricket, grasshopper, beetle, or roach. Perhaps cysts are taken in while the insect is drinking water or eating aquatic plants, but the processes of infection have never been actually observed.

Apparently, after being ingested, the larvae penetrate through the digestive tract of the host, as the remainder of development takes place in the insect's body cavity. When considerable growth has been attained, the larvae undergo a mild sort of metamorphosis to become adult. During transition such structures as the proboscis gradually degenerate, while the intestine elongates and the gonads and nervous system develop. Only during heavy rain or when the host is near water do the fully grown juveniles leave the host. Then, after molting, the new adults live in either mud or water for a short free existence.

THE NATURE OF PARASITISM

Except for a small phylum of pseudocoelomates described in the next chapter, all the major types of endoparasitic groups have now been reviewed. Thus none of the coelomate phyla and classes that are examined in the remaining ten chapters have become adapted as whole entities for a life totally within other organisms. To be sure there are crustaceans that are so highly modified for a parasitic existence that they are scarcely recognizable as an animal, let alone an arthropod, and similar statements can be made for certain mites that burrow into skin. Then there are other mites that enter the nasal cavity and some leeches that occasionally attach to the lining of the throat of horses. None of these, however, ever are far removed from the atmosphere, though highly specialized they may be for a parasitic existence. Furthermore, they constitute only small fractions of the major taxa to which they belong.

Hence, all the large groups of highly adapted endoparasites are restricted to such relatively primitive phyla as the mesozoans, the flat and round worms, the acanthocephalans, and the nematomorphs. The questions then can be raised: Why is endoparasitism limited to those lower levels of the metazoan organization represented by the acoelomatous and pseudocoelomatous phyla? And why have not many of the more complex coelomatous taxa been able to acquire an endoparasitic mode of existence?

In answer to these queries, several possibilities come to mind. One is that the acoelomates and pseudocoelomates, being relatively primitive, have therefore been in existence for a longer period than have the advanced groups; consequently they have had a longer time in which to undergo the changes necessary for an internal existence. However appealing though the idea may be, when it is recalled that the greater number of the endoparasites have coelomate hosts, it is seen to be faulty. Obviously the parasite could not have become adapted to its type of host until the latter arose, so both necessarily have had an equal amount of time.

A second possibility perhaps offers a more satisfactory solution—maybe conditions of the internal environment of organisms, including the scarcity of oxygen, are so harsh that only those forms which are relatively simple can make all the necessary changes. Suppose, for instance, that one organism has only four metabolic requirements for its existence, while a second one has fifteen. Obviously the one with only four basic needs, that is, the simpler animal, can more readily acquire by evolutionary means the fewer essential adaptations than the second one could. In other words, in advanced forms too many metabolic processes have reached a high level of complexity to permit their loss or to undergo the stringent modification required for survival in this unfavorable environment.

A third alternative also holds some attraction, one that is best exemplified by such multihost parasites as the broad tapeworm. If a typical life history is reviewed, such as that on page 112, it can be noted that the several hosts involved are at successively higher levels of advancement—for instance, the first one is a copepod, the second, a fish, and finally a mammal. Could it be that the earliest ancestral stock which led to modern tapeworms was at one time just a coracidium, that was fed upon by early copepods? And as millenia passed by, might not this form have evolved gradually into the simple oncosphere, which thus became able to live within this small arthropod? After the vertebrates eventually arose many thousands of years later and those early fishes fed upon the copepods along with other minute life, could not the procercoid have similarly become adapted for an existence in this new host and gradually have acquired the plerocercoid form? In like fashion after still more millions of years had passed and the mammals finally came into existence, it is possible that corresponding processes brought the tapeworm to its present adult form as further adaptation was achieved. This series of events then implies coevolution of a sort, the parasite evolving in response to the changes that occurred in the other organisms in its environment. It should be remembered that numerous additional organisms besides the copepod probably also fed upon the coracidium, and that many larger animals other than the fish likewise ate the copepod, and numerous others fed on the fish. But only in those taxa now containing the existing hosts did certain features happen to be favorable for the particular parasite and thus permitted the existing sequence of events to develop. By the same token, millions of other combinations proved unsuccessful. Thus long spans of time and enormous numbers of eggs, young, and mature individuals may have been involved in the processes of acquiring a complex type of endoparasitic existence.

QUESTIONS FOR REVIEW AND THOUGHT

1. State the chief characteristics of the phylum Nematoda.

2. What might have been some steps involved in certain nematodes' acquiring a role as parasites of plants? Of animals?

3. Name and describe three nematodes that parasitize man in which intermediate hosts are lacking. Which is the most serious of these and why do you say so?

4. What does the large number of ova deposited per day by ascarids imply about the advantages or disadvantages of a parasitic mode of living?

5. Describe and name four important nematodes that are parasitic in man or his domesticated animals which have intermediate hosts. What features of the life cycle are shared by all of these? Be as specific as possible.

6. Exactly what is meant by a pseudocoel? In what ways is that body cavity of nematodes typical and in what atypical?

7. Characterize the phylum Nematomorpha.

8. Describe the development of the young nematomorph. What is peculiar about its digestive tract? About its gastrula?

9. Define the following terms: spicule; phasmid; tripartite; syncytium; stereoblastula.

10. What reason might be given to explain the absence of large taxa of endoparasites from among the coelomate animals?

SUGGESTIONS FOR FURTHER READING

Barrett, J. 1976. Energy metabolism in nematodes. In *The organization of nematodes,* ed. N.A. Croll, p. 11–70. New York, Academic Press.

Croll, N.A. 1970. *The behaviour of nematodes: Their activity, senses and responses.* New York, St. Martins Press.

Croll, N.A. 1976. Behavioural coordination of nematodes. In *The organization of nematodes,* ed. N.A. Croll, p. 343–364. New York, Academic Press.

Leeg, D.L., and H.J. Atkinson. 1976. *Physiology of nematodes. Second edition.* London, The Macmillan Press, Ltd.

Van Cleave, H.J. 1932. Cell constancy and its relation to body size. *Quart. Rev. Biol.,* 7:59–80.

Zuckerman, B.M. 1976. Nematodes as models for aging studies. In *The organization of nematodes,* ed. N.A. Croll, p. 211–241. New York, Academic Press.

The Minor Pseudocoelomate Taxa

10

Now that the two more important pseudocoelomate groups have been examined, there remains a number of others of similar structure that contain relatively few species. Since these taxa are minor on the basis of numerical content, they are frequently omitted where time is limited; however, they have much to contribute towards a full appreciation of animal variety and its origins. Moreover, the organisms they include are often of much importance in ecological studies of freshwater and marine environments. That they are collectively a highly diversified group is demonstrated by the very first phylum treated below.

THE ROTIFERA

Animal specializations for immensity of size, like those shown by whales, elephants, and dinosaurs, although amazing, are nonetheless readily perceived to be extremely useful. What is difficult to comprehend is a reason for any multicellular organism to assume such microscopic dimensions as the 2,000 species of rotifers have. Yet such an adaptation must have its advantages, to judge from the frequency with which these animals occur. This possibility is further supported by the existence of two related phyla of similar habits and minute size. To assist in perceiving their likenesses and differences, a representative of each taxon is shown in diagrammatic fashion on a single plate (fig. 10.1). But striking though the small size may be, there are other traits in the Rotifera that are at least as spectacular.

Morphology and Physiology

About the size of *Paramecium,* rotifers resemble that protozoan also by bearing cilia, but the bristles in these animals are concentrated around one end in the form of a *corona* (fig. 10.1, A). Often the corona, which is Latin for "crown," is more like a funnel than a headpiece and eventually leads into the mouth. The latter in turn opens into another unusual adaptation, a pharynx or *mastax,* in which several movable parts serve as jaws. In action these structures, referred to as *trophi,* look more like rotating choppers and wheels than jaws, but serve the same end, that of grinding food. Since the diet consists of bacteria and bits of organic matter, the need for grinding is not immediately apparent, until the size of the rotifer itself is considered.

As in the nematodes, the body wall is largely epidermal, internally possessing similar scattered muscle bundles and externally covered by a tough cuticle. Frequently the body may be subdivided into rings that, by telescoping into one another, permit more flexibility than would otherwise be possible in its rigid coat (fig. 10.2, A). The excretory system consists of a pair of long convoluted collecting tubules and from four to fifty flame cells; the tubules, placed one on each side of the body, lead into a urinary bladder which opens into the cloaca. Besides a large brain located dorsad to the mastax (figs. 10.1, A; 10.2, A), the nervous system includes several pairs of fine nerve cords that extend to various parts of the body. Among the simple sense organs are an eyespot on the brain, a single (rarely paired) antenna dorsally on the "head," and scattered papillae or sensory hairs, depending on the species.

Often questions arise as to whether the pseudocoel of these animals and their relatives is empty, except for the organs. In the rotifers at least, the body cavity is

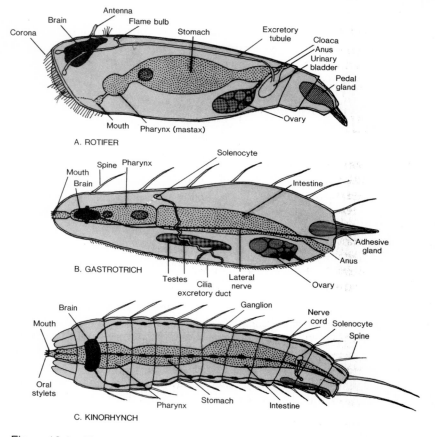

Figure 10.1 *Three rotiferlike taxa.* Three phyla of pseudocoelomates are similar in being microscopic in size and actively aquatic in habits. They differ sharply in structure, however, as the diagrams indicate.

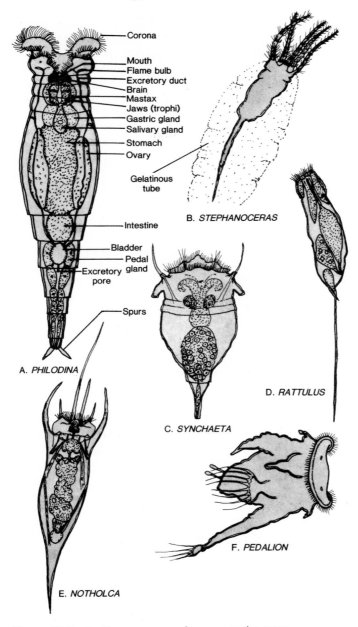

Labels on figure A (PHILODINA):
- Corona
- Mouth
- Flame bulb
- Excretory duct
- Brain
- Mastax
- Jaws (trophi)
- Gastric gland
- Salivary gland
- Stomach
- Ovary
- Intestine
- Bladder
- Pedal gland
- Excretory pore
- Spurs

A. *PHILODINA*

B. *STEPHANOCERAS*
- Gelatinous tube

C. *SYNCHAETA*

D. *RATTULUS*

E. *NOTHOLCA*

F. *PEDALION*

Figure 10.2 *Rotifer structure and representative types.*

filled with a clear, usually colorless fluid. To a large degree, this liquid appears to function much as blood does in more advanced phyla, despite its being sparsely supplied with cells. Apparently it carries digested foods and metabolic wastes, as well as gases that enter by way of the digestive tract. The cellular contents, however, play no role in the conduction of these substances. Some of these cells are merely stray spermatozoa, but the majority are amoeboid types, the specific functions of which still remain to be discovered.

Habits

By far the majority of known species are freshwater inhabitants, fewer than 100 occurring in marine or brackish water. No puddle, not even the water between the sand particles of moist beaches, is too small to harbor a few of these animals. Masses of damp vegetation, especially mosses, are also favored habitats. Most rotifers are free living, some being active swimmers while others are sessile and often provided with a vaselike envelope, or lorica. However, a number of symbiotic varieties are known; the majority of these are commensals, living externally on such freshwater invertebrates as insects and crustaceans. Others, like *Albertia,* are either ectoparasites or endoparasites of aquatic earthworms and similar invertebrates, whereas certain members of the phylum parasitize various algae. For example, *Proales parasitica* occurs quite commonly in the cavities of *Volvox* colonies.

In certain rotifers that inhabit mosses, a peculiar adaptation has evolved. Because their habitat is frequently subjected to protracted periods of drought, an ability to undergo extensive desiccation has developed. Without forming a cyst, under severe conditions the body loses water and becomes quite shrunken and spherical. The pseudocoel nearly disappears as the body is reduced to less than one-third of its normal size. Even the chromatin matter of the individual cells undergoes changes; instead of remaining as a mass centrally in each nucleus, it breaks into fragments that move to the inner surface of the *cell* membrane. Thus desiccated, rotifers can remain dry as dust for a considerable period, more than twenty-five years in one recorded case. When desiccated specimens happen to reach water, they rapidly absorb moisture and resume normal activity; recovery time may require only ten minutes or as much as a full day, depending on the species and circumstances.

Reproduction

Almost without exception the rotifers studied in the laboratory are of one sex—female! Male rotifers are known for but a handful of species, and these generally occur only during a definite period of the year. None of this sex ever live for more than three days, for, lacking a mouth and anus and frequently most of the rest of the digestive tract, they are unable to feed. As a rule they are much smaller than the corresponding female and are active swimmers, even in those species in which the females are sessile. Especially in forms that inhabit temporary ponds, males are found only near the close of the summer; after fertilizing the eggs, they live a couple of days and disappear until the same time the following year. Yet the appearance of members of this sex, brief though it may be, is essential to the survival of the species over winter, for only fertilized eggs are resistant to cold.

The mechanism that controls this absence and sudden appearance of males involves the production by the females of two kinds of eggs, *mictic* and *amictic*. The first type is produced by meiosis and is haploid like most eggs, whereas the second is formed without reduction in chromosome number and is therefore diploid. Moreover, the eggs differ in hatching requirements and in shell characteristics. Amictic (or *summer*) eggs hatch within a day or two after being deposited and have at most a thin shell, whereas mictic eggs have a thicker one (fig. 10.3). When not fertilized, mictic eggs have just a moderately heavy shell, and hatch within two or three days into males. In contrast, if fertilized, they become thick-shelled and remarkably resistant to freezing, drying, and other adverse conditions and require a rest period of several weeks or months before hatching into females.

In brief, a typical life cycle might commence with the thawing of the pond ice in spring, when the overwintering mictic eggs hatch into amictic females. As the name implies, these females lay amictic eggs, which hatch into similar females. After twenty to forty of such amictic generations, depending upon the species

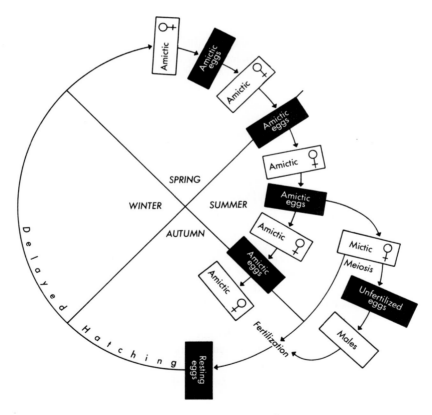

Figure 10.3 *The annual reproductive cycle in rotifers.*

and climate, when the pond waters undergo a slight cooling a number of females produce eggs meiotically (fig. 10.3). All the mictic eggs first produced, being unfertilized, within a few days hatch into males. Thereafter many mictic eggs are fertilized, and these resting eggs remain unhatched until the following spring. But until the waters become too cold, additional amictic females may continue to be produced as during the summer months.

THE PHYLUM GASTROTRICHA

At first encounter, the members of the phylum Gastrotricha (from the Greek words *gaster,* stomach, and *thrix,* hair) give the impression of being rotifers, for like them they are microscopic, active, aquatic forms. However, they are seen at once to be distinct in lacking the ciliated corona that marks the latter group. In the gastrotrichs, spines or scales usually cover the entire upper surface (fig. 10.4, A, B), while the undersurface bears a number of rows of cilia (fig. 10.1, B), whence the name of the phylum. In some freshwater genera, such as *Chaetonotus,* the body may be divided into a head, neck, trunk, and two tails, the latter being the only division that is clear-cut (fig. 10.4). In certain marine genera, like *Macrodasys,* the body is slender and cylindrical, subdivisions being totally lacking.

Habits

When swimming, these animals, only 0.06 to 1.5 mm in length, seem to glide along close to the substrate; suddenly they may stop and attach themselves momentarily by means of their posterior adhesive tubes, or they may curl up in pillbug fashion. In either case, they do not remain still long but quickly resume the gliding provided by the cilia. Their mouth is at the anterior end, surrounded by a raised band of cuticle called the buccal capsule; on each side of this are a number of sensory hairs or tufts, probably useful in detecting food. The diet consists of small algae and protozoans, as well as bits and pieces of matter from either plant or animal sources; in other words, all organic material that is sufficiently small is swept into the mouth as the gastrotrich glides along.

Internal Anatomy

All the internal systems are rather simple. From the mouth, food particles enter a muscular pharynx, which organ accounts for more than one-third of the total length of the *digestive tract.* In cross-section, the pharynx is seen to be tripartite and to have musculature quite like that of the nematodes (fig. 10.4, C); hence, in company with the pseudocoel, a relationship close to the Nematoda seems to be indicated. Behind this structure is a long tubular organ, variously named the stomach or stomach-intestine (fig. 10.4, A); its wall, like that of the pharynx, contains a number of unicellular glands, which are probably digestive in function. Farther caudad is a short rectum and a simple anus, located at the extreme posterior end of the body.

Only one order of gastrotrichs has excretory organs. In *Chaetonotus* and its allies a coiled tubule is located on each side of the body just before the middle, at

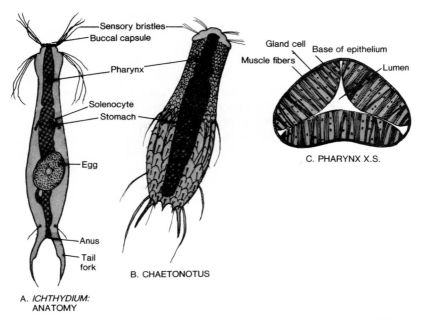

Labels in figure:
Sensory bristles
Buccal capsule
Pharynx
Solenocyte
Stomach
Egg
Anus
Tail fork
A. *ICHTHYDIUM:* ANATOMY
B. CHAETONOTUS
Gland cell
Muscle fibers
Base of epithelium
Lumen
C. PHARYNX X.S.

Figure 10.4 *Structure and examples of the Gastrotricha.* Some orders of the gastrotrichs are covered with scales, as shown by *Chaetonotus* (B).

the end of which is a solenocyte; this will be recalled as a uniflagellated modification of the flame bulb (p. 103). The *nervous system* is somewhat more impressive, for the brain consists of two rather large ganglia that fill much of the anterior region. From each ganglion, a longitudinal nerve trunk extends on each side of the body along the digestive tract. While the two ganglia are thus largely independent of one another, some degree of coordination is provided by a commissure that extends dorsally across the pharynx. Externally are several pits bearing sensory hairs, or, in marine forms, pistonlike structures, which are probably chemical detectors. Sensory hairs anteriorly possibly detect chemicals, too, but also respond to touch and to water current.

Reproduction and Development

Reproduction in these animals is somewhat remarkable and differs with the type. Marine forms, like *Macrodasys*, are hermaphroditic, as all individuals are provided with both testes and ovaries. In contrast, the freshwater forms are all females, the eggs developing without fertilization, that is, reproduction is parthenogenetic. Even the female system is extremely simple, consisting of one or two small ovaries located posteriorly, and a more anterior vitellarium that nourishes the eggs within the pseudocoel until they are ripe. In addition, it includes a saclike X-organ, which the ripe eggs enter before escaping through the genital pore. Thus the eggs leave the ovaries and grow a 100-fold or more in mass within the pseudocoel (fig. 10.4, A); however, most females produce only four or five eggs. A shell encloses the eggs while they are still within the body, but the covering does not harden until they have been deposited.

An annual *reproductive cycle* exists which recalls that of the rotifers. As there, the freshwater forms produce two types of ova. But in the present animals thin-shelled summer eggs are laid by younger females during the warmer months, whereas the thick-walled winter eggs are deposited by older individuals, when the waters begin to chill. A major difference from the rotifers is, of course, that all the ova of the freshwater gastrotrichs develop parthenogenetically, regardless of the season. The development of the embryo is still incompletely known. As a whole, the early processes seem to resemble those of starfish, gastrulation being by invagination as in those organisms. No larva develops, the young having the appearance of diminutive adults when hatching occurs.

THE PHYLUM KINORHYNCHA

The second taxon that resembles the phylum Rotifera in minute size and general body form, the Kinorhyncha, differs sharply from it in behavior. Unlike the members of the two preceding groups, those of the present one are mud-dwellers, rather than active swimmers, and all are stictly marine. The name of the phylum is from the Greek words *kinos,* spiny, and *rhynchos,* snout, and refers to the short curved stylets that surround the mouth (figs. 10.1, C; 10.5, A). Probably the most apparent distinction from the two preceding phyla is the obvious segmentation of the kinorhynch body. Usually 14, but sometimes only 13, segments are present, commonly referred to in the literature as zonites. The spines of the head and body (fig. 10.5, A) are adaptations for the peculiar form of locomotion. In creeping along the ocean floor, those of the head are inserted into the substrate as a sort of anchor. Then the head is retracted into the body, pulling the animal forward; it is then thrust forward again, the spines are anchored once more, and the whole process laboriously repeated over and over again.

Internal Structure

Structurally the *digestive tract* more closely resembles that of the gastrotrichs than that of the rotifers, but it is amply distinct from both. The mouth leads into a relatively short, thick pharynx, which in section is seen to be tripartite and to have musculature like that of the nematodes and gastrotrichs (fig. 10.5, B). However, the organ is distinct from the others in the muscles being outside the epithelial lining and having a peculiar crown at the anterior end, which may serve much as a valve. Posterior to the pharynx is a short, slender esophagus, which receives secretions from the so-called salivary glands, and behind this is the somewhat larger and thicker-walled midgut, that is supplied with secretions from the pancreatic glands. Still farther caudad is the intestine, a bulbous sac that constitutes over half of the entire tract (fig. 10.5, A). This organ is partially divided into anterior and posterior parts by a circular muscle. As the posterior portion is lined with cuticle, it is probably formed as an infolding of the body wall, much as the rectum of vertebrates is. It opens to the outside by way of an anus situated at the very end of the body proper.

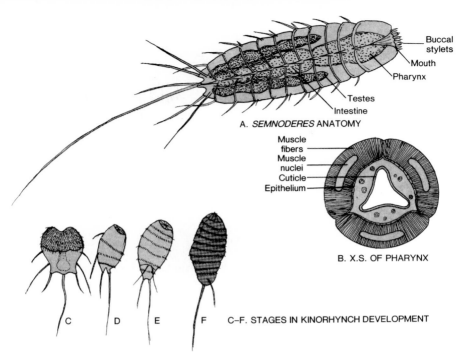

Buccal
stylets

Mouth

Pharynx

Testes

Intestine

A. *SEMNODERES* ANATOMY

Muscle
fibers
Muscle
nuclei
Cuticle
Epithelium

B. X.S. OF PHARYNX

C   D   E   F   C-F. STAGES IN KINORHYNCH DEVELOPMENT

Figure 10.5   *Anatomy and development in the Kinorhyncha.* The earliest developmental stages of the egg still remain unknown; only the larval stages have been described. It is of interest to compare the structure of the pharynx with that of the nematodes (fig. 9.1) and the gastrotrichs (fig. 10.4) with this one of the kinorhynchs (B).

The *nervous system* is somewhat less advanced than that of the gastrotrichs, especially in having the brain much smaller. In these kinorhynchs this organ is a thick strap around the pharynx that gives rise to four nerve trunks, one dorsal, one ventral, and two lateral, all provided with a ganglion in each body segment (fig. 10.1, C). These nerve cords, however, are embedded within the epidermis, a condition that is generally considered primitive. The ganglia of the segments serve the body musculature, which is rather well developed. Eyes of a very simple sort are often present and some of the body bristles appear to be sensory, too.

Excretion is carried out by means of the pair of multinucleated solenocytes, located one on each side of the eleventh segment. In these animals the solenocyte is peculiar in having two flagella, one long and the other much shorter, instead of a single one as usual. These excretory structures open directly to the outside through a pore, without intervention of any tubule (fig. 10.1, C).

Reproduction and Development

In the Kinorhyncha, the sexes are separate, but the two types of individuals are alike in appearance and structure. The two gonads (either testes or ovaries) are located in the posterior portion of the body (fig. 10.5, A). In the female, the ovaries are syncytial but have nuclei of two types, one of which develops into eggs while the other supplies the latter with food. The eggs remain within the ovary until mature; they then pass out through the short oviduct to exit through the genital opening. During this movement they appear to be fertilized while passing the seminal vesicle, an organ that stores the sperm received from the male. In the male this system is even simpler, as it consists only of a pair of testes, a short sperm duct, and the genital opening. It also includes two or three spicules which may serve in mating.

Almost nothing is known of the development of the embryo. However, the newly hatched larva consists of three segments, some of which bear long spines (fig. 10.5, C–F). As further growth occurs, new segments are added one at a time, until the full complement has been acquired.

THE PHYLUM ACANTHOCEPHALA

Although the relationships between the Nematoda and the several preceding groups are of a doubtful nature, the present taxon, the Acanthocephala, is universally treated as a distinct phylum. The reasons for separating these spiny-headed worms, as the members are called, from the nematodes and their relatives become immediately apparent as the structure is examined. On the outside, the worms, which may reach lengths up to 700 mm, appear not unlike thick-bodied nematodes, for the external surface is covered with a firm cuticle, devoid of bristles, segmentation, and other features, except for a large opening at the anterior end and another of varying size at the posterior (fig. 10.6). Because of the location of these openings they could readily be thought to represent the mouth and anus, but the anterior pore actually is the opening for the proboscis and the posterior one serves the reproductive system, the digestive system being completely absent.

Structure

The proboscis is densely covered with spines (fig. 10.6), and provides the basis for both the common and scientific names of the group (*acanthos*, spine; *cephalos*, head). Since all the known forms are parasites in the digestive tracts of vertebrates, this organ serves as an anchor, for it penetrates the lining of the host intestines, where it remains embedded. It is extruded and retracted in much the same fashion as the proboscis of the nemerteans. That is to say, extrusion is produced by increase in the pressure of the fluid within the proboscis sheath, resulting from muscle contraction, and retraction is brought about by contraction of muscles connected directly to the proboscis (fig. 10.6). The several tubelike bodies called lemnisci open into the proboscis receptacle and are usually thought to function as reservoirs for the fluid of that apparatus.

Little else can be noted within the body except the *reproductive system*. Even excretory organs are absent, except in the most primitive order, where a series of flame bulbs and tubules surround the reproductive organs. The sexes are

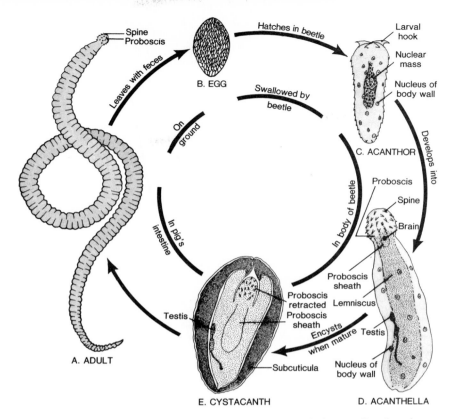

Figure 10.6 *Life cycle of Macracanthocephalus*. The beetle intermediate host is usually a May-beetle.

separate in this phylum and may be readily distinguished without dissection by the size of the posterior genital opening. A central suspensory ligament (fig. 10.6), thicker and longer in the male than in the female, bears the pair of testes or the uterus, respectively. In the female worms, the ovaries do not produce the eggs directly but first break down into ovarian balls, which then give rise to the eggs while floating free in the fluid-filled pseudocoel. The cement glands, located behind the testes in the male, are used to seal the female genital opening after mating has occurred.

Since a digestive system is lacking, food digested by the host apparently is taken in through the body surface of the worm, although in view of the tough cuticle that covers the entire parasite, questions arise as to how this is accomplished. A respiration system likewise is absent, so that energy from the breakdown of the absorbed foodstuffs possibly is gained by anaerobic processes, that is, they do not require oxygen.

The *nervous system* is quite small, consisting of a brain, a nerve trunk on each side of the body that activates the body muscles and genital organs, and a few small nerves that extend to the proboscis system. The brain is merely a simple ganglion located within the proboscis sheath, and the sense organs consist of only a few pits on the anterior end and on the tip of the proboscis.

Development and Life Cycle

During mating the sperm enter the uterus by way of the vagina and continue through that organ into the pseudocoel, where fertilization takes place. The zygote then undergoes a modified, somewhat distorted, spiral cleavage (fig. 10.6), developing through a stereoblastula (p. 63). Then the cell membranes break down so that the entire embryo becomes syncytial, that is, it becomes a single multinucleated cell, much as in the late nematode larva. Gastrula formation is marked only by the inward migration of several clumps of nuclei that enter into the growing reproductive system. Eventually development results in a peculiar larva known as the *acanthor*, because of the presence of six hooks at the anterior end. All this has occurred within the confines of the egg shell, still in the female's pseudocoel.

At this point the eggs are ready to be deposited, so the uterine bell at the anterior end of the uterus permits them to enter the latter organ at that time, but not previous to that stage of development. They then pass through the uterus and vagina into the intestinal tract of the host organism and eventually leave with the feces. If an egg is eaten later by the intermediate host, usually a certain type of insect or other arthropod, it hatches, and the liberated acanthor larva penetrates through the intestinal wall of the host into the body cavity. Here it lives for a time as it develops into a second type of larva referred to as the *acanthella* (fig. 10.6). This form continues to grow in size and develops all the parts of the adult except the reproductive system. At this point the worm is considered to be a juvenile and no longer a larva. Growth then ceases and remains arrested until the parasite is swallowed along with its intermediate host by the proper type of vertebrate. Once in the intestine of the final host, the juvenile attaches by its proboscis to the intestinal wall, resumes its growth, and is ready to engage in the reproductive processes.

An Important Species

All the species of Acanthocephala are parasites of vertebrates, particularly of birds and mammals, many of which have a lethal effect on the host. Since most of the species parasitized are wild, however, only a few of the worms are of economic importance. One acanthocephalan, *Polymorphus magnus*, does considerable damage to domestic ducks, but the species of greatest concern throughout the world is the spiny-headed worm of pigs, known as *Macracanthorhynchus hirudinaceus*.

The mature worms live in the intestinal tract of pigs, firmly attached to the intestinal wall by means of the spiny proboscis. As stated earlier, the female releases eggs already developed to the acanthor larval stage (fig. 10.6), which leave the host's body with the feces. When swallowed by the intermediate host, which is usually the larva of the June-beetle or closely related species, the para-

146   *The Minor Pseudocoelomate Taxa*

site emerges from the egg and, by penetrating through the wall of the insect's digestive tract, enters the body cavity. Here the acanthor develops further and undergoes two stages of metamorphosis, first becoming the *preacanthella* (fig. 10.6), and finally, the acanthella. These processes require a period of at least 4 or 5 months, but, if the egg had been deposited in late summer, it would not attain this final larval stage until the following fall. If the beetle larva or mature insect is then eaten by a pig, the worm enters the latter's intestine, where it inserts the proboscis into the wall; there it remains, reaching maturity in about 4 months, at which time it is about 600 to 650 mm long; usually its life span ranges from 1 to 2 years.

THE PHYLUM ENTOPROCTA

The members of this phylum are predominantly marine forms, although one genus (*Urnatella*) is confined to freshwater streams of North America and India. All are small, almost microscopic animals, always less than 5 mm in length, and are consistently sessile in habit, growing in colonies on submerged vegetation or rocks. Superficially the encrusting colonies appear like moss; hence, at one time they were combined with the similar-appearing coelomate taxon Ectoprocta to form the phylum Bryozoa (meaning moss animals). While somewhat resembling those ectoprocts in size, habit, and structure, they differ in development, in the anus being within the group of tentacles, and most of all, in having a pseudocoel.

Structure

In structure, except for some of the colonial hydroids (p. 90), these animals are probably unlike all others the student has seen. Essentially, the adult body consists of a *calyx,* in which the organs are contained, and a *stalk,* which attaches it to the substrate and provides *stolons* to the other members of the colony (fig. 10.7, A).

The calyx actually is arranged upside down, for when the larva is ready to undergo metamorphosis, it attaches itself by its upper surface to the substrate, an orientation that remains during subsequent growth. Hence the mouth and anus of the adult are situated on the upper side of the bell-shaped calyx, rather than on the lower side as might normally be expected (fig. 10.7, A). These openings are surrounded by a tentacular crown, which is folded inwardly when the calyx closes. The interior of the calyx is largely occupied by the *digestive tract,* which is heavily lined with cilia (fig. 10.7, B). The mouth leads into a long, narrow, buccal tube, the lower end of which serves as an esophagus, but the bulk of the tract is provided by the cavernous stomach, the intestine being much shorter and tubular. The latter is closed posteriorly by a sphincter muscle at the junction with the rectum, while another sphincter muscle surrounds the anus.

The food of these tiny animals consists of particles suspended in the water, such as unicellular algae, protozoans, and decaying vegetable matter, which are swept by the cilia of the tentacles down to the surface of the calyx. Here other cilia move them forward and into the mouth. Most digestive processes seem to

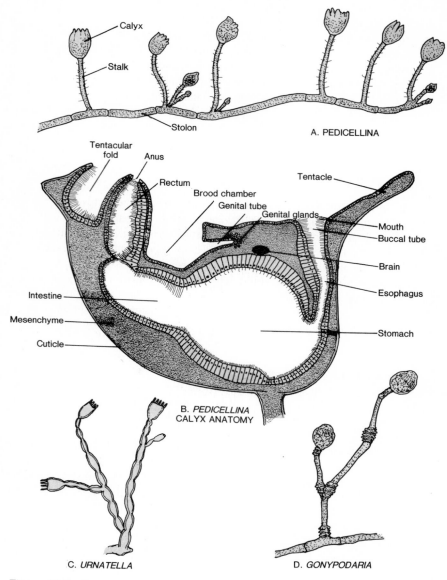

Figure 10.7 *Structure and representative types of Entoprocta.*

take place in the stomach, for its upper surface actively secretes various enzymes and mucus in which the food particles become ensnared. The resulting ropes of food and mucus are moved around by the cilia as the enzymes carry out their digestive actions.

The *excretory system* is extremely simple, for it consists only of a pair of flame bulbs located just above the stomach, connected by short tubules to the common excretory pore placed near the posterior border of the mouth. The *nervous system*, too, is relatively simple. A brain, which is really a double ganglion interconnected by a broad commissure (fig. 10.7, B), serves as the main center. From the sides of this organ extend a number of nerves that run to the calyx wall and gonads but, principally, to the series of sense organs contained in each tentacle. Others extend into the stalk and stolon, at least in some genera. The *pseudocoel* does not contain fluid but is completely filled with a gelatinous material in which are several types of mesenchyme cells. Many of these are starlike amoeboid cells, while others are attached to the internal organs. In the pseudocoel of the stalk and branches, the cells are of a rigid type known as tube cells.

The stalk is simply a prolongation of the calyx, with which it may be continuous, but sometimes the two parts are separated by means of a septum, depending on the genus. Although devoid of organs except for muscles, the stalk is often the most highly modified part in the colony and may be constricted or corrugated at a number of points (fig. 10.7, C, D); occasionally it may even bear spines or be otherwise ornamented. At its lower end is a disk, containing a pedal gland whose secretions provide attachment, while in the freshwater species there is a plate. These structures produce buds to give rise to other stalks and calyxes and thus result in small colonies. Usually, however, the disk produces the lateral shoots called stolons, which in turn bud to enlarge the colony.

Reproduction and Development

As just suggested, reproduction can be by *asexual* budding, the buds usually being produced solely as stated above by stalks, stolons, or base plates and resulting only in increasing the number of individuals contained in the colony. Contrastingly in one family (Loxosomatidae), buds are produced within the brood chamber, located on the wall of the calyx that overlies the intestine (fig. 10.7, B). In this case the buds grow only short stalks, but otherwise are like miniature adults that lack reproductive organs. When sufficiently developed, they break free and float about until they happen to land on a favorable substrate; then the stalk attaches and the young calyx grows to maturity, after which a colony develops as usual. It is of interest to note that these buds which are thus produced on the calyx wall are derived entirely from ectoderm and mesoderm; thus the entoderm of the young must be a subsequent product of the mesoderm.

Sexual means of reproduction are also of general occurrence among the entoprocts. As a rule, the sexes are separate and similar, but a given colony may or may not contain both types. the gonads are saclike organs located near the brain, the precise position varying with the genus. From each organ a tube extends medially, that unites with one another before opening to the surface with the common genital pore, located near the brood chamber (fig. 10.7, B). In the males, after the two vasa deferentia have united, the common duct thus formed may be expanded into a seminal vesicle. Following fertilization in the ovary or oviduct, the eggs are deposited in the brood chamber, where development into a free-swimming larva is completed. Cleavage is of a spiral type that eventually leads to the formation in succession of a typical morula, blastula, and gastrula, gastrulation being by the usual invagination processes (fig. 10.8, A–C). Eventually the processes result in a larva that is ciliated over much of the surface. In many of its features (fig. 10.8, D, E) it resembles the trochophore larva described in the chapter that follows (p. 162), except that it lacks the bands of long cilia and has flame bulbs instead of solenocytes. However, possibly the most unusual feature of this larva is that invertebrate zoologists have not provided it with a distinctive name.

EVOLUTIONARY SUMMARY OF THE PSEUDOCOELOMATES

In this summary of the pseudocoelomates, the types of problems that the zoologist encounters in his efforts to decipher the origins and past histories of the various phyla become particularly clear. Some of the phyla possessing this type of body cavity immediately seem to be closely related, while several appear quite

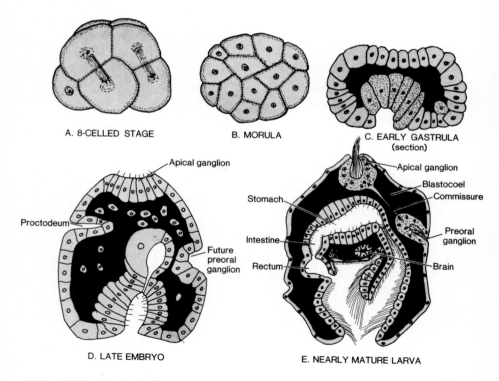

Figure 10.8 *Development of the larva in the Entoprocta.* (Based on Marcus, 1939.)

remote from the rest, despite their sharing important features. A few are obviously simple, others are quite as obviously complex, and no intermediate forms are to be found that might provide clues to the kinships. Larvae are present in many of the taxa and provide assistance in phylogenetic studies, but they are missing at many critical points. Moreover, simplicity in structure can arise in two different ways. First, it can represent an actual primitive state, that is, the organism concerned is a little-modified descendant of a primitive ancestral type, and second, it can be the product of degeneration. In such cases, the ancestors of the animal had been advanced forms, but in the descendants many of the complex parts have been lost secondarily through their being no longer useful to the present parasitic or sedentary way of life. As a result of all these uncontrollable variables, any number of interpretations of phylogeny are often equally valid.

One of the features valuable in tracing the pseudocoelomate phyla is the type of excretory organs that are present. To establish which variety, the flame bulb or the solenocyte, is the more primitive, the members of the Platyhelminthes can be examined as to this trait, since they are simpler animals than those of the present group in that they have no body cavity. Because those flatworms have the flame bulb, in which a tuft of cilia propels the water, that excretory structure can be considered to be ancestral to the solenocyte, in which a single (or sometimes double) flagellum performs that function. On this basis, two main branches of the pseudocoelomates can be recognized, a division that arose earlier, in which excretion is by means of flame bulbs, and a more advanced branch having solenocytes (fig. 10.9).

The less advanced branch might readily be viewed as having the Entoprocta closest to the ancestral stock. This phylum includes animals that are small, and its adult members are not far removed structurally from the larvae, except in

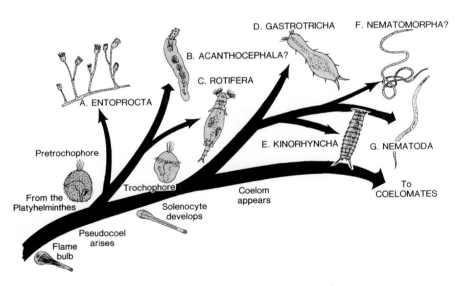

Figure 10.9 *Possible events in the evolution of the pseudocoelomates.*

being upside-down and in having an enclosure (calyx) and stalk. The budding type of asexual reproduction that prevails throughout the phylum also is suggestive of its being rather primitive. Above these animals, but still not greatly removed from the ancestral stock, are the rotifers; indeed, some invertebrate zoologists have considered these minute organisms as only slightly modified trochophore larvae. Since the latter, however, has the solenocyte, it is probably more correct to consider them slightly modified descendants of a pretrochophore. Finally, the Acanthocephala must be viewed as belonging to this branch, too, for those genera of spiny-headed worms that do possess excretory systems have flame bulbs. Where on the branch they should be placed is another matter, for they lack a digestive system and possibly entoderm. Thus they could be thought to be closely related to the acoel platyhelminths, with the absence of the digestive organs therefore representing a primitive condition. Alternatively they might be regarded, as here (fig. 10.9), as the terminal taxon on this branch, which has lost the digestive organs and entoderm secondarily.

The second branch similarly has groups of questionable status, but the presence of solenocytes in some phyla marks them collectively as more advanced than the preceding. Near the origin of this line of descent are the relatively simple and microscopic gastrotrichs and kinorhynchs (fig. 10.9), and far out near the branch's end are the highly diversified nematodes. Because these three groups share a typical form of pseudocoel and possess a tripartite pharynx, as well as other traits, their common ancestry appears clear-cut. However, the nematomorphs are problematic. Their lack of digestive organs may readily be accepted to be from secondary loss due to their parasitic habits, and hence, the phylum should probably be placed close to the nematodes. On the other hand, the form of the larva and mesenchyme-filled pseudocoel seem to suggest a primitive position for the taxon, possibly not far from the acanthocephalans. Here custom is followed and the first interpretation is illustrated (fig. 10.9); hopefully new data will be forthcoming some day that will make their actual relationships clear.

QUESTIONS FOR REVIEW AND THOUGHT

1. Compare the three phyla of minute aquatic pseudocoelomates to show likenesses and differences. Which have cilia externally? Which have a footlike part connected to a gland? How do the brains compare in size and location? How do the digestive tracts differ?

2. In what ways are the gastrotrichs and kinorhynchs more closely related to one another than they are to the rotifers?

3. Why are the kinorhynchs considered to be segmented and the rotifers to be falsely segmented, when both have similar-appearing folds on the body surface?

4. In what ways do the rotifers appear to be more closely related to the spiny-headed worms and entoprocts than to the gastrotrichs?

5. Characterize the phylum Acanthocephala. How do these spiny-headed worms differ from nematodes? In what ways do they resemble tapeworms? How do they differ from the latter?

6. State the life cycle of a spiny-headed worm.

7. Describe the principal features of the Entoprocta. How would you classify its body cavity and why? In what ways might it be advantageous for these animals to live upside down as they do?

8. By what means do entoprocts reproduce? Describe the chief steps in their development.

9. On what basis might certain of the taxa described as phyla in this and the preceding chapter be grouped together as the *phylum* Aschelminthes? What justifies the treatment given them here?

SUGGESTIONS FOR FURTHER READING

Donner, J. 1966. *Rotifers*. Translated and adapted by H.G.S. Wright. London, Frederick Warne and Co.

Ghiselin, M.T. 1969. The evolution of hermaphroditism among aminals. *Quart. Rev. Biol.*, 44:189–208.

Gilbert, J.J. 1966. Rotifer ecology and embryological induction. *Science*, 151:1234–1237.

Lanzavecchia, G. 1977. Morphological modulations in helical muscles (Aschelminthes and Annelida). *Internat. Rev. Cytol.*, 51:133–186.

The Segmented Worms

11

Near the top of the metazoan evolutionary tree are two major branches, each of which possesses a true coelom (fig. 5.4). Since certain phyla of each branch have been highly successful, as evidenced by their including the predominant animals of the land as well as the seas, they intimate the extensive evolutionary diversity which the advent of that cavity made possible.

While the coelom is usually well developed along both branches, it is formed in the embryo by two separate and distinct processes, as discussed in Chapter 5 (p. 66). Since the schizocoel-bearing animals are usually discussed first, that custom is followed here. Whether the earliest phylum of these schizocoelomates is represented by the Annelida or the Mollusca is still an unsettled issue in zoological literature, but treating the first of these two taxa as the earliest offers some advantages to clarity of discussion later, so that procedure is followed here.

THE PHYLUM ANNELIDA

Segmentation, a trait that also characterizes the members of this branch, at least primitively, puts in an appearance early in its evolutionary development. Perhaps this character, too, has contributed greatly to the success of these animals, for greater diversification occurs along this branch than anywhere else in the zoological world. But the number of species found among the schizocoels is part of another story and accordingly is held until later.

Since wormlike forms have dominated much of the earlier history of the metazoans, it is not at all surprising that this branch should have its origin in a phylum of similar habit. The Annelida are distinguished by their being the last such creatures to become highly successful, as indicated by the fairly large representation, for although one or two wormlike phyla are discussed later, they contain only a few species each.

Characteristics

While the principal traits of the phylum are made sufficiently clear by the diagram (fig. 11.1), several require brief discussion. The circulatory system is of the closed variety, resembling that of the nemertineans in having both arteries and veins. Sometimes the blood is red, as it contains hemoglobin similar to that found in human blood corpuscles; in the annelids, however, it is carried in the plasma, not in the blood cells. In most representatives the coelom is divided into

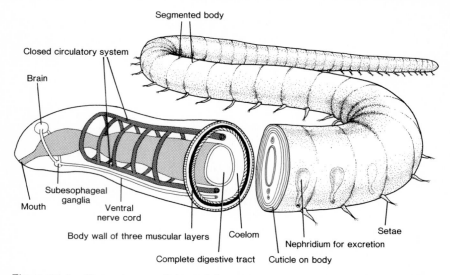

Figure 11.1 *The major morphological features of the Annelida.* Distinctive structural characteristics include a body made of segments, a closed circulatory system, a nerve cord located ventrally, a coelom, nephridia for excretion, and a body wall consisting of three layers of muscles covered by epidermis and a cuticle.

small chambers by cross-walls, called *septa,* extending between segments. The body segmentation is the basis for the phylum name, which in Latin means ringed ones. Although the digestive tract is often complex, the extent of its development varies widely among the several classes, the distinguishing features of which are summarized in table 11.1.

The Nervous System

In all annelids the nervous system consists basically of a ventral nerve cord enlarged in each segment to form a ganglion. In addition there is a brain (prostomial ganglia) to which a pair of subesophageal ganglia are connected by means of a commissure on each side of the pharynx. On a function basis the organization into two separate reflex systems is a distinctive feature. One set, the *intrasegmental reflexes,* coordinates the contraction of the muscles which compose the wall of each segment. Here two types of muscles oppose each other, the longitudinal muscles that reduce the length of the segment, and the circular ones that cause elongation. The reflexes are organized so that when one set of muscles has been stimulated to contract, the other is induced to relax. The second system, the *intersegmental reflexes,* coordinates the activities of corresponding muscles in adjacent segments. For example, if the circular muscles in segment 10 should be induced to contract by intrasegmental fibers, those in segment 11 are made to follow suit, followed by those in segment 12 and so on to the end of the body through the activities of the intersegmental nerves. In the meantine, the longitudinal muscles may have been activated in segment 10, so a correlated wave of contraction is initiated throughout the body. By use of the intra- and intersegmental reflexes in this alternating fashion, the normal mode of locomotion is brought about.

In addition to the short nerve fibers that comprise the reflexes, typically a system of *giant fibers* runs the entire length of the body. These fibers enable the whole organism to be brought under the control of the higher centers, the brain and the subesophageal ganglia. If these centers are strongly excited, as when the worm's anterior is grasped by fingers or a bird's beak, all of the longitudinal muscles are induced to contract. The brain has the additional function of inhibiting reflexes. If that organ of a live earthworm is removed, the animal moves about constantly, for nothing now suppresses the intra- and intersegmental reflexes. If both higher centers are removed, the animal becomes permanently quiescent, for nothing now excites the segmental reflexes into action.

The Class Polychaeta

The class Polychaeta is not the most primitive of the Annelida, but, because it possesses the majority of the distinctive structures found in this phylum, it is discussed first as a matter of convenience. Some 4,000 species have been described, almost all of which are marine.

Habits

There can be little doubt that the polychaetes show a greater degree of variety than any of the other classes of segmented worms. Three major lines of diversity exist, known as the errant, burrowing, and tube-dwelling types. In the first of these, the *errant* polychaetes (fig. 11.3, A), the worms have become especially adapted for actively creeping along the sea bottom. Many such species occur along sandy shores or in muddy sand in the intertidal zone, while others can be found under submerged stones; a number of forms, however, live at depths as great as 5,000 m. Although the errant species frequently burrow into the sea bottom, they have no special adaptations for that type of existence. In contrast, the *burrowing* polychaetes are adapted primarily for burrowing through the ocean floor in earthworm fashion. In these worms, evolution has largely involved the reduction of certain body parts; many genera, such as *Arenicola* (fig. 11.2, A), have the head inconspicuous and the pharynx shortened and not provided with jaws.

The most highly specialized, the *tubiculous* forms, spend their entire adult lives in tubes. Their specializations are often very complex and striking, sometimes to the point of being bizarre; the tentacles in particular are highly conspicuous. In *Sabella,* for instance, fifteen to twenty of these organs are present, all of which are plumelike, often highly colored, and perhaps two-thirds as long as the worm's body (fig. 11.2, B). When feeding, the worm remains within its tube but permits its tentacles to project into the sea water. Here the cilia with which these organs are clothed set up currents that sweep small particles inward to be captured in the tentacles' longitudinal grooves. Then the particles are conducted along these towards the mouth, but before entering that opening, pass through a

Table 11.1   The Classes of Annelida

	Classes	
Characteristic	Archiannelida	Polychaeta
Segments	Few, poorly indicated	Sharply marked internally and externally
Clitellum	Absent	Absent
Setae	Usually absent	Numerous, borne on parapodia
Suckers	Absent	Absent
Head	Distinct, with appendages	Distinct, with appendages
Sexes	Separate	Separate
Larva	Trochophore	Trochophore
Habitat	Marine	Marine
Common names	None	Clam worms, sand worms, etc.

sievelike chamber. This organ permits only the smallest particles to drop into the worm's mouth, rejecting the large ones altogether and sending the medium-sized bits into the tube, where they are used for adding to or repairing that structure. The form of the body also may be highly adapted for this mode of living. In most tubiculous species the segments are very broad anteriorly but gradually diminish in size towards the posterior end, so that the body is conical rather than cylindrical. Often it is divided into a distinct head, thorax, and abdomen, as exemplified by *Sabella*.

But the greatest specialization probably is found in *Chaetopterus,* a form that dwells in U-shaped tubes in the sea bottoms. While the characteristic tentacles of many other tube-dwellers are here reduced, there is a broad collar around the head with a tentaclelike fringe along the dorsal opening (fig. 11.2, D), and, just posterior to that, a pair of winglike parapodia bear a series of mucous glands. These glands secrete a bag that serves in filtering food particles from the seawater. It is so arranged that the particles collect in a cuplike elevation and are there rolled into small balls and passed forward to the mouth. Along the entire ventral surface of the thorax, the parapodia are modified as suction disks to secure the worm in its burrow, while dorsally three broad sets are specialized as fans. These beat rhythmically to circulate water through the tube and bring in food and dissolved oxygen. Behind them, the tapering abdomen lacks distinctive adaptations.

Structure

Highly diversified though they may be, the polychaetes, regardless of type, possess a number of features in common. A well-marked head is usually present,

Oligochaeta	Hirudinea
Sharply marked internally and externally	Well marked internally only
Present	Present
Several rows, on body	Absent
Absent	Present
Absent	Absent
United	United
Absent	Absent
Fresh water and terrestrial	Marine, fresh water, and terrestrial
Earthworms, limicolous worms	Leeches

consisting of two parts, a *peristomium* that contains the mouth and a rooflike *prostomium* that projects farther anteriorly. On the latter are two short tentacles and a pair of thick palps; in addition several pairs of eyes may be located on its upper surface. While the peristomium sometimes has a pair of parapodia, more characteristically it bears a number of tentaclelike structures called *cirri*. Frequently a segmented proboscis bearing a strong pair of jaws at its tip may be found projecting out of the mouth (fig. 11.3, A). Behind the head in the simpler errant types, the body consists of identical segments, each bearing a pair of parapodia, and at the very end of the body is a flaplike part called the *pygidium*.

The parapodia are probably the most characteristic structure of the polychaete annelids as a whole. Essentially they are paired lobes placed one on each side of every segment, as in *Nereis* (fig. 11.3, A, D). Although appearing merely as flaplike projections, a parapodium is actually an extremely complex organ, internally possessing a number of sets of muscles and an extensive network of blood vessels; the details, however, lie beyond present needs. Even externally these organs are far from simple and vary from species to species. First of all each is usually subdivided into two portions, an upper notopodium and a lower, smaller neuropodium (fig. 11.3, D). Both of these parts are themselves divided into two lobes, each of which in the notopodium serves as gills. In contrast, in the neuropodium only the ventralmost projection plays a role in respiration. In addition each podium bears a tuft of bristles. These must be of much importance in the economy of the worm, for the tufts are individually attached internally to a rodlike aciculum and can be retracted and exserted by complicated sets of muscles.

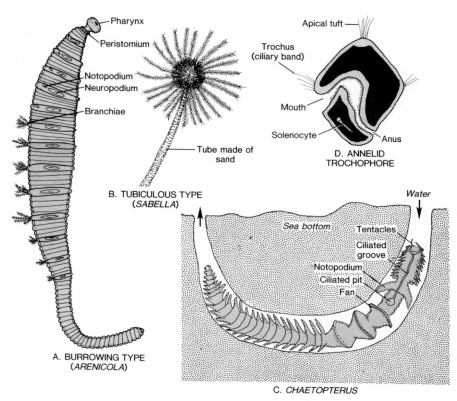

Figure 11.2   *Diversity among polychaetes.*

Reproduction

In many polychaetes, the gonads are located in most segments and are merely specialized areas of the coelomic epithelial lining. The sperm or eggs they produce are deposited directly into the body cavity, where they collect in large numbers, sometimes entirely filling the segment. After undergoing maturation, they leave the coelom either by way of the nephridial tubules or by rupturing the body wall.

Since the sexes are separate in the polychaetes, swarming is of frequent occurrence during the period of gamete release. When sexually mature, the worms, whether active bottom-dwellers or tube-formers, rise to the surface and swim about vigorously; then, after the gametes have been released, all return to the bottom once more. Not infrequently, soon after discharging the sex cells, the reproducing individuals perish.

Many adaptations for bringing the sexes together at swarming time have evolved. Among errant types, the parapodia frequently undergo radical changes as the sex organs mature; *Nereis* and its relatives become so modified that the sexual form is given the distinctive name *heteronereis*. As sexual maturity ap-

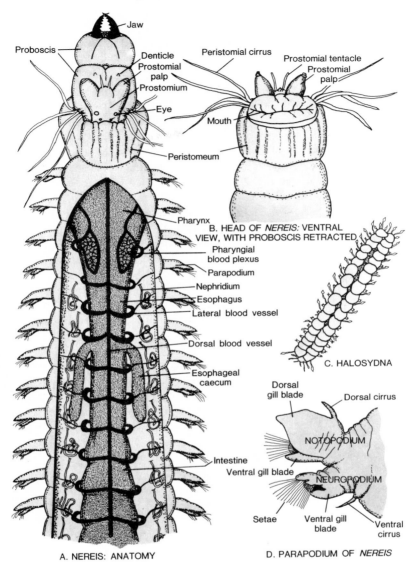

A. NEREIS: ANATOMY

B. HEAD OF *NEREIS:* VENTRAL VIEW, WITH PROBOSCIS RETRACTED

C. HALOSYDNA

D. PARAPODIUM OF *NEREIS*

Figure 11.3 *The structure of errant polychaets.* (B. after Richetts and Calvin.)

proaches in this genus, the body musculature breaks down and is consumed by leukocytes before new muscles of a different form begin growth. In the meantime the parapodia become modified by increasing in length, their several lobes enlarging into membranous frills. At the same time the old setae are lost, to be replaced with flattened ones that appear like so many oars. Moreover, the eyes increase greatly in size and the entire body of the worm becomes sensitive to light. While some of these developments doubtlessly are of value in swimming and floating, others enhance the efficiency of the gills for the very active mating period.

Other examples of diversity for reproductive purposes are provided by the palolo worm and others of the genus *Leodice*. In these inhabitants of coral reefs, the entire posterior half of the worm becomes filled with gametes, which ripen at a specific time of the year. In the West Indian species, breeding occurs only during the third quarter of the June-July moon. Then the posterior half of the worm breaks off and writhing actively, rises to the surface, where it discharges its contents into the sea. Often the worms are so abundant that the waters become turbid with released gametes. The palolo worm of the South Pacific behaves similarly but is still more specific as to the time of swarming. This activity takes place only at moonrise on that night during the latter half of October or early November when the moon attains its last quarter.

Among most polychaetes, the fertilized egg develops into a peculiar larva called the *trochophore* or *trochosphere*. In many ways the trochophore superficially resembles the pilidium of the ribbonworms, especially in having an apical organ at one pole. Instead of being ciliated over the entire surface, however, the present larva bears a band of cilia around its middle, and its digestive tract is of the complete type (fig. 11.2, F). Because it is found also in several other phyla to be described later, the trochophore is of great biological importance in suggesting relationships between otherwise quite dissimilar groups.

The Class Archiannelida

In occasional treatises of animal variety, the members of the class Archiannelida are considered to be merely aberrant polychaetes, but to treat them in this manner makes it impossible to define the latter taxon clearly. Here they are taken at their face value and accordingly are considered to be what they seem, remnants of a primitive class of Annelida whose members are now largely extinct. These are small forms of simple structure, which lack parapodia and usually setae, too. In some cases, such as in the genus *Dinophilus,* even external segmentation is wanting.

The largest members of the class are the several species of *Polygordius* that in some ways approach the errant polychaetes in structure. For instance, there is a prostomium that bears two tentacles (fig. 11.4, C), but the body is without parapodia and setae, and the segmentation is barely impressed. Internally the coelom is divided by septa, on the sides of which is located a pair of nephridia, as in the preceding class. Circular muscles are absent from the body wall, and the ventral nerve cord is not fully differentiated from the epidermis. While present, the circulatory system is far less extensive than that of *Nereis,* for instance.

The members of the genus *Nerilla* are much smaller than those of the foregoing taxon, having bodies consisting of only seven or eight segments. The head lacks a separate prostomial segment but bears three tentacles, a pair of palps, and several simple eyes (fig. 11.4, B). All body segments except the last have two sets of setae on each side, separated by a cirrus. The cirri of the head are so elongate that they appear as tentacles; the terminal segment also has a pair of long cirri but lacks setae. The digestive tract is simply a broad tube that tapers at each

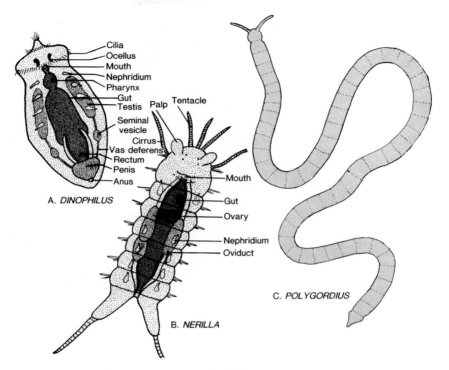

Figure 11.4 *Some representative archiannelids.*

end. Unlike most archiannelids, the sexes are separate. In males there are three pairs of testes, each having a separate sperm duct; however, these tubes unite posteriorly and open through a common genital pore. In females, there is a single pair of ovaries, each with an oviduct that has a separate genital pore. Nephridia are present in most segments, but the coelom is not divided by septa.

Dinophilus contains the smallest of all the species, which in body form appears not too unlike trochophores, except in being flattened ventrally (fig. 11.4, A). Merely five or six segments are present, indicated only by the tufts of setae and the pairs of nephridia, as segmentation is not impressed externally and internal septa are absent. The head bears two circlets of cilia and a pair of large ocelli. A circulatory system is absent, and body musculature and the coelom are greatly reduced, the latter nearly to the point of being wanting. As in the preceding genus the sexes are separate. The male has a muscular penis that penetrates the female's body wall during copulation to inject sperm into the latter's coelom.

The Oligochaeta

Many features of the polychaetes are absent in the present class, including the parapodia, protrusible pharynx, distinct head, and palpi. On the other hand, the reproductive system among the oligochaetes is better developed, as is also the circulatory system. Two major types are included, the terrestrial earthworms and the aquatic or limicolous (mud-dwelling) members.

Morphology

The main features of anatomy are made clear by the illustration (fig. 11.5), but a few points require comment. The *clitellum* is an organ of secretion found elsewhere only in the leeches. Although in large earthworms it is present throughout life, in the majority of species it becomes evident only with the approach of the breeding season, during which it plays two important roles (see below).

Externally the setae, usually eight per segment, are borne directly on the body wall, where they form rows along the ventral and lateral surfaces. A prolongation over the mouth, known as the *prostomium,* alone distinguishes the anterior end from the posterior, for no eyes or tentacles are present. While most species are measured in inches, in limited areas of Australia (fig. 11.6) and South America, giant forms feet long are encountered.

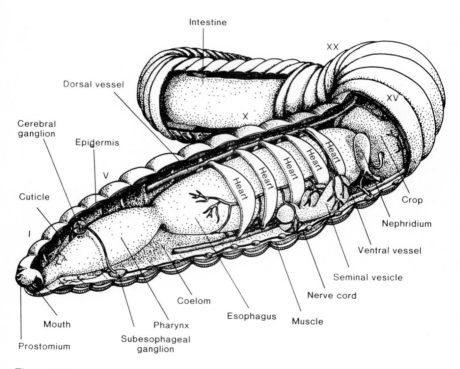

Figure 11.5 *The internal anatomy of an earthworm.*

Figure 11.6 *A giant earthworm from Australia.* Fully extended worms of this species (*Megascolides australia*) often reach lengths over three meters. Other giants, not quite so large as these, occur along the Andes and in South Africa and Sri Lanka. (Courtesy of the Australian Information Service.)

Reproduction

As oligochaetes are hermaphroditic, the reproductive organs typically include one pair of testes each in segments 10 and 11 and a pair of ovaries in segment 13. The ducts which carry the gametes have funnel-like openings internally, located just behind the gonads. The external openings of the oviducts are on that segment immediately following the ovaries, while those of the sperm ducts extend posteriorly as far as segment 15 or 16. As a rule the testes are enclosed in saclike *seminal vesicles* in which sperm are stored until ready for release. In addition, one or two pairs of *sperm receptacles* are found in the segment or segments preceding those that bear the testes.

Mating in *Lumbricus* and other large earthworms involves mutual insemination. The worms lie with ventral surfaces in contact, each with segments 9 and 10 adjacent to the clitellum of the other. The clitella then secrete mucous tubes over the anterior ends of the worms, while the sperm pass out through the sperm duct openings to flow to the respective clitella along seminal grooves on the ventral surface. How the sperm are conducted from the clitellum to the sperm receptacles for storage has never been established.

Several days after mating, oviposition takes place. The clitellum secretes a mucous tube over the anterior end as during copulation, but this time it serves as a cocoon. As the tube moves forward over the body, eggs are deposited into it along with an albuminous secretion; farther cephalad, the eggs are fertilized as they pass over the seminal receptacles. Finally, a series of strong contractions frees the cocoon from the body to remain in the ground while the eggs develop. After hatching, the young feed upon the enclosed albuminous material until they undergo a series of mild changes and emerge.

The Hirudinea

Unlike the Oligochaeta, in which the number of segments varies both with the age of the individual and from species to species, thirty-two segments plus a prostomium are uniformly present in the class Hirudinea, the leeches. Because the segments externally are subdivided into a series of rings, or annuli, the actual number is apparent only inside the body. Leeches differ from earthworms also in lacking setae and in possessing one sucker at each end of the body (fig. 11.7). Depending on the family, jaws or a protrusible pharynx may be present.

Kinship with the Oligochaeta is indicated by several shared traits, particularly by the presence of a clitellum during breeding. This gland functions here as in the preceding group, secreting tubes during mating and cocoons for the development of the young. The eggs, too, develop in similar fashion and the excretory and reproductive systems also resemble those of the Oligochaetes. Because of these likenesses and such others as the sexes being united, many European zoologists combine the two groups as a class named the Clitellata.

Habits

While the vast majority of the leeches live in fresh waters, a number are marine, and a few, particularly in the Old World, are terrestrial. In water most

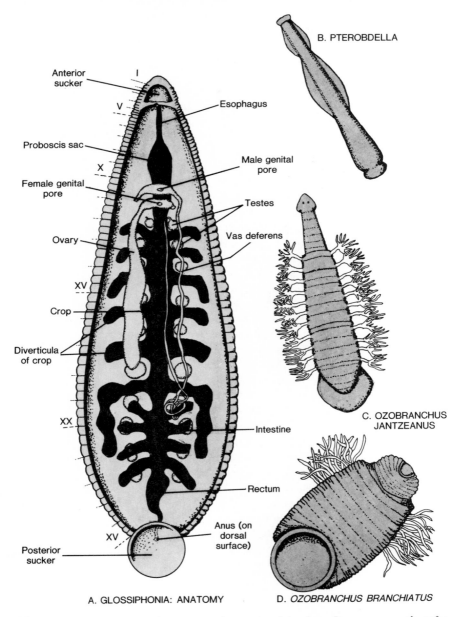

B. PTEROBDELLA

Anterior sucker

Esophagus

Proboscis sac

Male genital pore

Female genital pore

Testes

Ovary

Vas deferens

Crop

Diverticula of crop

Intestine

C. OZOBRANCHUS JANTZEANUS

Rectum

Anus (on dorsal surface)

Posterior sucker

A. GLOSSIPHONIA: ANATOMY

D. *OZOBRANCHUS BRANCHIATUS*

Figure 11.7 *Structure and representative types of leeches. Roman numerals refer to segment number.*

species are skillful swimmers; on dry land or mud they progress by a series of loops, much like those of a "measuring-worm," using the suckers to provide positive traction.

Food habits are quite varied. A number feed upon decaying flesh and are therefore scavengers, while a relatively few prey upon small animals, such as earthworms, snails, and insect larvae. Several are parasites in a strict sense, but the majority are notorious for their blood-sucking habits. For the latter mode of feeding a number of specializations have evolved. In gathering the fluid food, an anticoagulant is a necessity and is found abundantly in the saliva of such genera as *Hirudo*, the medicinal leech. Since prey of the proper kind may be encountered only ocasionally, a provision has been acquired that permits large blood meals to be consumed at one time, often to the extent of several times the worm's own weight. This feat is accomplished by means of the large crop and by lateral extensions on that organ called *diverticula*. After a full meal, the fluid part of the blood is absorbed into the leech's circulatory system, for elimination by the nephridia over a span of several days; in this way the body soon resumes nearly normal proportions. Digestion of the solid remains of the meal then proceeds slowly, as a rule requiring several months for completion.

So far as effects upon man and his economy are concerned, the aquatic species hold only a nuisance value, except for a small number that attack domestic animals. Perhaps the worst of these is the horse leech (*Limnatis nilotica*), a form that lives around the Mediterranean Sea and in the Near East. Although the adult feeds harmlessly on worms and small fish, the young often cause considerable damage. As the minute juveniles spend most of their time in the surface waters of ponds and tanks, they are frequently swallowed by horses, cattle, and even human beings while drinking. In passing through the mouth and throat, they attach themselves to the lining of these organs, occasionally in such numbers that the host dies from loss of blood.

The terrestrial species, particularly of the genus *Haemadipsa*, are undoubtedly the most detrimental. In all tropical regions of the world, but particularly in rain forests from India into Australia, the leeches occur in such large numbers that some areas are uninhabitable by man. In the forests the worms lie relatively inactive on grasses and low bushes until a vertebrate approaches. Then, detecting the host either by the vibration of its movements or by the warmth radiating from its body, they quickly move toward it by looping, as described above. A traveler along a jungle trail need pause for only a moment before he finds himself being converged upon by dozens or even hundreds of these leeches.

Internal Structure

While one or two internal structural features of the Hirudinea have been alluded to in the foregoing paragraph, several are deserving of closer attention. In the illustration (fig. 11.7, A), it is immediately evident that the internal organs are nearly entirely devoted to two functions, digestion and reproduction.

There, too, the crop and diverticula of the *digestive system* mentioned in the preceding section may be seen in their reduced state. Following a meal of blood, those organs almost completely fill the coelomic cavity, except for the anterior region, where the nondistensible esophagus and proboscis sac are located. Although the largest diverticula are found on the crop that makes up the greatest bulk of the tract, the intestine is also equipped with four pairs. The rectum that follows opens through a dorsally located anus.

As these worms are hermaphroditic, the two types of *reproductive systems* are present in each adult. Both sets are paired, but only one side of each is given in the illustration (fig. 11.7, A). The female tract is by far the simpler, as each half consists of only a long saclike ovary and a brief oviduct, that leads to a common female genital pore. In the male, there are nine pairs of rounded, segmentally-arranged testes, all on any one side being connected to a long coiled vas deferens by means of a series of vasa efferentia that are too fine to be indicated in the figure. The pair of vasa deferentia finally extends forward and fuses before exiting through a common male genital pore located anteriorly to that of the female system.

The nephridia are reduced in size but otherwise resemble those of the oligochaetes. In some genera, an unusual condition exists in that the several pairs of nephridial canals link to form a network before opening through a pair of excretory pores. The nervous system is in general similar to that of the earthworms, except that three or more of the anterior ganglia are fused into a large sub-esophageal mass.

Two Minor Taxa

Two small taxa of annelids, sometimes treated as separate classes, but often included in the Oligochaeta, are of importance in suggesting how the leeches may have arisen from an earthwormlike ancestor. The *Acanthobdellida,* containing only the single species *Acanthobdella peledina,* appears not unlike an oligochaete in structure (fig. 11.8, A)—even the internal anatomy shows a close resemblance. Nevertheless it has several traits like those of the leeches. In the first place, it has a definite and limited number of body segments—its 27 being slightly smaller than the 32 found among leeches but certainly much smaller than the oligochaetes. Secondly, the external false segmentation of the hirudineans is present here, too, and the first five segments have setae, an oligochaete trait, while the remainder have none, as in the leeches. Additionally, a posterior sucker is present, as in the latter taxon, while an anterior one is lacking, as in the former.

The second group, the Branchiobdellida, contains a small number of ecto-parasitic species found on the gills or body of crayfish; these similarly are intermediate in structure. As in the Acanthobdellida, they show a reduced and constant number of body segments, their 15 or 16 being far fewer than the number found in the leeches. In their other characteristics they likewise approach the leeches, for they are devoid of setae and possess both anterior and posterior suckers (fig. 11.8, B). Moreover, the buccal cavity contains a pair of small jaws used in feeding. However, the internal anatomy shows none of the leech characteristics, the simple, unpouched digestive tract being especially noteworthy. As

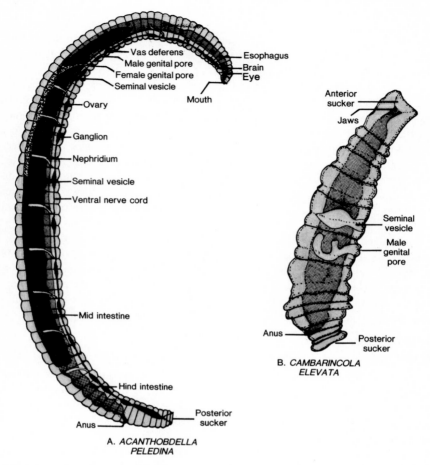

Figure 11.8 *Representatives of two minor taxa of Annelida.*

their mixtures of traits intimate, neither group probably is descended directly from the ancestral stock of the Hirudinea, but both have developed several parallel traits that indicate how some of the distinctive features of the leech may themselves have developed one by one.

THE ONYCHOPHORA

One peculiar evolutionary line developed during remote times by ancestral animals would have remained unknown to science were it not for a handful of species still surviving today, as the fossil record is devoid of all Onychophora. How many other soft-bodied groups similarly came and went during geological times without leaving any trace can only be conjectured. In the present group most of the seventy or so living species occur in such tropical places as the West

Indies, Borneo, Malaya, and the Congo, but a few are found in subtropical and temperate areas like New Zealand, Australia, and South Africa. Most frequently they live under the bark of fallen trees and in the litter of forest floors.

As might be expected of an archaic group, *Peripatus* and its allies do not fall readily into any existing phylum and have in bygone days been variously classed as annelids, slugs, and millipedes. Presently they are considered a separate phylum that perhaps represents an intermediate level in the origin of the Arthropoda.

Morphology

Resemblances to the Annelida are found in the muscular body wall and thin cuticle, the series of segmentally arranged pairs of nephridia, and the numerous legs which are not unlike parapodia in construction (fig. 11.9). In contrast to the Annelida, however, the body is not visibly divided into segments, segmentation being indicated externally only by the appendages and internally by the nephridia. Even the nervous system lacks any indication of serially arranged ganglia, consisting largely of a brain and two longitudinal nerve cords. The only sense organs specialized for a single function are the two simple eyes. In addition, a pair of tentacles on the head and several series of papillae on the dorasl surface serve both in touch and chemoreception.

The nephridia are constructed more like the arthropod organ than the annelid, for near each tubule's exit there is a bladder derived from the ectoderm, as in the crustacean's green or coxal gland. Also indicative of kinship with the arthropods

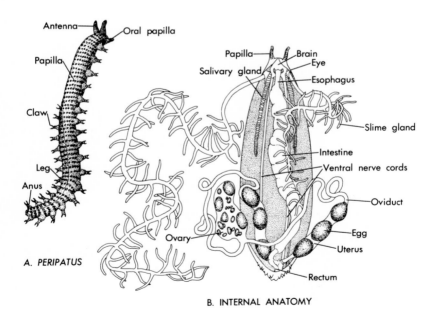

Figure 11.9 *Peripatus and its internal morphology.*

are the hemocoel and tracheae. The former will be recalled as a special cavity which serves as a part of the circulatory system, while the latter are fine tubes which conduct air from external pores directly to the various body parts. Unlike those of insects, the *spiracles,* as the pores are called, cannot be opened and closed; since water-vapor loss thus is uncontrollable, these creatures are confined to moister regions of the globe. It has been found that under similar atmospheric conditions, *Peripatus* loses body moisture at a rate twice that of an earthworm, forty times that of a caterpillar, and more than eighty times that of a roach!

QUESTIONS FOR REVIEW AND THOUGHT

1. Give the chief characteristics of the phylum Annelida. Of what value to the organisms might such characteristics be as the coelom, segmentation, and three layers of muscles in the body wall?

2. Name the four classes of annelids and give the distinguishing characteristics of each. Which is the most highly diversified in structure and habits? On what is your opinion based?

3. Describe the main features involved in annelid locomotion in general.

4. Distinguish between the three major types of polychaetes. Deriving a portion of the information from the figures, compare their food habits.

5. Describe a parapodium. What are some of the modifications it has undergone in the various types of polychaetes?

6. Compare the reproductive processes of the oligochaetes to those of polychaetes. Which of these two classes are the more advanced in this regard and why do you think so? How does a trochophore larva differ from a pilidium?

7. Describe any specializations the leeches may possess that adapt them particularly for their mode of life. In what ways do these worms resemble oligochaetes and in what ways are they distinct?

8. Supposing you were to include the two small taxa (Acanthobdellida and Branchiobdellida) in either the Polychaeta or Hirudinea. How would you then define the class in which you placed them in such a way as to include their traits in the definition and still keep the class sharply delineated from the other one? Now apply the same procedures to the Archiannelida, placing it in the Polychaeta. How would you then define the latter to distinguish it from the Oligochaeta?

9. Compare the phylum Onychophora with the Annelida. In what traits does it resemble the latter and in what ways does it differ? What features seem to resemble those of arthropods?

SUGGESTIONS FOR FURTHER READING

Ayala, S.C., C. Johnson, B. Morris, B. Rooney, A. Stuart, and B. Woodhull. 1972. A colony of giant Andean earthworms. *BioScience,* 22:299–301.

Baskin, D.G. 1976. Neurosecretion and the endocrinology of nereid polychaetes. *Amer. Zool.,* 16:107–124.

Benson, R.H. 1974. The role of ornamentation in the design and function of the ostracode carapace. *Geosci. Man.,* 6:47–57.

Callahan, P.S. 1975. *Tuning into nature.* The Devin-Adair Co., Old Greenwich, Conn.

Crisp, M. 1977. The development of the serpulid *Pomatioleios kraussii* (Annelida, Polychaeta). *J. Zool. Lond.,* 183:147–160.

Dyal, J.A. 1973. Behavior modification in annelids. In *Invertebrate learning,* ed. W.C. Corning, J.A. Dyal, and A.O.D. Willows, volume 1, p. 225–289. New York, Plenum Press.

Edwards, C.A., and J.R. Lofty. 1977. *Biology of earthworms.* 2nd ed. London, Chapman and Hall.

Fitzharris, T.P. 1976. Regeneration in sabellid annelids. *American Zoologist,* 16:593–616.

Gardner, C.R. 1976. The neuronal control of locomotion in the earthworm. *Biol. Rev.,* 51:25–52.

Hackman, R.H., and M. Goldberg. 1975. Peripatus: Its affinities and its cuticle. *Science,* 190:582–583.

Mann, K.H. 1962. *Leeches (Hirudinea): Their structure, physiology, ecology and embryology.* New York, Pergamon Press, Inc.

The Arthropoda
I. Crustaceans, Spiders, and Their Relatives

12

If the coelom and body segmentation started the annelid line toward achieving wide diversity, the advent of an efficient means of locomotion must surely have added great impetus. Within the present phylum, the Arthropoda, are embraced over a million known species, all of which are typically provided with jointed (segmented) appendages. It is this feature that gives the taxon its name, which is based on the two Greek words *árthos,* joint, and *podós,* foot. Those appendages are adapted for many purposes, as shall soon be seen, but their most widespread use is in locomotion. In carrying out this function great diversification similarly exists, for movement may be by creeping, walking, swimming, jumping, sailing, or even flying. Other important functions are defense and food-getting and are carried out by mechanisms that run the gamut from pincers on the legs to jaws that bite and fangs that inject poison, and from stingers on the tail to glands that secrete acetic acid, to mention only the more obvious adaptations.

In view of this diversity, it is not surprising to find that the phylum is divided into numerous classes. In order to facilitate their presentation, three closely interrelated ones are reserved for attention in the chapter that follows; the remainder discussed here are summarized in table 12.1, while the chief characteristics of the phylum are depicted in figure 12.1. In addition to the segmented appendages, the hemocoel, the external skeleton (exoskeleton) made of chitin, and segmented body are particularly diagnostic features.

THE CLASS CRUSTACEA

Although swimming is given above as a single mode of locomotion, the number of ways in which it is accomplished, even within the class Crustacea, is quite incredible. Most species swim forward in orthodox fashion, but many members of one group find they can go faster backwards or sideways, and those of another order navigate upside down (fig. 12.5, A). Because of these and the numerous other specializations that occur here, it is necessary to discuss at least the more important of the six subclasses into which the class is divided (table 12.2). Since the most advanced subclass, the Malacostraca, contains the majority of the larger and more familiar species, its characteristics are examined before the smaller and more primitive components.

The great diversity of habits and form displayed by the Crustacea certainly makes them a most interesting taxon; nevertheless, it also makes them very dif-

Table 12.1 The Classes of the Arthropoda

			Classes
Characteristic	Crustacea	Diplopoda	Chilopoda
Antennae	2 pairs	1 pair	1 pair
Mandibles	Present	Present	Present
Chelicerae	Absent	Absent	Absent
Body divisions	Head & thorax, or cephalothorax and abdomen	Head, thorax, & abdomen	Head & trunk
Thoracic appendages	2-11 pairs	3 pairs	
Abdominal appendages	Variable	2 pairs per segment	1 pair per segment
Respiratory organs	Gills	Tracheae	
Excretory organs	Antennal or coxal glands	Malpighian tubules	Malpighian tubules
Larva	Nauplius	Present	Absent
Habitat	Terrestrial	Terrestrial	Terrestrial
Common names	Crabs, crayfish, shrimp, sow bugs, etc.	Millipedes	Centipedes

ficult to define collectively, for almost every characteristic is absent in at least one order or subclass. For instance the appendages are not even segmented in one subclass, the Branchiopoda. Two pairs of antennae are usually present, the first of which, being smaller in the larger forms, are referred to as *antennules;* however, the larger second pair, the *antennae,* is absent in some of the subclass Branchiopoda. Typically the head and thorax are usually fused together as a cephalothorax (fig. 12.2), but this is highly variable from subclass to subclass, as shown in the pages that follow. Frequently there may be a firm covering, the *carapace,* over the cephalothorax, or even around the entire body. *Respiration* is by means of gills generally attached to the bases of the appendages, except in highly modified parasitic types, and *excretion* is by means of saclike glands located variously at the bases of the antennae or other appendages.

The Subclass Malacostraca

About two-thirds of the 40,000 known species of Crustacea belong to the subclass Malacostraca, and about half of these are the large and familiar types,

Insecta	Merostomata	Pycnogonida	Arachnida
1 pair	None	None	None
Present	Absent	Absent	Absent
Absent	Present	Present	Present
Head, thorax, & abdomen	Prosoma & opisthosoma	Prosoma & opisthosoma	Prosoma & opisthosoma
3 pairs legs, 0-2 pairs wings	6 pairs (prosomal)	7-9 pairs (prosomal)	6 pairs (prosomal)
None	6 pairs (opisthosomal)	None	None
Tracheae	Book gills	None	Book lungs or tracheae
Malpighian tubules	Coxal glands	None	Coxal glands; Malpighian tubules
Grubs, maggots, caterpillars, etc.	Trilobite larva	Present	Absent
Freshwater & terrestrial	Marine	Marine	Mostly terrestrial
Insects, bugs, beetles, moths, butterflies, etc.	Horseshoe crab	Sea-spiders	Spiders, mites, ticks, scorpions, etc.

such as the crabs, lobsters, and crayfish found throughout the temperate and tropical regions of the world. While many of these, including certain crayfish, are edible and of commercial importance, the smaller members also play important roles and are briefly discussed later. All are at once distinguished from members of the other subclasses by their having appendages on the abdominal segments (table 12.2); five pairs of these are known as *swimmerets* or pleopods, while a sixth pair, the *uropods,* are located on the *telson,* a flaplike structure at the end of the abdomen. Moreover, the eye is located at the end of a fleshy projection, a stalk (fig. 12.2), and the antennae near the base have a flat plate, known as a scale. The latter feature, however, is lacking in a number of smaller forms.

The Larger Malacostracans

The diagram (fig. 12.2) summarizes the more important structural features of the forms with long abdomens, such as the lobsters and crayfish, by far the

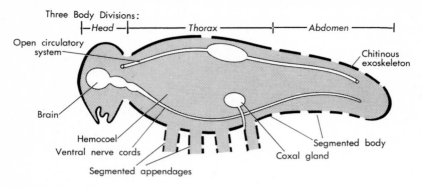

Figure 12.1 *The chief characteristics of the arthropods.* Among the principal diagnostic traits are a body made of segments and divided into three parts (head, thorax, and abdomen); a skeleton of chitin and located externally; the presence of variously modified, segmented appendages; an open circulatory system; the nerve cords placed ventrally; and the body cavity a hemocoel, the coelom being reduced.

majority of which are strictly aquatic. To the contrary, some crayfish are only semiaquatic and dig deep burrows in the ground in which to live. Each burrow is occupied by a single individual, except during the breeding season, and is always constructed in such a way that one portion extends well below the water table. Many burrowing species build chimneys of the mud pellets excavated during construction of the tube; the form of these is usually characteristic for each species. During the mating period, males actively defend their chimneys against invasion of other males, occasionally using the claws to repel aggressors. At least in certain species of the Gulf States, the chimneys serve as attractants for the females.

As a whole much more diversified than the long-abdomened crayfish and lobsters, the crabs have the abdomen reduced to a mere vestige that is folded downward and concealed in the lower surface of the carapace. Since the abdomen has thus lost all value in swimming, that function is carried out among strictly aquatic types by the walking legs. In such forms as the blue and lady crabs, the more posterior sets of legs are flattened like oars and serve in walking on the ocean bottom, as well as swimming. But most crabs do not possess this adaptation and are restricted to terrestrial habitats. During the day these forms occupy burrows built in the sand along seashores or conceal themselves in crevices in the rocks, from which they emerge at night to forage at the water's edge. A few, like the coconut crab, are strictly terrestrial and build burrows often at some distance inland from the sea. Several examples of the numerous types that are found are illustrated in figure 12.3

Other Important Malacostracans

Because of its obvious presence in the larger types, one tends to think of the claws as a characteristic feature of the malacostracans as a whole. That this is a false impression is quickly shown by the smaller members of the group. Collec-

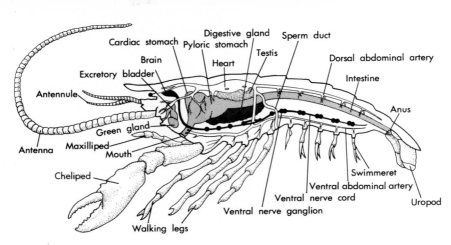

Figure 12.2 *The structure and appendages of the crayfish.*

tively these are much more highly diversified in form and habit than are the preceding types—indeed some are so highly modified that one hallmark of this subclass, the swimmerets, has been lost. Fortunately for crustacean specialists, in these species the uropods remain.

Among the many interesting forms that round out this subclass (fig. 12.4) are the mantis shrimps of the genus *Squilla* and its relatives. As the common name implies, these sea-going types appear remarkably like the dry-land preying mantids and have equally aggressive habits. About 200 species are known, ranging in size from 40 to 350 mm in length. Most of them occur in tropical oceans, especially around coral reefs, but some reach temperate waters, typically in water less than 300 m deep. Like their terrestrial counterparts, mantis shrimps lie in wait for their prey, concealing themselves in burrows or crevices in the coral rock. When an animal of suitable size swims close by, the large grasping front legs are shot out to secure the prey.

Quite in contrast to this active predator is another malacostracan of the shallower seas. These cumaceans are much smaller in size than *Squilla,* rarely exceeding 35 mm in length and live in burrows or tubes in muddy bottoms, the walls of which are made firm with a mucous secretion. In these structures, the crustaceans are largely concealed except for the head and anterior appendages (fig. 12.4, D), which they employ in feeding by filtering the sea water. Since the posterior portion of the carapace is buried in the mud, the water is pumped in at the front end of that structure by means of the maxillipeds and other appendages. It then passes over the mouthparts where ciliated structures catch the suspended organic matter; from there it flows over the gills, which extract oxygen before the water is forced upwards and forwards to be discharged above the head.

Two of the larger orders of the subclass are the Isopoda and Amphipoda, each of which includes about 4,000 known species. These two orders contrast sharply in body form, the first one being flattened dorso-ventrally as though

Table 12.2 The Subclasses of Crustacea

Characteristic	Subclass	
	Branchiopoda	Ostracoda
Carapace	Covers thorax, sometimes head and limbs too; occasionally absent	Bivalvular
Eyes	Compound, sessile or stalked	Simple or compound
Thorax	9–11 segments	2 segments
Thoracic limbs	5–11 pairs, usually broad and lobed, strongly bristled	2 pairs
Abdominal appendages	Sometimes present on basal segments, always on at least 3 apical segments	Absent
Habits	Free living, mostly fresh water	Free living
Common name	Fairy shrimp, brine shrimp, water fleas	Seed shrimp

Figure 12.3 *A blue crab molting.* The edible blue crab (*Callinectes sapidus*) is shown emerging from its hard carapace as a soft-shelled crab. (Photo courtesy of Virginia Institute of Marine Science.)

Copepoda	Branchiura	Cirripedia	Malacostraca
Absent	Formed from head, not thorax	Encloses much of body	Covers thorax, sometimes absent
Simple	Compound	Simple in adult	Compound, stalked
7 segments	5 segments	7 segments or less	8 segments
6 pairs	4 pairs	6 pairs or fewer	8 pairs
Absent	Absent	Absent	6 pairs
Free living or parasitic	Temporary parasites on fish	Free living and sessile, or parasitic	Free living
Copepods	Fish lice	Barnacles	Crabs, crayfish, lobsters, amphipods, isopods

stepped upon (fig. 12.4, A), whereas the second one is compressed, that is, flattened from side to side (fig. 12.4, C). Furthermore they differ in habitat to some degree, for the isopods are largely freshwater or land dwellers and the amphipods are either sea or freshwater inhabitants. A few of the latter taxon are terrestrial, however, the beach-flea that inflicts painful bites at certain months of the year being a common example. The terrestrial isopods are more familiar, for they are represented by the common sow- or pill-bugs that occur throughout most temperate and tropical regions.

Cave-Dwelling Crustaceans

In the central portion of the United States, extending from the southern Alleghenies through Indiana to eastern Kansas and southward into east Texas, is a great belt of caves, most of which contain streams and pools. Moreover, the streams frequently continue along low underground passageways many miles from actual caverns. In these subterranean waters are many species of Crustacea which have become especially adapted to the conditions of continual darkness. Often all pigmentation has been lost so that the integument is white or straw-colored. While the eyes are usually vestigal or absent, antennae are well-developed, as are also sensory hairs. Even forms as large as crayfish are specialized for this mode of life, but the cave-dwelling species do not generally become as large as above-ground inhabitants, about 3 inches being the maximum length.

Nearly all the subterranean forms in North American belong to the Malacostraca, including isopods, amphipods, and crayfish, but in Europe a number of the

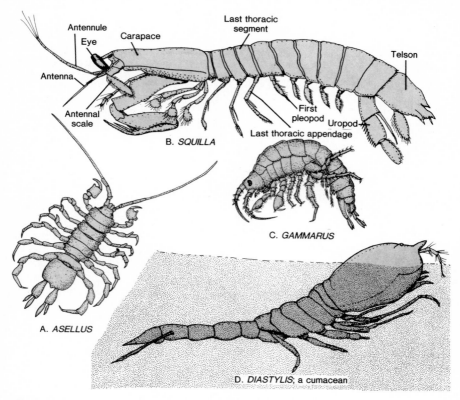

Figure 12.4 *A few of the numerous varieties of malacostracans.*

copepods to be discussed later have also been described from such habitats. The majority live within caves, but springs which open on the surface nearby are also frequently occupied. Occasionally isopods and amphipods are reported from wells many miles from any known cave. Their food, besides an occasional piece of vegetation that may be washed into cave waters, consist of the fine surface-scum of bacteria that coats underground rocks and soil particles.

Parasitic Species

Probably the most bizarre creatures of any animal taxon are parasitic crustaceans of the subclasses Copepoda and Cirripedia. Indeed, some are so highly differentiated from their relatives that they can be placed in the group only because of the free-living larval stage. The newly hatched nauplius shows few striking characteristics but, soon after attachment to the host, loses appendages and frequently segmentation also (fig. 12.8) in developing into the adult. Consequently, mature specimens appear like so many sacs or, at best, lice, rather than typical crustaceans. Freshwater and marine fish are the chief hosts, which the parasites occupy on the skin, fins, or gills; some of the parasitic barnacles, however, use crayfish and crabs as the host.

Other Important Subclasses

Since all the remaining subclasses of Crustacea lack the paired appendages of the abdomen that distinguish the Malacostraca, they were formerly grouped together in a single subclass termed the Entomostraca. Some years ago it was realized that such treatment obscured the real relationships of the animals, so the subdivisions employed here are the ones in current use. Since certain of these probably are still composite, the future will likely see even more subclasses erected. The most primitive taxon described immediately below undoubtedly will meet this fate in the decades to come, for reasons that are self-evident.

The Subclass Branchiopoda

As far as body form is concerned, it is difficult to perceive how the four different types of organisms assigned to the subclass Branchiopoda can actually be such close relatives (table 12.3). They do share several characteristics, however, which bind them into this single unit. Outstanding among these are the numerous similar appendages found on the thorax, most of which are unspecialized in function. As a rule they are flattened, leaflike structures, covered only by a flexible cuticle; hence, being soft and flexible, they lack segmentation, the hallmark of other arthropods. Thus the appendages are not too unlike elongated parapodia of annelids, from which structures some zoologists consider them to have been derived. This resemblance is further accentuated by the presence on each of a lobe used gill-like in respiration (fig. 12.5, A).

Many branchiopods characteristically are found in temporary ponds. The eggs, laid in the muddy bottoms at the close of the previous season, hatch in mid-winter. In these chilly waters, the young develop into adults, whose existence ends as the ponds become dry early in summer. Among these are the 10 to 25 mm long fairy shrimps (fig. 12.5, A), that swim gently through the waters on

Table 12.3 The Major Types of Branchiopods

Characteristic	Anostraca	Notostraca	Conchostraca	Cladocera
Carapace	Absent	Broadly ovate, covering head and thorax	Clam-shell-like, covering entire body, hinged	Covering thorax and abdomen, not hinged
Compound eyes	Stalked, paired	Sessile, paired	Sessile, paired	A single median compound eye, sessile
Thoracic appendages	11 to 19 pairs	Up to 60 pairs	10 to 28 pairs	4 to 6 pairs
Representative genus	*Artemia*	*Triops, Argas*	*Cyzicus*	*Daphnia*
Common names	Fairy shrimp, brine shrimp	Tadpole shrimp	Clam shrimp	Water fleas

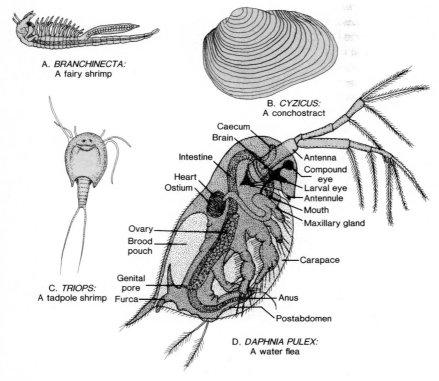

A. *BRANCHINECTA:*
A fairy shrimp

B. *CYZICUS:*
A conchostract

Caecum
Brain
Intestine
Heart
Ostium
Antenna
Compound eye
Larval eye
Antennule
Mouth
Maxillary gland
Ovary
Brood pouch
Carapace
C. *TRIOPS:*
A tadpole shrimp
Genital pore
Furca
Anus
Postabdomen
D. *DAPHNIA PULEX:*
A water flea

Figure 12.5   *Representatives of the subclass Branchiopoda.*

their backs. No carapace conceals the slender 11-segmented thorax of this form nor that of the related but saltwater inhabiting brine shrimps (*Artemia salina*).

In contrast, the carapace is a prominent feature of the remaining types of branchiopods. Especially is this true of the tadpole shrimps (fig. 12.5, C), whose broad carapace is reminiscent of the horseshoe crabs to be discussed later in this chapter. In the high plains regions of the United States, where wet springs occur infrequently, these 50 to 75 mm long animals may be absent for years. Then when a rainy spring does occur and the temporary ponds become full, they may appear by the hundreds of thousands, seemingly from nowhere. Actually their eggs are covered by a highly resistant shell that prevents desiccation for six or even more years; these remain in old pond bottoms or blow about with the dust until a favorable period eventually comes.

In collecting plankton, a novice may be shocked to see what appear to be miniature clams actively swimming around in his water samples, a most unorthodox behavior for those mollusks. But these creatures really are *clam shrimps,* whose carapace encloses their body completely, just as the shell does in their namesakes; a knoblike umbo is present on both types of animals that helps to accentuate the resemblances (fig. 12.5, B). However, antennae and the telson occasionally appear through the partly opened carapace of these clam shrimps and provide clues as to their being crustaceans. The final type included in this subclass, the *water fleas,* also are largely enclosed in a bivalvular carapace, but in their case, the head and its appendages are exposed (fig. 12.5, D). This taxon, however, is found in all types of bodies of water, small and large, fresh and salt.

The Copepoda and Ostracoda

Because of their prominent antennae and three-parted body, the Copepoda, a subclass containing about 5,000 known species, are readily recognizable as crustaceans. The body, however, is deceptively arranged, for what appears to be a cephalothorax is really the head fused with just the first one or two thoracic segments (fig. 12.6, C), and what seems to be the abdomen is largely the thorax. These are tiny forms, mostly only a few millimeters in length, that are abundant in marine and fresh waters, where they serve as intermediates in the food chain between microscopic and larger organisms. Food collecting is carried out by either filter-feeding devices, or as in *Cyclops,* by chewing on plant materials.

The antennules are longer than the antennae and are much more effective swimming organs in the copepods than are their relatively short or weak thoracic appendages and in the members of one order are especially highly developed (fig. 12.6, C). Not infrequently, copepods may be particularly adapted for floating, rather than swimming, and have developed elaborate featherlike structures whose resistance to water flow aids in maintaining their position in the water (fig. 12.6, D). Such specializations and the feathery antennules and other appendages many forms bear are particularly characteristic of deep-water species.

The members of the subclass Ostracoda are also small, mostly only 1 or 2 mm in length, but a few are relatively large, ranging up to 10 or 12 mm. At first sight, they may be mistaken for clam shrimps, for their carapace is similarly bivalved. Externally, however, the umbo is lacking, and the antennae and other appendages within the carapace are obviously segmented (fig. 12.6, A).

The 2,000 or so known species are highly diversified, some of which, particularly in view of the bivalvular carapace, have surprising habits. Equipped as they are with this shell, one would expect them to be mud-dwellers like clams, and indeed, a number of them are just that. These have few setae on the antennae and other appendages and merely push themselves along pond bottoms or on the ocean floor by means of the abdomen. In contrast, many other forms have long bristles at the tips of the antennules and antennae and are skillful swimmers. Even a few terrestrial situations have ostracod inhabitants. For instance, in the rainforests of Africa and New Zealand certain species burrow through the upper layers of wet humus, for which purpose the antennules have become modified into short, broad shovels.

The Subclass Cirripedia

Animals, which, like the Entoprocta and fairy shrimps, spend their lives dorsal side down, have previously been described, but here are animals that spend theirs standing on their heads. Among these *barnacles,* mature larvae preparing

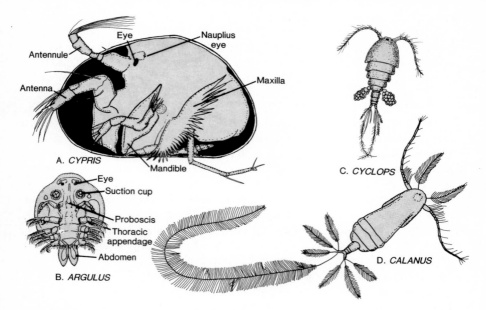

Figure 12.6 *Common members of the subclasses Ostracoda, Copepoda, and Branchiura.* A. The ostracodans, such as *Cypris,* externally resemble conchostrachs but lack an umbo; the appendages are segmented, however. B. *Argulus* is a common exoparasite of fish and is known as the fish louse. It is the representative type of the subclass Branchiura. C,D. *Cyclops* is an actively swimming, and *Calanus,* a floating type of copepod.

to undergo metamorphosis attach themselves to an object head downwards by means of cement secreted through pores near the base of the antennules (fig. 12.7 C–E). In one subgroup, the entire front part of the head then grows outwards to form a peduncle or stalk, leaving the antennules at the very base against the substrate. As growth of the stalk and body proceeds, the brain, mouth, and other parts become far removed from the original forepart of the head, ultimately attaining a location near the center of the enlarged "shell"-enclosed part, the *capitulum* (fig. 12.7, A). All of the nearly 1,000 known species are of economic importance as fouling organisms, for they frequently are nuisances on harbor facilities and sometimes occur in such numbers on ship bottoms that they retard progress.

Because of the calcareous plates that cover the organisms, barnacles were once considered to be mollusks, and a glance at the illustration of the anatomy (fig. 12.7, A) makes it easy to understand why such a misconception was possible. Few resemblances to other crustaceans can be noted, for segmentation is largely lost, the abdomen is absent, and the characteristic segmented appendages have been modified into the highly unorthodox tentaclelike flagella. Even the carapace is extremely atypical, being completely altered to form both the plates and the flexible membranous parts referred to as the mantle. These outer struc-

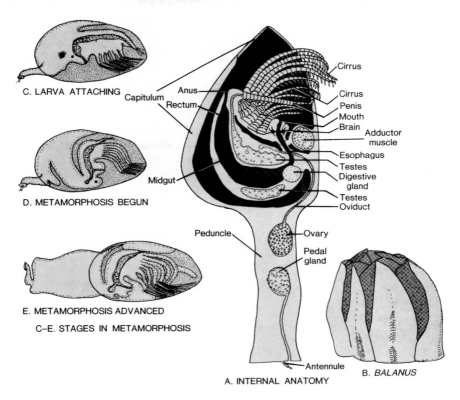

C. LARVA ATTACHING

Capitulum

Anus

Rectum

Midgut

D. METAMORPHOSIS BEGUN

E. METAMORPHOSIS ADVANCED

C–E. STAGES IN METAMORPHOSIS

Cirrus

Cirrus

Penis

Mouth

Brain

Adductor muscle

Esophagus

Testes

Digestive gland

Testes

Oviduct

Peduncle

Ovary

Pedal gland

Antennule

A. INTERNAL ANATOMY

B. *BALANUS*

Figure 12.7 *Structure and metamorphosis of barnacles.*

tures close tightly at low tide or at other unfavorable times but can be opened to provide an orifice through which the flagella emerge for feeding. By their beating movements these tentaclelike parts create a strong water current towards the mouth, where a series of fine hairs catch bits of organic matter. The material thus collected is removed by the maxillae and placed into the oral cavity. While most forms are therefore filter-feeders, larger species can also eat quite sizable organisms. In contrast, a number of barnacles, only a couple of millimeters in length, drill into the shells of mollusks or the calcareous skeletons of corals, and a wide variety of others are parasitic in starfishes, corals, and malacostracans in which they feed by absorption.

Parasitic Crustacea

In the chapter on nematodes, one section pointed out that *almost* no forms more advanced than the pseudocoelomates were endoparasites; it is the occurrence in the present class of a number of exceptional forms that make the qualifying word necessary. Here are found numerous species of Copepoda and Cirripedia that live as ectoparasites and a relatively few that are endoparasites, as intimated above. Indeed, some of the most bizarre creatures of any animal taxon fall into these categories—some are so highly modified that they can be placed as crustaceans only on the basis of the free-living typical larva, as described in the following section. Here only one example is given, drawn from the subclass Copepoda.

In this form the newly hatched larva (the nauplius) shows few distinctive features (fig. 12.8, A) until it attaches to the fish that serves as the host. Then it begins to elongate and develops reproductive organs. As it continues to mature, the appendages are lost and the abdomen becomes long and wormlike. Still later, the thorax and head lose all external features, while the abdomen swells until the whole animal resembles a twisted sac (fig. 12.8). As a rule, freshwater and marine fish are the chief hosts of parasitic copepods, whereas crayfish, crabs, corals, and starfish are used in that capacity by parasitic barnacles.

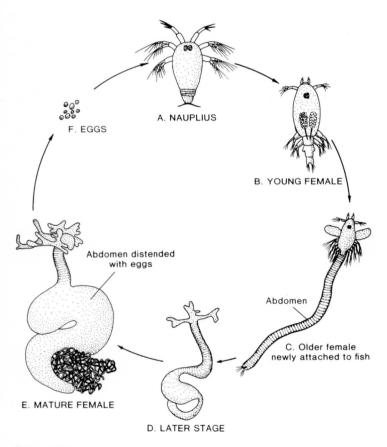

Figure 12.8 *The life cycle of a parasitic copepod.* Only the presence of a nauplius during the life cycle makes these highly modified parasites recognizable as crustaceans.

Reproduction in the Crustacea

Reproduction in the Crustacea is as varied as the organisms that class contains. Generally the sexes are separate, but in the barnacles, they are united. Parthenogenesis is not uncommon, being especially frequent in the branchiopods, in which group the annual cycles include summer and winter eggs and seasonal males, not unlike those of the rotifers.

Development of the egg leads into a series of larval types, depending on the taxon; none of these are such familiar types as the trochophore, for instance, for all are peculiar to this class of arthropods. While the number of different kinds of larvae is large, as might be expected in view of the plethora of subclasses, they are not really difficult, because of the repetition that exists. In the primitive taxa, like the fairy shrimps and water fleas, the first major type is found, the *nauplius* (fig. 12.9, A). This variety is found as the first larval stage in every taxon of crustaceans and is characterized by the presence of only three pairs of appendages. However, among crabs, lobsters, and crayfish, this stage is not free-living but remains within the egg.

In branchiopods, the nauplius gradually adds appendages with each molt, producing a series of larval stages called *metanauplii,* which have the same three pairs of functional appendages, but in addition have a number of small ones on the newly added segments (fig. 12.9, B). Before long, these undergo metamorphosis into the adult stage, which in the ostracods, it should be noted, includes members of the genus *Cypris* as well as numerous others. In the copepods, which are slightly more advanced evolutionarily than the two preceding classes, the metanauplius becomes somewhat modified into a form known as the *copepodid,* a type confined to the members of this subclass. Then in the Cirripedia another special larval type puts in an appearance; in these animals, the adult ostracod known as *Cypris* just mentioned is represented by a larval stage of similar structure (fig. 12.9, C). In these barnacles, the nauplius goes through the metanauplius stages as usual, but eventually undergoes a marked metamorphosis into a *cyprid*—it is these forms which attach their heads downwards to grow into an adult barnacle (fig. 12.7, C–E).

Among the malacostracans, comparable but contrasting series of changes have occurred. In these life cycles, nauplii are present as before but are confined to the egg, as stated earlier, as are the metanauplii also. In the primitive superorders, the eggs hatch into juveniles that resemble the adult in form, except for a smaller carapace, but beginning with the group that includes the opossum shrimps, two new larval types intervene. These are known as the *protozoea* and *zoea,* names almost as grotesque as the larvae themselves (fig. 12.9, D, E); both are distinguished by the absence of appendages on the last three thoracic segments, as well as on the abdomen. In more advanced groups another universal stage is added beyond the zoea, called the *mysis* larva, from its resemblance to the adult opossum shrimp belonging to a genus of that name (fig. 12.9, F); the shrimps of commerce (genus *Penaeus* and relatives) are the first line whose life cycle contains all these stages. In the lobster branch, the nauplius, protozoea, and zoea stages are passed within the egg; only the last larval stage, the mysis, is

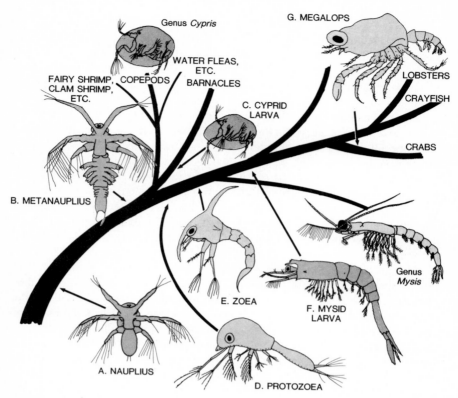

Figure 12.9 *The larval stages of the Crustacea.* By following the tree from its base to a given branch, one can determine its larval stages. For instance in going to the fairy shrimps, only the nauplius and metanauplius stages are passed through, whereas in going to the lobsters, these two stages, plus the protozoea, zoea, and mysid stages are passed through just as in the actual life histories.

free-living. Among crayfishes, even this stage is passed within the egg, so the eggs hatch directly into juveniles. Contrastingly, crab eggs hatch into zoea, after the earlier stages have been passed; as usual, this molts into a mysis, but another larval type, the *megalops,* is added before the adult form is finally assumed (fig. 12.9, G).

THE CLASS MEROSTOMATA

Among the arthropod classes are three which agree among themselves in certain essential features, while differing sharply from the others. None of this triplet have antennae (table 12.1), and, what is more unusual, none have jaws. Instead, they all possess leglike appendages in front of the mouth, called the chelicerae; although often highly modified, typically these are provided with pincers and are one of the outstanding traits of these classes. Accordingly they are sometimes grouped together as the Chelicerata, as opposed to the remaining ones, collectively called the Mandibulata. However, only two of the chelicerate taxa merit attention here.

The most primitive of these classes is the Merostomata, whose five known species rank it as a small group indeed; however, some 450 million years ago, its members were highly diversified and abundant in those early seas. Even now, these horseshoe crabs, as they are called, give one the impression of being something out of the remote past, as they actually are.

Structure

Viewed from above, a horseshoe crab seems to consist only of a large grayish carapace, with a short unsegmented abdomen and a long tail-like appendage trailing behind (fig. 12.10, A). On the carapace two sets of true eyes can be noted, the lateral ones of which are compound. Turned over on its back, however, the plethora of parts seen on the ventral surface more than compensates for the absence of dorsal features (fig. 12.10, B). The chelicerae are quite leglike, and like the first four pairs of walking legs, are provided with pincers. The fifth

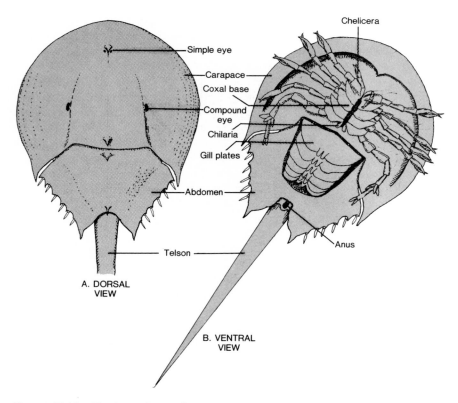

Figure 12.10 *The horseshoe crab.*

pair of legs is especially elongate and bears leaflike tips used to sweep away mud from the other body parts. Behind this last set of legs is still another pair of appendages, reduced to flattened knobs referred to as chilaria of unknown function.

No head nor thorax is present, it should be noted, for the entire body lacks the usual divisions. Here, as in other chelicerates, the forebody is termed the *prosoma* and the posterior portion, the *opisthosoma*. In these animals, the latter subdivision has six unpaired appendages medially, the first of which is modified into a flattened plate. Beneath this may be found the spongy book gills, used in respiration; one set of these is attached basally to each of the other five appendages, all of which are short and hingelike. Just before the spine, or telson, is a large opening, the anus, and on each side of the opisthosoma is a row of six spines, possibly representing the remnants of segmentation formerly present in some remote ancestor.

Habits and Reproduction

Typically horseshoe crabs are occupants of the muddy bottoms of shallow regions of seas, where they burrow in search of prey. Their food consists almost entirely of worms, especially errant polychaetes, which they capture by means of the clawlike chelicerae. Any larger specimens that happen to be caught are first crushed between the bases (coxae) of the walking legs, which being enlarged and flattened are well-adapted for this purpose (fig. 12.10, B). After thus being crushed, the fragments are passed to the mouth for swallowing.

Sexes are separate in the Merostomata and are quite similar in appearance and internal structure. The gonads are located medially in the opisthosoma above the intestine but extend forward into the prosoma; from there they descend to a location below the intestine as they recurve to the posterior part of the body. The oviduct or vas deferens then extends to the genital pores located on the platelike first appendage of the opisthosoma. After the female has built a nest in the sand, she oviposits while the male releases sperm over the eggs. The eggs are then enclosed in a leathery-textured capsule, in which they develop. Development leads to a stereoblastula and then to a stereogastrula.

In the latter stage at least one feature is of more than usual importance, for one series of changes undergone then suggests how a digestive tract like that of the acoels, having only one opening, gradually may have become a complete one, with mouth and anus. The mouth (blastopore) in the late stereogastrula leads into a simple stomodaeum. Later this pore begins to elongate, so as to become longer than wide (fig. 12.11). After this elongating has continued for a while, the middle portion of the hole gradually narrows somewhat, so that the slitlike blastopore grows shut medially. As a result two holes are formed, the anterior one becoming the mouth, the posterior one, the anus (fig. 12.11). Eventually the developing young breaks free of the egg as a peculiar larva, known as the *trilobite* larva, because of its resemblance to those extinct animals (fig. 12.11).

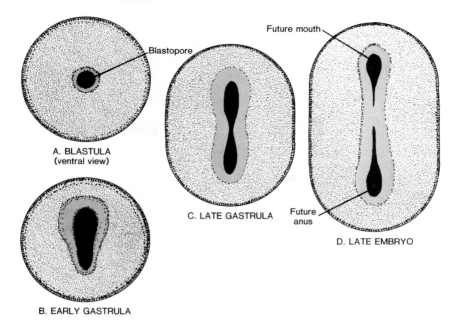

A. BLASTULA
(ventral view)

C. LATE GASTRULA

Blastopore

Future mouth

Future anus

D. LATE EMBRYO

B. EARLY GASTRULA

Figure 12.11 *Development in the horseshoe crab.*

THE CLASS ARACHNIDA

Although not as frequently studied in introductory courses as are the crustaceans, the class Arachnida is much larger and more greatly diversified, for it embraces around 55,000 described species. However, in body size they contrast very strongly, for whereas the largest crabs and lobsters are measured in feet, the biggest scorpions and tarantulas achieve measurements only in terms of inches.

The species are arranged into nine orders, but only the six that are of more importance are compared in the chart (table 12.4). Two of the three omitted include rare or minute forms largely confined to the upper layers of the soil and humus. There along with such other arachnids as mites, they play a major role in the soil formation and maintenance—as many as 160,000 individuals per cubic meter have been reported from the soil of grassland in England. Here space limitations compel the restriction of detailed attention to just the five largest orders, the scorpions, pseudoscorpions, spiders and tarantulas, harvestmen, and mites and ticks (fig. 12.12).

The Order Scorpionida

As the lands increased in extent and elevation during the Silurian period between 400 and 425 million years ago, the first legged animals to become adapted to this new and strange environment were members of the order Scorpionida. Since the climate was warm in those days, the present restriction of these

Table 12.4   Principal Orders of the Class Arachnida

	Orders	
Characteristic	**Scorpionida**	**Pseudoscorpionida**
Carapace	Single	In 2 pieces
Opisthosoma	Divided into mesosoma and metasoma	12-segmented, broad
Telson	Present	Absent
Pedicel	Absent	Absent
Chelicerae	Strong, 3-segmented	Weak, 2-segmented
Pedipalps	Strong, clawed	Strong, with poison-glands
Respiration	4 pairs of book lungs, no tracheae	2 pairs spiracles, tracheae
Common names	Scorpions	Pseudoscorpions
Habitat	Terrestrial	Beneath bark, etc.

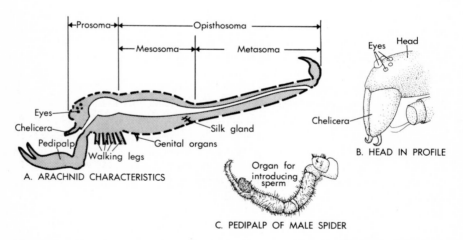

Figure 12.12 *Some distinctive characteristics of arachnids.* Among the salient features are the pedipalps, the four pairs of legs, chelicerae in place of jaws, the absence of antennae, and the body divided into two parts, the prosoma and opisthosoma.

Solpugida	Araneae	Acarina
Single	Single	Single
10-segmented	12-segmented, fused	No visible segmentation
Absent	Absent	Absent
Absent	Present	Absent
Strong, 2-segmented	2-segmented, with poison glands	Weak, 2-segmented, often adapted for piercing
Leglike	Leglike, modified in males	Clawed or leglike
3 pairs spiracles, tracheae	Book lungs and 2 pairs spiracles, tracheae	Spiracles and tracheae absent or present
Vinegaroons	Spiders, tarantula, etc.	Ticks, mites
Terrestrial	Terrestrial	Terrestrial or aquatic, often parasitic

arthropods to tropical and warm-temperate areas thus may be a reflection of the early adaptations having remained unchanged. Indeed, little about the scorpions has become greatly altered during those intervening millenia, for the relatively few species extant today (fig. 12.13) are little different in their basic features from their remote ancestors.

As in other chelicerates, the body is divided into a prosoma and opisthosoma, the former bearing six pairs of appendages, as in the horseshoe crab; in the present case, however, no appendages are apparent on the opisthosoma. Moreover, the latter body region is subdivided into a broad mesosoma of seven segments and a narrow metasoma, consisting of five segments and bearing a sting at the tip (fig. 12.13, A). Although the number of prosomal appendages is the same as in the horseshoe crab, only four pairs of these are walking legs, the former first walking leg now having been converted into the *pedipalp* (fig. 12.13, A) that characterizes all the members of the class Arachnida. In the present order, the pedipalps are more robust than are the walking legs and each bears a strong claw at its tip. In other orders, these pedipalps are not so large and are variously modified, more usually serving as leglike sensory organs, whence their name, from the Latin words *pes*, foot, and *palpare*, to feel.

Strictly speaking, the opisthosomal appendages are not really lacking as implied above but are so highly modified as to be no longer recognizable. The six pairs that were found in the horseshoe crab can be accounted for as follows: The first pair is actually absent, as it is lost during larval development, along with the entire first opisthosomal segment, while the second pair is reduced and fused together to form a covering over the genital pore that is located just behind the

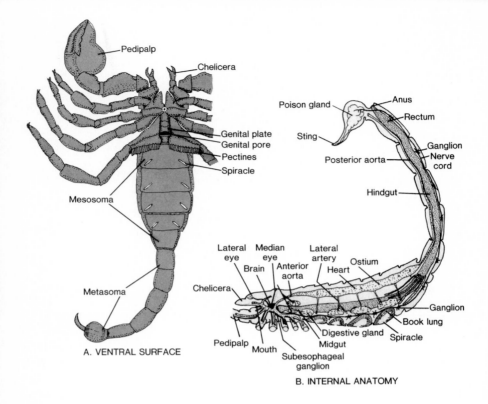

Figure 12.13 *Structure of scorpions.*

last pair of walking legs. The remaining four pairs are invaginated into the meso-some during development and carry book gills, as do the corresponding appendages in the merostomates; in the scorpions they are now more correctly called book lungs because they respire air. Their position is indicated externally by the slitlike spiracles of the undersurface (fig. 12.13, A).

The scorpions are nocturnal, carnivorous animals, whose prey consists largely of other arthropods, especially insects and spiders. Small or passive forms are not stung, but active or resistant prey are quickly quieted by use of the sting. To this organ is connected a pair of poison glands that secrete a neuro-toxin, which is effective immediately in the animals normally fed upon. The prey are captured by means of the pincers of the pedipalps and then torn into bite-sized pieces before being passed to the mouth by the chelicerae. The large scorpions of the tropical regions and southwestern United States are capable of inflicting a fatal injury on man, but the sting of such smaller forms as that which inhabits the Gulf region has been compared to a wasp sting in potency.

Figure 12.14 *Whip scorpion spraying acetic acid at a mouse.* Related to the scorpion but placed in the order Uropygida, the whip scorpions have a tubular whip instead of a sting at the tip of the metasoma. (Courtesy of Dr. Thomas Eisner, Cornell University.)

The Order Pseudoscorpionida

Sometimes when the humus of the forest floors is sifted or the bark of fallen trees is removed, one is surprised to see what seems to be tiny scorpions only a few millimeters in length, complete with claws on the pedipalps but no sting at the end of the body (fig. 12.15, A). These are really pseudoscorpions, for they differ from the true scorpions, not only in their diminutive proportions, but also in the opisthosoma lacking subdivision into meso- and metasoma and being more or less uniform in breadth throughout its length. While their food habits are like those of the true scorpions on a smaller scale, the chelicerae are modified so as to serve in web building. The silk web, however, serves as a shelter for survival during the winter or as a retreat in which molting can take place, rather than for catching prey.

The Order Acarina

The ticks, mites, and chiggers which comprise the order Acarina undoubtedly are the most highly diversified group of arachnids and are adapted to a wide variety of habitats (fig. 12.15, B). Probably the best known members are the common ectoparasites of mammals and birds, some of which are carriers (intermediate hosts) of certain viral and rickettsial diseases. Others are pests in grains and flour mills, at least one occupies the dust of households, a whole group is adapted for swimming in fresh and salt water, some are found in mosses, a number are predatory on other mites, one group occurs on the feathers of birds, others build galls on plants, a large group lives in the soil and humus, and a few drill into the skin or nasal cavities of mammals.

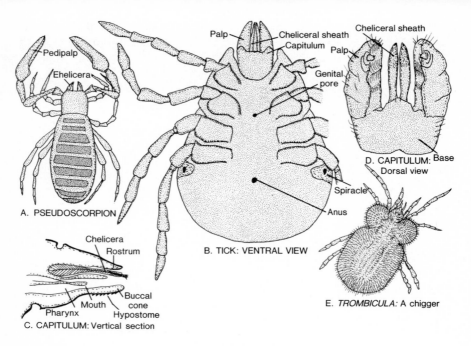

Figure 12.15 *A pseudoscorpion and tick structure.*

The body structure is peculiar, in the first place, in lacking subdivisions into distinct regions, segmentation being entirely absent; secondly, it is distinct in bearing a headlike part called the *capitulum*. This structure is not considered to be a head, because it consists almost entirely of the highly modified feeding appendages (chelicerae and pedipalps), along with the mouth. Although three sets of appendages are actually present on the capitulum, there appear to be only two, as a result of the dorsal and ventral sets (respectively the cheliceral sheath and hypostome) being rather closely associated (fig. 12.15, C). In feeding, the hypostome makes an opening in the food material, using the sawlike teeth with which it is often provided; in the process it is aided by the chelicerae, which can be partly extruded from the dorsally located cheliceral sheaths (fig. 12.15, C). Palps (the highly modified pedipalps) also may enter the opening to assist in feeding. In most members of the order, development is fairly direct, typically having two juvenile stages between hatching and the adult stage. As a rule the juveniles, known as *nymphs,* are similar in form to the mature animal, except that only three pairs of walking legs are present, instead of the four of the adult.

Possibly the most familiar members of the order are the chiggers, a widespread family whose nymphs are ectoparasites, whereas the adults are free-living. The eggs are deposited on soil or vegetation where they hatch into tiny, 6-legged young; these wait on vegetation, typically in brushy dry areas, for a warm-blooded vertebrate to pass by. When an opportunity arises, they creep onto the host, and soon make a minute wound in the skin with the hypostome and chelicerae. The saliva which enters the puncture contains enzymes that digest the surrounding host tissues, providing food particles for the chigger to feed on and a miniature pit in the skin to live in. Here it completes its first nymphal stage, drops off the host, and becomes free-living.

The Orders Araneae and Opiliones

The spiders and tarantulas that comprise the order Araneae are certainly the best known members of the Arachnida, while the harvestmen (daddy-long-legs) of the order Opiliones can scarcely be far behind in familiarity. Popularly no distinction is usually made between these two types, both groups being considered to be spiders, but they are quite divergent in structure. The most obvious distinction is that spiders have only a slender, almost stalk-like connection (the pedicel) between the prosoma and opisthosoma, whereas the harvestmen have the two body parts broadly interconnected.

Habits

The two groups differ in food habits, too. Obviously enough, the spiders feed on insects, which are captured as described later. In feeding the fanglike second segment of the chelicerae can, when necessary, inject poison from venom glands to subdue the prey. Usually these fangs are too short or weak to penetrate human skin, but in some species like the tarantulas, black widow, and brown recluse, severe bites may be inflicted by these organs, in some cases proving fatal.

In contrast the harvestmen are quite diversified in dietary habits. Although live insects and other arthropods are the main fare, they also consume dead animals of various kinds and even eat fruit and vegetation on occasion. Some species are known to attack terrestrial snails, in addition to the standard items of their diet. Whatever its nature, the food is held by the claws of the pedipalps while the chelicerae and bases of the pedipalps and anterior sets of legs tear it into bits.

Internal Structure of Spiders

Relative to the size of the animal itself, the spider's *digestive system* is quite small, but this condition probably stems from the feeding habits. As stated above, insects are the main staple in the diet and are secured by the variety of methods described later. However, a few large forms, like *Mygale,* can attack other animals up to the size of sparrows. When the prey has been captured, the spider injects poison into it from the glands located in the chelicerae (fig. 12.16); then after the prey has become quieted, the salivary glands of the buccal cavity actively begin to secrete a fluid that contains a number of enzymes. In some species, the fluid is merely poured over the insect, whereas in others the prey is first crushed between the bases of the chelicerae. After a few moments, the contents of the insect have been well digested and the spider merely sucks up the resulting juices.

With digestion being thus largely external, the digestive tract does not need to be large. It consists of a short buccal cavity followed by an esophagus, part of

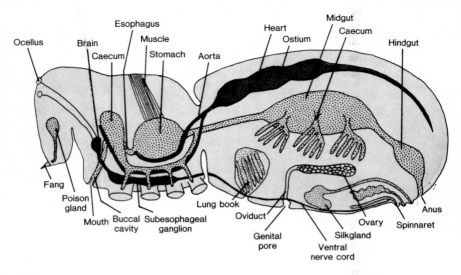

Figure 12.16 *The internal anatomy of a spider.*

which is expanded into a stomach. This entire fore region is derived from ectoderm, as is also a large portion of the hindgut; accordingly both of these regions are lined with chitin. The so-called stomach is supplied with strong external and sphincter muscles, which make it an efficient pumping organ. Hence, functionally it corresponds to the pharynx of other organisms, but it is referred to by the name cited largely on the basis of its shape. The midgut that follows this organ is provided with two anterior pairs of caeca that sends branches into each set of walking legs, and a single but larger posterior part that extends into the abdomen. Farther posteriorly it has several highly branched digestive diverticula, which tend to occupy much of the abdominal cavity. The hindgut consists largely of a short cloaca, into which the Malpighian tubules also open.

The tubules just mentioned are arranged as dual pairs and are part of the *excretory system,* which includes two other types of structures in addition. The first of these are absorptive cells found in the lining of the midgut that seem to function also in the storage of digested foods. A second type of cell is in the form of the so-called nephrocytes, located in the upper surface of the prosoma.

The *nervous system* has undergone extensive modification from the type found in the crustaceans. Although the dorsal brain is not especially enlarged, the ventral ganglion is quite extensive. During development of the embryo, all the ganglia, which at first have the primitive arrangement of one in each of the segments, as in the annelids and crustaceans, move forward and combine into this subesophageal ganglion—the remains of as many as seventeen ganglia can be found here, although the precise number varies from species to species. The brain proper receives tracts from each of the eight eyes and thus is largely sensory, with vision its predominant function. All the eyes are simple ocelli, some of which receive light directly, while others have the neural receptor away from the focal point of the light beam and thus receive visual stimuli indirectly. In addition there is a taste-sensory pouch in the esophagus, and males, at least, have chemoreceptors on their tarsi, which respond to scent emitted by females. Finally, the pedipalps are elongate and serve in tactile and other sensory functions.

Reproductive systems in spiders tend to be quite simple, with the sexes separate and the organs located beneath the digestive tract. In the female there are two ovaries, each with an oviduct, which leads into a single uterus; this is followed by a vagina that opens through a genital pore situated medially on the ventral surface of the abdomen (fig. 12.16).

In the male the testes are multiple and arranged in two parallel rows along the floor of the abdomen. The sperm is transferred from the genital pores to the vagina of the female by means of a specialized organ on the pedipalps of the male (fig. 12.12, C). After copulation has taken place in this manner, the male may be eaten by the female, but this behavior characterizes only a small proportion of the species, including the black widow.

As mentioned previously, book lungs are a common type of *respiratory organ* in arachnids in general, and spiders are 'not exceptional (fig. 12.16). In addition, a number of unbranched tubes called tracheae are often present; these open through pores known as spiracles placed on the ventral surface of the abdomen, generally posterior to the usually paired openings of the book lungs. The exact number of book lungs and spiracles present, however, varies with the family. Moreover, the abdomen contains the silk glands (fig. 12.16), whose numbers and characteristics are more clearly enumerated in the following discussion of preying behavior.

The *circulatory system* plays a role in locomotion, as well as in the usual ones of conducting oxygen, foodstuffs, and hormones. It, too, is a simple system, consisting largely of a heart that extends medially along the roof of the abdomen. This is a saclike tube, tapering at each end and equipped with three pairs of ostia along each side. An ostium is a valvelike pore through which blood enters the heart in lieu of auricles. Thus the heart corresponds to a ventricle of other animals. This pumps blood anteriorly through a short aorta that divides into two arteries to pass along each side of the subesophageal ganglion and brain, where they terminate. Each artery in turn sends fine branches into the legs. However, no veins are present, the deoxygenated blood returning to the heart between the muscles and other organs and in the body cavity called the hemocoel. While thus free in the body, it is constantly kept under pressure. This detail is of particular importance, for it is this pressure that straightens (extends) the legs and other appendages after the musculature has bent (flexed) them. If a spider experiences dehydration through injury or the absence of water, the legs become curled under the body due to the loss of blood pressure, so that the animal is unable to move. Rehydration effects an immediate return to active, motile behavior.

Evolution of Prey Capture

Though major evolutionary lines within the arachnoid orders are readily indicated, the wide range of specialization within the several families cannot even be intimated. To suggest what possibly has occurred—but, of course, along different lines in each case—the food-procuring habits of spiders will be outlined briefly.

The most primitive methods are undoubtedly those of wolf spiders and relatives that catch terrestrial insects by sheer strength and speed. Some larger species, especially in tropical and subtropical regions, are strong and fast enough to capture birds or mammals. While silk glands are present, all are of one variety and are employed solely in wrapping the eggs into a "cocoon." Jumping spiders, while feeding in much the same fashion, have evolved somewhat further and are more at home on vertical walls than on the bare ground. To assist in holding fast to upright surfaces, their tarsi are provided with adhesive tufts of hairs; the spider, moreover, uses a specialized silk gland to spin a strand which trails behind it, much as the rope of mountain climbers. The two anterior pairs of eyes, too, are especially adapted to assist in leaping accurately, being provided with a series of muscles that centers them upon the intended victim.

Among still more highly evolved spiders, greater variety in the silk-producing glands is gradually acquired. Probably the next step in elaborating the use of silk is represented by the trap-door spiders, forms that conceal the entrance to their burrows by trap-doors made of silk and earth. These species, like all that follow, wait for prey to approach, rather than actively foraging as the primitive types do. More advanced forms combine a sheet of silk with the burrow, while still higher ones make a funnellike tube of silk above ground. Among the latter are the North American black widow and the Australian redback spiders, which have an additional adaptation in the form of an especially toxic poison. This poison is not believed to be a defense against vertebrate enemies, but an effective means of quieting their prey, which consists largely of beetles and other active heavy-bodied insects.

The very top of the spider world undoubtedly is represented by the orb-weavers whose intricate web-building habits are too well known to require description here. It can be pointed out, however, that in these forms no fewer than five kinds of silk glands occur. The tubuliform glands, absent from males, are employed in making the egg cocoon, while the aciniform set secretes silk for wrapping prey caught in the web. The remainder are used solely in web making. Of these, the pyriform provides silk to anchor the long radial lines secreted by another set, the ampulliform, while the fifth set, the aggregate, furnishes both the silk for the spiral threads and the viscid fluid that covers them.

QUESTIONS FOR REVIEW AND THOUGHT

1. Characterize the phylum Arthropoda and the seven classes as fully as you can. On what structures are the classes principally distinguished?

2. What are some of the more striking adaptations found among crustaceans? On what body parts are the subclasses distinguished from one another?

3. The subclass Malacostraca is generally considered to be the most advanced taxon in this class. Would you agree? Why or why not?

4. Name as many types of appendages of a crayfish as you can. Would you consider the stalked eye to be an appendage? Give the reason for your answer.

5. Describe some of the habits of malacostracans. What are some of the smaller types of this subclass?

6. The branchiopods contain highly diversified groups of animals. Describe some of the principal types. Do you think them really closely related or not? On what do you base your opinion?

7. Describe the development of barnacles. What develops into the stalk? The flagella? The plates and mantle?

8. Name the larval stages found in the crabs. In barnacles. In lobsters. In clam shrimp. In copepods. In ostracods. In shrimp. How does a nauplius differ from a metanauplius?

9. Give the distinctive characteristics of the class Merostomata. What other class has chelicerae? What other features indicate relationships between these two taxa?

10. Name the members of five orders of arachnids. How do scorpions differ from horseshoe crabs? From spiders? In what ways are scorpions more primitive than other arachnids?

11. In what ways are ticks and mites unique among the arachnids? Of what does the hypostome consist? The capitulum?

12. Differentiate between spiders and harvestmen. How do they differ in feeding habits? Outline a scheme how a complex mechanism of prey-capture may have evolved among spiders.

SUGGESTIONS FOR FURTHER READING

Anderson, D.T. 1973. *Embryology and phylogeny in annelids and arthropods.* Oxford, Pergamon Press.

Benson, R.H. 1974. The role of ornamentation in the design and function of the ostracod carapace. *Geoscience and Man,* 6:47–57.

Blest, A.D. 1978. The rapid synthesis and destruction of photoreceptor membrane by a dinopid spider: A daily cycle. *Proc. Roy Soc. Lond.,* B200:463–483.

Caldwell, R.L., and H. Dingle. 1976. Stomatopods. *Sci. Amer.,* 234(1):80–89.

Cisne, J.L. 1974. Trilobites and the origin of arthropods. *Science,* 186:13–18.

Factor, J.R. 1978. Morphology of the mouth parts of larval lobsters, *Homarus americanus,* with special emphasis on their setae. *Biol. Bull.,* 154:383–408.

Fahrenbach, W.H. 1975. The visual system of the horseshoe crab, *Limulus polyphemus. Int. Rev. Cytol.,* 41:285–349.

Lahue, R. 1973. The chelicerates. In *Invertebrate learning,* ed. W.C. Corning, J.A. Dyal, and A.O.D. Willows, vol. 2, p. 1–47, New York, Plenum Press.

Lawrence, J.M. 1976. Patterns of lipid storage in post-metamorphic marine invertebrates. *American Zoologist,* 16:747–762.

Manton, S.M. 1974. Segmentation in Symphyla, Chilopoda, and Pauropoda in relation to phylogeny. *Symposia Zool. Soc. Lond.,* 32:163–190.

Momot, W.T., H. Gowing, and P.D. Jones. 1978. The dynamics of crayfish and their role in ecosystems. *Amer. Midl. Nat.,* 99:10–35.

Neil, D.M., D.L. Macmillan, R.M. Robertson, and M.S. Laverack. 1976. The structure and function of the thoracic exopodites in the larvae of the lobster, *Homarus gammarus* (L). *Philos. Trans. R. Soc. Lond., B.* 274:53–68.

Steinacker, A. 1978. The anatomy of the decapod crustacean auxillary heart. *Biol. Bull.,* 154:497–507.

Vermeij, G.J. 1977. Patterns in crab claw size: The geography of crushing. *Syst. Zool.,* 26:138–151.

The Arthropoda
II. Insects and Relatives

13

Since in the preceding chapter, the crustaceans and the more important classes of chelicerate arthropods were discussed, all that remains for review are three closely allied classes that share such fundamental characteristics as a single pair of antennae, well-developed jaws, and branching tracheae for respiration. Because the first two of these taxa are similar in having legs on the abdomen as well as the thoracic region, for many years they were treated as subdivisions of a single class known as the Myriapoda. More recently, it has come to be realized that the differences between them are more important than this one seemingly unifying trait, for actually the arrangement of abdominal legs differs greatly between the two. Hence, today they are consistently treated as separate classes, as here.

THE CLASS DIPLOPODA

The millipedes that constitute the class Diplopoda are rather unfamiliar, as they are usually slow-moving vegetation-eating creatures that rarely come indoors. Their common name means "thousand-legs," but that term is more usually applied popularly to the members of the following class. Most of the millipedes are less than 40 mm in length, slender in form, and with a fringelike set of numerous, short legs along each side (fig. 13.1). As a rule they are found beneath logs and bark, and in humus and moist plant litter. The relatively few species are grouped into four subclasses (table 13.1), the first of which, the Pauropoda, is sometimes treated as a separate class.

Occasionally the body is considered to be divided into only a head and a trunk, but more usually the latter division is treated as consisting of a thorax of three segments and an abdomen. The abdominal segments have become fused by pairs, so that two pairs of legs occur on what thus has become a single unit; since fusing has not occurred on the thorax, only one pair of appendages per segment is present there. In addition, one head segment is not fused with the rest and forms the collum, a sort of collar between the head proper and the thorax (fig. 13.1).

The mouthparts, which are highly modified, consist of a pair of mandibles and the second pair of maxillae, the first pair being lost during embryological development. In addition, parts of the ventral portion of the posterior head segments are combined with the maxillae to form what is referred to as the chilognatharium; to some extent this part corresponds to the labium of insects (p. 212).

Table 13.1   The Subclasses of Diplopoda

Characteristic	Subclass			
	Pauropoda	Pselaphognatha	Opisthandria	Proterandria
Gnathochilarium	Present	Absent	Present	Present
Collum appendages	Absent	Leglike	Absent	Absent
Trunk segments	11	10–12	11–20	18–31
Eyes	Wanting	Present	Present	Present
Antennae	Branched	Unbranched	Unbranched	Unbranched
Legs	6-segmented	7-segmented	7-segmented	7-segmented

However, it is not present in one subclass (the Pselaphognatha), the maxillae there being free and the collum bearing leglike appendages. Antennae are present throughout the class, for the most part being short and rather club-shaped, while in the subclass Pauropoda they branch near the apex (fig. 13.1).

The legs, although numerous, are short and weak, so movement in all the members of the class is slow; speed, however, is not especially advantageous to consumers of vegetation and decaying matter. Except in the pauropods where there are only six, the legs are comprised of seven segments. The larger number results from division of a primitively single segment, called the trochanter, into

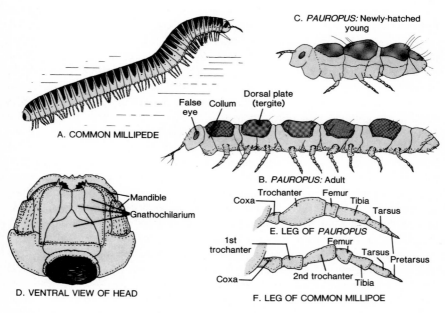

Figure 13.1   *A pair of millipedes and some characteristic structures.*

two in the more advanced forms (fig. 13.1). While the legs individually are weak, in unison they can exert considerable force, a trait particularly useful in burrowing into soil as these animals do. With their aid, the millipedes also are able to thrust themselves into tight crevices in fallen timber or beneath bark. As might be expected, the movement of these multitudinous legs is coordinated by integrated ganglia, two of which are found within each abdominal segment. Almost all of the legs are identical in structure; males, however, are exceptional in having either the sixth or the terminal pair modified for transferring sperm during copulation, serving much as do the pedipalps of male spiders. In both sexes the genital ducts of millipedes open on the second thoracic segment posterior to the basal segments of the legs.

Development is not especially striking, for the newly-hatched young is not too unlike the adult, except in having fewer legs. Consequently, growth from young to adult stages involves the addition of one abdominal segment and thus two pairs of legs with each successive molt. Growth by means of additions of segments as here is said to be *anamorphic*.

THE CLASS CHILOPODA

Centipedes of the class Chilopoda are opposites of the millipedes in almost every one of their traits. Their bodies are long, flexuous, and flattened, rather than cylindrical; the antennae are elongate, containing 12 or more segments; the legs are long and powerful and movement is exceedingly swift; and they are carnivorous in food habits. Most species are moderately small, but some tropical members may be as long as 300 mm. Beneath litter and bark of decaying logs, under rocks, and in humus are among the numerous habitats of these animals.

The head is followed by a trunk which varies in length with the species from 15 to as many as 180 segments, each of which bears a single pair of legs. Often, as in *Lithobius,* the body segments are alternately long and short, while in others like the geophilids, all are of equal length (fig. 13.2, C). In still others, the segments have the appearance of being equal, whereas actually short ones intervene between the long ones; however, the former are so reduced as to be concealed by the dorsal covering of the large components. Short segments bear legs in all cases but often lack spiracles. The very last abdominal segment, known as the telson or pygidium, lacks appendages, except sensory structures called cirri.

The mouthparts approach those of the insect rather closely in structure, consisting of an upper lip (labrum), a pair of mandibles, and maxillae; however, there are two pairs of the latter organ, compared to one in the insects and millipedes. An additional difference from the diplopods is that the bases of the second maxillae are fused to form a lower lip or labium, as in the insects.

The legs are usually elongate and slender and typically consist of seven segments, as in most millipedes. As in those animals, too, there are two trochanters, except in the subclass Symphyla, in which there is only one, and thus only six segments in the legs. Members of that subclass are also atypical in not having the first pair of legs especially modified, as is the case with the others. In each of the

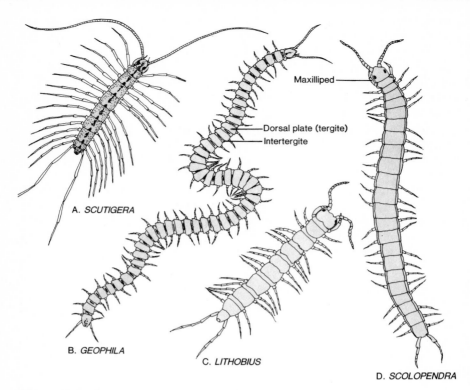

Figure 13.2 *Some representative centipedes.*

latter, that pair is modified into maxillipeds which bear a fang equipped with a poison gland on the tip, used in killing prey (fig. 13.3). In some genera like *Scutigera* (fig. 13.2, A), the hindmost pair of legs is usually held outwards above the substrate and is modified to serve as a posterior pair of antennae.

Centipedes have a highly developed *respiratory system,* consisting of tracheae that branch and unite with one another freely; however, the details vary with the order and subclass. In the Epimorpha, spiracles are present on all trunk segments except the first and last; each leads into tracheae that branch but largely remain within the individual segments. In others a number of segments do not bear spiracles, so that most of the main tracheae are elongate and run the length of the body, sending off numerous branches as they do so. In those centipedes that have somites of differing sizes, only the large ones may bear spiracles. Finally, in the Symphyla the system is so drastically different that it provides one of the principal reasons for considering that category as a separate class, rather than a subclass. In this taxon a single pair of spiracles is located on the sides of the head. These openings connect to branching tracheae that serve the tissues of only the head and first three trunk segments. The remainder of the body thus must receive oxygen either from the blood or by diffusion through the body wall.

A

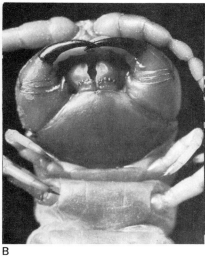

Figure 13.3 *A common centipede of the genus Scolopendra and its poison fang (maxilliped).* (Photographs courtesy of Dr. F. Schlemmer.)

B

The *reproductive system* is short, with the gonads being dorsally located. Often the males have certain pairs of legs modified to serve in sperm transfer, but in other cases the male genital openings are each equipped with a penis for copulation. One of the more unusual features of reproduction in centipedes is the brooding of the young. Usually the eggs are deposited in clusters in the soil or leaf mold, but some species prepare nests or cocoons. The eggs are then guarded by the female until they hatch, which protection may be extended to the young afterwards for a period. Protection is largely directed against the growth of fungus, rather than predators, as such plants are possibly the greatest hazard experienced by the eggs and early juveniles. Growth is anamorphic, a larval stage being absent.

THE CLASS INSECTA

No one can seriously question the coordinate role insects play with man as the dominant forms of animal life on earth today. The biological importance of the members of the class Insecta in nearly all types of environment also is unquestionable—only in certain marine habitats are they of little significance. In the open seas the marine water striders of the true bug genus *Halobates* alone are known to occur, but brackish water, salt marshes, and sandy beaches abound with individuals and species of this class. Soils, fresh waters, forests, grasslands, deserts, swamps, mountain tops, and lush valleys, all have a wide diversity of insect inhabitants. Moreover, other animals externally and plants both internally and externally have numbers of pest species belonging to this taxon.

Often the insect's wings have been held to be responsible for the major part of the success of this class, but in view of the ample numbers of wingless forms, like fleas, lice, spring-tails, and bedbugs that have achieved a similar degree of success, it is improbable that any single physical trait can be given sole credit.

More than likely, it is their general adaptability that underlies much of it—if evolution is occurring today, most probably it is doing so among insects, according to the studies of such geneticists as Dobzhansky, Patterson, and many others.

The more than a million known species of insects are classed into 25 to 33 orders, depending upon the author. Within these categories, the numbers are far from being evenly distributed, for one order of primitive wingless forms, the Protura, contains less than one hundred species, while the order Coleoptera, the beetles, includes about 800,000—it has been said that at least one out of every four species of living things is a beetle!

Metamorphosis

The orders of insects fall into four more or less natural subdivisions on the basis of the type of metamorphosis that the young undergoes in attaining adulthood. In the most primitive of these categories, the Ametabola, all stages beyond the egg are alike in appearance and structure; as wings are absent, no change except in size occurs during the life cycle. Undoubtedly the most abundant representative ametabolic types are the silverfish and springtails (fig. 13.4, A).

In a second type of metamorphosis, development is gradual in that the wings of the adults are acquired in a series of slight changes. The newly hatched young are wingless in this Paurometabola subdivision; then at the first molt, brief wing pads are acquired. At the second molt, these pads are elongated a bit to become still longer with the third, and so on, until at the last molt, the wings are fully developed. Every stage thus resembles the mature form except in wing size, and, perhaps, in the proportions of the several body parts. For instance, in the grasshoppers and their allies, which represent this group, the heads are proportionally much larger in the young, or *nymphs,* as they are called, than in succeeding stages. Mantids, roaches, termites, lice, true bugs, and cicadas are among the numerous orders which undergo this type of metamorphosis (fig. 13.4, C).

The third type, the Hemimetabola, experiences marked changes in body form during growth. Its members include certain orders in which the juvenile stages are aquatic, whereas the adults are aerial, such as the dragonflies and mayflies (fig. 13.4, B); consequently, the young possess gills and food-getting organs not present in the adult, and of course, lack the wings of the latter. Hence, the immature forms, referred to as *naiads* (really larvae, zoologically speaking), do not resemble the mature forms. However, all stages are active; thus in the absence of a quiescent stage, this subdivision is called the Hemimetabola, with an incomplete type of metamorphosis.

The inactive stage, or *pupa,* is confined to the Holometabola, the forms in which metamorphosis is thus complete. In all the holometabolic orders, the young are drastically different from the adults and are referred to as *larvae.* The pupa, too, differs in form from the adults as well as the larva; this stage may be enclosed in a cocoon, in a cell in soil or plant material, or merely in the last larval skin. Among the numerous orders included here are those containing the dobson flies, ant lions, beetles, flies, butterflies and moths, fleas, and the bees, wasps, and ants (fig. 13.4, D).

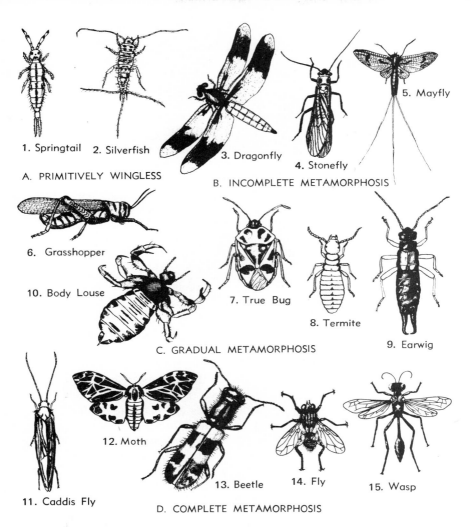

1. Springtail   2. Silverfish

A. PRIMITIVELY WINGLESS

3. Dragonfly

4. Stonefly

5. Mayfly

B. INCOMPLETE METAMORPHOSIS

6. Grasshopper

10. Body Louse

7. True Bug

8. Termite

9. Earwig

C. GRADUAL METAMORPHOSIS

12. Moth

11. Caddis Fly

13. Beetle   14. Fly

15. Wasp

D. COMPLETE METAMORPHOSIS

Figure 13.4 *Representative insects.* Each figure represents one of the thirty-odd orders of insects, as follows: 1, Collembola; 2, Thysanura; 3, Odonata; 4, Plecoptera; 5, Ephemerida; 6, Orthoptera; 7, Hemiptera; 8, Isoptera; 9, Dermaptera; 10, Anoplura; 11, Trichoptera; 12, Lepidoptera; 13, Coleoptera; 14, Diptera; and 15, Hymenoptera.

External Structure

In spite of the diversity of its members, the class Insecta is a well-marked group. The body is consistently divided into three distinct regions, the head, thorax, and abdomen (fig. 13.5). One pair of antennae is always present, except in the order Protura, a primitive taxon of admittedly doubtful relationship; these organs are often modified to an extreme extent. Three pairs of walking legs provide another consistent trait, and wings typify the vast majority of species. In

Three body divisions:

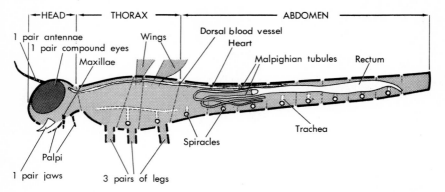

Figure 13.5 *Distinctive features of insects.* Included in the list of distinctive structural traits are the three pairs of segmented legs, a single pair of antennae, spiracles and tracheae for respiration, complex mouthparts, compound eyes, and Malpighian tubules for excretion. Although wings typically are present, they are reduced or absent in several orders.

fact, the various modifications to which the latter organs have been subjected provide many of the major characteristics employed in defining the numerous orders.

Another portion of the insect useful in distinguishing the several orders are the mouthparts (fig. 13.6). Four main types of structures are included: a single upper lip (labrum), followed by a pair of jaws (mandibles) and a single pair of maxillae. The latter usually function in holding and handling the food, rather than in chewing it. Finally, the mouth is closed on the ventral surface by a single lower lip (labium); this and the pair of maxillae are provided with palpi on the sides (fig. 13.6). Actually the labium is derived from the fused bases of the second set of maxillae, as pointed out previously for the centipedes. Internally there is also a tongue (lingula or hypopharynx) that bears the salivary ducts. While many forms like grasshoppers, beetles, and dragonflies have chewing mouthparts as described, others have them greatly modified, especially for sucking. In bugs and their close relatives, the leafhoppers, the labium is modifed for piercing, while the mandibles and maxillae are reduced to threadlike parts which help form a siphon used in sucking plant or animal juices (fig. 13.6, F, G). Butterflies, too, have siphonlike parts, but in their case the maxillae comprise almost the entire structure (fig. 13.6, H, I).

Other prominent external features found throughout the class are the compound eyes located on the sides of the head and frequently two or more simple ocelli on the dorsal surface. Along each side of the body are found porelike spiracles to which the tracheae are attached; while each abdominal segment usually bears one spiracle on each side, only the two posterior thoracic segments do so. Finally, at the tip of the abdomen may be found various appendages, such as claspers used in reproductive activities, caudal filaments or cerci, and forceps in the earwigs.

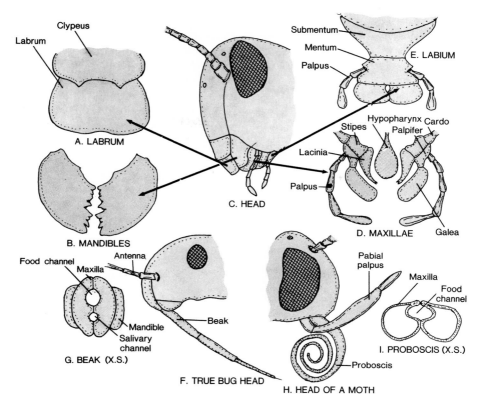

Figure 13.6 *The mouthparts of a representative insect and some specializations.*

Internal Anatomy

· Although no single example can be truly representative of the highly diversified internal structure of insects, the grasshopper is sufficiently unspecialized that it at least shows all the parts found among the other orders. Accordingly, this insect provides the example here (fig. 13.7, A). The *digestive tract* is nearly a straight tube. Following the mouth is a short pharynx that leads into a widened portion, the esophagus, and then into a large saclike part, the crop. At the end of the latter are twelve small sacs, or gastric caeca, six of which project forward, the remainder backwards. Farther posteriorly is a thick-walled, muscular grinding organ, known as the gizzard or proventriculus; usually its inner walls are ridged and provided with chitinous teeth, spines, or other structures suitable for grinding. Behind this is the midgut or ventriculus; sometimes, as in the grasshopper, this organ is considered to consist of an anterior pyloris, a medial ileum, and a posterior colon, the last being greater in diameter than the other two divisions. A rectum, which opens through an anus, completes this system.

Just under the median dorsal line of the thorax and abdomen lies the elongate heart, which makes up almost the entire *circulatory system* (fig. 13.7, A). This somewhat resembles the corresponding organ of spiders but has ostia in each abdominal segment; in addition, there is a terminal valve posteriorly that similarly admits blood into this organ. The heart pumps blood forward through an aorta to just behind the brain, where that vessel terminates. As in other open systems, the blood circulates freely thence through the body cavity and appendages, being moved along by the muscular activities of the body as a whole, but especially by the wing muscles where those organs are present.

Excretion is by means of Malpighian tubules, which are located on the digestive tract at the junction of the proventriculus and midgut. The number of tubules varies widely from order to order, ranging from 4 to 100 or more; in the aphids, however, they are completely absent. *Respiration* is by means of tracheae, which ramify throughout the body (fig. 13.7, B). Unlike the condition in the spiders, the tubules are highly branched, dividing into finer and finer tracheoles, so that the final divisions conduct air to the individual clusters of cells. Near their external ends the tubes may be expanded into a number of air sacs; in many orders two especially large ones fill much of the dorsal region of the thorax. The larger tracheae are lined with cuticle that is shed during molting of the skin.

A large complex brain is an obvious feature of the *nervous system*. As a rule this organ consists of three major subdivisions (proto-, deuto-, and trito-

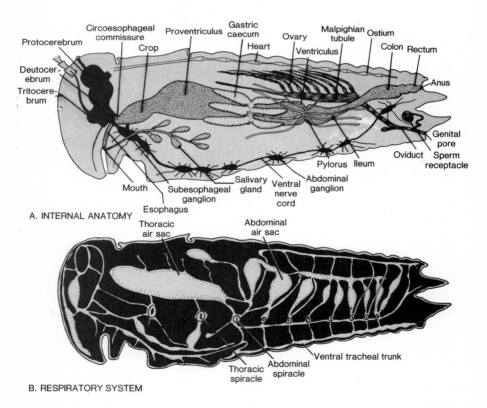

A. INTERNAL ANATOMY

B. RESPIRATORY SYSTEM

Figure 13.7 *Internal anatomy of an insect.*

cerebrum), and prominent optic lobes extend from the sides to each compound eye (fig. 13.7, A). In addition, anteriorly a stalk or pedicel runs to each ocellus and antenna. Then on each side of the lowest brain subdivision (the tritocerebrum) are the paired circumesophageal commissures that connect to the subesophageal ganglion. Although the latter complex organ is involved in coordination of muscle activities, its most important function is in a secretory role in the regulation of molting and maturation of the individual. Behind this is a series of ganglia, primitively one in each thoracic and abdominal segment, connected to one another by a double nerve cord. Frequently the thoracic components in particular are fused into two and sometimes even into a single ganglion; the abdominal members, too, may be partially combined, but this condition is of less frequent occurrence. All of these structures, as in the annelid worms, coordinate muscle contraction in their individual or combination of segments.

The *reproductive system* is frequently quite elaborate. Generally the sexes are separate, but parthenogenesis occurs in some instances, especially in aphids and a few beetles, males being either absent or seasonal in occurrence. The paired gonads are located in the abdomen dorsally and laterally to the digestive tract. In the testes are a number of follicles, while in females the ovaries consist of a series of elongate ovarian tubes (fig. 13.7, A). These subdivisions in each sex connect to a pair of genital tubes (vasa deferentia and oviducts, respectively). Often the vas deferens expands into a seminal vesicle for the storage of sperm, and oviducts have one or more accessory glands which secrete the shell. These paired ducts then unite below the rectum to form a single ejaculatory duct in the male and a vagina in the female. In the latter sex there is frequently a sperm receptacle in which the sperm received during copulation are stored. Both systems finally open through a genital pore, located at various positions on the external genitalia, including the penis or ovipositor.

The various internal systems and organs not only differ greatly from order to order but have undergone extensive diversification in the methods of carrying out their functions. Because whole books would be required to discuss these specializations in detail, a few examples only are provided. These selections, it is hoped, should enable each student individually to discover that, striking though the morphological differences may be between a beetle and butterfly or a dragonfly and an ant, far greater but less evident ones exist in insect internal functionings.

Evolutionary Adaptations in Feeding Habits

Under this heading, the discussion could logically be devoted to the numerous specializations to which the mouthparts have been subjected. But highly modified though these are, the methods of treating the foods after being secured and swallowed show even more numerous diversifications.

As in human beings and other vertebrates, foods are digested by enzymatic action and, in such omnivorous forms as the roaches, series of enzymes are present to break down proteins (proteases), fats (lipases), carbohydrates (carbohydrases), and nucleic acids (nucleases). Insects adapted to a special diet often show a deficiency of one or more types of enzymes. In tsetse flies, which feed on blood, all carbohydrases are absent, whereas among adult blowflies, whose food is rich in carbohydrates, most of the proteases as well as the lipases are lacking. Sometimes this type of diversity has evolved to great extremes, as among leaf-mining caterpillars. These extremely small, flat caterpillars spend their entire life within the interior of a leaf, feeding upon a single region of cells. In some cases, a species may feed upon the upper, or columnar, layer of leaf cells, while others consume only the lower, or spongy, layer. If by chance the egg of one such species is deposited in the wrong layer of the leaf, the caterpillar soon perishes because it lacks the enzymes necessary to digest the proteins of those cells.

Many insects burrow through trees or feed on plant tissues, but few are actually able themselves to utilize the cellulose of the tissues. The larvae of long-horned beetles are among the exceptions that possess the essential enzymes. On the other hand, plant-eating caterpillars cannot utilize cellulose but have enzymes that penetrate the cell walls and digest the protoplasm within. In other wood-eating insects, such as termites, certain woodroaches, and deathwatch beetle larvae, symbiotic organisms in the intestine carry out the actual digestion of cellulose, a fact already pointed out in the discussion of certain protozoa. Still others, like the beetles that drill extensive burrows beneath bark, do not in reality feed upon the wood but eat the fungi which grow in the tunnels.

In a number of groups that saliva serves both in digesting and ingesting food. For example, among the larvae of tiger beetles and flesh flies, the protease-rich saliva is poured out upon the prey and then lapped up after the proteins have been digested. Consequently, these insects depend upon external digestion to a large degree. Feeding mainly upon nectar and pollen, bees are so highly specialized that they have four types of salivary glands. The secretion of certain glands attacks nectar, and that of others, pollen, while the remainder add formic acid, apparently to prevent spoilage of the foods during storage in the honeycombs.

Specialization for Escape

Undoubtedly the elementary and secondary schools have already supplied a familiarity with insect adaptations which assist in escaping attacks of predators. Such things, then, as bodies that imitate plant spines or bird droppings, scent glands that secrete a repellant, or wings that resemble leaves need not receive attention. Here mention is made only of two adaptations of night-flying insects that seem to be employed for defense against nocturnal insect-eating mammals and birds.

The first of these, the production of light by fireflies, apparently serves to some degree for recognition purposes and for sexual attraction, but its major value may be an indirect one in defense. When fireflies are fed to a young insect-eating bird, for example, on the first occasion they are usually quickly rejected and thereafter steadfastly refused—facts suggesting that the beetles possess an unpleasant taste. While such a repugnant quality might provide ample protection to an insect against day-feeding insectivorous vertebrates, who quickly learn to discriminate between edible and inedible forms, it can be of little value to a nocturnal species unless some other device enables its predators to recognize it before capture. Among the fireflies the flashing light provides such a recognition character, so that night-feeding birds and bats avoid attacking these insects.

The second example is a peculiar adaptation that evolved in moths in reaction to the unusual method of food-locating employed by bats. These mammals, while flying at night, emit extremely high-pitched sound waves, the echoes of which are detected with sensitive ears; in this fashion they avoid obstacles and locate their food (flying insects). Recent experiments by F.A. Webster and others have shown that bats actually can plot the course of a steadily flying object and intercept it, so that feeding on insects is a fairly routine procedure. However, against this subtle "sonar," one family of moths has acquired an effective means of defense in the form of well-developed ears that detect the bat's sound waves. K.R. Roeder, A.E. Treat, and others are experimenting upon these insects using high-speed cinematography in conjunction with a floodlight and tape recordings of bat calls. They have found that upon exposure to the sounds, some moths immediately respond by an angular change in direction of flight and others by flying in bewildering circles, but the majority react by diving headlong into vegetation.

A number of species of moths belonging to the family Arctiidae have also acquired a defense mechanism against predation by bats. In this case, however, the defense involves "jamming" the bat's sonar system by the moth's making a series of similar sounds; these are produced by buckling a row of fine ridges or microtymbals located on a ventral sector of the thorax. The rapid clicks are emitted when the moths are handled, but particularly when they are exposed to the sounds made by insectivorous bats. That this defense mechanism is effective against predation is shown in laboratory experiments; for instance, if tape-recordings of the arctiid clicks are played, bats refuse to eat even preferred foods. The moth sounds have been demonstrated to be probably a defense mechanism by the click-producing arctiid's occurring during months while bats are active. In contrast, those species that occur only before bats have returned for the summer consistently lack the click-producing devices.

QUESTIONS FOR REVIEW AND THOUGHT

1. Describe the members of the class Diplopoda and state their chief distinctive traits. On what characteristics are the subclasses principally based? Why is the Pauropoda sometimes placed as a separate class?

2. What evidence is provided by certain members of the Diplopoda that the head in the higher mandibulate arthropods has probably resulted from a fusion of several anterior segments? Since no other invertebrate of any type has more than one neural ganglion per segment, how do you suppose the millipedes acquired two per segment?

3. Compare the members of the class Chilopoda with the millipedes. On what basis might it be logical to combine these two classes into a single one, the Myriapoda, as was the former practice? What reasons are there for separating them, as here?

4. In what ways do the centipedes show closer kinship to the insects than the millipedes do?

5. Present several items of evidence that indicate the insects to be one of the most successful taxa of living things.

6. Name and describe the four patterns of metamorphosis found among insects. Also give the common names of one or more representative types and the name of the immature forms in each instance.

7. Name and describe the several mouthparts of a generalized kind of insect. What parts are often involved in modifications?

8. What are some of the adaptations in feeding habits that have been acquired by insects? For escape from predators?

SUGGESTIONS FOR FURTHER READING

Buck, J., and E. Buck. 1978. Toward a functional interpretation of synchronous flashing by fireflies. *Amer. Nat.,* 112:471–492.

Butler, C.G. 1967. Insect pheromones. *Biological Reviews,* 42:42–87.

Carroll, C.R., and D.H. Janzen. 1973. Ecology of foraging by ants. *Annual Review of Ecology and Systematics,* 4:231–257.

Cloudsley-Thompson, J.L. 1958. *Spiders, scorpions, centipedes and mites.* New York, Pergamon Press.

Gould, J.L., M. Henerey, and M.C. Macheod. 1970. Communication of direction by the honey bee. *Science,* 169:544–554.

Horridge, H.A. 1977. The compound eye of insects. *Sci. Amer.,* 237(1):108–120.

Lewontin, R.C. 1978. Adaptation. *Scient. Amer.,* 239(3):213–230.

Manton, S.M. 1953. Structure, habits, and evolution of the Diplopoda. *Journal of the Linnean Society of London, Zoology,* 42:299–368.

McElroy, W.D., and H.H. Seliger. 1962. Biological luminescence. *Scient. Amer.* 207(December):76–84.

Roeder, K.D. 1966. Auditory system of noctuid moths. *Science,* 154:1515–1521.

Sherk, T.E. 1978. Development of the compound eyes of dragonflies (Odonata) III. Adult compound eyes. *J. Exp. Zool.,* 203:61–80.

Wigglesworth, V.B. 1970. *Insect hormones.* Edinburgh, Oliver and Boyd.

The Mollusca 14

In relation to the two coelomate lines of evolution, the precise position of the Mollusca remains subject to question. Because the phylum shares a number of traits with the Annelida, including such important ones as a spiral type of cleavage and a trochophore larva, it undoubtedly needs to be placed close to that taxon. But there are three points on the phylogenetic tree where it could be placed, any one of which would be just as logical as the other, and therein lies the basis for differing opinions. For instance, as already pointed out in Chapter 11, the Mollusca could be considered to belong on the same line of ascent as the segmented worms, but the question is, should it be treated as being earlier or later than that group? Or alternatively, it could be regarded as being near the base of a second line of ascent that branched off from a common ancestral stock along with the annelid line. These are problems that have perplexed zoologists for many years—and shall probably continue to do so for many more.

Up to 1957 only five classes of the phylum Mollusca were known to be represented by living forms, but early in that year a Danish zoologist, H. Lemche, reported an exciting specimen he had taken by dredging at depths exceeding 11,000 feet off the coast of Costa Rica. This mollusk, which he named *Neopilina galatheae*, was the first modern representative ever captured of a class previously known solely from Paleozoic times, none of which are less than 300,000,000 years old. Thus this member of the class Monoplacophora can be considered a "living fossil" in a very real sense. Since then the number of classes has been incresed to seven by the current practice of subdividing the former class Amphineura into the Aplacophora, containing the solenogast portion, and the Polyplacophora, including the chitons.

CHARACTERISTICS

As most of the characteristic features of this phylum are readily discerned in the illustration (fig. 14.1), only a few remarks are necessary, particularly in regards to those traits that are unique to the mollusks.

Structure

The body as a whole is diagnostic for these animals, especially in its being soft—it is this condition that is referred to by the phylum name, which is from the Latin *molluscus,* meaning soft. Perhaps this aspect of the body is best

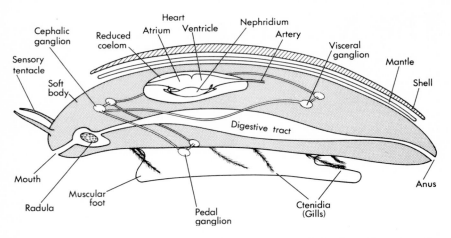

Figure 14.1 *Salient features of the mollusks.* Among the distinctive traits are a soft body, usually unsegmented and covered by a calcareous shell that is secreted by a mantle; coelom reduced; a single muscular foot located ventrally; circulatory system open; nervous system double, forming a triangle; and a rasping organ called the radula.

exemplified by the snails and oysters. In addition, a head is present, except in the bivalves, but segmentation is absent, except in *Neopilina,* in which the several pairs of hearts, nephridia, and gills indicate its presence internally. Usually the coelom is reduced to cavities surrounding the heart and gonads, but the extent of reduction varies from class to class. Nothing is especially remarkable about the *digestive tract,* except the peculiar organ called the *radula* (fig. 14.2), present in all classes other than the bivalves. Each radula consists of a chitinous strap, on one side of which are numerous, fine, horny teeth. In use these organs are moved back and forth by muscles and serve in obtaining food and tearing it into small pieces.

The *mantle* is another unusual structure. This is a fold of the body wall, that in most classes secretes a shell, and in the squids and octopuses makes up much of the body surface. Between the mantle and the body wall is a mantle cavity, outside of the body proper, in which the gills (often called ctenidia) are enclosed. Here, too, are to be found the terminal openings of the digestive, excretory, and reproductive systems.

The *nervous system* is unusual in consisting of three pairs of ganglia, often arranged as a triangle. Although much variation exists, typically the members of each pair are interconnected by transverse commissures, while dual nerve cords connect the ganglia in series. Because the cephalic ganglia generally are no larger than the others, they are not regarded as brains; the squids and octopuses are exceptional in having these ganglia extremely well developed and organized into a highly complex brain.

Figure 14.2 *Scanning electron micrograph of the radula of a snail.* The numerous teeth are evident that make this distinctive feature of mollusks an effective scraping organ. X 3200. (Photo by Alan Solem, Courtesy Field Museum of Natural History.)

The Shell

In general the shell provides the principal basis for diversity among the Mollusca. That its specializations have been abundant is attested by the large number of known species of mollusks—nearly 100,000 living today and more than half again that number preserved as fossils. Even at the level of the classes, the major distinctions are provided by the form of the shell (table 14.1); the only taxon which has a covering other than this structure is the Aplacophora, a group of wormlike forms known as solenogasters, in which calcareous spicules cover the body. In the class that includes the oysters and clams, known as the Pelecypoda, the shell is divided into two valves, and in another, the Polyplacophora or chitons, it consists of eight, but in the remaining four classes, in which only a single valve is found, special features in each set them off sharply from one another. These distinctions are brought out more clearly as the chief features of each class are reviewed in the following pages.

THE CLASS MONOPLACOPHORA

The living fossil, *Neopilina,* mentioned in the introduction has proven to be even more interesting than suspected when first discovered. One of the distinctive features, the single shell, is referred to by the name of the class Monoplacophora, which is derived from Greek words meaning "one-plate-bearer." In shape this shell is tentlike, being nearly circular in outline and rising to a peak near the center. From above, the appearance of the one and one-half inch shell is reminiscent of the limpets, but the animal enclosed by it is obviously different.

Table 14.1 The Classes of Mollusks

Characteristic	Monoplacophora	Polyplacophora	Scaphopoda
Shell	Single, cup-shaped	Of 8 plates or absent	Tubular, open at both ends
Foot	Discoidal	Discoidal or rudimentary	Reduced
Body	Segmented internally	Unsegmented	Unsegmented
Gills	5 pairs, external	6 to 80 pairs, around foot	Absent
Sense organs	Sensory tentacles	Absent	Sensory tentacles
Habitat	Marine	Marine	Marine
Common names	—	Chitons: solenogasters	Tooth shells; tusk shells

From beneath, the most evident feature is the large circular foot, surrounded by five pairs of segmentally arranged gills (fig. 14.3, A). Near the anterior end is a mouth, which is merely a rounded opening provided on both sides with a ruffled membrane called a *velum*. Each of the latter is covered with large numbers of cilia, whose beating movements sweep food particles into the mouth. Behind these structures are several branching tentacles that also are concerned with food gathering. The only other feature visible ventrally is the edge of the mantle which protrudes briefly between the body and the shell. When the foot and surrounding features are dissected away, the internal structure is found to bear little resemblance to that of most other mollusks (fig. 14.3, B), the eight pairs of segmentally arranged shell muscles and six pairs of kidneys being especially noteworthy.

These strange creatures, first collected at a depth of 11,000 feet from the Pacific Ocean floor about 250 miles off the Central American coast, have subsequently been dredged from locations farther north and south of the original site and also from near Hawaii. Since more recently some have also been found in the Atlantic Ocean, the species is evidently widespread in distribution. A second species has now been discovered in the South Atlantic; this form is much smaller than the other, being less than 2 mm long when mature. An additional difference is in its having six, rather than five, pairs of gills.

Pelecypoda	Gastropoda	Cephalopoda
Bivalvular	Tubular, often spiral, sometimes flat or absent	Reduced or absent
Wedge-shaped	Flat	Modified into 8 or more tentacles
Unsegmented	Unsegmented	Unsegmented
2 pairs, internal	1 pair, 1, or none; respiration sometimes by lungs or mantle	1 or 2 pairs
Palpi, eyespots; sensory tentacles absent	Sensory tentacles, eyes	Eyes very well developed; sensory tentacles absent
Marine and fresh water	Marine, fresh water, and terrestrial	Marine
Clams; oysters, mussels, etc.	Snails, slugs, conchs, whelks, earshells, etc.	Squids, nautili, octopuses

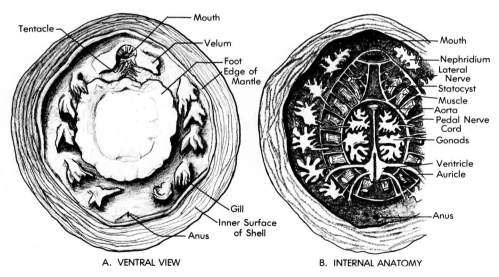

A. VENTRAL VIEW   B. INTERNAL ANATOMY

Figure 14.3 *Neopilina, a "living fossil."*

THE CLASS APLACOPHORA

There is little doubt that few persons would recognize the wormlike soleno-gasters that comprise the class Aplacophora as being mollusks, for they lack the mantle, shell, head, foot, and nephridia present in the typical members of the phylum. Actually the single noncontroversial molluscan trait to be found in these animals is the radula; only that structure, the embryonic development, and larva provide a basis for their inclusion here. One external feature that at once distin-guishes the solenogasters from all other wormlike animals is the elongate slit on the ventral surface that is headed anteriorly by a deep pit (fig. 14.4), but this feature characterizes only the members of the Neomeniomorpha, one of the two orders in this class. In lieu of a shell, the body is covered with scalelike spicules, but these are so small that their presence can be detected only by the silky sheen they impart. They are secreted individually by single cells in the epidermis and consist of calcium carbonate embedded in an organic matrix of an undetermined nature. Only in the larvae do the spicules actually form a continuous covering (fig. 14.4, E, F).

A total of about 150 species of aplacophorans have been described to date, all of which are marine animals living at depths of 18 to 4,000 m. Most are small,

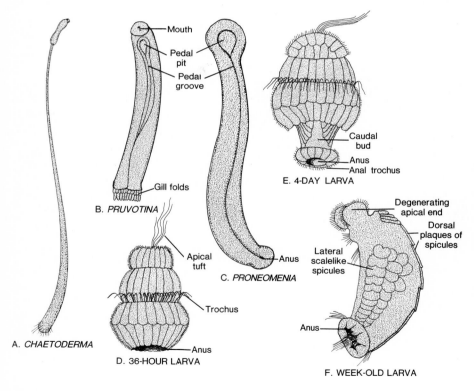

Figure 14.4 *Representative types and larvae of solenogasters.* (In part based on Pruvot, 1890.)

averaging around 25 mm, but a few grow as large as 30 cm. Since they consistently occur far below the intertidal zone, they are captured only by dredging operations in deep seas; consequently, their habits remain poorly known. The members of the second order, the Chaetodermatoidea, containing approximately 40 species, inhabit muddy bottoms, where they drill burrows by forcing their anterior end downward into the substrate by muscular contraction and expansion. Usually they remain thus head downward, leaving the gills on the posterior end exposed at the surface. These and the members of the first order, the Neomeniomorpha, which do not burrow, are alike in being sluggish in their movements and in remaining immobile for hours at a time. The surface dwellers of this latter taxon creep by unknown means and are characteristically found in tangles of seaweed or entwined about hydroids or corals. The associations between these solenogasters and the other organisms seems to be species specific—that is, one particular species of these mollusks is always found coiled around a certain species of hydroid, another always with a given kind of seaweed, and so on. The food habits are still largely mysteries, but studies of stomach contents suggest that the mud-dwellers are filter-feeders, while the surface forms feed on the particular organism with which they are found associated. The principal features of development of the trochophore larva are made clear in the illustration (fig. 14.4, D–F), where the definitive young may be noted to form by budding from the ventral end of the larva. After a while, the anterior parts atrophy and are resorbed.

THE CLASS POLYPLACOPHORA

The chitons, placed in the class Polyplacophora, represent another strictly marine taxon which is difficult to recognize as belonging in the Mollusca. Instead of a shell enclosing much of the entire animal, here a row of eight plates usually covers less than two-thirds of its upper surface. Moreover, these organisms are flat and ovate in shape (fig. 14.5, A, B) and could as easily be an insect larva as a relative of a snail. However, when the animal is examined more closely, the resemblances to arthropods disappear one by one and the molluscan traits gradually become reinforced.

Structure and Habits

While most chitons are somewhat flattened and broadly ovate as stated above, a small number are elongate and narrowly ovate to the point of being wormlike (fig. 14.5, D). It is the presence of these exceptional types in this class that formerly provided the logical basis for also including the solenogasters here. Most chitons do not exceed 50 mm in length, but *Acanthopleura echinata* of Chile reaches 135 mm and *Cryptochiton stelleri* of the North American Pacific Coast occasionally is 330 mm long. In addition to the longitudinal row of valves, which vary in form with the species, the upper surface may be ornamented with spines, scales, or bristles, but most usually only a naked mantle covers the sides of the dorsal region. The undersurface, too, is not complex. A large muscular foot occupies most of the midregion (fig. 14.5, B), preceded by a muscular head

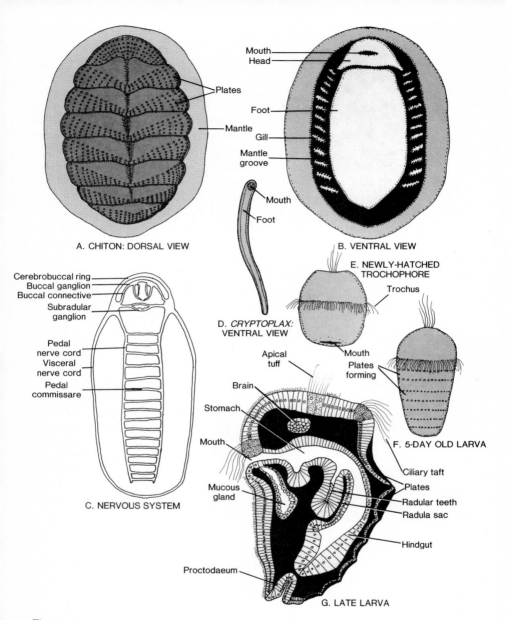

Figure 14.5 *Chiton anatomy and larval structure.* (In part based on Kowalevsky, 1883, Pelseneer, 1899, and Nierotrasz, 1905.)

containing the mouth. Around the entire head and foot is a deep groove, called the mantle groove, that contains the gills (fig. 14.5, B).

The *nervous system* is probably the only internal structure that needs attention here. As a whole this system agrees with the corresponding parts of other molluscan classes, essentially being dual and arranged as the two sides of an angle. However, it is greatly modified. No pair of cephalic ganglia can be recognized; instead there is a cerebrobuccal ring that corresponds to the circumenteric ring of other phyla, accompained by a pair of buccal ganglia (fig. 14.5, C). Since visceral and pedal ganglia are also lacking, the cephalic parts form a loose sort of neural centralization. The pedal nerve cords are complexly interconnected by numerous commissures (fig. 14.5, C) in a pattern found among the following class also. In some forms, similar commissures extend to each lateral nerve cord. Sense organs consist of simple eyes, or ocelli, embedded in the valves, where sensory pits of unknown function are located, too.

Chitons are typically confined to the intertidal zone of rocky shores, but a few exceptional forms descend to depths exceeding 4,000 m. During the daylight hours the shore dwellers remain attached to rocks where waves can wash over them at low tide, adhering by means of the foot and ventral surface of the mantle. Normally the edges of the latter are slightly elevated here and there to permit water to circulate over the gills, but when the animal is disturbed, the mantle is clamped down on the rock's surface so firmly that it cannot be removed without extensive injury. If detached, chitons roll up in armadillo fashion and may remain in that condition anywhere from 30 minutes to several hours before becoming relaxed. Progress over the surface is by means of waves of muscular contraction passing over the foot's surface from the anterior toward the posterior region; each wave requires about one-half minute to traverse the length of the foot and moves the animal forward a distance of 4 to 8 mm. Thus the average chiton travels along at a speed of about 25 mm per minute. At night these mollusks emerge from the water to scrape algae and other live material from the rock surface by means of the radula, or to feed on seaweed. Toward daybreak, each returns to near its former position on the rock, its entire territory usually not exceeding a meter in diameter.

Reproduction

Among chitons the sexes are separate, except in one species (*Trachydermon raymondi*), whose members begin life as females but become males with maturity. None of the chitons mate but merely deposit the sex cells directly into the sea, under the influence of seasons, temperature, time of day, and other factors that vary with the species. As a rule the eggs merely scatter through the water soon after they are released, but in a few forms the female carries them in the mantle groove adjacent to the foot.

Development is spiral and quite rapid, requiring only from 1 to 3 days from fertilization to hatching. The newly hatched larva is a typical trochophore, except that it bears a series of seven small, clear cells dorsally (fig. 14.5, E, F); these later grow into seven valves, which number seems to be the primitive complement—indeed the oldest known fossil adult had only that many valves. On the trochophore the ventral surface is densely ciliated, reflecting a primitive creeping habit; this region eventually thickens and acquires a heavy musculature to become the foot (fig. 14.5, G). Internally can be found a well-developed radula and radula sac, but the digestive tract is incomplete and the body cavity is a pseudocoel (fig. 14.5, G). Within perhaps a week's time from hatching, the larva drops to the sea floor, becomes flattened, and undergoes metamorphosis, losing the apical tuft, the ciliary ring, and eyes, and developing a coelom and complete digestive tract to become a juvenile chiton.

THE CLASS GASTROPODA

By far the greatest portion of the molluscan variety mentioned earlier arises through that displayed by the gastropods—some 80,000 species of snails, slugs, limpets, and other types belonging to this class have been described, arranged in three subclasses (table 14.2). In these animals much of the ventral surface is occupied by the foot, the characteristic responsible for the class name, derived from the Greek words, *gáster,* stomach, and *podós,* foot.

The Shell

In view of the immense number of species, it is not surprising that the gastropod shell comes in a nearly infinite array of sizes, shapes, and colors (fig. 14.6). Almost always it consists of a single valve, but about a score of years ago, a species captured off the coast of Japan had paired valves like a clam. Later investigations into museum collections of bivalves turned up a small number of other species with this same trait whose real kinships had not been recognized previously. In some other species the shell becomes covered by the mantle, so that the mollusk appears to be naked, and in such forms as the slugs and sea-slugs (fig. 14.6, C), the shell has actually been completely lost.

Some varieties of shells have diverged so greatly from the typical coiled pattern that it is difficult to perceive how they could have originated from that type, but the development of the limpet shell illustrates the processes clearly. These 35 mm long keyhole limpets have tent-shaped shells and are abundant along seashores, often literally concealing the surface of rocks or posts in the intertidal regions. At the top of the tent is an opening shaped like a keyhole, hence their common name. Immediately following metamorphosis, the very young limpet is covered with a spiral shell that is ornamented with a series of ridges and provided with an elongate notch anteriorly on the right side (fig. 14.7, C). The shell is carried posteriorly, leaving the head and tentacles of the juvenile protruding beyond the edge, in typical snail fashion. As this time the mollusk is only a few millimeters long. As it grows, its mantle deposits new material along the entire periphery of the shell, closing off the formerly open notch to form a slit. Later deposition occurs more rapidly along the hind edge, so that the coil that was originally posterior gradually comes to assume a median location; by this time the slit is reduced in length as the edge recedes ever more distantly from

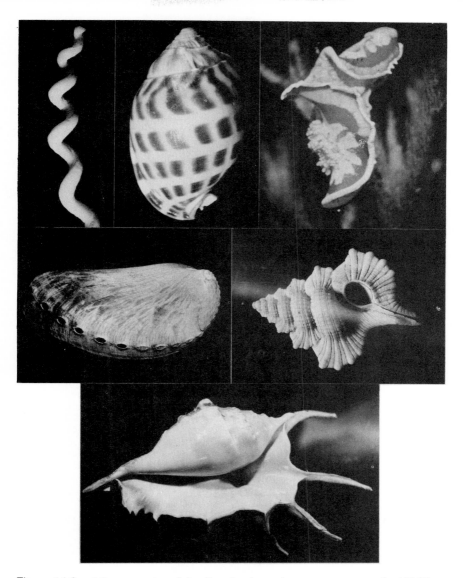

Figure 14.6 *A few examples of the diversity that exists among gastropods.* (A) The worm shell resembles a worm burrow, but is actually a snail shell. (B) The checkerboard helmet shell. (C) Slugs, including nudibranchs (sea slugs) like this one, have lost the shell completely. (D) Although this ear shell looks like one-half of a bivalve, it is actually a highly diversified type of snail shell. (E) The kookaburra shell resembles that bird. (F) Like all the other examples shown, the smooth spider shell is from the South Pacific.

Table 14.2 The Subclasses of the Gastropoda

	Subclasses		
Characteristic	**Prosobranchia**	**Opisthobranchia**	**Pulmonata**
Mantle cavity	Anteriorly located	Along right side or wanting	Along right side
Head	Marked	Marked	Not indicated
Tentacles	1 pair	1–3 pairs (usually 2 pairs)	1 or 2 pairs
Eyes	Near tentacles	Well behind tentacles	Near base of anterior tentacles or on top of posterior ones
Shell	Well developed	Conical, reduced or concealed in mantle; rarely bivalved; often wanting	Moderately developed; rarely within mantle or absent
Respiration	One, rarely two gills, anterior	One gill, posterior; or dorsal body outgrowths	Gills absent; mantle cavity modified into lungs
Heart	One or two auricles, lateral or anterior to ventricle	Two auricles, one posterior to ventricle	One auricle, anterior to ventricle
Reproduction	Sexes separate	Hermaphroditic	Hermaphroditic
Habitat	Mostly marine; some freshwater and terrestrial	Marine	Fresh water and terrestrial, few marine

it (fig. 14.7, D, E). With further increase in shell size, the old coil is nearly lost, the keyhole attains the extreme apex, and the limpet now completely covered by its tentlike shell (fig. 14.7, F) secures a position on a firm surface. The holes of abalone shells (fig. 14.6, D) arise in like fashion. In both of these types of gastropods, the slits or holes are associated with internal respiratory structures.

Frequently some species of these mollusks are able to retract themselves completely into the open end of their spiral shell. Typically such forms possess an operculum with which to close the orifice; this is attached near the posterior end of the foot (fig. 14.7, B), the last part to retreat into the shell. Like the shell, it is secreted by the mantle, material being deposited equally around the edges, as shown by lines of growth; its increase in size is correlated to that of the shell, so that it always is just the right size to close the opening tightly. Among some land-dwelling species, the operculum is cemented shut during severe droughts or other unfavorable situations, preventing the animal from becoming desiccated.

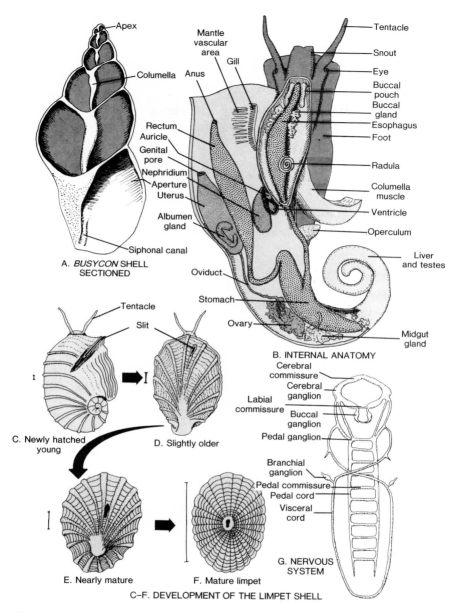

Figure 14.7 *Structure of snails.* (Based in part on Souleyet, 1852, Boutan, 1885, and Woodward, 1901.)

Internally the shell is quite simple in structure, the smooth spiral lumen occupying all of the interior except for a median upright strut called the columella (fig. 14.7, A). Each turn of the spiral tube is referred to as a whorl; the largest of these, the last, is termed the body whorl, and its opening, the aperture, through which the foot and anterior portion of the body can be protruded. Since the aperture is carried forward, it is considered to be anterior and the apex posterior. Particularly in the subclass Prosobranchia, a siphonal canal, through which a fold of the mantle projects for respiration (fig. 14.7, A), is associated with the body whorl.

Internal Structure

Internally the body of gastropods shows a number of adaptations in response to its inhabiting a posteriorly-located coiled shell, the *digestive tract* in particular being appropriately modified. This system begins in the buccal mass, in which is enclosed the pharynx, the radula, and complex musculature needed to operate the latter. The pharynx is followed by a long esophagus, which, instead of entering the elongate stomach at its anterior end, actually connects to it at its middle (fig. 14.7, B). The anterior end of this organ leads into the intestine, and the latter extends forward and terminates in the anus, which is located just to the right of the mouth. Consequently, the posterior portion of the stomach is a blind pouch. Salivary and gastric glands may also be noted in the figure.

The *respiratory system* is highly variable, depending on the subclass and the habitat of the species in question. Although the number of gills is subject to a slight variation (table 14.2), most usually only one is present, except in the pulmonates which have none. When in their normal position, the gills are located to the right side of the head, but the adjacent region of the mantle often is richly supplied with blood vessels to assist in the respiratory processes (fig. 14.7, B), even in species that have gills.

Since the *circulatory system* is an open one, it shows some unusual features. The heart, located in the pericardial cavity, one of the remaining portions of the reduced coelom, consists of a strong muscular ventricle and one or two thin-walled auricles. From the heart, blood passes through anterior and posterior aortas to the various regions of the body. As no capillaries or veins are present, it returns to the heart by way of interconnected sinuses located among the organs and muscles. Before entering the auricles, it first passes through the single nephridium where waste materials are removed, and then through the gills to be oxygenated. Thus no separate subsystems exist for pumping oxygenated and nonoxygenated blood; when two auricles are present, they merely receive blood from their respective sides of the body, not from specialized organs. In fact only about one-fourth of the blood follows the path through the nephridium and gills as described; most enters the auricles directly from the sinuses, without becoming oxygenated or purified.

The *nervous system* shows some advances over that of the chitons, especially anteriorly. Here are found two well-developed ganglia that together serve as a brain (fig. 14.7, G). In addition, there is a much smaller part of ganglia in the buccal pouch that probably coordinates the intricate movements of the radula and other mouth structures. The pedal ganglia, while poorly marked, can be found at the anterior end of a ladderlike pair of interconnected cords that coordinate the foot musculature. In contrast, the two visceral ganglia are quite distinct, but lack the usual transverse commissures. In response to the spiraling of the body, the right and left visceral nerve cords and ganglia are transposed in these animals (fig. 14.7, G).

Reproduction and Development

Since the sexes are separate in the subclass Prosobranchia, little needs to be said about reproduction in those forms, except that the eggs develop spirally into a free-living trochophore larva (fig. 14.9). On the posterior surface of the young larva, a shell gland soon appears and begins to secrete the shell, giving rise to the larval type known as a veliger (fig. 14.9).

The members of the subclass Pulmonata, however, are hermaphroditic, all mature individuals actively secreting both sperm and eggs. In some species, the ovaries and testes make up a common mass, whereas in many others, they are separate as shown (fig. 14.7, B). As far as is known, mating always involves two individuals and is mutual, self-fertilization rarely occurring. In terrestrial species at least, mating is preceded by a ritual, the significance of which is not understood. These preliminary procedures center around the mutual exchange of small objects known as darts, that are secreted by a sac on the oviduct. After these rites have been completed, the penis of each member of the mating pair is then inserted into the other's genital pore. Sperm are then transferred in the form of a bundle called a spermatophore, after which the snails separate. Later each deposits one or more clusters of eggs in damp places, under decaying logs, or in burrows, depending on the species. Often the eggs are covered with a gelatinous coat, but, in the edible snail, they are encased in a snowy white covering and have the size and appearance of pearls. Development is direct, the young emerging as minute snails.

THE CLASS SCAPHOPODA

The class Scaphopoda, whose members are called tooth- or tusk-shells because of their shape, contains only around 350 living species, most of which do not exceed 50 mm in length. These are marine forms that live in sandy bottoms, mostly in shallow, offshore waters, but sometimes at depths exceeding 4,600 m. There they lie obliquely buried in the sand, with only the apical portion of the shell free in the water (fig. 14.8). The apex of the shell is not closed, so that water may be taken in through the opening to provide oxygen and food particles. Since the lower opening is buried, however, the water must be pumped out through the same opening by muscle contractions.

Burial is accomplished by means of the broad, boat-shaped foot, a characteristic alluded to by the formal name, from the Greek word *scaphos*, meaning boat. Although some food particles are brought in as described above, the fine

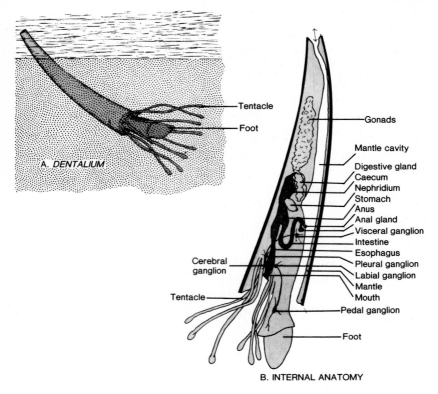

Labels in figure:
Tentacle
Foot
A. DENTALIUM
Gonads
Mantle cavity
Digestive gland
Caecum
Nephridium
Stomach
Anus
Anal gland
Visceral ganglion
Intestine
Esophagus
Cerebral ganglion
Pleural ganglion
Labial ganglion
Mantle
Tentacle
Mouth
Pedal ganglion
Foot
B. INTERNAL ANATOMY

Figure 14.8 *Habits and structure of tooth shells.*

tentacles that surround the mouth also seek out and capture minute organisms that live in the sand. The nervous system has the general characteristics of other members of the class. The reproductive processes also offer little of particular note, sexes being separate and development leading into a free-swimming trochophore. After a short active period, the larva develops a mantle and becomes a bottom-dwelling form. A shell then is secreted by the mantle, and a life similar to that of adults is commenced.

THE CLASS PELECYPODA

Except for the few unusual species of gastropods, the 7,000 species of clams, oysters, mussels, scallops, and other bivalves are readily distinguished from other mollusks and placed into their class, the Pelecypoda, because shell diversification is not one of their outstanding attributes. In size they range from about 1 mm to 1 m, the largest form being the giant clam of the South Pacific atolls. Although some live in lakes, ponds, or rivers, the vast majority are marine inhabitants; there they commonly occur in the shallow waters along the shore, but a number of forms descend to depths as great as 5,000 m. Most live on muddy or

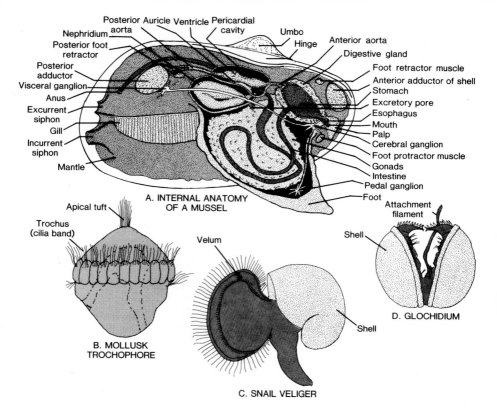

Figure 14.9 *Structure of pelecypods.*

sandy bottoms, where they move along on the edges of the partly opened shell, pushing themselves by their long, muscular foot. A number of others become permanently attached to submerged rocks, pilings, or other objects, a few drill burrows into rock or submerged wood, and some like the scallops can swim actively about.

Structural Organization

The basic pattern of organization of bivalves is relatively simple. If one valve is carefully removed, the thin but rather resistant mantle is exposed, at one end of which two sets of folds may be noted (fig. 14.9, A). These folds on one flap of the mantle coincide with those of the second to form two tubes of various lengths, depending on the type. In most clams and oysters, the siphons, as the tubes are called, are short and are not protrusible; on the other hand, in such species as the razor clams that bury themselves deeply, the siphons when in use protrude for a foot or more. Between the two flaps of the mantle is the mantle cavity, in which the gills, foot, and labial palps are located, as well as the body proper, or visceral mass. Muscles for closing the valves and for positioning the foot also are visible here (fig. 14.9, A).

The gills are subject to much variation among the pelecypods and often serve in food gathering as well as in gas exchange. Typically, each of these is an elongate sheet, suspended from the floor of the visceral mass and comprised of numerous so-called filaments. The gill is a refolded structure, so that in cross-section it is W-shaped, the filaments being continuous from one side to the other. Inside these are the blood vessels that carry out the actual gas exchange processes; however, much variation exists, both in superficial and internal organization. One other feature characterizes the external surfaces of the gills—a dense coat of cilia that serve in two functions. The first is that of keeping the surface clean of debris which might interfere with respiration—the importance of this function becomes clear if it is recalled that the majority of species are mud-dwellers. The second is that of food gathering, for almost all pelecypods are filter-feeders, as described in the next paragraph.

Internal Anatomy

To understand the peculiar method of filter-feeding which these animals employ, it is first necessary to examine the structure of the *digestive tract*. The mouth is simply the open end of the short tubular esophagus that leads into a large saclike stomach (fig. 14.9, A). No radula is present nor are any salivary glands, but a large digestive gland surrounds the stomach. After emerging from one side of the latter organ, the intestines wind through the cavity of the foot and then reach along the dorsal surface before ending in an anus located near the excurrent siphon. In feeding, most pelecypods remove fine particles from the water brought in through the incurrent canal by means of the cilia that cover the gills, as mentioned earlier. These particles are then delivered to the palpi where the coarse ones are sorted out and rejected. The remainder, after entering the mouth, are moved by ciliary action through the esophagus to the stomach. Often this organ is subdivided into specialized areas, including some for sorting, others for digesting, and a groovelike part for transport into the intestines. Actually very little breakdown of the foodstuffs occurs in this organ, for in the so-called digestion areas, the particles merely pass through pores in the walls to enter the digestive glands, where they are broken down intracellularly. If by chance items that are too large or resistant enter the glands, they are eventually rejected and enter the intestine by way of the groove mentioned above. Here in this long coiled tube the final digestive processes are carried out enzymatically, while indigestible by-products pass out through the anus.

Unlike that of other mollusks, the *circulatory system* is largely a closed one. The heart lies in the pericardial cavity, a remnant of the coelom, and consists of a thin-walled auricle and a thick muscular ventricle. From the latter the blood flows both posteriorly through a major artery to the large adductor muscle and anteriorly through a second one to the digestive glands, returning by way of veins through the gills, mantle, and auricle. The pair of large, folded nephridia is closely associated with this system, and lies in another portion of the coelom. The intake pores, or nephrostomes, are located in the pericardial cavity, while the excreta leave through excretory pores in the mantle flaps.

The *reproductive system* is quite as simple in structure as it is in function. Most species have the sexes separate, with a pair of gonads located around the intestines in the foot. From these glands, the sperm or eggs leave by way of short ducts that open through genital pores in the mantle near the excretory pores. As a rule, fertilization occurs in the water, where the eggs develop into a veliger not unlike that of snails, except that the velum is circular, not bilobed (fig. 14.9, C). In some cases, however, the eggs are retained in the mantle cavity, where development takes place. Certain other forms, including the freshwater mussels, have the gills serve as a brood chamber. Rather than forming veligers, the eggs of mussels develop into glochidia (fig. 14.9, D), which spend a short parasitic existence on the gills of fishes.

EVOLUTION OF THE CEPHALOPODA

There are two good reasons besides size for choosing the present class to illustrate the origins of variety in the mollusks. In the first place, the squids and octopuses hold a particular fascination for most persons, and secondly, the history of the group is clearly documented in the fossil record. Some of the clarity stems from the unique shell, which besides fossilizing readily, can be identified with certainty. Like that of the modern chambered nautilus, the shell is divided internally by a series of transverse *septa,* through which a tube called a *siphon* extends (fig. 14.10, A). In addition, the exterior of the shell beneath the outermost horny covering is marked with transverse *sutures,* corresponding to the edges of the internal septa.

This group is represented first in the Ordovician, a period of the Paleozoic that began about a half billion years ago. In deposits of that age are found straight, conical shells known as *orthocones,* which have all the characteristics described above for members of this class (fig. 14.10, A). Since the fossil shells sometimes achieved a length of 15 feet, their inhabitants were by far the largest animals then in existence. Obviously still earlier forms must have existed in which the sutures, septa, and siphon were gradually developed, but nothing suggestive of these preliminary steps has been encountered in geologic deposits. The primitive straight cones later became slightly curved and subsequently increasingly more strongly so, until, among still later representatives, the typical spiralled condition was achieved (fig. 14.10, B–D).

During Devonian times, about 100 million years later, one branch showed the beginnings of a new modification, the function of which is difficult to deduce. Up to this point, the sutures had been straight, but with the advent of this branch, they began to undulate slightly. In still later fossil forms, the undulations were more pronounced; it is to this ancient group, the *nautiloids* (fig. 14.10, E), that the chambered nautilus of today belongs. Eventually the simple wavy sutures themselves became sinuous and led to the formation of a group of cephalopods called the *goniatites* (fig. 14.10, F). These creatures were highly successful, for they persisted for the more than 200 million years that remained in the Paleozoic. In the Mesozoic era which followed, the doubly sinuate sutures

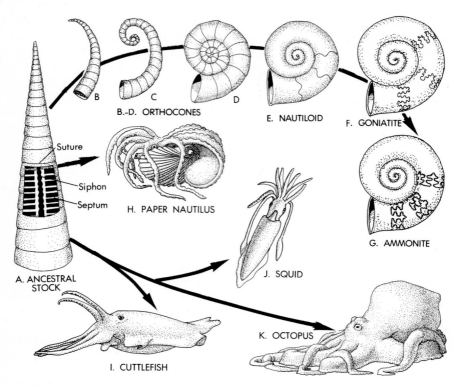

Figure 14.10 *Evolutionary paths among the cephalopods.* Evolution appears to have occurred along three major lines of specialization from a common ancestral stock (A). The first line (B–G) is marked by coiling of the shell and elaboration of the sutures. In the second (H), the shell became modified as an egg-container, whereas in the third (I–K), it became internal and, later, degenerate.

suddenly increased in complexity and became so intricate as to suggest the tracery of frost on a windowpane. The explosive speciation that followed resulted in more than 6000 known species of *ammonites,* as this type of fossil has been named (fig. 14.10, G). All during the 100 million years of the Mesozoic these animals were the dominant invertebrates of the seas and ranged in shell size from 4 inches or less in diameter to nearly 15 feet. Yet at the end of that era, all the ammonites, goniatites, and other advanced forms disappeared, leaving only the ancient line of nautiloids to survive to the present.

Other types of specializations were acquired by descendants of the Ordovician stock; as these are not well supported by fossil forms, the modern species must be used in suggesting what probably occurred. Along one path of evolution, represented today by the paper nautili (fig. 14.10, H), the shell is not attached to the body by muscles as is usual and is present only in the female. This is held around the body to provide protection, a specifically adapted pair of tentacles being used to hold it in place. In addition, the shell serves as a depository for the eggs, where they remain until hatched.

The third and final line of development which began in the same ancestral stock is marked by the increasing muscularity of the mantle, which provides greater speed in swimming. As the ability of these cephalopods increased to escape attack by taking flight, the shell was no longer needed for protection but became more and more a handicap. Consequently, among successively higher stages it is gradually reduced in size. In early representatives the mantle then surrounded the reduced shell, so that eventually it became internal, as in the cuttlefish of today (fig. 14.10, I). Among still more advanced forms like the squids, the shell is reduced to a featherlike rod known as the pen, while the true octopuses at the very end of the branch lack the shell entirely (fig. 14.10, K).

EVOLUTIONARY SUMMARY

With the discussion centered on but a single phylum, a evolutionary summary must be brief indeed, and the present instance is no exception. Brevity, however, does not necessarily contribute to clarity, so the evolutionary history and, particularly, the origins of the phylum Mollusca remain quite obscure. The trochophore larva that appears briefly during embryological development suggests, along with a number of other traits, that the beginnings were close to those of the Annelida. Whether they arose independently from the early trochophore or after that ancestral stock had developed some annelid traits cannot be decided at present (fig. 14.9). Nevertheless the derived type soon acquired some distinctive molluscan traits, especially in the form of a small shell that developed on the lower aboral surface. The acquisition of this characteristic brought into existence the veliger larva typical of the phylum. Much of the subsequent diversification into five classes has resulted secondarily from modifications in the growth of the shell. Usually the shell remained external and single as it increased to conceal most of the growing larva, as in the Amphineura and Gastropoda. In the Pelecypoda, however, a hinge formed in the mid-dorsal region, so that a bipartite shell is formed, in which the young is entirely surrounded. The shell in some cephalopod larvae is itself enclosed within the animal as a consequence of the mantle growing over it.

QUESTIONS FOR REVIEW AND THOUGHT

1. Which characteristics of its allied phylum, the Annelida, are missing or greatly reduced in the Mollusca? Which appear unique to the Mollusca? Why or why not may the shell of a molluscan be considered to be an exoskeleton?

2. Chracterize the six classes of mollusks. Which one appears to show the greatest diversity?

3. In what ways is *Neopilina* of particular importance to biologists. Describe the chief anatomical features and then state which appear to indicate a degree of segmentation.

4. To what class do the chitons belong? What are their chief distinctive features? Do these really characterize all the members of this class? Explain your answer. How do the wormlike members differ from solenogasters? On what basis might the latter animals be placed into the Polyplacophora? What justification is there for treating them as a separate class?

5. What are the principal traits of the gastropods? Which of those you have named do not apply to all the members of this class?

6. Name the three subclasses of gastropods. On what characteristics are they primarily distinguished?

7. What internal structures most clearly indicate the effects that the coiling of the shell has had upon the internal organization of snails?

8. Describe the habits of tooth-shells. Remembering that the boat-shaped foot is a highly muscular organ, how do you suppose it might serve in burying these animals?

9. List as many common names of representative types of pelecypods as you can. Which are edible? What members do you suppose could be harmful to the human economy?

10. Name the most important distinctive features of the Pelecypoda. In what ways is the digestive tract distinct from that of all other mollusks? What are some of the peculiarities that exist in the functioning of this system? What striking differences in internal structure do you find between the pelecypods and gastropods?

11. Describe the chief developmental features of mollusks, and name the several larval types you have noted. Which type occurs in all the more important classes? Which is found in only a limited number of pelecypods? Which is harmful to a degree? How does the veliger of gastropods differ from that of pelecypods?

SUGGESTIONS FOR FURTHER READING

Anderson, W.A., and P. Personne. 1976. The molluscan spermatozoan: Dynamic aspects of its structure and function. *American Zoologist,* 16:293–314.

Arnold, J.M., and L.D. Williams-Arnold. 1976. The egg cortex problem as seen through the squid eye. *American Zoologist,* 16:421–446.

Cousteau, J.Y., and P. Diolé. 1973. *Octopus and squid. The soft intelligence.* Translated from the French. Double Day and Co., Inc., Garden City, New York.

Denton, E.J. 1974. On buoyancy and the lives of modern and fossil cephalopods. *Proc. Roy. Soc. London,* B185:273–299.

Hart, A.D. 1978. The onslaught against Hawaiian tree snails. *Natural History,* 87(10):46–57.

Lawrenz-Miller, S. 1977. Locomotion in gastropod mollusks and evolution of the brain. *Ann. N.Y. Acad. Sci.,* 227:26–34.

Linsley, R.M. 1978. Shell form and the evolution of gastropods. *Amer. Sci.,* 66:432–441.

Lowenstam, H.A. 1978. Recovery, behaviour, and evolutionary implications of live Monoplacophora. *Nature,* 273:231–232.

Luchtel, D.L. 1976. An ultrastructural study of the egg and early cleavage stages of *Lymnaea stagnalis,* a pulmonate mollusc. American Zoologist, 16:405–419.

Solem, A. 1974. *The shell makers: Introducing mollusks.* New York, John Wiley and Sons.

Willows, A.O.D. 1973. Learning in gastropod mollusks. In *Invertebrate learning,* ed. W.C. Corning, J.A. Dyal, and A.O.D. Willows, volume 2, p. 187–271. New York, Plenum Press.

Willows, A.O.D., D.A. Dorsett, and G. Hoyle. 1973. The neuronal basis of behavior in *Tritonia.* I. Functional organization of the central nervous system. *J. Neurobiol.,* 4:207–237.

The
Echinodermata

15

In contrast to the annelid-arthropod branch, in which a number of adult structural features and embryonic developmental traits lend a degree of credibility to the suggested relationships, the second coelomate line of ascent brings together odd bedfellows indeed. On the surface, there appears to be no justification for considering a sea squirt to be kin to a sea lily, let alone treating a starfish as related to mammals. Yet the life histories of certain primitive stocks intimate that such conclusions, unbelievable as they may seen at first glance, are amply substantiated. But before these relationships can be discussed, the characteristics of the various organisms with the enterocoel type of body cavity (Chapter 5) must receive attention.

CHARACTERISTICS

The very first phylum that appears to have branched off the enterocoel line, the Echinodermata, sets the stage for the variety of animals that follows. Of all the taxa of organisms probably none is more peculiar than this one. Only here is a radial type of symmetry acquired by the adults secondarily from bilaterally symmetrical larvae, and its members alone possess a hydraulic system to operate expandible tubes that serve in locomotion. All 8,000 known living species are bottom-dwellers in the oceans and are universally arranged into five classes (table 15.1). In addition, innumerable fossil forms have been described, including representatives of five extinct classes.

Morphology

Although highly divergent from the other phyla and specialized along five separate lines, the modern echinoderms within each major division are remarkably undiversified. Perhaps this lack of important modification helps to account for the relative paucity of living representatives.

In addition to the hydraulic mechanism mentioned above, called the *water-vascular system,* and the extensible *tubefeet* (fig. 15.1), a number of other traits are unusual. First among these is the skeletal system, which is of the endoskeletal type, found elsewhere only among the vertebrates; in the present animals it is also distinctive in generally consisting of plates. These plates, made of calcium compounds, interlock to form a sort of shell, or *test;* in starfish and most classes the plates are moveable but in the sea urchins they are rigidly attached to one

Table 15.1   The Modern Classes of Echinodermata

		Classes
Characteristic	Crinoidea	Holothuroidea
Position of oral surface	Upward	On one end
Body form	Spherical or ovoid with numerous tentaclelike brachioles; often stalked	Elongate, cylindrical
Tubefeet	Primarily food-catching; on upper surface of arms	Locomotory, not in grooves; sometimes absent
Endoskeleton	Of immovable plates	Of scattered ossicles
Larvae	Doliolaria	Auricularia and doliolaria
Common names	Sea-lilies	Sea cucumbers

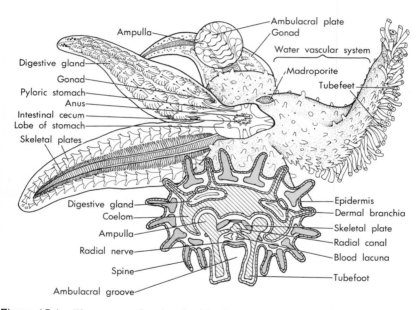

Figure 15.1   *The structural traits of echinoderms.*

another. Among the sea cucumbers the skeletal plates are replaced by small ossicles embedded in the dermis. This same group also lacks another feature of the skeleton present in all the others, the spiny projections on which the technical name of the phylum is based (*echino,* meaning "spiny," and *derma,* "skin").

The circulatory system is peculiar too, for the blood, instead of flowing through vessels, travels through channels in the coelom. These channels, called *lacunae* because they lack complete walls, are especially well developed in the

Asteroidea	Echinoidea	Ophiuroidea
Downward	Downward	Downward
Starlike or discoidal, with 5 or more arms	Globular or discoidal; often covered with long spines	Starlike, with 5 slender arms
Locomotory, in grooves on oral surface of arms	Locomotory, not in grooves	Reduced to sensory papillae, not in grooves
Of movable plates	Of immovable plates	Of movable plates
Bipinnaria and brachiolaria	Pluteus	Pluteus
Starfish	Sand dollars, sea urchins	Brittle stars, sea baskets

sea cucumbers and sea urchins, in association with the digestive tract. Hence, the blood more than likely aids in the distribution of digested material. Probably, along with the body wall in general, it assists also in excretion and respiration, as special organs for these functions are lacking. For many years no heart was known to exist in the echinoderms, but recently one has been demonstrated to be present in the so-called axial gland, located close to the water-vascular system.

Except among the sea cucumbers, in which the tract extends throughout most of the body's length, the digestive system is quite short. Rather than the intestine providing the bulk of the system as in other animals, the stomach along with its associated glands is the largest organ. This condition stems from the manner of feeding. By way of illustration, the starfish, whose principal food consists of bivalves, forces open a mollusk shell and everts its stomach around the prey. Then the digestive fluids are poured out and the enzymes permitted to act upon the bivalve's tissues. When these are sufficiently broken down, the stomach and its enclosed digested materials are retracted into the body.

Reproduction

Little that is distinctive exists in the basic processes of reproduction. Except in the few hermaphroditic species of sea cucumbers and brittle stars, the sexes are separate, and fertilization almost always takes place in the seas. But the larvae resulting from the fertilized eggs are most remarkable.

Although most classes have unique larval types, these share far more characteristics than their diverse names indicate (table 15.1). Unfortunately, the earliest stages, which might resemble the trochophore, are passed within the egg, so their traits do not become apparent; consequently, even the simplest larva is already highly modified when first hatched. The most primitive type, known as the *auricularia* and found in the sea cucumbers, shows the beginnings of one striking peculiarity of echinoderm larval stages, the extension of the ciliated bands into folds (fig. 15.2, A) that project outward from the body. In this form, as in all other echinoderm larvae, the presence of a *hydrocoel*, or water sac, is a noteworthy feature. Beyond this basic larval type, two major branches of diversification may be considered to develop. Along the first of these, oddly enough, the ciliated folds are reduced in extent, so that the cilia become arranged to form a number of nearly horizontal rows encircling the body; this stage is represented by the *doliolaria* (fig. 15.2, B) characteristic of both the crinoids and sea cucumbers.

The second evolutionary trend is just the opposite, for the folds become greatly extended. In the *pluteus* larva of brittle stars and sea urchins (fig. 15.2, C), the ciliated lobes become so prolonged as to be armlike; four, six, or even eight pairs may be present, each supported internally by a slender skeleton. In contrast, the folds of starfish larvae not only elongate but also become intricate in arrangement and number. The first larva to develop (fig. 15.2, D, E), the *bipinnaria*, possesses eleven long arms; later, when three preoral ones in addition have formed, it is known as the *brachiolaria*. Regardless of type, the larva when mature undergoes marked metamorphosis in acquiring the adult body form. During the transition, the hydrocoel ultimately develops into the unique water-vascular system that characterizes the echinoderms as a whole.

THE CLASS ASTEROIDEA

The starfish of the class Asteroidea are certainly the most abundant and familiar members of the Echinodermata. Although the greatest diversity is to be found in the tropical seas, especially on coral reefs, some of the 2,000 known

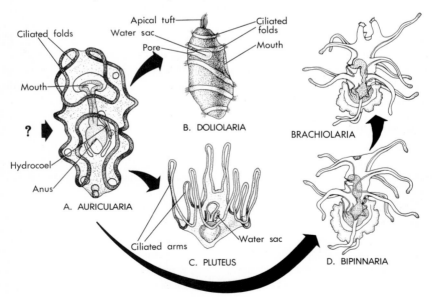

Figure 15.2 *Diversification among echinoderm larvae.*

species can be found in every ocean, even in the coldest waters. Aside from coral beds, rocky shores are the favored abode of the starfish, but these animals are by no means restricted in habitat preference.

As a general rule, starfish have five rays (arms) that grade into a central disk, but extensive variation exists in number and length of the rays, thickness of the body, and armature of the surface (fig. 15.3, A, B). Size, too, is variable, but remains within the range from 25 to 400 mm, one of the largest being the crown-of-thorns starfish (*Acanthaster placi;* fig. 15.3, C). A population explosion of the latter species aroused considerable concern among marine ecologists recently. For a while, it was feared that the resulting excessive grazing activities of these over-abundant animals would denude and permanently destroy some of the coral reefs of the Pacific, but the populations returned to normal proportions within a few years under natural influences. It is to be noted in the illustration that this, like a small number of others of the class, has 21 arms.

External Anatomy

As in other radially symmetrical animals, the two major surfaces are not referred to as dorsal and ventral (Chapter 5), but as oral and aboral, according to the location of the mouth. Since in starfish the two sides contrast strongly in their external features, it is advantageous to begin with the simpler, the aboral surface. The central disk of this part bears only one obvious structure peculiar to it, a small low knob, known as the madreporite, located near the junction of two rays. This contains pores through which water is filtered as it enters and leaves the water-vascular system. In addition, the anus is located at the very center of the disk, but is quite inconspicuous. The remaining features are found also on the rays. Among these is a characteristic trait of the phylum as a whole, the numerous spines that are attached to the skeletal plates, called ossicles. Around the bases of these are grouped tiny pedicellariae, which are of three main types, straight, crossed, and alveolar, the latter being located in shallow pits (fig. 15.4). All are really modified spines and have jaws that serve in defending the body surface from carnivorous worms or other pests and in removing bits of debris. Between the spines are soft, thin-walled extensions of the coelom, called papulae or dermal branchiae; these structures function in gas exchange (respiration), supplying the coelomic fluid with oxygen and permitting carbon dioxide to escape.

On the oral side of the disk is the very large mouth, surrounded by a soft membranous peristome and a number of spines. Each ray medially is occupied by a broad, deep ambulacral groove, in which are found the very numerous, slender tubefeet (fig. 15.5), arranged in either two or four rows, depending on the species. At the tip of each ray is a reddish spot, called the optic cushion, in which are a number of simple ocelli.

Internal Structure

Within the disk and the rays alike is the *digestive system* (fig. 15.1), filling most of the interior; yet, in spite of its extensiveness, this system is markedly

Figure 15.3 *Diversity of form among starfish.* A. The aboral surface of this five-rayed sea star (*Astropecten* sp.) resembles tooled leather. B. A pincushion starfish (*Culcita* sp.) lacks rays and is thick bodied. C. The crown-of-thorns star (*Acanthaster plancki*) underwent a population explosion that damaged a number of coral atolls through over-grazing of the coral animals. All three species occur on the Great Barrier Reef of Australia.

simple. The mouth leads directly into a large, saclike cardiac stomach, which in turns opens into the smaller, rather flattened pyloric stomach. As intestines are absent, the latter terminates directly in the anus, stated earlier as being at the center of the disk. From the pyloric stomach a cylindrical tube runs to each ray, where it branches into two. In turn, the branches send out myriads of pouches to form what is referred to collectively as a pyloric caecum; the number of such caeca present, of course, corresponds to the number of rays.

The *water-vascular system* can be followed readily. From the madreporite may be found a long, hard tube called the stone canal that runs towards the oral surface where it connects to a ring canal around the mouth. From that central ring one radial canal extends to each ray, from which in turn brief lateral canals attach to the tube feet (fig. 15.1). The individual tubefeet are contracted and extended by means of an ampulla located on their tips, and their outer ends are provided

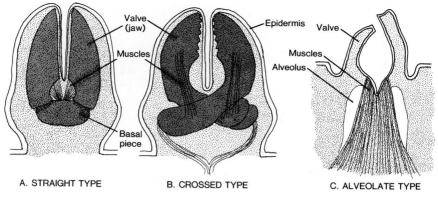

A. STRAIGHT TYPE   B. CROSSED TYPE   C. ALVEOLATE TYPE

Figure 15.4   *The types of pedicellaria of starfish.*

with a sucker that can be securely attached to such firm objects as rocks or shells of mollusks.

In starfishes the *nervous system* consists of three poorly integrated divisions. The first of these, the *oral nervous system,* is closely associated with the water-vascular system and consists largely of a circumoral ring surrounding the mouth. In addition, this ring sends out a radial nerve to each ray, located just under the corresponding radial canal. The second, the *deep nervous system,* is made up of a double circumoral ring immediately above that one just described, which gives off paired branches placed on each side of the radial nerves. The third, the *aboral system,* begins in an anal nerve ring and sends out a nerve cord along the dorsal surface of each ray. Although nerve nets interconnect the three divisions, a central control unit, such as a brain or ganglion, is conspicuously absent.

Sexes are separate in the Asteroidea, but their *reproductive systems* are identical, the type of gonad present being distinguishable only by microscopic examination. A pair of gonads is found near the base in each ray, located somewhat dorsally; usually these glands are rather small, except during breeding season when they become quite extensive. No oviducts or sperm ducts are present, as the organs simply open through minute pores in the body wall of each ray on the aboral surface. Thus their products are discharged directly into the sea, where fertilization occurs, usually during early summer. In a certain few species, however, the females brood their eggs by cupping their bodies over the egg mass; here they remain without feeding until the eggs have hatched. Usually such forms have larger eggs, containing more yolk than those of nonbrooding species, and deposit only a few hundred eggs or less, in contrast to the millions released by the others.

Locomotion and Feeding Habits

The means of locomotion in starfishes is particularly distinctive. Since much of their behavior is manifested in this manner, extensive attention has been given to the water-vascular system, tubefoot action, and the coordination of their parts—which is considerable in spite of the relatively poor nervous system. Con-

Figure 15.5 *Tubefeet of a starfish.* The large tubefeet in an ambulacral groove of the crown-of-thorns starfish are shown.

trary to popular notion, the tubefeet do not pull the starfish along, except on vertical surfaces, but they provide a stepping action that exerts a push. During locomotion a tubefoot is extended outwards until it contacts the substrate; then the central area of the sucker is contracted to produce a vacuum, and mucus is secreted to assist in securing a tight hold. Still fully extended, the tubefoot is then swung inwards, thereby moving the animal as though each were a leg. When the movement is completed, the vacuum is broken to release the grip of the sucker, and the tubefoot is extended outwards once more to repeat the entire operation.

In these activities the tubefeet of the entire animal participate—even those out of contact with the substrate undergo movement in a coordinated fashion. If, however, the circumoral ring of the oral nervous system is transected on each side of a radial nerve, the tubefeet of that ray move entirely out of harmony with those of the others. Perhaps they may work in an opposite direction or become active while the others are quiescent. If a ray is completely detached from the body, its tubefeet carry out locomotion in normal fashion, although usually the rate of progress is slower than ordinarily.

The water-vascular system is also of great importance in feeding. As a whole starfish are carnivorous and generally take any animal food. While they appear to show preference for clams and oysters, they readily accept snails and various crabs and even injured and dying fish. In some species, small mollusks are swallowed whole; when the contents of these have been digested, the shells are ejected through the mouth, for the anus is too minute to permit the passage of any

Figure 15.6 *A starfish with its stomach everted.* (Photo courtesy of Virginia Institute of Marine Science.)

except the finest indigestible particles. The most characteristic method of feeding, however, is by everting the stomach through the mouth (fig. 15.6). In a typical sequence of events, the starfish arches its body around a clam or oyster in such a way that its oral surface of the disk is adjacent to the aperature of the pelecypod's shell. The tubefeet then secure firm holds on the shell and the struggle begins, the mollusk attempting to keep the shell shut while the echinoderm does its best to open it. As a rule it is believed that the latter animal is capable of exerting a pull for a longer period of time than the shellfish, so that the latter finally becomes fatigued and the shell opens. It may be, however, that sometimes the tubefeet are able to open the shell just widely enough—a gap of only 1 mm would be sufficient—to permit the starfish's stomach to enter and thus speed the weakening of the bivalve. Once this organ has been everted around its prey, digestive enzymes are abundantly secreted; after they have had time to function, the predigested food is swallowed as the stomach is retracted.

THE CLASS OPHIUROIDEA

The brittle stars (fig. 15.7, A) of the class Ophiuroidea have received their common name because of the ease with which their rays become detached from the disk. As in the starfishes, around 2,000 species have been described, but since these animals tend to conceal themselves beneath rocks or in the sand, they are less familiar than the asteroids. Unlike the latter the brittle stars have no pedicellariae or papulae on the body surface, and ambulacral grooves are lacking. Tubefeet are few in number and are called tentacles in this group, as they play only a limited role in locomotion. While they do pass food to the mouth, they are largely sensory in function.

The disk and rays are sharply delimited in the brittle stars. On the former part, both the mouth and madreporite are to be found on the oral surface; here too occur the tentacles, arranged two at the base of each ray, which continue across the surface nearly to the mouth. Around the latter are five sharp teeth (fig. 15.7, B), between the bases of which may be seen the paired tentacles mentioned

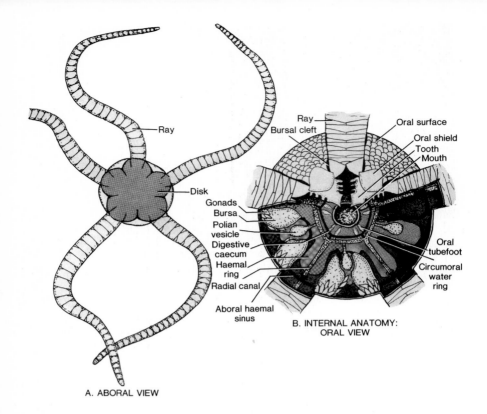

Figure 15.7 *Structure of a brittle star.*

above. The rays consist largely of ossicles that give them a segmented appearance and are often densely covered with spines; in some species, however, the surface may be quite smooth. In many cases the rays are branched and in the forms known as sea baskets, the branching occurs repeatedly (fig. 15.8). In the order Ophiurae, the skeletal ossicles are jointed in such a manner that arm movement is confined to the plane of the disk, but in the second one, the Euryalae, the arms are extremely flexuous in all directions.

Within the rays, the only visible parts are the coelom and a radial canal, the relatively few organs being concentrated within the disk. The *digestive system* consists of only the mouth and stomach, intestines and anus being wanting. The stomach is large, filling much of the interior and bearing ten large caeca. In addition, a pair of gonads can be noted closely associated with two bursae that lie at the bases of the rays. The bursae, unique to this class, are prominent sacs that open individually through large, slitlike openings on each side of the ray bases; through these slits water can enter to provide oxygen to the animals. The bursae also are employed as ducts through which the gametes can leave the body from the gonads, and sometimes they serve as brooding chambers for the eggs. The water-vascular system consists simply of a circumoral ring and five radial canals.

Figure 15.8 *A basket star, relative of brittle stars.* (Courtesy of the New York Zoological Society.)

THE CLASS ECHINOIDEA

Sharply distinctive body forms may be lacking in the brittle stars and basket stars, but that certainly is not the case with the sea urchins and sand dollars that make up the closely related class Echinoidea. Probably the most consistent features in the present taxon are the absence of rays and the strongly flattened oral surface of the body. To a large degree, the members fall into three categories, the sea urchins, whose nearly spherical bodies are usually covered with long spines (fig. 15.9, A, B), the sand dollars that are discoidal and provided with very short

A   B

Figure 15.9 *Some Caribbean sea urchins.* A. A group of long-spined sea urchins (*Diadema antillarum*) have denuded an area around a brain coral by over-grazing. B. This unusual species (*Tripneustes ventricosus*) camouflages itself with bits of seaweed. (Both photos courtesy of Dr. John C. Ogden, West Indian Laboratory.)

spines, and the heart urchins, with ovate bodies and moderate-sized spines. However, in technical treatments the class is subdivided into seven orders, largely on the basis of the plates that make up the skeleton, or test.

When the spines and other surface coverings have been removed, the test of a sea urchin is an attractive object, for the plates that comprise it are symmetrically arranged, as are the tubercles to which the spines had been attached. Five double rows of very fine, ambulacral plates can be noted (fig. 15.10, A), toward their sides bearing minute pores through which tubefeet had projected in life. Between them are five double rows of interambulacral plates, and at the very top of this aboral surface is a disk of five genital plates, surrounding the centrally-located anus and each bearing a genital pore. In addition a madreporite is found on one plate. The oral surface of the test varies widely from order to order; the most important constant feature is the mouth and the membranous peristome that surrounds it. In the living urchin, a series of thin-walled extensions of the latter outline the mouth and serve as gills.

In sand dollars, the very fine spinules that cover the entire body permit surface features of the disk to show through. Particularly to be noted is the whitish pattern that resembles a five-petalled flower, produced by the very narrow ambulacral plates and the pores for the tubefeet. Also present in keyhole sand dollars are a number of slits called lunules, whose function remains unknown.

The habits of the members vary widely. Most are common to all seas of the world, usually in the off shore reaches, but a few descend to depths of 4,000 m or more. Sand dollars live just below the surface of sandy bottoms; if by accident they become exposed, they make a small heap of sand in front of them and then push themselves into it. Heart urchins have rather similar habits but show a preference for muddy bottoms, where they make burrows, the walls of which are supported with a mucous substance. As a whole, sea urchins do not burrow but conceal themselves in crevices of rocks; certain species, called boring urchins,

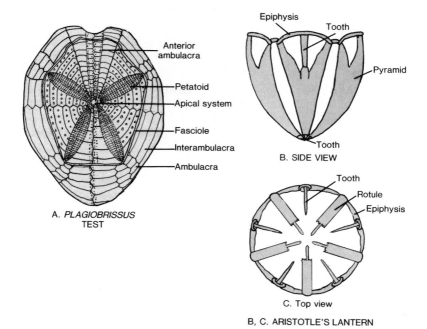

Figure 15.10 *Structural features of echinoids.*

enlarge the crevice with the teeth that form part of Aristotles lantern, one of the unique features of the internal anatomy of the echinoids (fig. 15.10, B, C). They also use the spines in such operations.

The spines are employed with unexpected dexterity by the animals in a number of activities. If accidentally exposed, members of certain species have been found able to cover themselves with fine gravel in several minutes by means of the spines and pedicellaria. In many types, the spines are of different sizes, longer ones being used primarily in locomotion and defense and short broader ones in excavation. Sometimes some of the long ones are exceedingly sharp and can inflict painful punctures, and in a few cases, venom glands are present that increase the seriousness of such wounds.

THE CLASS HOLOTHUROIDEA

The sea cucumbers of the class Holothuroidea are marine animals, in shape often well compared to their namesake-vegetable, but some are more snake-like in form, and others, including the 21 × 100 cm *Stichopus variegatus* from the Philippines, could more appropriately be likened to a watermelon. Although most of the 500 species are found in shallow water, a number occur at depths as great as 6,000 m.

These animals lack some of the attributes of the other members of the phylum, their body being soft and leathery, rather than firm, and spines are absent (fig. 15.11, A). What is even more notable is that the five-parted radial symmetry also is lacking, a character which is supposed to distinguish this phylum. While the body is essentially cylindrical, one side is flattened or otherwise modified to serve as a ventral surface, and the mouth tends to be ventral and the anus dorsal. Thus the developmental history of the body organization is quite complex. It begins in the early larva as bilaterally symmetrical but at metamorphosis becomes secondarily radial; then with subsequent growth, it tertiarily regains bilaterality.

Not only spines, but the pedicellaria and papulae of other classes are absent in the Holothuroidea, and tubefeet vary with the order. In the Aspidochirota, they are densely arranged on the ventral surface to form a creeping sole but are absent elsewhere. In another order, the deep-sea Elasipoda, the tubefeet are arranged in two or more longitudinal rows, in the Molpadonia they are reduced to papillae around the anus, and in the Apoda they are completely absent. All orders have a number of related but larger structures which serve as tentacles.

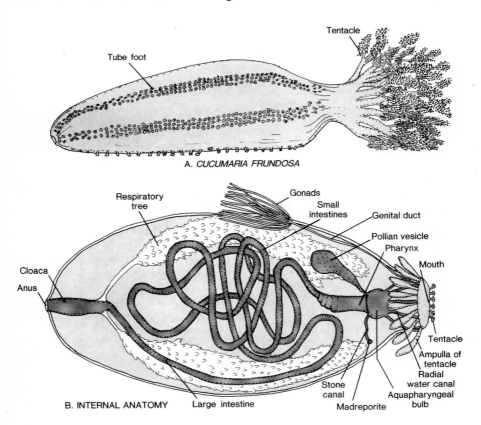

Figure 15.11 *The external and internal anatomy of a sea cucumber.*

THE CLASS CRINOIDEA

As a rule the 700 species of sea lilies and feather stars that represent the class Crinoidea today are confined to deeper waters (fig. 15.12), so are not as familiar as are the starfish and sand dollars. They nevertheless are quite abundant where they grow, for as many as 10,000 specimens have been taken in a single haul of a deep-sea net. While the class is relatively small today, it was exceedingly diversified during the Mississippian period about 340,000,000 years ago, for more than 5,000 fossil species have been described, arranged in four orders. Only one of the latter survives today, however, the Articulata, to which all extant species belong.

The body of all crinoids consists of a corona and a stalk, the latter part in feather stars being shed at the close of the juvenile stage. The corona is inverted, so that the aboral surface, which is covered by a calyx of tight-fitting ossicles, is associated with the stalk or its remnant. The oral surface, or tegmen, is largely membranous, usually having fine ossicles embedded in the softer parts. At the junction of the aboral and oral surfaces a series of five rays arises; often these are repeatedly branched, so that as many as 200 may be present. On each of the ossicles that comprise the individual rays is a pinnule, made of finer ossicles and sometimes branched. Extending to the mouth on the oral surface of each ray is an ambulacral groove, the epidermal lining of which bears numerous cilia instead of

Figure 15.12 *A patch of comatulid sea lilies.* This photograph of the sea bottom was taken at 2000 ft. depth off the Galicia Bank, Atlantic Ocean. (Courtesy of A.L. Laughton, National Institute of Oceanography, England.)

tubefeet; the latter structures are confined to the sides of the groove and the outer surface.

Various algae and protozoans are the principal food materials and are collected by a sort of filter-feeding mechanism. As the unicellular forms settle onto the surface of the rays, the tubefeet move them into the groove, in which mucus is actively secreted. This mucous rope and adhering particles is slowly moved toward the mouth by ciliary action. The digestive tract consists of a mouth, esophagus, intestine, rectum, and an anus, the latter being situated at the tip of an elevation of the oral surface. Usually the intestine is somewhat greater in diameter than the esophagus and in some cases bears several caeca.

As in most echinoderms, fertilization occurs in the seas. Generally in the separate sexes maturation of the gametes occurs simultaneously, but the males release the sperm first. The presence of sperm then induces females of the same species to release the eggs. For instance, a Pacific species called *Comanthus japonica* has been found to spawn between 3 and 5 P.M. on one day during the latter portion of October when the moon is either in its first or last quarter—even laboratory specimens behave in identical fashion.

QUESTIONS FOR REVIEW AND THOUGHT

1. Cite as many traits that are unique to the Echinodermata as you can. Can you name another phylum that has so many truly distinctive characteristics? Which feature do you think is most unusual?

2. Characterize the five classes of this phylum. Are tubefeet really a feature of the entire taxon? Explain your answer.

3. Describe the members of the class Asteroidea. How are tubefeet expanded and contracted? Tell how starfish travel and then how they feed on clams or oysters. What are the three types of pedicellaria and how do they differ?

4. In what ways do brittlestars differ from, and in what traits resemble, the starfishes? Would you say that the rays of brittle stars are homologous or analogous to those of starfish? Why do you think so?

5. Describe the three types of animals that comprise the class Echinoidea. In what ways does the structure of sea urchins more closely resemble that of starfish than it does the brittle stars, to which they are usually considered to be related?

6. Sea cucumbers differ in a number of characteristics from the other members of the phylum. List these distinctive traits and then state whether the class should accordingly be considered more primitive or more advanced than the rest.

7. Characterize the members of the Crinoidea. Describe the method of feeding in sea lilies.

8. Compare in detail the reproductive processes of the several classes.

9. Describe the various larvae that occur in this phylum and tell in which class or classes each type occurs.

SUGGESTIONS FOR FURTHER READING

Binyon, J. 1972. *Physiology of echinoderms.* New York, Pergamon Press.

Burnett, A.L. 1961. Enigma of an echinoderm. *Natural History,* 70(9):10–20.

Cameron, R.A., and R.T. Hinegardner. 1978. Early events in sea urchin metamorphosis; description and analysis. *J. Morph.,* 157:21–32.

Feder, H.M. 1967. Organisms responsive to predatory sea stars. *Sarsia,* 29:371–394.

Glynn, V.W. 1973. *Acanthaster:* Effect on coral reef growth in Panama. *Science,* 180:504–506.

Kanatini, H. 1973. Maturation-inducing substances in starfishes. *Annual Review of Cytology,* 35:253–298.

Meyer, D.L., and D.B. Macurda. 1979. Alive and well after millions of years. *Natural History,* 88(1):58–69. [On crinoids.]

Ogden, J.C., R.A. Brown, and N. Salesky. 1973. Grazing by the echinoid *Diadema antillarum* Philippe: formation of halos around West Indian patch reefs. *Science,* 182:715–717.

Weber, J.N., and P.M.J. Woodhead. 1970. Ecological studies of the coral predator *Acanthaster planci* in the South Pacific. *Marine Biology (Berlin),* 6:12–17.

Winsor, M.P. 1976. *Starfish, jellyfish, and the order of life: Issues in Nineteenth-Century science.* New Haven, Conn., Yale University Press. Chapters 2, 3 and 8 are especially recommended.

Chordate Origins 16

Between the invertebrate taxa and the vertebrate animals, there exists a series of forms that are transitional in a number of ways. In the first place, lacking a vertebral column as they do, they must be considered invertebrates; nevertheless, at least as larvae, they possess the structure around which the backbone eventually is based. In addition, all have some morphological parts that are typical of the invertebrates but possess others that are found elsewhere only among the vertebrates. In a sense, then, these provide an interlude between the vertebrate-haves and have nots, and a strange interlude it will be seen to be.

THE HEMICHORDATA

Like the onychophorans, the seventy known modern species of Hemichordata provide a link between phyla that would otherwise have forever remained undetected, for these soft-bodied forms are not represented in the fossil record. Moreover, in this case, the existence of living members is of particular importance, for the evidence of interrelationships is furnished largely by a minute larva.

Morphology

One of the most surprising discoveries for a beginning student is that the stock whose ancestors gave rise to the phylum to which he himself belongs is today represented by worms. These *acorn worms,* which spend their lives burrowing in the ocean bottom, are striking in appearance because of a peculiar adaptation for creeping. In the place where a head is usually located a thick *proboscis* occurs (fig. 16.1, A), the shape of which provides the basis for the common name. This organ and the elevated *collar* that lies just behind it can be distended with water and then deflated by muscular contraction. By becoming inflated and contracted in alternating fashion, the two structures function together to provide locomotion.

The principal adult trait that relates the present taxon to the Chordata is the presence of *gill slits* that open into the pharynx in both groups. A second feature possibly indicative of interrelationships is found in the nervous system. Although this system consists almost entirely of nerve tracts that are not completely differentiated from the body wall, in the dorsal region of the collar there is a hollow nerve cord like that of the chordates.

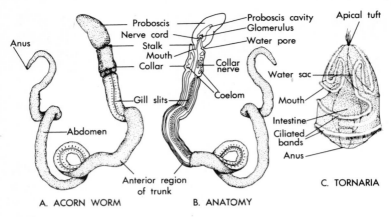

Figure 16.1 *An acorn worm and the larva.* The presence of gill slits in the pharynx suggests that these worms are related to the chordates.

The Larva and Relationships

While certain adult characteristics thus suggest a relationship between the Hemichordata and the Chordata, the larva is of the utmost importance in implying remote kinship with another phylum. The newly hatched form of the acorn worms, called the *tornaria* (fig. 16.1, C), shares many unique traits with the echinoderm larva. Among the common traits are the transparent body, undulant rows of cilia that become elevated as lobes, similar digestive tracts, and a marine habitat. In addition, each has a hydrocoel correspondingly located and of like origin. Since the majority of these characteristics are unique to these larvae, common descent is strongly indicated.

THE CHORDATA

The end products of the annelid line of development, the Arthropoda, have gained predominance among living things of today largely through diversification into nearly countless thousands of species, for no representative has ever achieved great body size. In contrast, the present phylum, including perhaps 70,000 living species, is relatively poor in numbers but has developed the most immense animals ever to inhabit either seas or land. Not that all its members are gigantic, for mice and hummingbirds too belong here, as well as certain fish which do not exceed an inch in length. But no terrestrial animal ever has surpassed the 90-foot *Diplodocus* in length, nor has any marine invertebrate even approached the 110-foot extent found in certain fossil sharks.

Only four structural characteristics are shared by the members of the Chordata (fig. 16.2), and these are frequently confined to the larva or embryo. Generally the phylum is divided into three subphyla (table 16.1), only one of which, the Vertebrata, is abundantly represented by extant forms. To show the diversification and interrelationships of the group as a whole, a synopsis of these major

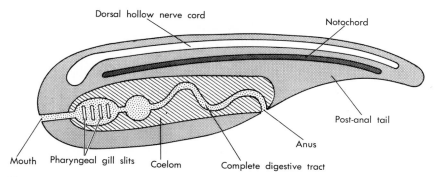

Figure 16.2 *Chordate characteristics.* Four traits distinguish the phylum Chordata as follows: nerve cord hollow, dorsally located; a notochord during part of the life cycle; gill slits in the pharynx; and a tail behind the anus.

Table 16.1   The Subphyla of the Chordata

Characteristic	Subphyla		
	Urochordata	**Cephalochordata**	**Vertebrata**
Notochord	Well developed in larva, usually reduced in adult	Well developed	Well developed at least in embryo or larva; usually reduced in adult
Vertebral column	Absent	Absent	Usually present in adult
Nerve cord	Extends to middle of length of the larval tail; reduced in adult	Well developed	Well developed
Tunic	Usually well developed	Absent	Absent
Atrium	Present	Present	Absent
Head	Absent	Absent	Present
Endostyle	Present	Present	Usually absent
Branchial sac	Present	Present	Absent
Habits	Sessile or free-floating, marine	Live in burrows, marine	Free living, rarely semi-parasitic; marine, fresh water, and terrestrial
Common names	Tunicates, ascidians, sea squirts	Lancelets	Fish, snakes, birds, mammals, toads, etc.

subdivisions will be provided first, while the following chapter will outline the most successful subphylum in greater detail.

The Subphylum Urochordata

The members of the subphylum Urochordata are a highly diversified lot of approximately 3,000 species, arranged in three classes (table 16.2). All are marine, but the components of the several taxa have widely divergent habits. The Larvacea and Thaliacea are predominantly deep-sea forms, the former occupying surface waters, the latter occurring at greater depths. On the other hand, the tunicates that comprise the third order, the Ascidiacea, are sessile and are found attached to rocks and pilings along the shore or on the ocean bottom. Varied though these types may be, they share several characteristics that unite them into this single subphylum, the more important of which is the confinement of the notochord to the tail, as implied by the taxon's name (Greek *ourá,* tail, and *chordé,* cord). In addition, all secrete a covering about themselves, and all are hermaphroditic.

The Class Larvacea

The class Larvacea contains fewer than 100 species of tiny forms, mostly around 5 mm in length, whose transparency of body adds to the difficulty of observing them in nature. Fortunately the animals secrete a gelatinous covering (a capsule) about themselves, many times their own size (fig. 16.3, A), that makes them easier to detect. Were it not for the tail, the larvaceans would be minute, indeed, for that appendage is perhaps five times as long as the body. These two parts bear a strange anatomical relationship to one another, for the tail is attached near the middle of one side, rather than at one end (fig. 16.3, B). It is an efficient organ of locomotion, as it is provided with strong musculature, the firm notochord, and a flat fin, or finfold, along the entire dorsal and ventral edges—quite like that of a tadpole in appearance, but much longer in proportion to the width.

The tail not only serves in locomotion but also provides circulating sea water when the animal is in its capsule. The latter structure varies in complexity from species to species, in some cases being little more than a bubble expanded around the mouth, but in one of the commoner genera, *Oikopleura,* it is quite elaborate. At the center is a large chamber in which the animal dwells, to which is connected an anterior and a posterior tube (fig. 16.3, A), through which water enters and leaves, respectively, under the propelling influence of the tail. Over the entrance is a fine filter, which is augmented by several filtering channels within the central cavity. In addition there is an emergency escapeway, through which the larvacean leaves when it abandons its covering, a rather frequent occurrence. After a brief period of freedom, the chordate rapidly secretes a new capsule by means of its epidermal glands.

The name Larvacea is in reference to a prevailing belief that the adults fail to undergo metamorphosis as an unknown ancestor is suspected to have done, and thus retain the larval form throughout life. Retention of juvenile characteristics is

Table 16.2 The Classes of the Subphylum Urochordata

Characteristic	Classes		
	Larvacea	Ascidiacea	Thaliacea
Adults	Tailed, actively swimming	Tail absent; sessile	Tail absent; active
Atrium	Absent	Large, opens dorsally	Large, opens posteriorly
Stolon	Absent	Simple, if present	Complex
Gill clefts	Simple, few in number	Numerous, divided into stigmata by external bars	Numerous, not divided
Habitat	Surface waters of the open seas	Close to shore	Deep sea

referred to as *neoteny,* and characterizes such amphibians as the axolotl of Mexico to be discussed in a later chapter. Two unusual features shared by all urochordates, as well as by some groups that follow, are found here, although in simple form. The *branchial sac,* or *branchial basket* is either a portion of the large pharynx as here (fig. 16.3, B) or makes up the entire and greatly expanded pharynx, as in the later classes. Typically this is distinguished by the presence of vascularized walls through which a large number of gillslits penetrate, often subdivided into pores called stigmata, but in the Larvacea only two gillslits occur. The second unique feature, the endostyle, is associated with this chamber, and is

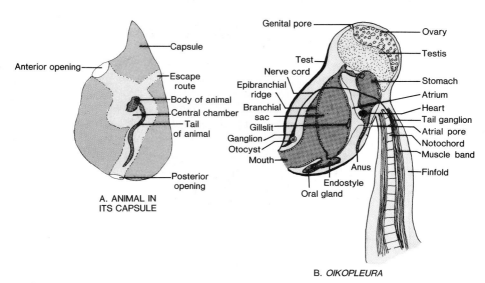

Figure 16.3 *Capsule and structure of a larvacean.*

located in the floor of the branchial apparatus in the form of an elongate groove bearing a dense covering of cilia (fig. 16.3, B). Together these parts form an elaborate filter-feeding device. After water has entered into the branchial basket from the mouth, the rate of flow is diminished, so that organ acts as a settling basin. Food particles present thus drop to the endostyle, which secretes a heavy mucous rope; this rope with the adhering particles then is propelled by the cilia into the intestines where the entire conglomeration is digested. In the present group, the water leaves by way of the two gillslits into a small cavity called the atrium, from which chamber it leaves through the atrial pore into the sea.

The Class Thaliacea

In habits the salpians that collectively form the class Thaliacea are not unlike the larvaceans, but on a much larger scale. Here, too, the animals inhabit transparent capsules as they swim about, feeding by filtering the sea water as they go. But there all resemblances cease. The adults are tailless and are shaped much as a barrel open at both ends (fig. 16.4), which resemblance is accentuated by the series of muscle bands that encircle the body like so many hoops. At the respective ends are the funnel-like oral and cloacal siphons, on each side of which are a series of broad tentacles. The former leads into the voluminous branchial sac, which is provided with a longitudinal endostyle and numerous stigmata. These open into the atrium, that typifies all the primitive chordates; this cavity is far more extensive than in the larvaceans and leads to the outside by way of the cloacal siphon. Relative to the pharynx, the remainder of the digestive tract is small indeed, for it consists of only an intestine having an anus that opens into the atrium. In addition a U-shaped heart is present but no vessels, the blood circulating through sinuses extending around the organs. A large and one or two small ganglia on one side and a series of radiating nerve cords represent the entire nervous system. Gonads that open into the atrium are present near the posterior end of the body.

Circulation of water through the animal for feeding is responsible also for locomotion through the seas, so that both activities occur concurrently. The muscular bands mentioned earlier contract rhythmically, forcing the water within the body outwards through the cloacal siphon. Upon relaxation of the muscles, the body wall resumes its normal dimensions, bringing water through the oral siphon. Thus these animals travel by jet propulsion at one end and vacuum at the other. The body wall, made up largely of a dermis overlaid by epidermal cells, secretes a tough tunic about itself. This envelope is made of a complex carbohydrate called tunicin, chemically related to cellulose; it is known to occur only among urochordates and hemichordates.

Development involves an unbelievably complex cycle of events. Fertilization occurs in the sea by gametes discharged from hermaphroditic individuals, the zygote becoming a tadpolelike larva (fig. 16.4, B). After growth is completed, the larva undergoes metamorphosis, losing the relatively short tail in the processes, including the notochord. Such sexually-produced transformed individuals, called oözooids (fig. 16.4, C), now reproduce asexually by budding on a special

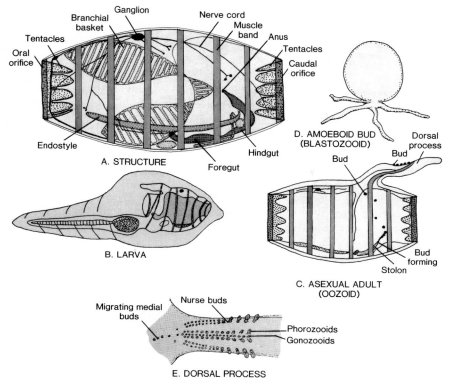

Figure 16.4 *Structure and life cycle of a salpian.*

ventral process termed a stolon. The resulting buds, or blastozooids, are tiny amoeboids that crawl about on the oözooid until they reach what is known as the dorsal process. Here they arrange themselves in three double rows, one set medially and one set on each side (fig. 16.4, E). The lateral rows never leave the parental body, but become modified to serve as nurse buds; the medial ones, however, develop into two additional types of buds, which join one another before breaking free. One type, the phorozoid, serves as a carrier for the second type, the gonozoid, which ultimately produces a sexually-reproducing individual. Thus there is an alternation of generations as in many plants, an asexual generation intervening between sexual ones. In these organisms, the unique feature is that five types of asexual individuals—one oözooid and four kinds of buds—are needed to produce one sexually reproducing animal.

The Class Ascidea

The tunicates of the class Ascidea are larger than the other members of the subphylum but rarely exceed 300 mm in length. Some colonies, however, may become a meter or more in diameter. These, as well as solitary species, are the most widespread of the urochordates, ranging from Arctic to Antarctic waters and from the shoreline to abysmal depths. Before the organization of the colonial types can be understood, it is necessary to examine the structure of a solitary type, for these animals possess some unusual features. A worn brown bag, attached to the substrate at one end and with two holes near the top, provides a close analogy to the external appearance of a tunicate. The wrinkled leathery covering is, of course, the tunic, made of tunicin as mentioned earlier, and provides protection to these otherwise defenseless creatures. Of the two holes, the uppermost leads into the incurrent (oral) siphon, whereas the lower one is the excurrent siphon or atrial pore, homologous to the cloacal siphon of salpians (fig. 16.5, A). If the tunic is removed, a more or less transparent body wall (or mantle) is exposed, composed of a thick dermis overlaid by a thin epidermis and provided with muscular bands running in diverse directions. The latter supply a degree of form to these skeletonless creatures and can propel a stream of water at an intruder through the atrial pore when the animal is exposed at low tide—hence, their common name, sea-squirts.

Internally the structure is not too dissimilar from the salpians, except for the U-configuration. The incurrent siphon leads into the branchial sac through an oral funnel, fringed with tentacles as in the Thaliacea. Here, too, is an endostyle lined with cilia that secretes a mucous rope to catch food particles. At the end of the branchial sac is a digestive tract, which is much larger than that of any other urochordate. As in the salpians, the gillslits are subdivided into numerous stigmata and likewise open into an atrium; the latter, however, is much more extensive and empties through the excurrent siphon. Nearby this exit are located both sets of gonads and their associated ducts, as well as a heart, lying in what little remains of the coelom. Since the genital pores and anus open near the excurrent siphon, that region of the atrial cavity is generally referred to as the cloaca.

Colonies are produced by individuals undergoing bud-formation, which processes are carried out in diverse manners, depending on the species. In such colonies the degree of structural intimacy among the members also varies widely, largely as a result of differing extents to which a common tunic and atrial cavity are shared. In the simplest types, the individual members (zooids) of a colony are budded off a stolon sent out by the parental members, forming loose colonies not unlike those of the Entoprocta in principle. A more advanced type has the new zooids arising in such a way that the tunic is partly shared, and in still more complex types, the tunic is completely shared by all the zooids. In the latter case, the colonies tend to be symmetrical, as in *Botryllus* (fig. 16.6). Some colonies formed in this way actually are free-swimming, although the zooids themselves are sessile, *Pyrosoma* perhaps being the commonest example. Here the minute animals form a dense colony, all the members of which are oriented in like fashion with their oral funnels outward and the atrial pores inwards around a common cloaca (fig. 16.6). Thus the whole colony forms a cylindrical mass, at one end with the cloacal opening surrounded by a velum which serves as a valve. Thus the movement of water through the individual zooids combines into a common jet stream that propels the entire colony from one place to another. Recently it has been discovered that alignment of the young individuals with the

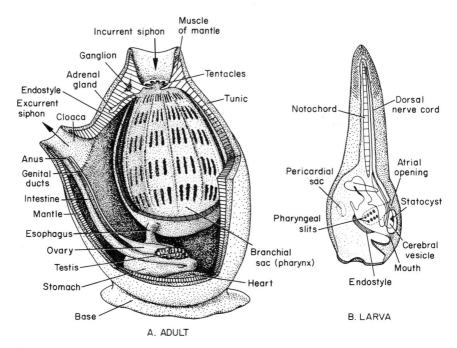

Figure 16.5 *The structure and larva of the tunicates.*

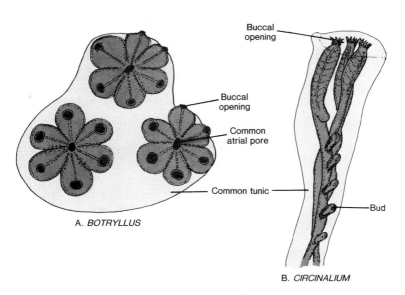

Figure 16.6 *Colonial representatives of the Ascidea.*

parent involves some sort of attractant or secretion, and results in some interesting behavior patterns. Several of the readings present the fascinating details.

Whether the eggs are fertilized by the same individual or not is still a moot point. All that is definitely established is that the fertilized eggs develop free in the sea water. Development is by radial cleavage through the usual series of steps, including a hollow blastula and gastrula and terminates in a tadpolelike larva, not unlike that of the salpians, except in having a longer tail (fig. 16.5, B). As there, the larva does not feed, so soon undergoes metamorphosis. The tadpole attached itself to the substrate, anterior end downwards, by means of the so-called anterior papillae, as shown. Here it undergoes a remarkable series of changes, partly arising from absorption of existing structures and partly by differential growth. The region between the attachment papillae and the mouth grows very rapidly, so that the mouth ultimately reaches the extreme upper end of the organism. In the meanwhile, the tail, including the notochord, muscles, fins, and nerve cord, undergo complete degeneration, leaving only a ganglion in place of the brain. Also during this period, the atrium increases manyfold in size and the pharyngeal gillslits become subdivided into stigmata.

The Subphylum Cephalochordata

When alive, the 75 to 200 mm long *lancelets* that comprise the subphylum Cephalochordata appear quite like small fish, but closer examination reveals that the eyes, opercula, and fishlike tail are absent. Nor do these animals behave strictly like fish, for during the daylight hours, they remain buried in sand, leaving only the anterior portion of their bodies exposed. Here in shallow waters of the oceans, they feed by means of a filtering device not too unlike that of the tunicates. At night, they emerge from the sand and actively swim about, but with the approach of dawn, they drill their ways into the sand head-foremost by rapidly vibrating the anterior part of the body. Progress into the sand is quite fast. After a few seconds of drilling, when about half the body is buried, the lancelets make a U-bend and continue burrowing until their heads emerge above the surface. The tunnels are strictly temporary structures, being abandoned at least daily; thus the walls are not supported by mucus nor cement of any kind.

Structure

In general terms, the structure of these lancelets is not unlike that of a tunicate but is housed in a fishlike body (fig. 16.7); however, a number of important features have been added. A noted zoologist many years ago pointed out that: "Though specialized in some particulars and degenerate in others, the lancelets represent a grade of organization not far removed from the main line of early vertebrate ancestors." Externally the peculiar segmentation provided by the muscle bundles (myotomes) is a striking feature. No head is to be seen, but a fold, called the oral hood, that bears a number of prominent cirri, marks the entrance into the mouth (fig. 16.7). The mouth leads into a cavernous branchial sac, which is provided with an endostyle along the ventral surface and a large number of gillslits on the sides. Unlike those of most of the urochordates, the gillslits are not subdivided into stigmata. Through these, water passes into an atrial cavity to emerge from the body through the atriopore.

The *digestive tract* is rather voluminous but straight, consisting of an intestine which opens through an anus and a caecum near its anterior end, here called the liver diverticulum. Above this lies the notochord, the main part of the skeletal system. In these animals it is unique in that it not only extends to the tip of the tail but also reaches the very anterior tip of the body—in other words it extends anteriorly through what should be the head. The name of the taxon, of course, refers to this peculiarity of structure. In addition, the fin rays found throughout the length of the finfold that encircles the body make up the remainder of the system. The nature of this finfold should be especially noted, because it enters into later discussions.

The *circulatory system* is entirely closed. Although no heart is present, it is quite similar in pattern to that of vertebrates. Blood is moved forward beneath the branchial sac by the contractile ventral aorta, much of it being diverted upwards to pass over the gillslits. Here no gills are present, the vascular surface itself serving in the gas-exchange processes. A number of dorsal aortas then conduct the blood posteriorly to the various organs of the body, including the myotomes.

The *excretory system* provides a strong link between the chordates and earlier invertebrates, for it consists of true nephridia particularly recalling those of the annelids. A number of these organs occur within the coelom along the walls of the branchial sac between the gillslits. Each nephridium consists of a folded

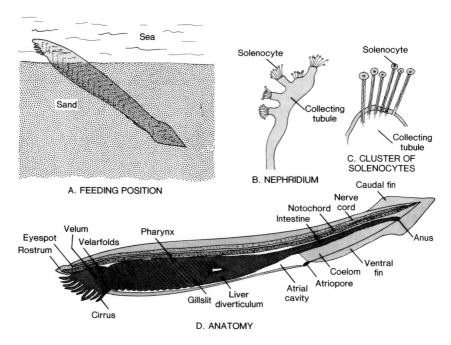

Figure 16.7 *A lancelet and its anatomy.*

L-shaped sac, bearing large numbers of solenocytes and opening into the atrium (fig. 16.7); waste products are received from the coelomic fluid, augmented by nearby blood vessels.

A *nervous system* consists largely of a hollow nerve cord that runs the length of the body just dorsad of the notochord. Although in the larva there is an opening to the outside that leads into the nerve cord, this, the so-called olfactory funnel, becomes closed in the adult. The anterior region of the nerve cord is generally referred to as the brain, but except for the enlarged cavity it contains and the eyespots, it is scarcely differentiated from the rest of the nerve cord. Actually the eyespot is more like an ocellus than a true eye. From this central system a number of sensory and motor nerves extend to the various parts of the body, many being segmentally arranged.

Reproduction and Development

In contrast to the urochordates, lancelets have the sexes separate. In both sexes the gonads, mere pouchlike derivatives of the coelomic walls, are segmentally arranged and can be noted externally from about the 10th to 30th somites. During summer these become enlarged and, when fully distended with ripe eggs or sperm at the arrival of breeding time, they rupture into the atrium. As a rule spawning takes place at sunset when both sexes simultaneously release their gametes into the open seas, where fertilization occurs. Here in subsurface waters development of the embryo is completed.

Development is radial and includes the usual hollow blastula, gastrula, and a coelom from enterocoelous origins (fig. 16.8). In the midgastrula stage, a peculiar series of steps occurs that characterizes the vertebrates, too. Externally the ectoderm of the dorsal region first becomes somewhat thickened into what is termed the neural plate. After this is formed, it sinks inward a bit as the ectoderm on each side and at the posterior end begins to grow over top of it (fig. 16.8). Inward growth of these neural folds, as they are called, continue until the plate is completely covered. Towards the close of these processes, the neural plate sinks inwardly still farther, but the sinking this time is confined to its midline, and a cavity is formed (fig. 16.8). The sides of the neural plate then rise dorsally and fuse at the top in such a way as to surround the cavity and create a tube—the dorsal hollow nerve cord. In longitudinal section, the successive changes can be noted to leave a neural pore open to the exterior at the anterior end and at the posterior end to produce a connection with the digestive tract, the so-called neurenteric canal. Further growth and elongation of the embryo soon leads into a free-swimming juvenile. Metamorphosis includes loss of part of the anterior region and movement of the mouth from the left anterior side of the juvenile to its definitive position. Moreover, the buccal funnel and cirri form, the gillslits become subdivided, and the gonads develop.

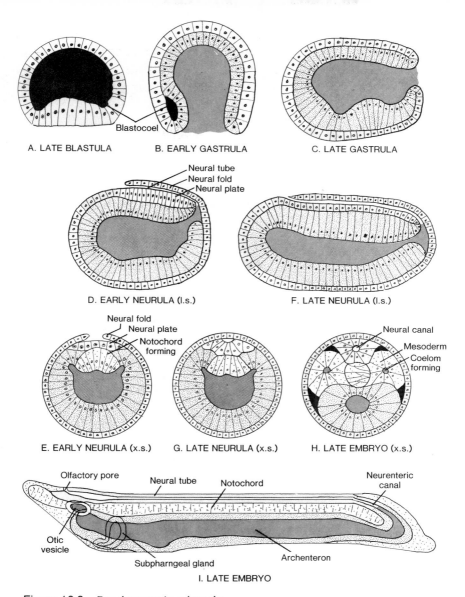

Figure 16.8 *Development in a lancelet.*

ORIGIN OF THE CHORDATA

Since the Chordata is an important phylum to mankind, its possible origins have received much attention, and many theories accordingly have been proposed. Included among the ancestral stocks supposed to have given rise to this line are members of nearly all the invertebrate phyla, including jellyfishes, flatworms, earthworms, horseshoe crabs, and those fossil arthropods known as trilobites. All these concepts have now faded into oblivion, yielding the field to two of more recent vintage, one based on the Nemertinea and the other in part on echinoderm larvae. This pair alone then needs to be considered.

Actually the nemertine theory was first advocated nearly a century ago, when a number of ribbon worm traits were pointed out that could represent the beginning of certain features of chordates. As will be recalled (p. 115), these marine animals have an elongate proboscis, housed when at rest in a proboscis sac that occupies much of the dorsal portion of the interior. This sac is enclosed by a strong muscular sheath, which upon contraction forcibly everts the proboscis to secure food (fig. 16.9). Because of its location and general structure, the sheath was suggested possibly to represent the primitive forebear of the notochord. Later, other zoologists proposed that the eight longitudinal nerve cords of the nemertineans might serve as a model for the origin of the hollow nerve cord of chordates. The two lateral and four ventral nerves supposedly atrophied, and the remaining two dorsal ones fused in such a way as to produce a tube.

For a while this theory became forgotten until in recent years it was readvanced in a more sophisticated fashion. This revised concept suggested a series of model steps to indicate in detail how such simple vertebrates as the hagfish (Chapter 17) might have been derived from the nemertinean order Hoplonemertina. The notochord itself was shown to be a complex organ in that it consists of an outer sheath made of a fibrous tissue, enclosing a cylindrical body of a gelatinous nature. Within the latter in turn is a median flattened fiber, known as the notochordal strand. On the basis of these data, the theory then advocates that the proboscis of these ribbon worms degenerated and, as it did so, the muscles of the outer sheath became noncontractile and eventually were converted into the fibrous sheath of the forming notochord. The cylindrical gelatinous body of the latter organ is conceived as having resulted from concurrent increase in viscosity of the fluid contained in the proboscis sac, and the central notochordal strand represents remnants of the former retractor muscle (fig. 16.9). The tongue worms and early chordates, like the tunicates and lancelets, are considered to have been derived along with the echinoderms from the hagfish by a series of degenerative steps.

In the second theory advanced by a number of theoretical zoologists, the chordates are considered to have had common ancestry with echinoderms, because of certain characteristics shared by the larvae of primitive members of both phyla. Among the traits common to the tornarian larva of the acorn worms and the early larval types of echinoderms are the oblique rows of cilia on a transparent body, that also bears an apical tuft. In addition, there is a pair of hydrocoels, or water sacs, present on the super posterior surface, which usually fuse into a single sac; this organ is of especial importance in these views because the hydro-

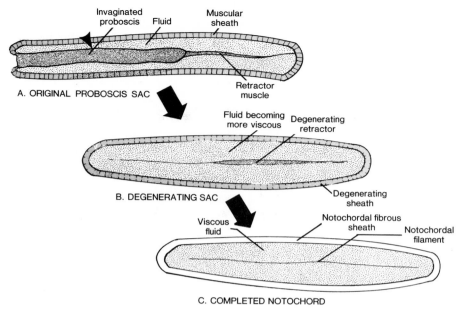

A. ORIGINAL PROBOSCIS SAC

Invaginated proboscis   Fluid   Muscular sheath

Retractor muscle

B. DEGENERATING SAC

Fluid becoming more viscous   Degenerating retractor

Degenerating sheath

C. COMPLETED NOTOCHORD

Viscous fluid   Notochordal fibrous sheath   Notochordal filament

Figure 16.9   *The nemertine concept of chordate origins.*

coel gives rise to some of the unique adult traits that characterize the several phyla. In the echinoderms, for instance, the sac grows around the larval digestive tract to form a ring canal; later this canal gives rise to five tentacles (tubefeet), from each of which grows a row of additional tubefeet as the larva matures. Thus in this phylum, the hydrocoel provides the basis for both the water-vascular system and the five-parted radial symmetry on the adults. Among the acorn worms the hydrocoel develops chiefly into the cavity of the adult proboscis, which it distends with water during locomotion.

However, in addition in the acorn worms, the hydrocoel becomes associated with the apical organ and its derivatives, and thus seems to play an elementary role in neural activities. Most likely it functions in olfaction to a degree, at least by bringing in particles of food and dissolved substances. Later this role can be deduced to have become enhanced in importance, because, as shown by urochordate tadpoles, the sac became enlarged and its walls thickened to the point that it grew partially through the back into the tail. In the cephalochordates, the lengthening continued, until it extended the entire length of the body and ultimately joined the digestive tract just before the anus to form the neurenteric canal, as is the case now in the larvae. This connection primitively would have increased the efficiency of the chemoreceptive apparatus by permitting sea water to flow into the olfactory funnel through the brain and neural cord to exit through the anus. In these animals, as in the vertebrates, the hydrocoel, greatly modified in structure, thus gradually became transformed into the chordate dorsal hollow nerve cord. As shown in the diagram, other chordate peculiarities underwent concurrent changes as the nervous system was thus developed (fig. 16.10).

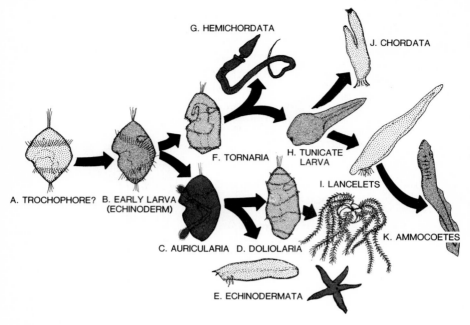

G. HEMICHORDATA

J. CHORDATA

A. TROCHOPHORE? B. EARLY LARVA
(ECHINODERM)

F. TORNARIA

H. TUNICATE
LARVA

I. LANCELETS

C. AURICULARIA D. DOLIOLARIA

K. AMMOCOETES

E. ECHINODERMATA

Figure 16.10 *Steps in the echinoderm concept of chordate origins.*

QUESTIONS FOR REVIEW AND THOUGHT

1. What are the distinctive features of the phylum to which acorn worms belong? In what traits do they show possible kinships to the chordates?

2. In what ways are remnants of formerly large taxa, such as the Hemichordata, of particular importance in biology? Make a list of all the metazoan taxa that could be considered ''living fossils'' like these acorn worms.

3. What are the four distinctive traits of the phylum Chordata? Which of these has enabled some of its members to achieve great body size? Name the three subphyla and tell how they are distinguished from one another.

4. Name the three classes of urochordates. Which is the most complex in structure? In reproductive habits? Which is the most active as adults? Which has swimming colonies?

5. What is meant by neoteny?

6. Describe the life cycle of a salpian. In what two ways do tunicates reproduce?

7. Give the chief characteristics of the lancelets. In what ways do they resemble fish? How do they differ from the urochordates?

8. Outline the nemertine theory of chordate origins. List the factual evidence that seems to support the concept. Is there any factual evidence that the urochordates and lancelets are degenerate fish?

9. Give the principal features of the echinoderm theory of chordate origins. In what characteristics does the tornarian larva resemble those of echinoderms? What other evidence might support this concept?

SUGGESTIONS FOR FURTHER READING

Barrington, E.J.W. 1965. *The biology of the Hemichordata and Protochordata.* San Francisco, W.H. Freeman & Co., Publishers.

Bone, Q. 1960. The origin of the chordates. *J. Linn. Soc. Lond., Zool.,* 44:252–269.

Dillon, L.S. 1965. The hydrocoel and the origin of the chordates. *Evolution,* 19:436–466.

Fell, H.B. 1948. Echinoderm embryology and the origin of chordates. *Biol. Rev.,* 23:81–107.

Jefferies, R.P.S. 1975. Fossil evidence concering the origin of the chordates. *Symp. Zool. Soc. London,* 36:253–318.

Jensen, D.D. 1963. Hoplonemertines, myxinoids, and vertebrate origins. In *The lower Metazoa,* ed. E.C. Dougherty, p. 113–128. Berkeley, Calif., University of California Press.

Jollie, M. 1977. The origin of the vertebrate brain. *Ann. N.Y. Acad. Sci.,* 299:74–86.

Rickards, R.B. 1975. Palaeoecology of the Graptolithina, an extinct class of the phylum Hemichordata. *Biol. Rev.,* 50:397–436.

Russell, G.J., and J.H. Subak-Sharpe. 1977. Similarity of the general designs of protochordates and invertebrates. *Nature,* 266:533–536.

Stebbing, A.R.D. 1970. Aspects of the reproduction and life cycle of *Rhabdopleura compacta* (Hemichordata). *Marine Biology,* 5:205–212.

Webb, J.E. 1975. The distribution of Amphioxus. *Sym. Zool. Soc. London,* 36:179–212.

Willmer, E.N. 1975. The possible contribution of the nemertines to the problem of the phylogeny of the Protochordates. *Symp. Zool. Soc. London,* 36:319–345.

The Earlier Vertebrates

17

Probably nowhere in the zoological world are the processes of evolution better illustrated than among the Vertebrata. Proceeding from the simpler to the more advanced representatives of this subphylum presents a clear picture of the successive stages that occurred in their progress. In brief, the account shows how the vertebrate animals first became increasingly adapted for an active aquatic existence; then after the marine and freshwater habitats had been fully mastered, later members of the taxon invaded the lands and gradually became more completely adapted for that environment. This, the first of two chapters concerned with the broad aspects of the taxon, is devoted to the strictly aquatic and transitional classes, while the second reviews the terrestrial forms.

The fishes, then, are the subject for much of the present discussion—fish of all sorts, with and without jaws, scaled and scaleless, backboned and otherwise, and even finned and finless. These are followed by the frogs, toads, and other amphibians that provide a glimpse into the first major steps required in converting aquatic adaptations to terrestrial ones. Thus a great diversity of forms are embraced within these few pages.

THE CLASS CYCLOSTOMATA

The two alternative names available for this class, Cyclostomata and Agnatha, are equally descriptive of one of the outstanding characteristics of its members, the circular, jawless mouth. These terms are derived respectively from the Greek *cýclos,* circular, and *stóma,* mouth, and *a,* not, *gnáthos,* jaw. As a whole, the taxon is distinguished more by what it lacks than by its possessions, for no scales are present here, and neither are paired fins nor a vertebral column. Bony tissue, too, is absent, as is a stomach. Two major types of eel-like fish are included here, classified as either subclasses or orders: lampreys, the species of which are more or less equally divided between marine and freshwater forms, and hagfishes, which are entirely marine (table 17.1).

The Lampreys

The approximately 30 species of lampreys that represent the Petromyzontia are somewhat more advanced structurally than are the hagfish of the second subdivision in some particulars but more primitive in others. For example, the finfold that was seen to be continuous in the lancelets is divided dorsally into two strong fins, and only seven pairs of gillslits, each opening separately to the outside, penetrate the pharyngeal wall (fig. 17.1). Thus one salient feature of the tunicates and cephalochordates, the atrium, can be noted to be absent in the present animals, as is the case also with the remainder of the phylum.

Habits

Lampreys, which range in length to nearly 500 mm, have received much attention since their depredations to fish during the 1840s and 1950s nearly ruined commercial fisheries in the Great Lakes. Much of the damage arose through the feeding of the common species, *Petromyzon marinus,* of which several populations exist. Some of these inhabit the two sides of the Atlantic Ocean, while others are inhabitants of the Finger and Great Lakes, presumed to be landlocked since the recession of the Great Ice Sheet about 10,000 years ago. Typically adults feed by attaching themselves to the lower sides or ventral surface of a fish by means of their suckerlike mouth, aided by the piston-action of their thick tongue. Here with the sharp horny teeth that line the buccal cavity, they rasp away the flesh to obtain blood, using an anticoagulant to promote free bleeding. When fully gorged, they release their hold, but frequently the wound they make

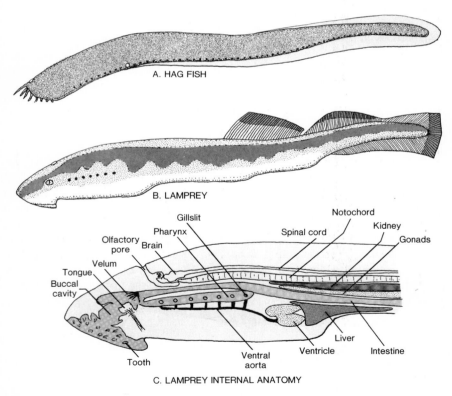

Figure 17.1 *Cyclostome representatives and their structure.*

Table 17.1 The subclasses of Cyclostomata

Characteristic	Subclass	
	Petromyzontia	**Myxinoidea**
Dorsal fin	Divided	Continuous or absent
Eyes	Present	Vestigial
Oral cavity	Funnel-like, with numerous horny teeth	Suctorial, only 1 horny tooth
Oral tentacles	Absent	6 present
Gills	7 pairs, with separate ducts	6–14 pairs, with a common excurrent canal
Semicircular canals of inner ear	2 present	1 present
Larva	Ammocoetes	None
Sexes	Separate	Hermaphroditic
Common name	Lamprey eels	Hagfish, slime eels

is large enough to be fatal. Adults feed in this manner for about one year's time; however, in some species they do not feed at all, so the buccal cavity and digestive tract have become degenerate and nonfunctional.

Internal Structure

The *notochord* of the primitive chordates persists here throughout life, too, but in adults small rodlike structures of cartilage, known as arcualia, form dorsally along its length. These rods are usually believed to be forerunners of the neural arches of the true vertebrae found in all higher vertebrates. The cranium, made of a cartilaginous floor and encased by a series of cartilage bars, generally is not considered homologous to the head parts of higher forms; in contrast, the membranous sheath that covers it is often viewed as the actual precursor. Within the cranium are two pairs of semicircular canals in the inner ear, used in maintaining equilibrium, as well as the relatively simple brain (fig. 17.2). It should be observed that the olfactory pore does not open directly into the brain as is the case in the cephalochordates, but into an adjacent elongate sac bearing two multifolded caeca in which branches of the olfactory nerve are embedded (fig. 17.1). The brain includes a recognizable cerebrum and the rudiments of a cerebellum, but the larger portion is occupied by the olfactory and visual parts and the medulla. A pair of well-developed eyes is also present.

As mentioned earlier, the *digestive tract* begins in a large buccal cavity, the walls of which bear numerous horny teeth; this is followed by a wide pharynx that ends in a blind sac. In the latter are contained the seven pairs of gillslits, each of which opens individually directly to the outside. Because of the peculiar feed-

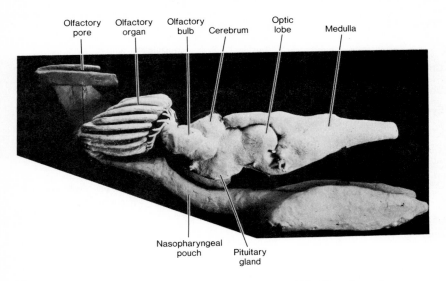

Olfactory pore Olfactory organ Olfactory bulb Cerebrum Optic lobe Medulla

Nasopharyngeal pouch Pituitary gland

Figure 17.2   *Model of the lamprey brain.* (Courtesy of H. Kleerekoper.)

ing habits, which seal off the mouth for hours at a time, water both enters and leaves through these openings during such periods. From a midpoint of the pharynx dorsally, a slender esophagus leads into an equally slender intestine, a stomach being absent. On the wall of the intestinal lumen is a low fold, called the typhlosole, that is slightly spiralled—a small point but noteworthy nevertheless. This structure is believed to enhance the absorptive powers of the digestive tract by increasing the available area. Near its posterior end, the intestine is slightly enlarged to form a rectum which terminates in a ventral anus. Secretion of digestive enzymes is carried out by a liver and a series of small glands on the outer surface of the intestine, collectively called the pancreas. The former is peculiar in not being attached to the remainder of the tract, so that its products are carried to the intestine in the blood stream.

The *excretory system* is of particular importance in understanding the phylogenetic level of a given vertebrate, and these simple forms are no exceptions. In the larva, the kidney is of the *pronephros* type, in which the coelomic fluid alone is filtered, since no close association exists with the blood capillaries (fig. 17.3, A). Later in life, the adult gains a *mesonephros* type, which filters not only coelomic fluid, but also the blood by way of a knot of capillaries. This glomerulus, as it is called, is enclosed within a double-walled cuplike structure, the Bowman's capsule (fig. 17.3, B). A simple U-shaped tubular structure, divided into two chambers (auricle and ventricle), serves as a heart, pumping blood forward through a ventral aorta to pass dorsally through the gills and thence through a dorsal aorta in a typical vertebrate pattern.

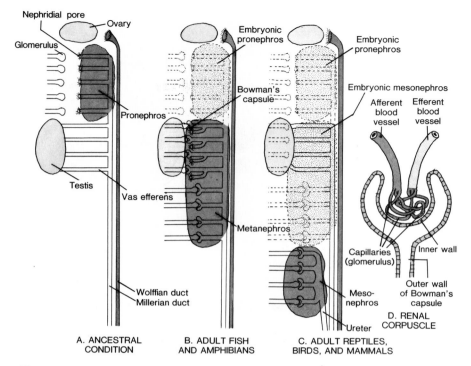

Figure 17.3 *The types of kidneys found among vertebrates.* A. The anteriorly located pronephros filters only the coelomic fluid, and (C) the posteriorly located metanephros filters blood only by way of glomeruli. B. The mesonephros is intermediate both in location and in function.

Reproduction and Development

In spring both the marine and freshwater types migrate upstream to spawn in the shallow upper reaches of streams. Here males work in small groups to remove pebbles from an area, carrying them in the buccal funnels. When an area of suitable proportions has been cleared, a pit is made by vigorous movements of their bodies; once this is sufficiently deep, the females anchor themselves by their buccal funnels to pebbles rimming the area. Such nests serve small communities of breeding pairs. Males wind their tails about the females and discharge sperm over the eggs as they are deposited into the pit. After spawning the lampreys soon die. The eggs hatch in about two weeks into peculiar larvae; after the *ammocoetes,* as they are called, have attained a length of about 10 mm in the nest, they move out into quiet waters, where they burrow in the muddy or sandy bottom. Here they remain, with their heads exposed in lanceletlike fashion, feeding by means of a filtering device that involves a large branchial basket, endostyle, and ropes of mucus, just as in those cephalochordates (fig. 17.4). One notable difference exists, however, in that the endostyle moves the mucous ropes and adhering particles by muscular contractions rather than ciliary action.

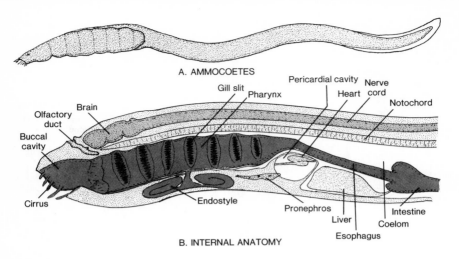

A. AMMOCOETES

B. INTERNAL ANATOMY

Figure 17.4 *The ammocoete larva of a lamprey.* A number of structural resemblances to the lancelet (fig. 16.7) may be noted.

After two to seven years depending on the species, when the larva has attained a length of about 135 mm, the ammocoetes begins to undergo metamorphosis. Usually in *P. marinus*, these changes commence around the middle of July and extend into the following May. The first indication of metamorphosis is in the formation of eyes, which are absent in the larvae. This is followed by alterations in the structure of the mouth, the oral hood and velum of the young giving way to the buccal funnel of the adult. Concurrently the nostril migrates dorsally, the liver loses its connection to the intestine, the pronephros is replaced by a mesonephros and arcualia develop across the notochord. No food is consumed during this ten month period, but when metamorphosis is completed, the young adults feed for a few weeks before migrating downstream to the places in the seas, lakes, or lower reaches of rivers where the parental stock had originated.

The Hagfish

Although the 45 species of hagfish and slime eels of the Myxinoidea show many similarities in appearance to the lampreys, they differ sharply in a number of ways. In the first place, they tend to be larger than lampreys, attaining lengths of 900 mm in some instances, and dorsal fins are absent, being replaced by a finfold as a rule, but even that structure is wanting in some species. No buccal funnel is to be found, the mouth being suctorial and equipped with only one horny tooth, and around the mouth are six sensory tentacles. The nostril is located anteriorly, and the body bears a row of very active mucous glands on each side.

Internally are found six to fourteen pairs of gills, but these open into a common duct, so that only one gill aperture is found on each side of the body. The nervous system is even less impressive than that of the lamprey, for the brain is smaller relative to body size, and neither a cerebrum nor a cerebellum can be detected (fig. 17.1). Eyes are absent, and only a single semicircular canal is found in the inner ear. The digestive tract is not unlike that of the lamprey, being largely a straight tube and without a stomach; the liver has a gall bladder, however, and a tube leading into the intestine. In addition, there is a strong tongue actively used in feeding.

In habits the hagfish and slime eels are often considered parasitic. After the animal has attached to the gill covering of a fish, it penetrates into the body using the rasping tongue as a drill, and there consumes all the internal organs, so that only an empty shell remains. During the day the animals bury themselves in the sea bottoms at depths of 600 m or more, and feed at night in the fashion described. Reproductively they are peculiar among vertebrates in being hermaphroditic; however, they can produce only one kind of sex cell during a given season. A single individual thus may be functionally a male one year and a female the next, and so on. No larval stages, and hence, no metamorphic changes occur in the Myxinoidea.

THE CLASS CHONDRICHTHYES

Between the foregoing early vertebrates and the next level represented by living forms, many developments occurred, most of which are not clearly shown even by fossils. Among the most important structures gained during this interval are jaws, two sets of paired fins, and vertebrae. In spite of all these additions which involve the skeleton, no true bone is as yet present, but only cartilage as before; reference to this condition is made by the technical name Chondrichthyes, that is, "cartilage-fish." The sharks, rays (fig. 17.5), and related forms constitute this class.

Characteristics

If the embryology of this group is to be believed, the jaws originated by modification of those cartilages that support the first pair of gill slits. While these were undergoing elaboration, related parts were being acquired that illustrate one way in which new structures may develop. The novel parts referred to are the *teeth,* without which the jaws would have remained inefficient organs of mastication indeed. All available evidence points to the peculiar scales covering the body as the source from which teeth have been derived. These placoid scales found among Chondrichthyes consist of minute rhomboidal platelets, each provided on the outer surface with a sharp projection. As the hard portion of the scales consists of dentine, capped with an enamel-like layer, the structural resemblance to teeth is at once apparent. One can readily imagine that, when the ancestral jaws first formed, the rough scaly skin around the mouth moved inward to assist in mastication; when the older scales wore out, replacements were provided by further inward growth of skin. By evolutionary processes, the orginal minute scales slowly and gradually enlarged and later became embedded as teeth in the jaws. In this connection it is interesting to note that many sharks and even certain mammals of today can replace lost teeth an indefinite number of times.

Figure 17.5 *A stingray.*

The majority of sharks and rays have just five pairs of gill slits in addition to a porelike opening, the *spiracle*. The latter represents the remnant of the primitive first gill slit's upper portion; later in terrestrial vertebrates it becomes connected with the middle ear as the Eustachian tube. Equipped thus with efficient organs for respiration, locomotion, and ingestion, the sharks and rays became the dominant vertebrates in the seas and maintained their supremacy for more than 100 million years. Among the 600 or more species extant today are such extremely diversified forms as hammerhead and angel sharks, sawfish, electric rays, devilfish or manta, chimaeras, and elephant fish. Included here are the largest living vertebrates next to the whales, for whale sharks reach lengths of 12 to 16 meters and man-eating sharks of the genus *Carcharodon* often grow to 9 meters.

Internal Structure

The *digestive tract* shows a number of advances over that of the preceding class. The mouth is ventral, not anterior as in most vertebrates, and leads into a broad, but not cavernous, pharynx, the walls of which are penetrated by five sets of gillslits, as already mentioned. Following this organ is the esophagus that opens into a J-shaped stomach. The latter in turn leads into the intestines, within which is the peculiar spiral valve (fig. 17.6) that increases the surface area available for absorption. This is followed by a much narrower rectum, provided with a rectal gland, and then a cloaca, which empties through the anus. A liver,

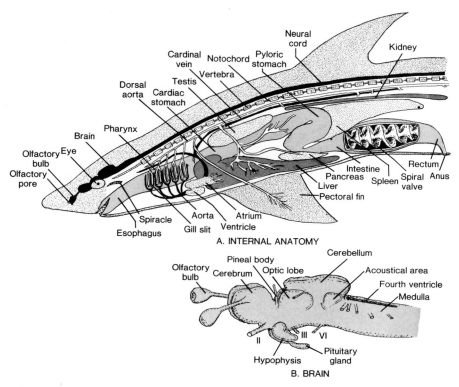

Figure 17.6 *Internal structure of a shark.*

complete with a gall bladder, and a pancreas connect to the intestine to supply digestive fluids.

The *circulatory system* is basically little different from that of the cyclostomes. The heart is similarly tubular, S-shaped, and two-chambered, and the pattern of blood vessels is comparable, except for those modifications made necessary by the two pairs of appendages. However, the brain shows considerable development in having a well-marked cerebrum and cerebellum (fig. 17.6). Another less evident advancement is found in the nerves which here are medullated, except for the sympathetic nerves, whereas none are thus sheathed in the lampreys or hagfish.

The *excretory system* consists of a pair of mesonephric kidneys, to the tubules of which the reproductive system is closely associated; thus the products of the gonads leave the body by way of ducts, not by way of the coelom as in cyclostomes. Two sets of tubes are present, one of which, the *Wolffian,* corresponds to the mesonephric ducts, while the second, the *Müllerian,* is of unknown relationships and origins.

Both sexes employ these tubes but in greatly different ways. The male system begins with a pair of elongated, straplike testes, located above the esophagus.

From these runs a series of very fine tubules, the vasa efferentia, which attach to the Wolffian duct, the Müllerian being reduced; thus the Wolffian duct is referred to as the vas deferens. Just before the latter empties into the cloaca by way of a genital pore, there is an enlargement, the seminal vesicle, in which sperm is stored. The mesonephros also connects to this tube, so the posterior portion of the Wolffian duct in the male serves in dual capacities as the vas deferens and ureter.

In contrast, in the female, the Müllerian ducts are greatly elongated and form a pair of oviducts. These lead posteriorly from the usually single ovary, located on the right side above the esophagus, but are enlarged here or there to form yolk or shell glands, according to the species. However, they are not actually connected to the ovary, but open into the coelom by a large, common opening beneath the esophagus (fig. 17.6). Consequently, eggs enter the coelom from the ovary and then find their way into the oviducts, through which they are then moved into the cloaca by means of the cilia that line those tubules. Thus in the female, the Wolffian duct is strictly the ureter. In a number of species, the oviduct (Müllerian tube) may be modified into a uterus in which the eggs develop into young.

THE CLASS OSTEICHTHYES

Although the sharks and their relatives were able to become highly successful in face of the lower level of competition provided by their predecessors, the jawless fish, they in turn have now been largely replaced by the still better-adapted forms that constitute the present class.

Characteristics

The successors of the Chondrichthyes are classified together by many specialists under the name Osteichthyes, meaning "bony fishes," whereas other workers in this field of research prefer to term them the Actinopterygii, signifying "ray-finned fishes," after the nature of their fins. However, many other treatments have been accorded the 50,000 or more species belonging here, and a wide variety of names have been applied. Their skeletons usually consist of bony tissue, although the sturgeons and certain other members retain the cartilaginous condition or have reacquired it secondarily. The body is covered with scales that are outgrowths of the dermis alone, whereas the placoid scales of sharks and rays are products of both the dermis and the epidermis.

As in the cartillaginous fish, there are five pairs of gills, but the spiracles have migrated inwards and become associated with the inner ears as the Eustachian tubes. The opercula, or gill coverings, which made their first appearance with the chimeras of the Chondrichthyes, occur consistently in the present group. Actually these structures are extensions of the cranium and serve, not only in protecting the gills from injury, but also in retaining water in the gill cavity. For instance, eels in migrating up rivers often need to clamber up rocks or over dry land to pass around such insurmountable objects as very high water falls. To prevent desiccation of the delicate vascularized tissue that makes up the gills, the fish close the opercula during such excursions, trapping water within the gill chambers. In the bony fish group as a whole, the heart remains unchanged from that of the sharks, but the brain is somewhat more elaborate.

Types of Caudal Fins

As in the preceding taxon, the fins are of the ray-fin type and thus show no notable improvement; however, the tail structure has undergone extensive modification. Five types of caudal fins are recognized among chordates, the most primitive of which is the protocercal variety found in lampreys, certain juvenile fishes, and tadpoles (fig. 17.7, A). This consists merely of a continuous, more or less uniform finfold around the notochord or vertebral column. In sharks, sturgeons, and a few other primitive fish is found a more advanced type, known as the heterocercal, in which the ventral portion of the fan is broad and the dorsal part narrow (fig. 17.7, D, E). A few unusual primitive fishes and the ichthyosaurs among the reptiles developed the opposite arrangement; that is, the ventral portion is narrow and the dorsal broad—a type called the hypocercal (fig. 17.7, C). In being symmetrically developed, the diphycercal caudal fin recalls the protocercal; however, it differs in having strong fin rays and not being continuous with the other fins (fig. 17.7, B). A modification of this type, called the gephyrocercal and found in the lungfishes to be discussed later, is distinguished by the tail blade being drawn out to a point. Finally, the most advanced type, the homocercal tail of most ray-finned fish, is characterized by the outer rays being longer than the central ones, giving a forked appearance to the blade, and, more

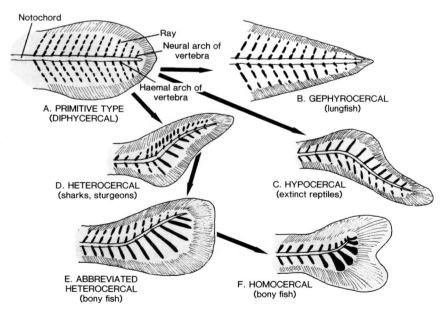

Figure 17.7 *Types of caudal fins of fish and their evolution.*

importantly, the rays are largely terminal. Its origins from the heterocercal type are strongly indicated by the internal structure (fig. 17.7, E, F).

Other Specializations

In adapting to the numerous varieties of aquatic habitats that exist, the Osteichthyes have undergone a number of specializations, but unfortunately only a few of these can be discussed here. One peculiar change that has taken place is the forward displacement of the pelvic fin. In sharks, sturgeons, gars, and other primitive types, the pair of pelvic fins are located well behind the middle of the body. With further evolutionary advancement, however, they are found in front of the center and, ultimately in the most specialized of these fishes, are located on the thoracic region.

Another organ that has undergone a number of adaptations is the swim bladder, a structure that is absent in the Chondrichthyes. At the lowest levels of organization, as in the primitive African bony fish *Polypterus*, the swim bladder is indicated to have arisen as a pair of sacs connected to the esophagus (fig. 17.8, A). In this genus, however, the organ has already made some advancement in that the two sacs are unequal in size, the right one being much the larger (fig. 17.8, B). In the bowfin of southern North America, the organ with this primitive arrangement has become highly vascularized to serve as simple lungs, a peculiarity that occurs occasionally at all levels of development. With further advancement, as in *Neoceratodus*, the Australian lungfish, only the right sac remains, but the tube still opens ventrally into the esophagus. At the highest stages of development, the bladder's connection to the esophagus has migrated to the dorsal side, rather than the ventral, and this condition is followed by total loss of any connection, both variations being found in the advanced bony fish (fig. 17.8, D, E). Besides its respiratory and floating functions, this organ has become

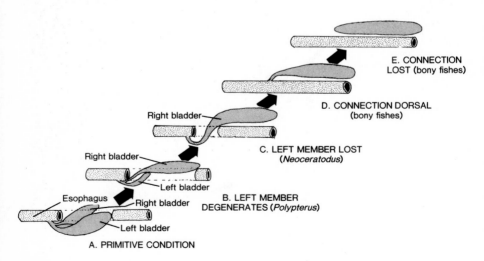

Figure 17.8 *Evolutionary changes in swim bladder structure.*

adapted for sound production in many fishes, but in a variety of ways. The toadfish and the sea robin, by way of illustration, produce sounds by contractions of special sets of muscles connected to the bladder, and in the triggerfish the pectoral fins beat upon an area of the sac that is located close to the body surface. At more elementary levels the structure merely serves as a resonator for sounds made by the fish grinding its teeth together.

The scales of bony fish also have undergone vast changes from the placoid type of the sharks and rays. Probably the earliest derivative of this toothlike type was the ganoid, of which several varieties exist among the primitive members of the class, including sturgeons, paddlefish, and other cartilaginous types. All variations agree in being platelike and bony and covered on both the inner and outer surfaces with an enamel-like substance called ganoin. At all higher levels many of these hard layers have been lost and later all are lacking. First their absence leads to the formation of the thin, circular cycloid variety of scales, such as those of catfish, and later to the ctenoid, which has an elaborate series of teeth at the free edge, as in most bony fishes (fig. 17.9).

TWO TRANSITIONAL CLASSES

That the bony fish possess all the features essential for an existence in water is clearly demonstrated by the presence of 50,000 species on earth today. These occupy nearly every body of water of whatever size or nature, from the smallest freshwater pond to the very depths of the oceans. Consequently, it is difficult to perceive how the vertebrates could undergo any additional major diversification in an aquatic environment. Yet several structures absent among the forms described above are needed before the first steps toward an existence on land could be taken.

The Coelacantha

Among the requisites is a mechanism to provide locomotion in a terrestrial situation; hence, the predecessor's fins must include features which can be modified for the purpose. The essential fin traits are found among ancestral

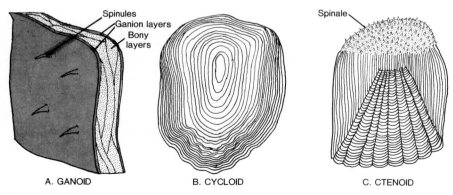

A. GANOID B. CYCLOID C. CTENOID

Spinules
Ganion layers
Bony layers
Spinale

Figure 17.9 *Structure of scales among fishes.*

coelacanths, represented today by a single species discovered in recent years off the coast of east Africa. This form, *Latimeria chalumnae* (fig. 17.10) which lives in the ocean depths, has secondarily lost much of the typical lobe-fin structure that its fossil forebears possessed. These had fins far more robust than those of the ray-finned fish, for the bony elements, instead of forming transverse rows, were arranged in long series (fig. 18.21). How the lobefins proved of value to the ancestral stock cannot even be guessed; perhaps they supported the body weight as the fish rested on the lake bottoms or served during migration from one pond to another. But all that is actually known is that the fins existed and that they doubtlessly played a role vital to their possessors.

The Choanichthyes

The lungfishes, now represented by three genera in tropical regions, show other features needed before vertebrates could venture onto dry land. Lungs instead of gills obviously must exist when a terrestrial habitat is entered, but on the surface it would appear that an air-breathing mechanism could hold no value at all for a gill-bearing aquatic organism. To the contrary, even fish may require lungs under particular conditions. The Australian lungfish (*Neoceratodus forsteri;* fig. 17.11), for example, inhabits lakes which become deficient in oxygen during the long dry periods of Queensland, so that it surfaces frequently to fill its lungs with fresh air. The lungs, however, do not serve only for emergencies, but are an essential supplement to the gills at all times; even in well-oxygenated water, it has recently been shown, the lungfish will perish unless permitted to surface for air from time to time. Its lungs, which are modified from the swimbladder, open into the esophagus, are well supplied with blood to be oxygenated, and are sacculated internally for greater efficiency.

Africa and South America also have lungfish, belonging to the genera *Protopterus* and *Lepidosiren,* respectively, which are much more advanced than the Australian species. The several which occur in Africa have recently received thorough study in their native habitats. Instead of living in temporary ponds that evaporate completely during periods of drought as once believed, the lungfish

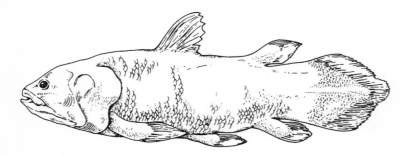

Figure 17.10 *Latimeria chalumnae, a "living fossil."* The only species of coelacanth known to exist today lives at considerable depths in the Indian Ocean, off the coast of East Africa.

Figure 17.11 *The lungfish of Australia.* This freshwater fish grows to a length exceeding 3 feet and a weight up to 15 pounds. (Courtesy Australian News and Information Bureau.)

were found to live in the large rivers, which never go dry. Nevertheless, each year as the rivers recede to their usual channels with the onset of the dry season, these fish move up to the terraces where in the mud they build "cocoons" which are cemented with mucus. Here in these chambers, breathing air that enters by way of a tubular aperature, the fish aestivate until the rainy season raises the water level to flood stage once more.

The technical term for this class refers to a second adaptation for respiration that its members have acquired, the nostrils. While a nostril-like tube leading from an olfactory pore into the mouth cavity is present in several earlier groups, including the hagfishes, a special pair of tubes for respiratory purposes occurs first in this group. Moreover, the primitive heart has become three-chambered, for the single atrium of the lower fishes is subdivided by a septum to form right and left atria (fig. 17.12, A). The latter chamber receives only oxygenated blood from the lungs whereas the former receives deoxygenated blood from the remainder of the body. Special structures, like the spiral valve in the base of the aorta, assist in preventing the two types of blood from mixing as they pass through the ventricle. The latter is partially subdivided by a thin septum.

Figure 17.12 *A poison arrow frog.* Poison from the skin of this striking tree frog (*Atelopus varius*) from Costa Rica is employed by the native Indians on their arrow points in killing game. Its brilliant coloration, black and white with red markings, is often considered by zoologists to warn predators of its poisonous nature and thus serves as a survival mechanism. (Photograph courtesy of Kenneth T. Nemuras.)

THE CLASS AMPHIBIA

Between the foregoing two classes of fish that possess features which could be converted to use on land and the class Amphibia in which that conversion is consummated, a great gap exists, for many of the intermediate steps are absent, even from the fossil record. Yet a knowledge of the precursorial parts, together with the primitive structures found among the frogs, toads, and salamanders that constitute the present class, permit the steps taken to be deduced with a high degree of confidence. Further, these deductions are often aided by the existence of several levels of evolutionary development within this taxon, as becomes obvious in the paragraphs that follow.

General Characteristics

The class Amphibia is generally considered to consist of three major types of organisms, the lizardlike salamanders, the familiar frogs and toads, and the subterranean caecilians (table 17.2). Since the latter are represented by only a handful of species today, they need to receive only passing mention here. While the anurans, the frogs and their allies (fig. 17.12), are a compact group, the salamanders include a wide diversity of forms, some of which possess a number of primitive structures, whereas the others are quite advanced. Consequently, it is necessary to discuss such forms as the water pup and congo eels separately from salamanders proper.

Undoubtedly the terrestrial adaptation of greatest importance found within the taxon is the conversion of the former finlike appendages into true legs. It is not fully perfected here, however, for the tips of the digits are not provided with protective devices such as claws or nails. Among other changes that are noteworthy is the loss of the scales that characterize the fishes—only in primitive salamanders are scales present, and then only on restricted areas of the body

Table 17.2 The Orders of Amphibia

Characteristic	Orders		
	Gymnophiona	Urodela	Salientia
Common names	Caecilians	Salamanders; newts; efts; Congo eels, etc.	Frogs; toads; tree frogs
Body form	Wormlike	Lizardlike	Short, more or less quadrate
Tail	Short or absent	Present	Absent
Legs	Absent	Short, weak; sometimes reduced or absent	Front pair short; hind ones elongate, used for jumping
External ear (tympanum)	Absent	Absent	Present
Gills	In larva only	In larva and sometimes in adult	In larva only
Fertilization	Internal	Internal	External
Habitat	Subterranean; rarely aquatic	Aquatic or terrestrial	Terrestrial, larva aquatic
Number of species	50	300	2700

surface. Since scales would seem to be highly desirous as a protection against the sharp stones and spines frequently encountered in terrestrial habitats, their loss in these animals cannot help but raise questions as to the advantage thus gained. No answer is clear-cut, but the most logical one appears to be related to respiratory requirements. The lungs of amphibians differ only slightly from those of lung-fishes, being mere bags whose thin walls are vascularized. So inefficient are they that they are usually supplemented by vascularized areas of the skin—indeed the most advanced salamanders have lost the lungs entirely and respire solely by means of the skin. Since scales would interfere with gas exchange, the loss of their protection may be outweighed by the increase in respiration their absence permits.

Changes in Heart Structure

Although a summary of heart evolution within the phylum as a whole is given at the close of chapter 18, its purpose is to provide an overview of the whole sequence of events and thus omits details. Certain of these details nevertheless are of much pertinence in providing insights into such problems as how an S-shaped tube became cone-shaped and how the posterior entrance for the blood became an anterior one. In this discussion the terminology is simplified some-what and a number of less important features are omitted, so as not to obscure the essentials. For instance, the parts correctly known as the conus arteriosus and truncus arteriosus are referred to merely as the aorta, of which they are a part functionally, if not structurally.

In the sirens (genus *Siren*), a type of primitive salamander that lacks hind legs, the heart is nearly identical to that of the lungfishes. The organ is essentially S-shaped when viewed from the side, with the atria placed dorsally to the ventri-cle (fig. 17.13, A). In these forms the ventricle is ovate in shape and incom-pletely divided by a septum, precisely as in the lungfishes, conditions found nowhere else in the Amphibia. The chief distinctions between the heart of the sirens and that of the lungfish is in the atrium being more completely divided and the aorta slightly less bent than in the latter animals.

The mudpuppies of the genus *Necturus* have the ventricle somewhat triangu-lar, the aorta nearly straight, and the atria placed farther anteriorly. This forward movement of the atria is continued in the caecilians, so that the sinus venosus is located just posterior to the anterior end of the ventricle (fig. 17.13, B, C). The latter is still elongate triangular, however, as in the mudpuppies. Then in the heart of the robust, aquatic salamander known as the hellbender (genus *Crypto-branchus*), the ventricle acquires a short, triangular or conical form, a shape that persists throughout the remainder of the amphibians, as well as in the higher classes. Rather than being placed dorsad to the ventricle, the atria are anterio-laterad to that chamber; the sinus venosus, however, is no farther anterior than previously (fig. 17.13, D).

Only in the advanced salamanders do the atria become nearly entirely an-terior to the ventricle; here, too, the sinus venosus has moved forward from its posterior location and now leads into those chambers on one side. These steps are

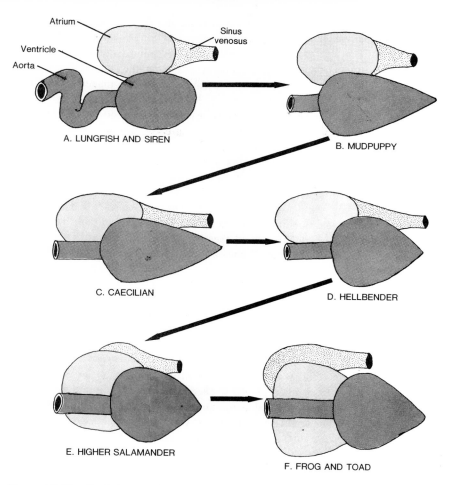

Figure 17.13 *Evolutionary changes in heart structure among amphibians.* A. In the lungfish and sirens, the ventricle is divided by a septum into two compartments, a condition lost in more advanced forms.

continued to their ultimate ends in the frogs and toads, in which the atria have become fully anterior to the ventricle and the sinus venosus relocated to enter the atria at their anterior end (fig. 17.13, E, F).

Reproduction and Development

Reproductive habits differ greatly among the three orders of Amphibia. In caecilians the details are poorly known but involve internal fertilization—the cloaca of males, being protrusible, serves as a penis during copulation. The eggs then are deposited in moist ground close to a body of fresh water, but the resulting larvae may be either aquatic or as usual in this class the entire larval development may be completed within the egg. In still other caecilians, such as those of the South American genus *Typhlonectes,* the eggs are retained within the uterus where development of the young takes place. No placenta is formed, however, as in the live-bearing, or *viviparous,* mammals; in instances where zygotes merely undergo development within the body, the species is said to be *ovoviviparous,* while ordinary egg-laying forms are distinguished by the term *oviparous.*

Among the salamanders fertilization is largely internal, too, but in the primitive aquatic types, it occurs externally. Among some of the latter, mating is often preceded by elaborate courtship behavior patterns, in which special, temporary glands on the chin or other body parts of males play a significant role. These rituals terminate in the males depositing their sperm in irregularly-shaped capsules called spermatophores, which are placed on sticks, leaves, or other objects. These are picked up and placed in the female's body by the so-called cloacal lips that border the cloacal opening. After being taken in, the walls of the capsules break down to release the sperm and thereby effect fertilization. The eggs are then deposited, typically in long chains or clusters in the water, but some of the lungless species deposit them in moist earth. At least one species, the European *Salamandra salamandra,* is known to be ovoviviparous. Development leads to a salamander-like juvenile, which differs from the adult most notably in having external gills. Usually these are lost at the close of the juvenile period, but in the axolotl of Mexico they are retained throughout life, since no metamorphosis occurs. As pointed out earlier (p. 265), retention of such juvenile traits is referred to as neoteny. Experimental treatment of the neotenous adults with thyroid extract leads to metamorphosis and the concommittant loss of the gills.

The mating behavior of frogs and toads also involves elaborate mating rituals, in which activities the vocal cords and eardrums play important roles. In view of their being the first vertebrates to have a voice to make, and a tympanic membrane to detect, sounds, the vocalizations are quite varied and even modestly complex. The calls of frogs are not employed solely in reproductive activities but function in establishing territories and in communicating, albeit at a simple level. In contrast to the salamanders, nearly all frogs and toads have external fertilization. When the female engages in depositing the eggs, the male holds firmly to her and releases the sperm over the eggs.

Because of the rather large quantity of yolk the eggs contain, development of the embryo is altered from the typical pattern. The first two cleavages are normal, but thereafter division is unequal, the cells of the yolkless animal pole being smaller than those of the yolk-saturated vegetal pole (fig. 17.14, A, B). Consequently, in the blastula the blastocoel is located off-center (fig. 17.14, C). Since the ventral, yolk-bearing cells are obviously too large to sink into the blastocoel, the gastrula is formed by cells of the animal pole growing over the vegetal cells in the form of a sheet (fig. 17.14, D). The sheet of cells does not completely envelop the yolk cells but for a time leaves an opening known as the yolk-plug through which those cells are visible. As in the lancelets, a neural plate bordered by neural grooves develops on the dorsal region, to give rise to the neural tube (fig. 17.14, E, F). The embryo eventually develops into the familiar

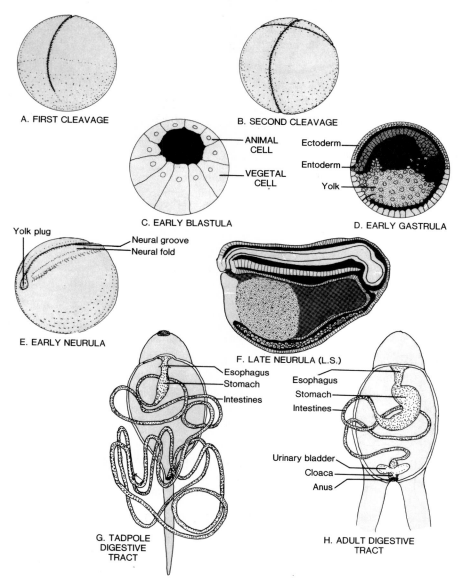

A. FIRST CLEAVAGE

B. SECOND CLEAVAGE

ANIMAL CELL

VEGETAL CELL

C. EARLY BLASTULA

Ectoderm

Entoderm

Yolk

D. EARLY GASTRULA

Yolk plug

Neural groove
Neural fold

E. EARLY NEURULA

F. LATE NEURULA (L.S.)

Esophagus
Stomach
Intestines

Esophagus
Stomach
Intestines

Urinary bladder
Cloaca
Anus

G. TADPOLE
DIGESTIVE
TRACT

H. ADULT DIGESTIVE
TRACT

Figure 17.14 *Development in amphibians.*

tadpole, which is essentially herbivorous, unlike the adults that are carnivorous. Thus as the legs are gained and the tail is resorbed at metamorphosis, extensive changes occur internally, that can be especially noted in the digestive tract (fig. 17.14, G, H). The kidneys, too, undergo radical modification, the pronephros of the young being replaced by the mesonephros of the adult.

QUESTIONS FOR REVIEW AND THOUGHT

1. What characteristics must an organism possess to qualify as a fish, as that term is generally used?

2. Define the class Cyclostomata and differentiate between the two major types of its representatives. What characteristics of the class indicate it to be a group of primitive vertebrates? In what ways does the ammocoetes larva suggest relationships to the lancelets?

3. What features suggest the hagfishes to be more primitive than the lampreys and in what traits more advanced? Compare breeding and feeding habits, too.

4. Compare the three types of kidneys that occur among vertebrates as to their structure and function.

5. What three types of organisms are placed in the class Chondrichthyes, and what are their major common characteristics? List the structural advancements over the cyclostomes that have been made in this class. What important anatomical items are missing?

6. Compare male and female reproductive systems of sharks.

7. Compare the Osteichthyes first with the Coelacantha and then with the Choanichthyes. In what way, if any, do either of these latter groups show features that make them better adapted for an *aquatic* existence than the bony fish? Is *Latimeria* any more of a living fossil than are such lungfish as *Neoceratodus* for example? Why or why not? What function does the lobe fin serve in *Latimeria*?

8. In what ways are nostrils essential to a life on land? What other features were required before vertebrates could live on land? What most clearly intimates that the Amphibia descended from an aquatic ancestor?

9. What evolutionary changes have occurred in the caudal fin of fish? In the swim bladder? In the heart of amphibians?

10. In what ways does the development of amphibians differ from that of invertebrates studied earlier? What features suggest kinships to the lancelets?

SUGGESTIONS FOR FURTHER READING

Blight, A.R. 1977. The muscular control of vertebrate swimming movements. *Biol. Rev.*, 52:181–218.

Compagno, L.J.V. 1977. Phyletic relationships of living sharks and rays. *Amer. Zool.*, 17:303–322.

Erlich, P.R. 1975. The population biology of coral reef fishes. *Ann. Rev. Ecol. and Syst.*, 6:211–247.

Løvtrup, S., V. Landstrom, and H. Løvtrup-Rein. 1978. Polarities, cell differentiation and primary induction in the amphibian embryo. *Biol. Rev.*, 53:1–42.

Nieuwenhuys, R. 1977. The brain of the lamprey in a comparative perspective. *Ann. N.Y. Acad. Sci.*, 299:97–145.

Perks, A.M. 1977. Developmental and evolutionary aspects of the neurohypophysis. *Amer. Zool.*, 17:833–849.

Potter, I.C., G.M. Wright, and J.H. Youson. 1978. Metamorphosis in the anadromous sea lamprey, *Petromyzon marinus*. L. *Can. J. Zool.*, 56:561–570.

Sawyer, W.H. 1977. Evolution of active neurohypophysical principles among the vertebrates. *Amer. Zool.*, 17:727–737.

Scadding, S.R. 1977. Phylogenic distribution of limb regeneration capacity in adult Amphibia. *J. Exp. Zool.*, 202:57–68.

Schaeffer, B., and M. Williams. 1977. Relationship of fossil and living elasmobranchs. *Amer. Zool.*, 17:293–302.

Shaw, E. 1978. Schooling fishes. *Amer. Sci.*, 66:166–175.

Stocum, D.L. 1978. Regeneration of symmetrical hind limbs in larval salamanders. *Science*, 200:790–793.

Thorson, T.B., R.M. Wotton, T.A. Georgi. 1978. Rectal glands of freshwater stingrays, *Potamotrygon* spp. (Chondrichthyes: Potamotrygonidae). *Biol. Bull.*, 154:508–516.

Wourms, J.P. 1977. Reproduction and development in chondrichthyan fishes. *Amer. Zool.*, 17:379–410.

The Advanced Vertebrates

18

As has been seen in the preceding chapter, the acquisitions of legs by itself was not sufficient to free the vertebrates from a dependency on aquatic environments. This incomplete adaptation to the terrestrial habitats shown by the amphibians, while most marked in reproductive requirements, was not completely confined to those needs. A large number of other specializations, notably in the skeleton, respiratory and circulatory organs, development, and excretion, had to be acquired before vertebrate animals could be said to be thoroughly adapted to the land. In a sense, then, this chapter is concerned with the steps that completed the conversion of these animals for a terrestrial existence. But, animals being natured as they are, a wide diversity of forms also arose that eventually enabled the vertebrates to reach from pole to pole and from the highest mountains to the deepest seas.

THE REPTILIA

The Reptilia as a whole are far better adapted for a life on land than are the amphibians, one of their important acquisitions being the scales that cover the body. These are not homologous with the scales of fish, which are of dermal origin; rather they represent a derivative of the epidermis and may be viewed as dead horny plates made of keratin, a protein found in epidermal cells in general. Scales, however, characterize only the members of the Squamata (table 18.1), the most abundant order of living reptiles. Instead of scales, turtles have large scutes (fig. 18.1), which increase in size by additions to their lower surfaces, and the crocodilians have leathery scutes on the dorsal surface and scales on the ventral. Most scaled forms, like the snakes and lizards, shed their skin periodically, usually fairly intact, but some slough off isolated patches here and there more or less continually. These coats protect not only against abrasion and injury but also against desiccation; consequently a number of lizards and snakes are found in desert regions where few amphibians can live.

Other Characteristics

Another adaptation reptiles have acquired is found in the skull as a result of relocation of the eardrums. From their original location near the shoulder, those organs migrated forward and into the skull, where they are still exposed at the surface but had a firm bony base to assist in increasing their efficacy. This set of

Table 18.1   The Extant Orders of Reptiles

	Order			
Characteristic	Testudinata	Rhynchocephalia	Squamata	Crocodilia
Body covering	Plates of dermal origin	Epidermal scales above, plates beneath	Epidermal scales	Horny scutes
Teeth	Absent; with horny beak	Present	Present	Well-developed
Vertebrae	Fused to carapace	Concave front and rear	Concave anteriorly	Concave anteriorly
Quadrate of skull	Immovable	Immovable	Movable	Immovable
Anal slit	Longitudinal	Transverse	Transverse	Longitudinal
Parietal eye	Absent	Readily visible	Absent	Absent
Habitat	Freshwater, marine, and terrestrial	Terrestrial	Mostly terrestrial	Freshwater and marine
Number of species	500	1	7000	25
Common names	Turtles, tortoises, terrapins	Tuatara	Lizards, geckos, snakes, vipers, etc.	Crocodiles, gavias, alligators

developments receives detailed attention later. Still another adaptation involves the nostrils. In the frogs and their relatives, these openings lead directly into the anterior portion of the mouth cavity, whereas in reptilians a bony partition has formed, so that they open internally at the back of the mouth or in the throat. Thus a crocodile can breathe while it holds prey under water to drown.

The legs have made progress, too, although not in a spectacular way—the acquisition of a claw on each toe does not sound especially important (fig. 18.2). However, when one considers the modifications made to the claw among mammals in the form of hoofs, nails, and the like, its significance becomes more manifest. The leg, nevertheless, is still in its primitive position, being attached to the body at right angles to the sides. Many of the dinosaurs and related forms did acquire vertically-oriented legs, but those animals have become extinct. In contrast, the musculature of the legs has far outstripped that of the amphibians and approaches that of mammals in complexity.

The internal organs, too, have undergone improvement, especially those of the respiratory and excretory systems. Semicircular rings of cartilage now support the trachea, and the lungs no longer are simple sacs, save in the tuatara and snakes. Moreover, movable ribs have been developed. Thus the lungs are not

Figure 18.1 *A turtle from the Galápagos Archipelago.* This giant of turtles (*Testudo elephantopus*) contrasts strongly in size with the recent hatchlings; it ranks among the largest of extant species of reptiles, since a full-grown adult may weigh as much as 400 pounds. (Photograph by Ron Garrison, courtesy of the San Diego Zoo.)

filled with air merely by means of hyoid (throat) movements, as is the case with the amphibians, but by bellowslike action of the rib cage. In the excretory system, a metanephros now is the functional organ. This differs from the mesonephros in lacking openings into the coelom, so that it filters only blood, by way of glomeruli. Furthermore, it is located posterior to the mesonephros and empties by way of a tube that is not derived from the Wolffian duct but is a separate organ, the ureter (fig. 17.3). The brain has become larger relative to body size and has all its divisions well-developed, including 12 pairs of cranial nerves in contrast to the ten of the Amphibia.

The Embryonic Membranes

Undoubtedly the most remarkable of the new acquisitions of the reptiles is found in the developing embryo. Rather early in development, four characteristic membranes form around the embryo, each of which serves in a capacity formerly provided by the aquatic environment in which the eggs of earlier vertebrates were deposited. The outermost of these, the chorion, extends around the egg shell and assists in respiration (fig. 18.3). The yolk sac, the second member, contains the yolk and thus assists in nutrition; quite likely this membrane originated as a diverticulum of the archenteron in some ancestral stock. The third sac, the allantois, connects to the digestive tract farther posteriorly and stores the nitrogenous wastes received from the kidneys. Finally, the amnion is a liquid-filled sac enclosing the whole embryo; thus it acts in absorbing shocks and prevents the

Figure 18.2 *A gecko from Thailand.* The Tokay gecko (*Gekko gecko*) easily climbs such smooth surfaces as walls and ceilings of buildings by means of the pads on its digits. These lizards are usually welcome in homes, because their insect-eating habits help in controlling flies and mosquitoes. (Photograph courtesy of Kenneth T. Nemuras.)

growing young from adhering to the egg shell or other membranes. Only the presence of this series of membranes finally permitted higher vertebrates to be free of aquatic ties for reproduction.

Modifications to the Skull

In order to understand the nature of the variety that exists and has existed among the reptiles, the modifications that have occurred to two additional organs need to be reviewed. Discussion of the changes to one of these, the heart, is more meaningful in context with the organ in other vertebrate taxa; consequently, it is reserved for the summary of this section (p. 332). In contrast, the second one, the skull, is more applicable to present purposes as it makes clear some features used in distinguishing the orders (table 18.1). Moreover, it enters into considerations of the two higher classes of vertebrates that follow, the birds and mammals.

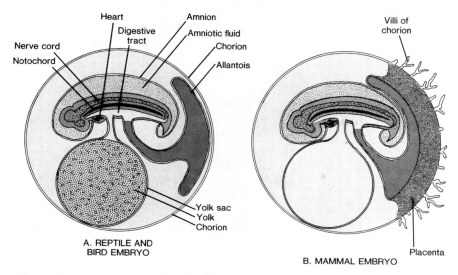

A. REPTILE AND
BIRD EMBRYO

B. MAMMAL EMBRYO

Figure 18.3 *The embryonic membranes of the egg in higher vertebrates.* All the advanced vertebrates have four membranes present around the embryo during development of the egg.

In order to understand the problem, it must first be realized that none of the living amphibians and nearly all the fossil ones lack some of the characteristics necessary to have given rise to the reptiles—by way of illustration, the structure of their vertebrae is unsuited to being ancestral to the corresponding parts of the higher vertebrates. One fossil group, the Eoreptilia, is exceptional, however, in that it possessed a vertebral structure similar to that of reptiles, but its skull morphology was closer to that of amphibians. Accordingly the more advanced members of this group, the seymouriomorphs, are classified either as Amphibia or Reptilia, depending on the author. Thus they were obviously close to the boundary between these two taxa and admirably suited for the role of ancestor to that latter class.

By using *Seymouria* and its allies as a starting point, a logical evolutionary path for the existing reptiles can be traced. As shown by several fortunate fossil finds, the tympanum of this early ancestral stock was located against the posterior rim of the skull, not within it as in the modern forms nor near the shoulder as in frogs and toads. The skull was quite solid, the only openings being the nostrils, the orbits of the eyes, and the parietal eye (fig. 18.4, A). Thus the two pairs of openings in the temporal region found in many advanced types were missing. These are viewed as forming two pairs of arches, so the animals that possess them accordingly are referred to as Diapsida; those groups like the turtles, which lack openings and thus arches, are referred to as Anapsida. In the turtle skull it can be noted, however, that a deep otic notch exists on each rear corner of the skull and that the upper surface is strongly cut out on each side at the base (fig. 18.4, B). The otic notch marks the point where the tympanum has

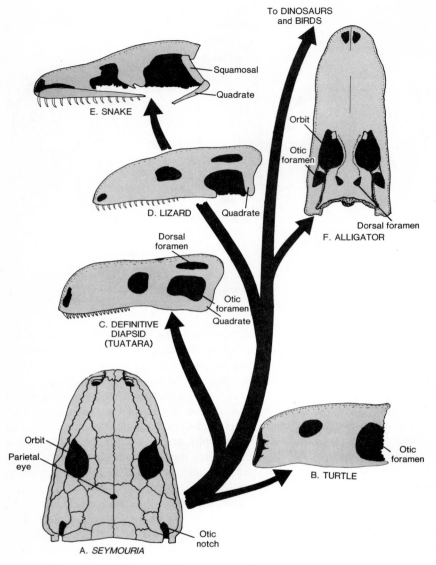

Figure 18.4 *Evolutionary changes in the skull of diapsid reptiles.*

become partly embedded in the skull, but the function of the upper excisions is not known. In forms like the tuatara, the otic notch has migrated forward somewhat, as have the upper excissions also; both sets of openings are now closed behind, forming two temporal arches. Hence, the tuatara is generally considered the earliest living diapsid (fig. 18.5).

Figure 18.5 *The tuatara of New Zealand.* The sole survivor of a formerly large taxon (the Rhynchocephalia) lives on rocks along the seashore. (Courtesy of New Zealand National Publicity.)

The lizard and snake skulls have undergone modification from this basic pattern in that one or both arches have been lost, although they are present in the embryo. When both arches are in place, as in the tuatara, the posterior cranial bone known as the quadrate is immovable. Since it is with this bone that the lower jaw articulates, the mouth is necessarily restricted in forward and backward movements. In adult lizards the lower arch has become lost, so the quadrate is capable of a degree of horizontal movement (fig. 18.4). In the snake skull, the upper arch also has been lost, permitting the quadrate wide latitude in movement. Thus snakes are able to swallow prey as large as their own diameter, or even greater on occasion, whereas lizards can do only about half as well. It can be noted in the diagram (fig. 18.4) that in snakes the arches below the orbits and nostril openings have also been dispensed with, but the significance of this loss remains a mystery.

The crocodilians have retained the same basic pattern found in the tuatara, but some changes in relative position of the two temporal openings can be observed (fig. 18.4). One point is especially pertinent relative to the class that follows. While in adult birds so many secondary modifications occur that the fundamental design is obscured, the skull of the fetus shows the same pattern of structure as the alligators and crocodiles.

THE CLASS AVES

As suggested in the foregoing paragraph on the skull, the birds of the class Aves show many internal similarities to the reptilians—in fact, they are sometimes referred to as glorified reptiles. These relationships can be brought out better in a later section; our immediate concerns are the adaptations these animals have acquired in becoming adapted for flight, song, and their other familiar traits.

General Characteristics

Approximately 10,000 species of birds are extant today, arranged in 25 to 30 orders. These, while relatively few in numbers, represent a whole spectrum of evolutionary advancement from fairly primitive to highly advanced. For instance, the ostrich of Africa, the emu and cassowaries of Australia (fig. 18.6, B), the rhea of South America, and kiwis of New Zealand (fig. 18.6, A) are representatives of primitive flightless birds (ratites), whose fore appendages have become reduced or even lost entirely. These forms are primitive in that they lack the keel on the breastbone of flying species, a structure that provides a base for the attachment of the powerful flight muscles. As a whole, these few species are not closely related to one another and are classed in four separate orders; thus they appear to be remnants of formerly more abundant and widely diversified taxa.

Many other birds are flightless but are thought to have lost their former powers of flight secondarily through specialization, for they all have a well-developed keel. For instance, the penguins (fig. 18.7) cannot fly, because their wings have become adapted as paddles for swimming beneath water. While thus advanced in having a keel, they lack the light bone structure and other specializations of higher types; consequently, the order to which they belong (the Sphenisciformes) is usually ranked among the lowest of keeled forms.

As just intimated, many adaptations for flight other than wings, feathers, and keel have been acquired by birds. For instance, the rib cage has become rigidly fused to the breast bone, so that while providing the greater strength to the skeleton needed to cope with the stresses imposed by flight, it no longer can serve in respiration. Instead there is an extensive system of air sacs distributed between the internal organs and extending into some of the larger bones. These do not serve in lightening the body of birds, for they actually contribute to the gross

A   B

Figure 18.6 *Two primitively flightless birds.* (A) One of several species of kiwi, wingless nocturnal forms that nest in burrows. (Courtesy of New Zealand National Publicity.) (B) The cassowary of tropical Australia is one of the few remaining large species of flightless birds. (Courtesy of Australian News and Information Bureau.)

weight; rather, they aid in cooling the internal organs, and more importantly, help in inhaling and exhaling air. Air is taken into the lungs and these sacs, which are connected to them, by means of contractions of muscles on the ribs and other body parts that enlarge those organs by pulling on their surfaces. During expiration, the musculature of the thorax and abdomen contract to compress the respiratory organs and sacs, thereby forcing the air out. The flight muscles also help to such an extent that the air of the lungs and sacs is completely replaced in respiration.

Figure 18.7 *Penguins, secondarily flightless birds.* Penguins, like these emperor penguins from Antarctica, appear to have been derivatives of ancestors that could fly, for they have a keel on the breastbone. However, they lack the hollow bones and airsacs of higher forms. (San Diego Zoo Photo.)

Other flight adaptations are found in the excretory system. The urinary bladder is lacking, so that no watery secreta add unnecessary weight to the body. Instead the products from the kidneys are stored in the cloaca, where moisture is removed, and pass out of the body with the excreta. As in reptiles, the nitrogenous waste is in the form of nearly insoluble uric acid, rather than the readily soluble urea; consequently, it is not necessary to waste water in removing the nitrogenous by-products of metabolism. Since during migration or other long flights, water is difficult to obtain, this adaptation has considerable survival value. Its importance is accented by an adaptation that numerous seabirds have acquired. Many such birds, including albatross, gulls, terns, and shearwaters, often spend long periods at sea without returning to land. Obviously the only water available to them is that of the oceans, which is 4% salt. Since the blood of birds, like that of other vertebrates, is only about 0.6% salt, the excess chemical taken in by drinking must be quickly eliminated. For this purpose, salt glands have evolved in these birds, located either above the eyes or near the base of the upper beak. These organs remove salt from the blood and secrete it at the base of the beak or through the nostrils.

Diversification

Aside from modifications of feathers, such as those exhibited by the lyre bird, the adaptations of birds are chiefly centered on beak and leg structure. Among specializations of the latter are included the running legs of the cassowary (fig. 18.7, B) and ostrich, the webbed feet of swimming birds such as those of gulls and terns as well as ducks and geese, and the stout legs of the kiwi, especially useful in digging its burrow. Others with which the student doubtlessly is familiar are the elongated appendages of herons, willets, and other waders, the powerful talons of hawks and owls, the weak legs of hummingbirds and swifts reduced almost to the point of uselessness, and those of canaries, sparrows, and other finches specialized for perching.

Much diversification in beak structure has been associated with specializations in food preferences. That of the kiwi is long and tubular (fig. 18.7, A) and is particularly adapted for probing the earth for worms and insects, whereas the sharp strong one of the cassowary is specialized for the fruit and berries on which it feeds. Usually the bill structure is characteristic for whole orders of birds, such as the hooked one used for tearing flesh by eagles, hawks, and other carnivorous forms, or the strong seed-eating type characteristic of all finches. However, occasionally, as among the family Drepaniidae (fig. 18.8) of Hawaii, wide divergence in beak structure may occur in relatively small taxonomic units.

Reproductive Adaptations

Perhaps the most remarkable adaptations are associated with reproductive behavior. Intricate courtship patterns often precede pairing activities (fig. 18.9), and differences in color between sexes (sexual dimorphism), as in cardinals and house sparrows, are of frequent occurrence. Complex song patterns, which have evolved along with the development of a distinctive voice box, or syrinx, are

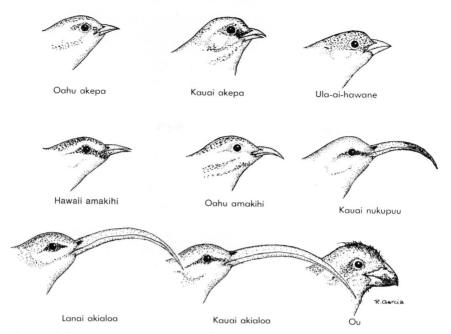

Oahu akepa

Kauai akepa

Ula-ai-hawane

Hawaii amakihi

Oahu amakihi

Kauai nukupuu

Lanai akialoa

Kauai akialoa

Ou

R.Garcia

Figure 18.8 *Diversification within a single family of birds.* Among birds, specializations in food habits typically involve concomitant changes in the bill. For example, in the Hawaiian family of honeycreepers, the akepas catch insects on the wing, the amakihis search out insects on leaves, the akialoas pry out insects from crevices of bark and also feed on nectar, and the ous feed on seeds. (From Dillon, Lawrence S.: *Evolution,* 2nd ed., St. Louis, 1978, The C.V. Mosby Co.)

often part of these proceedings, too. In addition to their role in courtship, calls are used for communication between members of the same pair or family groups, and in defending the territories set up by breeding males. After the courtship rites are consummated, the actual laying and incubation of the eggs and care of the young following hatching are likewise associated with numerous intricate behavioral traits.

Nests, a familiar feature of the reproductive processes, are frequently absent among the primitive types. By way of illustration, the female emu merely lays eggs on the ground wherever she may happen to be in her mate's territory. The male, then, gathers the six or more eggs which make up a clutch into one spot where he incubates them (fig. 18.10). Many of the somewhat more advanced types, including the brush turkey of eastern Australia, let decaying vegetation provide the heat needed during incubation. The male builds a mound, at least 1 m high and 3 m in diameter (fig. 18.11), out of fallen leaves and other plant debris in various stages of decay. When ensured by the resulting heat production that fermentation is proceeding satisfactorily, the female commences to deposit eggs and continues over an extended period of time until 30 or more have been

Figure 18.9 *Courtship in the bobolink*. The male spreads his wings and tails as he sings. Note also the marked differences in coloration (sexual dimorphism). (Photo courtesy of Stephen G. Martin.)

Figure 18.10 *Emus and their eggs*. The male emu gathers the eggs that females deposit into a group on the bare ground where he will incubate them.

A

B

Figure 18.11 *Mound-building birds of Australia.* Several species of birds build mounds of decaying vegetation and use the heat of fermentation to incubate their eggs. A. A mound built by a male brush turkey (*Alectura lathami*). B. The female mallee fowl (*Leipoa ocellata*) has just laid the egg barely visible in front of her; the male standing behind her will cover the egg with the sand and vegetation that makes up the mound. (Both photographs courtesy of H.J. Frith and Division of Wildlife Research, C.S.I.R.O., Australia.)

laid. During the subsequent incubation period, the male adds or removes the vegetable matter to regulate the temperature of the mound carefully. Such mounds are used over a period of years, new debris being added each season—it is sometimes believed that several females may use the same mound. Other fairly primitive birds, including the killdeer, lay their eggs in a group of pebbles on the surface of the ground (fig. 18.12), whereas the intricate nests of advanced species built in trees are too well known to need description.

Among the more primitive orders of birds, including the flightless ones as well as quail, turkey, chickens, ducks and geese, and most waders and shore birds that build nests on the ground, the newly-hatched young are covered with down and can run or swim almost immediately. In contrast to these precocial forms, the new young of the higher orders are naked and quite helpless for a period before they are able to leave the nest and are referred to as altricial. The two kinds of young are alike in requiring parental care for an extended period after they leave the nest, for both must be protected against weather hazards and predators. In addition, the altricial kind requires continual feeding, a difficult task as most juveniles consume a quantity of food exceeding their own body weight each day. Food requirements of the young often contrast with those of the adults. For example, adult cardinals feed almost exclusively on seeds, but they make special efforts to capture moths and other insects to feed their young. On the other hand, mockingbirds as adults have a diet consisting largely of insects, but feed their young on berries, especially in spring.

The Origins of Birds

Some years ago, in the lithographic limestones of Germany a very exciting fossil was discovered, in the form of a skeleton of a bird that had teeth like those of reptiles and a long, bony tail. Fortunately the fine grain of the stone in which it was embedded preserved intact many delicate features, such as the tracery of the

Figure 18.12 *The eggs and nest of a killdeer.*

feathers which had covered the bird in life. This oldest known bird, named *Archaeopteryx* (fig. 18.13), lived during Jurassic times, about 160 million years ago. Without the imprints of the feathers, this fossil would have been considered just another small bipedal dinosaur, for there would have been little to indicate otherwise. The teeth would certainly have suggested it to be a reptile, as would the elongate tail. Although wings were present, they were too feeble for flight and at their tips were three fingers, each provided with a claw. None of the bones were hollow nor was there a keel on the breastbone; furthermore, the structure of the pelvis and hind legs resembled those of the small running dinosaurs.

Two concepts have developed to suggest the mechanisms which might have led to the origins of the feathers and wings. The first of these, the arboreal theory, proposes that the early parental stock consisted of tree-dwelling species whose fore limbs and long tail were edged with broad, flattened, overhanging scales that served much as a parachute to break the force of the fall as these creatures leaped from limb to limb. Gradually these scales elongated and slowly became modified into feathers as we know them today and as found on *Archaeopteryx*. The wings then were still weak, but as these organs became strengthened over the millenia, they first were useful in gliding from one tree to another, much in the fashion of flying squirrels. Finally, when additional strengthening and musculature had been gained, the birds were actually able to fly.

The second concept suggests essentially similar processes but begins with ground-dwelling forms, as the bipedal dinosaurs proper obviously were. In this set of ideas, the flattened, overhanging scales of the fore limbs and tail were viewed as providing buoyancy and, by thus increasing the animal's speed, had great survival value in escaping the numerous predatory reptiles that abounded in

Figure 18.13 *One of the better-preserved specimens of Archaeopteryx.* (Courtesy of the American Museum of Natural History.)

those times. As in the foregoing concept, this cursorial theory considers the scales to have developed into the feathers of *Archaeopteryx,* and the fore limbs gradually to have become strengthened into wings suitable for flight. This hypothesis has recently received support by the discovery of a third skeletal fossil specimen in a museum collection. In this latest example, the claws of the toes are much more clearly preserved and have been shown not to be fitted for climbing as had been believed earlier, but resemble those of ground-dwelling reptiles.

THE CLASS MAMMALIA

Although birds are found in large numbers in all areas of the world, including the seas and the lands from pole to pole, in a sense they have not generally mastered the severer climates. For rather than becoming adapted to them completely, they migrate to more favorable climates when winter sets in. Of course, there are a number of exceptions, like the penguins that remain in Antarctica throughout the year. On the other hand, the mammals, lacking the ability to migrate over great distances, are in a stricter sense adapted to the regions they occupy. And they, too, occur throughout the marine and terrestrial environments of the world. However, they are not as highly diversified as are the avians, for only around 4,300 species are known to be extant, arranged in three subclasses and only 19 orders (table 18.2). Perhaps the phylogenetic tree (fig. 18.14), based on a widely accepted scheme of classification, most clearly indicates the highly varied specializations that have developed. The diagram not only brings out the existing diversity but also suggests the complex manner in which comparable adaptations have been acquired. For example, three orders (whales, seals, and sirenians) have become adapted for aquatic life, yet they are distantly related to one another.

Other Characteristics

Also in contrast to birds, mammals possess a number of traits found in no other taxon. Among the most outstanding of these are a covering of hair, sweat glands in the skin, a muscular diaphragm that aids in respiration, a lower jaw that consists of only one bone, three ossicles in the middle ear (incus, malleus, and stapes; birds and reptiles have only the stapes), teeth of four different types, and mammae (milk glands). Moreover, in addition to several other traits that can be better pointed out in later discussions, the red blood cells become enucleated just prior to their entrance into the blood stream.

Improvements in respiration and circulation also provide prominent features of mammals. Probably the most noteworthy new adaptation in the first of these functions is the diaphragm mentioned in the foregoing paragraph. This muscular organ, in conjunction with the movable ribs, enables the lungs to be emptied and filled more completely than is possible in almost all the other vertebrates. The only group that compares favorably in this action are those birds that have well-developed air sacs, which in flight replace the air of the lungs 100%. Other resemblances with birds exist, including endothermy (warm-bloodedness) and a

Table 18.2 The Subclasses of Mammals

| Characteristic | Subclasses | | |
	Prototheria	Metatheria	Eutheria
Egg	With leathery or membranous shell; abundant yolk present	Membranous shell usually present, yolk reduced	Shell lacking, yolk absent
Nipples	Absent; tufts of hair only	Present, with tufts of hair	Present, untufted
Pouch	Absent or temporary	Usually present in female, becomes scrotum in male	Modified into external genitalia and scrotum
Legs	Placed at right angles to body	Arranged upright	Arranged upright
Pelvic girdle	Coracoid well-developed throughout life	Coracoid present in embryo only	Coracoid absent
Marsupial bones	Present	Present	Absent
Right ventricle	Valves muscular	Valves membranous	Valves membranous
Representatives	Platypus and echidna only	Opossums, kangaroos, bandicoots, marsupial mice and cats, phalangers, etc.	Mice, cats, wolves, elk, badgers, moles, mink, camels, horses, cattle, etc.

four chambered heart, provided with only a single aorta, but in the present group the left aorta remains while the right one of the reptilian ancestors has been lost. Consequently this organ, although superficially alike in the two taxa, is considered to have been independently derived from the partially septate ventrical of the ancestral stock.

Reproductive Habits

In these animals probably the most outstanding adaptations are found in the reproductive traits. Interestingly enough, these begin in nesting habits not too dissimilar from those of certain birds. The most primitive mammals of today, a monotreme known as the duck-billed platypus (fig. 18.15, A), digs a burrow adjacent to streams, where the female builds a nest in which to deposit the clutch of two eggs. The latter are covered with a leathery shell quite like that of turtle and snake eggs, and are similarly supplied with an abundance of albumen and yolk. Hatching occurs after 10 to 14 days. It is only then that the sole improvement over reptilian and avian reproductive habits that can be noted is found, for the young are then fed milk. However, as nipples are absent in the female, the

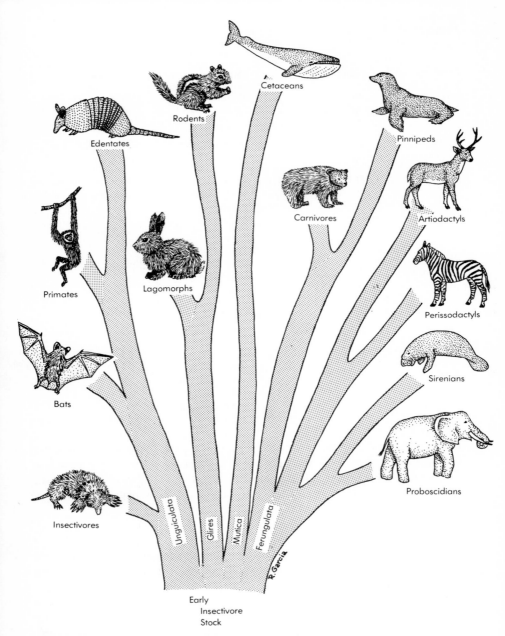

Figure 18.14 *A phylogenetic tree of mammals.* This tree shows in diagrammatic fashion the relationships of the various mammalian orders as presented by a currently popular scheme of classification. (From Dillon, Lawrence S.: *Evolution,* 2nd ed., St. Louis, 1978, The C.V. Mosby Co.)

A   B

Figure 18.15   *The two diverse types of egg-laying mammals.* All such monotremes are
confined to Australia and New Guinea region. A. The duck-billed platypus daily
consumes large quantities of earthworms and other soft-bodied invertebrates. B. In
contrast, the echidna is adapted to a diet of ants and other small insects. (Courtesy of the
Australian Information Service.)

young obtain the milk by means of hair tufts along which the milk flows from the
glands. Nursing continues for 11 weeks, but the young do not emerge from the
burrow for an additional 6 week period.

The second monotreme, the echidna or spiny anteater (fig. 18.15, B), shows
several improvements over those of the platypus in egg structure and reproductive habits. Although the egg is covered with a shell, no calcium salts are deposited in it, so the covering is soft, not leathery (fig. 18.16). No nest is built;
instead when the single egg of the year is laid, the female catches it on one paw
and places it in an open pouch that forms on the abdomen only during the breeding season. There hatching takes place in between 7 and 10 days, but the young
remains in the pouch for about 8 weeks, feeding on milk in the same manner as
the platypus young. Since the juvenile's spines begin to form at the end of this
time, the female removes it from the pouch and conceals it in a sheltered spot for
a period.

The marsupials (fig. 18.17) display a number of advancements over the reproductive processes of the monotremes. Here the egg has only a thin shell,
consisting of but one of the original set of three membranes, and only a small
quantity of albumen and yolk is present. After fertilization has occurred, the
embryo is retained in the uterus where it becomes attached and nourished by
means of a placenta, usually for a period of 10 to 14 days. In some marsupials,
however, the intrauterine period continues for about 6 weeks. At best the young
are poorly developed at birth, with mere vestiges for hind legs and many internal
organs still in a rudimentary condition (fig. 18.18, A). When born, the young

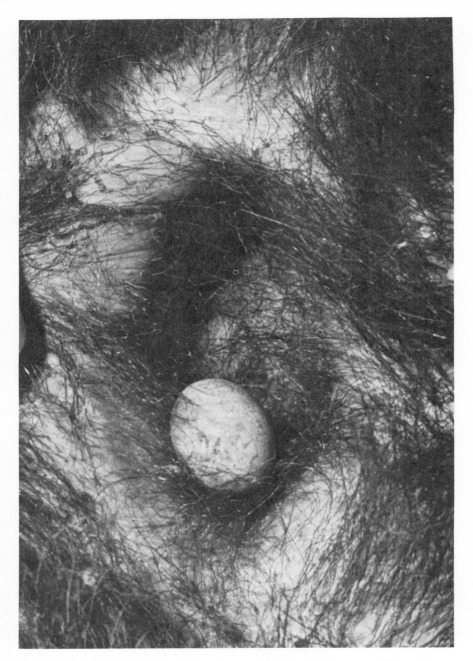

Figure 18.16 *The egg of an echidna in the temporary pouch.* The cover of the echidna egg is soft and delicate, quite unlike the leathery one that covers the platypus egg. (Courtesy of Ederie Slater and the Division of Wildlife Research, C.S.I.R.O., Australia.)

A

B

Figure 18.17 *Diversity among marsupials.* A. Among the most advanced types of marsupials are the kangaroos, whose bipedal mode of rapid locomotion is well illustrated by these red kangaroos of New South Wales. B. The Australian "native cat" (genus *Dasyurus*) is one of many carnivorous types; it grows to about 18 inches in length. C. The Tasmanian tiger may no longer be in existence; if still extant, it is confined to the wilderness of southeastern Tasmania. D. The wombat is a social animal living in clusters of burrows; it is a vegetarian, not unlike the North American ground hog in habits. (Photo courtesy of the Australian Information Service.)

Figure 18.17—*Continued*

C

D

works its way along hair tracts on the female's body to the pouch, using the fore legs alone for locomotion. There in the pouch the young attaches to a nipple (fig. 18.18, B), each of which bears a tuft of hair; the mouth then becomes immobilized, so the young is securely fastened. Nursing continues in this fashion for periods ranging from 55 days in bandicoots (insect-eating, ratlike marsupials) to 6 or more months in kangaroos. Then the eyes open, the jaws relax, and the young is free to emerge from the pouch, but returns to it frequently for food and shelter. In male marsupials, the pouch of the fetus develops into the scrotum, here located anterior to the penis.

In the eutherians, or placental mammals, the egg lacks a shell entirely and is totally without albumen and yolk, although the yolk sac remains. After the developing early embryo has become embedded within the folds of the uterine wall, a placenta forms as described shortly, and a rather protracted period of intrauterine development and growth begins. The outcome is a juvenile which is equivalent in its development to that which young marsupials gain in the uterus plus that which they undergo in the pouch. Such gestation periods in placental mammals range from 12 to 16 days in many shrews to 16 months in the sperm whale. As in the birds, the newly born young vary in degree of development. In the rodents, carnivores, and primates, the young are born naked, often sightless, and with muscles too feeble to support the body, while at the other end of the scale, as in deer, horses, and whales, the infant is capable of locomotion within a few minutes after birth. A pouch forms on fetuses of both sexes, that of males becoming a scrotum, located behind the penis, and that of females becoming the external genital parts.

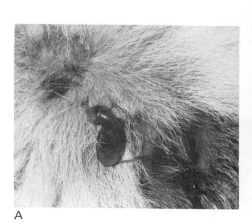 

A   B

Figure 18.18 *Early events in the life of a new-born kangaroo.* A. The tiny new-born here is still attached to the parent's uterus by the umbilical cord. Note that the young is scarcely longer than the parental hairs and lacks hind limbs at this stage. B. The young has found its way to the pouch and is now attached to a nipple. (Courtesy of Ederie Slater and the Division of Wildlife Research, C.S.I.R.O., Australia.)

As seen in the two foregoing paragraphs, the embryos of both the marsupials and placental mammals develop a placenta during the intrauterine period. First it should be clear that, while in the uterus, all mammalian young are supplied with food to some extent—even in the monotremes, the zygote undergoes considerable development in the reproductive tract before the egg shell is finally added, during which period of growth the embryo absorbs fluid nutritive material secreted by the uterine walls. Furthermore, in the American opossum, the embryo retains the thin eggshell throughout development, thus precluding close contact between it and the uterus. Hence, no placenta can possibly exist, yet the growing young is supplied nourishment from the parent in the form of a nutritive fluid secreted by the uterus.

Most usually in marsupials, the eggshell is absent or ruptures early in embryogeny, and a placenta develops. In the majority of forms, the placenta consists solely of yolk sac derivatives. For this role of absorbing foodstuffs, the yolk sac is particularly well suited, for its walls are heavily vascularized in reptiles and birds, as well as in mammals. In the several genera of bandicoots, the placenta consists of derivatives of the allantois and chorion, just as it is in all the placental mammals themselves. Several varieties of the placenta of eutherians are known, all made from these same basic membranes, but the details of structure are of no pertinence here.

Origin of Mammals

The origins of many of the unique traits that characterize mammals will likely always be less clear than those of the birds, where intermediate forms between the Aves proper and the ancestral stock are still alive to supply livers, hearts, brains, and kidneys, organs that are never known to fossilize. Since all the predecessors of mammals have long since been extinct, the origins of that group must accordingly be based on parts like the skull and teeth that do fossilize readily. Fortunately these parts are quite distinctive in the present taxon and fossils sufficiently abundant, that a reasonably probable restoration of the major events in their establishment can be made. And in following the development of these structures, light is also cast on the origins of an unexpected third part, the bones of the middle ear.

It will be recalled that the birds and living reptiles are classed as Diapsida, on the basis of the presence of two pairs of openings in the temporal region of the skull. Contrastingly, in mammals only one pair of temporal arches is present, so these animals are considered to be members of a branch called the Synapsida. This line, too, had its origins in *Seymouria,* in which the eardrums were located at the base of the skull, and the subsequent events show that the pair of openings was originally formed by the inward migration of the eardrums. In this case, the latter penetrated into the upper surface of the skull, rather than into the sides as in the Diapsida. At first the openings merely penetrated the roof of the cranium, as in *Eothryis* and *Lycosuchus* (fig. 18.19, A, B), two representatives of a group called the pelycosaurs. Later the openings and the eardrums migrated laterally somewhat, forming a broad arch on the sides (fig. 18.19, C). Then in a second,

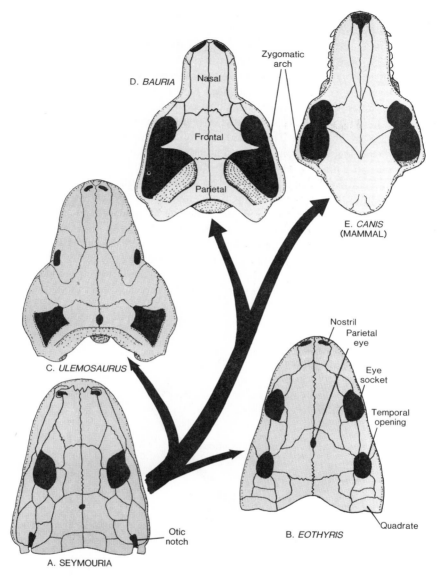

Figure 18.19 *Changes in skull structure among the synapsid reptiles.*

more advanced group known as Therapsida, or mammal-like reptiles, the lateral movement resulted in the zygomatic arch that forms part of the cheek bone in mankind (fig. 18.19, D–F). Still later the tympanic membranes became engulfed by the skull bones below the arch, so the latter no longer served as a supportive structure.

While this characteristic was developing, two other sets of changes were proceeding concurrently, one of which involved the teeth. Whereas all modern reptiles have teeth of only one type, some of the therapsids mentioned above began to acquire specialized types, until eventually in the most advanced therapsids the four varieties found in mammals were present. But the more important of the two sets was concerned with changes in the structure of the lower jaw. Among most reptiles, the lower jaw consists of no fewer than eight distinct bones, but here for simplicity's sake, the changes in only the four located on the outer surface are followed. These four are the dentary, in which the teeth are embedded, the angular, surangular, and articular; as its name implies, the latter bone provides the hinge with the cranium, the point of articulation being on the quadrate, a skull bone that is also involved in these events.

At the earliest known levels among the mammal-like reptiles, the dentary has already become larger than the corresponding bone in typical forms, and during the ensuing events, it carries this trend further (fig. 18.20). As this bone steadily increases in relative size, the other three jaw bones decrease correspondingly. One by one (fig. 18.20) they continue to become reduced in size, until each has attained diminutive proportions. On the skull, the quadrate, too, has undergone reduction; eventually it is so small that it becomes detached from the skull, but

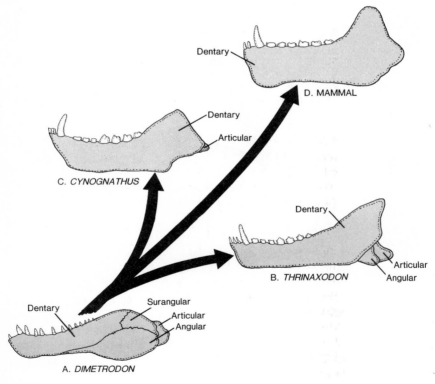

Figure 18.20 *Evolutionary development of the mammalian lower jawbone.*

still retains its articulation with the lower jaw. About this time the dentary has become quite extensive and has sent a process upwards toward the skull, so for a while, the jaw has two points of articulation on each side. With the advent of this new hinge, the angular and surangular are lost entirely, while the articular breaks free, leaving the lower jaw to consist of only the dentary (fig. 18.20).

In mammalian embryos, the quadrate and articular bones develop just behind the rear angle of the lower jaw, as indicated above. Here for a time they lie attached to the skin and other tissues of the region, but then the pair migrates inwards and becomes connected to the stapes. The latter is already associated with the eardrums, a condition that prevails even in frogs. As development continues, the three bones become the ossicles of the middle ear. Because the therapsid reptiles have so many characteristics which gradually merge into those of the Mammalia, it has sometimes been proposed that those reptiles should be classed in the latter taxon. Thus both the Aves and the present class display traits which indicate an origin from a reptilian stock. Perhaps these relationships will become even more clear as the historical changes in several important chordate structures are summarized in the section that follows.

EVOLUTIONARY CHANGES IN THE VERTEBRATES

While the foregoing discussions make clear the major changes that occurred during the evolutionary development of the vertebrates, these in turn are underlain by other, less obvious alterations which are of at least equal significance. Some of these modifications that occurred over the long span of geologic time involve technical points which are beyond the scope of this text. There is a sufficiency of others, however, that can be summarized here to indicate the more profound nature of many adaptations acquired by organisms as their lineage develops from a primitive to a highly advanced state.

Evolution of Paired Appendages

One of the more evident requirements of active animals, regardless of whether aquatic or terrestrial, is the presence of an efficient locomotory apparatus. In providing a clear-cut idea, both of the major steps required in evolving an effective system and the alterations necessary thereafter in adapting to new ecological situations, the vertebrate series of events is paramount.

The sequence may be viewed as beginning with a type resembling the lancelets, one which is equipped with only a single adaptation for swimming, the laterally flattened tail. Nothing between this simple state and the next more advanced type exists, so it is not possible to suggest on solid grounds how the *finfold* of the lampreys arose. All that is confirmable with evidence is that these most primitive of existing vertebrates have such a fold. This swimming device consists of a single, flat, dermal flap that extends along the middorsal line to the tail web. Then from the lower tip of the tail, it continues forward along the abdomen nearly to the anal opening, where it forks; from there each fork continues forward as a lateral fold along the side to terminate near the gill openings (fig. 18.21, A).

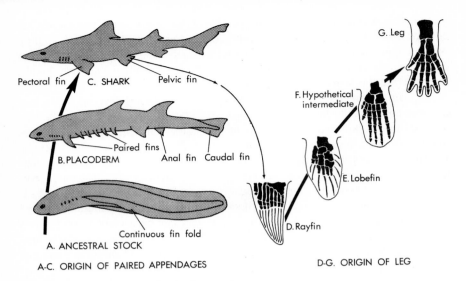

Pectoral fin   C. SHARK   Pelvic fin

Paired fins

B. PLACODERM   Anal fin   Caudal fin

Continuous fin fold

A. ANCESTRAL STOCK

A-C. ORIGIN OF PAIRED APPENDAGES

G. Leg

F. Hypothetical intermediate

E. Lobefin

D. Rayfin

D-G. ORIGIN OF LEG

Figure 18.21   *Evolution of paired appendages.*

Among a number of ancient fossil fishlike forms known as placoderms, several types intimate how this relatively cumbersome organ began its progress toward becoming efficient fins. As shown in the illustration (fig. 18.21, B), parts of the lateral finfold became reduced and eventually lost, leaving about seven fins on each side, so that a series of *paired fins* was created. These seven pairs were in addition to a number of unpaired fins behind the anus, on the tail, and on the back. With additional progress, the number of paired fins was gradually reduced in the fossil placoderms, first to five pairs, then to four, and three, until ultimately the descendants of this group, the sharks (fig. 18.21, C), had only the two pairs that characterize the more advanced vertebrates.

Later the flat *rayfin* type of paired appendages found originally in the sharks developed to their highest level of efficiency as the modern fish arose and evolved. Possibly the evolution of these fins explains, in part at least, how their possessors, the 50,000 species of fish living today, were able to conquer all possible types of aquatic environments, ranging from tiny springheads to the oceans in size, from fresh to brackish and saline in quality, and in temperature from frigid polar to the quite warm springs of desert areas.

Why or how the coelacanths modified the efficient flattened rayfin to a thick cylindrical type known as the *lobefin* remains a mystery. Nevertheless, the short flattened bones found at the base of the rayfins appear to have fused or otherwise become reduced in number. Then they elongated as a strong musculature developed around them, so that the resulting organs appeared somewhat like thick digitless legs (fig. 18.21, E). In the modern African and South American lungfish, the lobefins have been modified into long, slender fibers, practically worthless for swimming and obviously of no value in digging into the soil during cocoon formation. In the Australian species, however, the lobefin is still a functional swimming organ (fig. 17.11).

Some intermediate form, thus far not found in the fossil record, must have existed between the early lobefin fishes and the next stage in the evolution of paired appendages (fig. 18.21, F). Certain of the bony elements of the lobefin are believed to have elongated greatly so that they formed a bony support for the swimming web. Then, when the vertebrate stock began its adaptation for a terrestrial life, the web gradually was reduced between the terminal bones so that digits resulted (fig. 18.21, G). Certain primitive salamanders have simple legs such as that figured, with relatively poor musculature; moreover, no amphibian has protective armature on the digit tips. Only with the advent of the reptiles did the digits receive their claws. And with the development of this armature, the central evolution of the paired appendages was brought to a close. All other adaptations for climbing, running, flying, or swimming involve mere modifications of the basic structural pattern.

Evolution of the Respiratory Apparatus

The major steps in the development of the breathing apparatus have already been alluded to during the discussion of the various vertebrate classes. A brief summary, however, may make the chief events clearer.

Again the series begins with the lancelets or the lanceletlike ammocoetes larva. In these early forms, a great number of gills are located in the disproportionately large *branchial basket* into which the pharynx is modified—as many as 34 pairs of gills may line the walls of the pharynx (fig. 18.22, A). In the lancelets, as in their relatives, the gill slits open outwardly into a special cavity called the atrium. This outer cavity is absent in ammocoetes, so that the gill slits open directly into the surrounding waters, as in more advanced types.

After this first progressive step of the loss of the atrium had been taken, the gills must have undergone reduction in number—that is, they increased in respiratory efficiency—since adult lampreys and hagfish have only 8 to 15 pairs (fig. 18.22, B). Still greater functional capacity seems to have been acquired by the gills in the placoderms, accompanying the development of the paired appendages, for modern sharks and rays possess only 5 pairs of functional gills. In addition there is a *spiracle* (fig. 18.22, C) on each side, which is the remnant of an anterior gill slit; this, too, opens into the pharynx but appears to be vestigial.

Later in vertebrate evolution, as among the rayfin fish, the spiracle became modified into the Eustachian tube and therefore no longer is considered an active part of the respiratory system. For the greater part the number of functional gill slits (fig. 18.22, D) continued at the shark level of five pairs during much of the remainder of the evolutionary history of this system. Further improvement first came about with the addition of *lungs* as in the lungfish, but the predecessor of these organs, the *swimbladder,* had arisen much earlier among the rayfin fishes. Although it was vascularized in some rayfin fishes to supplement breathing, this ancestral organ mostly served a nonrespiratory function until the lungfish arose.

In the lungfish (fig. 18.22, E) the lungs are essential supplements to the gills, which provide the major part of oxygen to the blood, and in the amphibians, too, they play only a supporting role. The gills do not persist in most adult salaman-

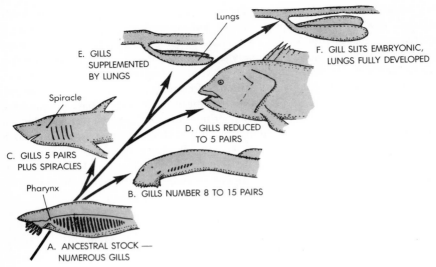

Lungs

E. GILLS
SUPPLEMENTED
BY LUNGS

F. GILL SLITS EMBRYONIC,
LUNGS FULLY DEVELOPED

Spiracle

D. GILLS REDUCED
TO 5 PAIRS

C. GILLS 5 PAIRS
PLUS SPIRACLES

Pharynx

B. GILLS NUMBER 8 TO 15 PAIRS

A. ANCESTRAL STOCK —
NUMEROUS GILLS

Figure 18.22   *Major changes in the respiratory system of vertebrates.* At the highest
level, the gill slits become nonfunctional, as well as confined to the embryo.

ders and frogs, for the moist skin provides the major oxygen-absorbing organ,
not the lungs. However, in the reptiles lung structure becomes vastly improved,
so that supplementary devices of all sorts are lost (fig. 18.22, F). Among the lost
adjuncts are the gills, for now only gill slits ever appear, and these are confined to
the embryo, in which they are reduced to just four pairs.

Evolution of the Heart

Improving the methods for introducing oxygen into blood by way of better
ventilating organs can provide little real benefit until the system concerned with
moving the blood also has made progress. In biology, this does *not* mean that an
improved locomotory system makes a better respiratory system necessary, and
that the acquisition of the latter necessitates improved circulation. Rather, the
interrelation would be expressed in terms suggesting that the acquisition of adaptations for more effective locomotion gave an adaptive advantage to any mutation
which provided more efficient respiration. And in turn, the latter imparted survival value to any genetic changes which induced improvements in the circulation
of the blood. In the latter point of view, the relations are not one of cause and
effect; rather, the principal ingredients are chance genetic changes and a slightly
bettered rate of survival among the descendants, processes repeated again and
again over long periods of time.

Among vertebrates, the heart is the prime mover of the blood, and a clear
series of stages in its elaboration exists in the several classes. In the lancelets,
only a pulsating blood vessel is present, but, in the lampreys, a slightly twisted
two-chambered heart exists, suggesting that in some unknown intermediate stock
the pulsating vessel become modified into a straight two-chambered heart (fig.

18.23, A, B). The simple twisted stage is found among sharks and rays, as well as among the rayfin fish and coelacanths (fig. 18.23, C).

With the advent of the lungs in the lungfish, however, the heart underwent extensive improvement, for the atrium became subdivided into two chambers, a structural device permitting the partial separation of the oxygenated and deoxygenated blood (fig. 18.23, D). Later, when the earliest amphibians came into existence, the heart remained fundamentally unchanged, as shown by the congo eel of today. Then in more advanced salamanders, the twisting of the heart continued, so that eventually the atrium which had formed the posterior portion of the heart came to be located anteriorly, as in the frogs and toads (fig. 18.23, E). Then in later steps, best seen among the living reptiles, the ventricle acquired a short septum, as in the turtles (fig. 18.23, F); later, as in the snakes and lizards, this septum elongated and nearly subdivided the ventricle (fig. 18.23, G). Still later, the heart attained its ultimate development, when, as in crocodilians, birds,

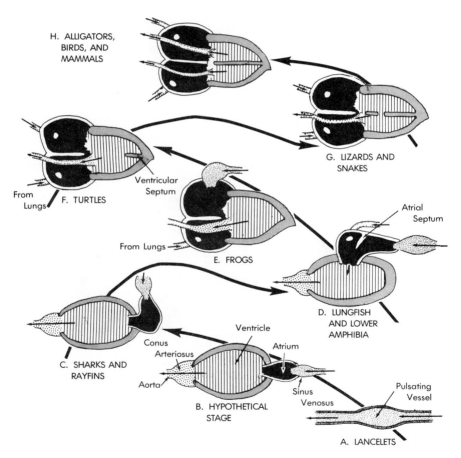

Figure 18.23 *Some steps in the evolution of the vertebrate heart.*

and mammals, the original single ventricle became completely divided into two (fig. 18.23, H), forming the very efficient four-chambered condition.

Unfortunately space limitations do not permit descriptions of the evolution of the other systems of vertebrates. But equally remarkable series of changes can be found in their brains, reproductive organs, and digestive systems, and are detailed in some of the readings suggested below.

EVOLUTIONARY SUMMARY

To judge from the similarities of habits and body structure, there can be little doubt that a lanceletlike form ultimately led to the development of an ammocoeteslike type and that from this early stock all the vertebrates were derived, one step at a time. The first surviving descendant group, the lampreys and hagfishes, lack many of the traits of the higher types, including bone, jaws, and paired fins (fig. 18.24, B). While the next extant group to arise, the sharks and rays, had acquired the latter two characters, they still lacked bone. However, teeth and much improved respiratory and other systems also had been developed. Although some very early, extinct groups had had bony *exo*skeletons even before the cyclostomes arose, bone in the *endo*skeleton was developed only with the advent of the ray-finned fishes; these animals had gained a still more efficient respiratory system also, as well as opercula and a swim bladder.

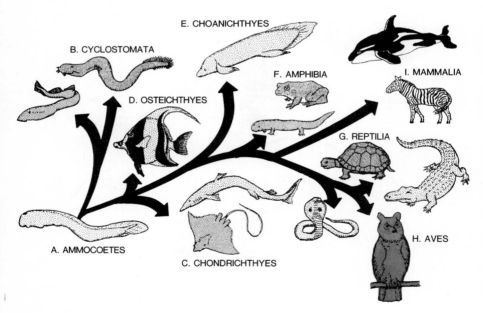

E. CHOANICHTHYES

B. CYCLOSTOMATA

F. AMPHIBIA

I. MAMMALIA

D. OSTEICHTHYES

G. REPTILIA

A. AMMOCOETES

H. AVES

C. CHONDRICHTHYES

Figure 18.24 *A phylogeny of the vertebrates.*

In later groups, such characteristics as lobefins (fig. 18.24, E), nostrils, lungs (from the swim bladder), and a three-chambered heart made lungfish and others that possessed them increasingly adapted for a terrestrial habitat. Beyond this point, a number of intermediate groups doubtlessly existed that showed the conversion of a fishlike body to the cylindrical one of land dwellers, but they have not as yet been encountered in the fossil record. Thus the next more advanced group extant today, the Amphibia, has fully developed walking legs, slender body, strong skeleton, and other features required for a land existence. It should be noted that this taxon possibly is not entirely a natural one, for several of its branches show stages that are intermediate in the evolution of the tubular heart of the lungfish to the conical one of frogs and all higher forms. Vocal cords and auditory tympani appear also to have been acquired in several stages of this vertebrate group.

After a post-amphibian stock had developed the firm-shelled egg, claws, and epidermal scales that mark the higher vertebrates, several main branches of advancement were followed. One of these, terminating in the birds, includes all extant reptiles. In the hearts of these latter creatures, a series of steps is shown that indicates how the three-chambered heart of the frog gradually was converted into the four-chambered ones of the birds and mammals. Along a second major branch, the reptilian representatives have long been extinct, so the mammals are the sole survivors. Fossil finds, however, have been of great value in suggesting how the characteristics of the mammalian skull, lower jaws, teeth, and middle ear were evolved.

QUESTIONS FOR REVIEW AND THOUGHT

1. In what specific ways are the Reptilia better adapted for an existence on land than are the Amphibia? Why was it necessary for a new type of scale to arise in this class to provide a protective coat? That is, why were not the types found in fishes merely modified for the purpose?

2. Describe the two paths by which the eardrums entered the skull of reptiles. How are the two lines of ascent named? What are their respective terminal products?

3. Name the four embryonic membranes that surround the developing embryo of reptiles, birds, and mammals, and give their principal functions. Why is it that the earlier vertebrates lack such membranes during development?

4. Cite some of the adaptations for flight that have been acquired by the more advanced forms of birds.

5. The female crocodilian, to which group birds are very distantly related, builds a nest in which her eggs are laid and then guards it until hatching has occurred. Beginning with this knowledge, outline a series of possible events involved in the development of the reproductive habits of the higher birds.

6. Distinguish the cursorial and arboreal theories of bird origins, giving their chief resemblances and differences.

7. List the distinctive features of mammals.

8. By examining the reproductive habits of mammals, outline the major series of events possibly involved in the evolution of the egg, placenta, and pouches, in the latter case including those of male mammals.

9. Describe the changes that have occurred in the dentition and lower jaw structure as the mammals evolved from the primitive reptilian ancestral stock.

10. Outline the major changes that have occurred in the evolution of the paired appendages of vertebrates. Then do likewise for the respiratory apparatus and heart.

SUGGESTIONS FOR FURTHER READING

Bard, J.B.L. 1977. A unity underlying the different zebra striping patterns. *J. Zool. Lond.*, 183:527–539.

Borgens, R.B. 1977. Skin batteries and limb regeneration. *Nat. Hist.*, 86(8):84–89.

Calder, W.A. 1979. The kiwi and egg design: evolution as a package deal. *BioScience* 29:461–467.

Cole, C.J. 1978. The value of virgin birth. *Nat. Hist.*, 87(1):56–63.

Davis, D.E. 1976. Hibernation and circannual rhythms of food consumption in marmots and ground squirrels. *Quart. Rev. Biol.*, 51:477–514.

Eccles, J.C. 1977. Evolution of the brain in relation to the development of the self-conscious mind. *Ann. N.Y. Acad. Sci.*, 299:161–179.

Garrick, L.D., and J.W. Lang. 1977. The alligator revealed. *Nat. Hist.*, 86(6):54–61.

Gunderson, H.L. 1978. Under and around a prairie dog town. *Nat. Hist.*, 87(8):57–61.

Heatwole, H. 1978. Adaptations of marine snakes. *Amer. Sci.*, 66:594–604.

Kirsch, J.A.W. 1977. The six-percent solution: Second thoughts on the adaptatedness of the Marsupialia. *Amer. Scient.*, 65:276–288.

Le Maho, Y. 1977. The emperor penguin: A strategy to live and breed in the cold. *Amer. Scient.*, 65:680–693.

Meanker, M., and N. Zimmerman. 1976. Role of the pineal in the circadian system of birds. *Amer. Zool.*, 16:45–55.

Ostrom, J.H. 1974. *Archaeopteryx* and the origin of flight. *Quart. Rev. Biol.*, 49:27–47.

Packard, G.C., C.R. Tracy, and J.J. Roth. 1977. The physiological ecology of reptilian eggs and embryos, and the evolution of viviparity within the class Reptilia. *Biol. Rev.*, 52:71–105.

Pivorunas, A. 1979. The feeding mechanisms of baleen whales. *Amer. Scient.* 67:432–440.

Ralls, K. 1976. Mammals in which females are larger than males. *Quart. Rev. Biol.*, 51:245–276.

Regal, P.J. 1975. The evolutionary origin of feathers. *Quart. Rev. Biol.*, 50:35–66.

Woolfenden, G.E., and J.W. Fitzpatrick. 1978. The inheritance of territory in group-breeding birds. *BioScience*, 28:104–108.

BTHOH.

BARBARA

BIRCH,

BARBARA

The Primates and Human Origins

19

Since the human species shares all the fundamental traits of other mammals, there can be little doubt of its being a member of that class, and since it also has all the characteristics of other members of the Primata, it is accordingly placed in that order. Even in 1758 when the first modern system of classification was advanced, long before the theory of evolution had been firmly introduced into zoological science, man was classified as a primate.

GENERAL CHARACTERISTICS

Actually there is only a single trait that is totally confined to the primates. On the digits of these animals are broad nails, rather than claws or hoofs, a structure found nowhere else in the animal world, but at the elementary levels of the taxon, this characteristic is almost absent. Although the group then is not sharply defined on the basis of any single character, the members possess a number of others, which, while not unique individually, in combination serve to differentiate these mammals clearly from all others. This combination of features includes the following, many of which may be perceived to be related to a tree-dwelling existence:

1. Nails on digits.
2. All four types of teeth present. Advanced primates have 32 teeth, including 8 incisors, 4 canines, 8 premolars, and 12 molars. In turn this generalized dentition reflects an unspecialized diet, vegetable and animal matter alike being consumed.
3. Highly developed vision, including color perception. The eyes are directed forwards to provide stereoscopic vision; such depth and range perception is of particular advantage in leaping from limb to limb.
4. Poorly developed olfaction, a sense of relatively little value in the trees.
5. Shoulder bones (clavicles) are present, bones that serve as struts in animals that use the fore limbs over the head in climbing.
6. The first digits (thumb and great toe) are opposable to the others, and thus aid in climbing about the tree tops.
7. Mammary apparatus (breasts) reduced to only one pair located on the chest.
8. Eye sockets posteriorly enclosed with bone.
9. The skull with an enlarged, rounded braincase.
10. Central nervous system highly developed.

11. A menstrual type of reproductive cycle present in all except the primitive species. This is characterized by the occurrence of a periodic bleeding from the uterus.
12. The hair follicles are clustered into small groups, or islands.
13. The sweat glands of the body surface are of the type called the eccrine, which in nonprimate mammals are confined to the soles of the feet.

THE PROSIMIANS

Although the foregoing characteristics hold for the order Primata as a whole, a number of representatives exist which lack several of them. Especially is this true among the more primitive species collectively known as prosimians. In habit these animals are more like squirrels than monkeys, as they run along tree branches on all fours. Moreover, they have elongate muzzles, lack a semierect carriage, and usually have the hind limbs longer than the front. At least six different types are present, of which only the three more important need to be considered.

The group with the greatest abundance of forms are the lemurs, of which 16 species are known. All of these are now confined to the island of Madagascar off the east coast of Africa, but an abundance of fossil representatives occur in Europe and North America. Like the ruffed lemur shown (fig. 19.1, A), these are long-tailed and long-legged creatures that travel with great agility in the tree-tops or on the ground. Their relationships to the rest of the primates are indicated beyond question by the nails on all digits, although the one of the second digit is clawlike, and the hair follicles are arranged in islands. While most lemurs have only two mammae, located on the chest, others have an additional pair on the abdomen. As a whole they have 36 teeth, three premolars being present on each side of each jaw, rather than the two of advanced primates. Eccrine sweat glands are absent from the body skin, being confined to the soles of the feet and hands as in nonprimate mammals, and the orbits posteriorly are not completely closed by bone.

Another group of prosimians that show both primate and nonprimate traits are the two genera of lorises (fig. 19.1, B) from southern Asia and the two related genera of pottos from Africa. So slow moving are these thick-bodied, nocturnal animals as they climb hand over hand in trees that in Sri Lanka they are often referred to as sloths. Tails are absent or virtually so, the four legs are nearly equally long, and external ears are very short. Larger in size than those of lemurs, the eyes are set in orbits that are almost completely enclosed posteriorly by bone. As in the lemurs, four mammae are present, including two on the abdomen, all digits have nails, the second one being clawlike, and 36 teeth are present, with three premolars on each side of both jaws. While the hair is arranged in islands, eccrine sweat glands are lacking except on the soles and palms.

If the eyes are large in the lorises and allies, they can only be described as enormous in the three species of prosimians of southern Asia and Philippines known as tarsiers (fig. 19.1, C). These are small creatures, only 6 inches long,

A

B

C

Figure 19.1 *Some representative prosimians.* A. The lemurs, like this ruffed lemur, occur on Madagascar and adjacent islands, but have no close relatives elsewhere. B. The slender lorises *(Loris tardigradus)* and related forms are slow moving, not quick like the lemurs. C. Tarsiers are strictly nocturnal inhabitants of the large islands of southeastern Asia; the form illustrated is the Mindanao subspecies *(Tarsier syrichta carbonarius)*. (San Diego Zoo photographs.)

and as might be supposed from the size of the eyes, they are strictly nocturnal. Also they are nearly exclusively arboreal and travel through treetops in froglike fashion, often leaping distances of six feet or more, the elongate hind legs being especially fitted for this mode of travel. The digits, besides bearing ordinary and clawlike nails, have pads at their tips which act somewhat as suction disks and aid in securing firm holds on the tree limbs and trunks. The great toe, but not the thumb, is opposable. The tail is nearly twice the length of the body but is naked and slender, more rat- than squirrel-like as in other prosimians. These animals secure food, including insects, small lizards, and other small prey, by leaping at them and catching them with both hands, closing their eyes as they do so. The teeth are like those of the other prosimians, except that two incisors are absent from the lower jaw, reducing the total to only 34. As elsewhere among prosimians, the orbits are only partially enclosed by bone. Tarsiers are nearly nonsocial in habit, usually living singly or in pairs, but sometimes occurring in groups of three, or rarely, four.

ANTHROPOIDEA

All the remaining primates are classed together as the suborder Anthropoidea, a name referring to the humanlike appearance, particularly the long legs, grasping fingers, semi- or fully-erect carriage, and reduced muzzle. The forward-directed eyes accentuate the hominoid[1] appearance, and the relatively high level of intelligence contributes to behavioral resemblances. Three subdivisions are generally recognized: The flat-nosed monkeys of South and Central America, the longer-nosed monkeys and lesser apes of Asia and Africa, and the hominoids (Hominoidea), the great apes and man. In all types, only one pair of mammae are present, located on the thorax, and almost all have eccrine sweat glands over the body surface in general, usually along with apocrine as well.

The American Primates

The nonhuman primates of the New World are of two major types, the marmosets and monkeys. In many ways these animals resemble the prosimians, particularly in having 36 teeth, including three premolars on each side of the jaws. They differ notably in having the muzzle short and in lacking the shiny nosepad, such as that of dogs and the prosimians (fig. 19.2, A). As may be noted in the illustration, the nostrils are often widely separated, with the intervening septum quite broad; however, in such more advanced forms as the howler monkeys, the septum is much narrower as it is also in Old World species. While the great toe is opposable, the thumb usually is only partially so, because the ball of that digit cannot be rotated. As is the case also in the prosimians, menstruation does not occur in the smaller of these primates where the typical estrous cycle prevails, but such larger forms of as the spider and howler monkeys do have a menstrual cycle.

The squirrel-like marmosets and tamarins are small animals with long, bushy tails, whose primate relationships are revealed by the flat faces and short muzzle like those of monkeys. But kinships with prosimians also are indicated, especially by the elongate hind legs and the presence of clawlike nails. Unlike the lorises, lemurs, and their kin, progress through the trees is not by leaps but by running along branches and up and down tree trunks with all the agility of squirrels. Insects are the chief food of these diurnal animals, captured mostly in the trees but to some extent in tall grass, too. As a rule they live in small bands.

The remaining tropical American forms are definitely monkeylike in appearance, having long legs, the front pair often exceeding the hind ones in length. Possibly the most primitive and abundant of all are the squirrel monkeys (fig.

1. It should be noted that the term *hominoid* refers to any creature that somewhat resembles a human being, and that *hominid* is applied to any type of mankind.

A

B

Figure 19.2 *New World monkeys.* A. As in many other South American monkeys, the nasal pad is like that of cats and dogs and has a broad septum between the nostrils. (From Dillon, Lawrence S.; *Evolution,* 2nd ed., St. Louis, 1978, The C.V. Mosby Co.) B. The red howler monkey (*Alouatta villosa*) is one of the largest New World native primates. (San Diego Zoo photograph.)

19.2, A), a small species that still possesses certain squirrel-like traits of prosimians, in particular a long, bushy tail. However, they do not scamper along limbs or up and down tree trunks in squirrel fashion but grasp the branches with feet and hands as they climb about. Usually they remain in large troops, often containing 100 members and at times in excess of 500.

Another common type is the capuchin, four species of which are distributed throughout much of tropical Central and South America. These have the tail prehensile and use it freely in climbing and in carrying objects. Because of their intelligence and tractibility they are frequently trained to perform in circuses and carnivals and are also extensively used in biological research.

Another group of prehensile-tailed forms includes the five species of howler monkeys (fig. 19.2, B), found from southern Mexico to Bolivia and southern Brazil. These are the largest of the American monkeys, ranging to nearly a meter in combined head and body length. Usually they remain associated in small troops, containing from 4 to 20 members, but occasionally there may be up to 40 individuals, led by one or two old males. Definite territories through the treetops are established and defended by each band. While partly nocturnal, they are most active at dawn and late afternoon, when they engage in the howling that gives them their common name. The calls, resonated by enlarged jawbone angles and throat bones, carry for 3 km over the jungles and nearly twice as far over lakes.

Old World Monkeys

The Old World anthropoids, beginning with the monkeys and lesser apes, differ from the New World relatives in having the thumb as well as the great toe completely opposable—these digits can rotate from the ball, not just the next joint, to oppose the other fingers in grasping objects. All also possess the definitive pattern of dentition, with 32 teeth, including just 2 premolars but 3 molars on each side of the jaws. A menstrual cycle occurs among all species of Old World primates, including these monkeys as well as the great apes. It should be noted that the term ape does not necessarily pertain to a strictly taxonomic unit but is applied to any fair-sized monkey whose tail is short or absent.

Two groups are recognized, sometimes treated as families and at others as subfamilies, which differ on one hand by having prominent pouches in the cheeks and on the other by having the stomach enlarged to digest the leaves that make up their diet. Among the 38 pouched forms are such familiar African inmates of zoos as baboons (fig. 19.3, A, B), guenons, vervets or grass monkeys, mandrills, and Barbary apes. The last of these is particularly distinct in lacking a tail completely and in having a vermiform appendix, two traits shared with only the great apes and man. Among the Asiatic representatives is the rhesus monkey, an essentially arboreal form that also spends much time foraging on the ground. Through the use of this species as the experimental subject, much progress has been made in medicine, biology, and space technology.

Relatively few of the 32 species of the leaf-eating group are found in Africa, the most outstanding being the black-and-white colobus, whose attractive coat has led to its being reduced to an endangered species. It occurs, although in

A

B

Figure 19.3 *A species of baboon, one of the Old World monkeys.* A. A female baboon grooms her young, removing ticks, other parasites, and debris. B. A dominant male challenges two other males. Here the large canines of the higher primates may be readily noted. (Courtesy of Irven DeVore and Anthro-Photo.)

reduced numbers, in a broad belt from Ethiopia west to the Cameroons (fig. 19.4, A). Lichens vary its main diet of leaves and fruit obtained high in the trees, but occasionally it also descends to tall grass to feed on seedpods. The greatest portion of this group live in southeastern Asia, including the major islands. Among the largest of these is the proboscis monkey, which occurs only on the island of Borneo, where it forms small bands that are active in the daytime, especially in early morning. Males commonly attain a combined head and trunk length of 750 mm and may weigh as much as 23 kg; while females may attain a length of 600 mm, they are much more lightly built, weighing less than half as much as males. While the nose is quite prominent in females (fig. 19.4, B), in large males it becomes long and pendulous, sometimes attaining a length of 3 inches. The function of this peculiarity remains a complete mystery.

Although obviously different in food habits, the two major groups of Old World monkeys are not really highly divergent, but largely parallel one another closely in structure and habits. As a whole, both types travel doglike quadripedally, the fore and hind limbs being subequal in length; however, when carrying such objects as leaves or food, bipedal locomotion may be engaged in, either in the treetops or on the ground. The elongate canines, especially those of the males (fig. 19.3, B) are prominent features of many of these species of both groups. To provide room for these fangs when the mouth is closed, a gap, or diastema, is present in front of the canines of the upper jaw and behind those of the lower. While giving these animals the appearance of being carnivorous, the diet, as already indicated, is largely of vegetable matter.

Actually the fangs are believed to be of value mostly in defense and in aggressive fighting between males of the often well-organized bands. Not infrequently large groups of such forms as the rhesus and other macaques, as well as baboons, are divided into subgroups. In these the central area of the band is occupied by one or two dominant males, associated with females and infants. Young of both sexes and subordinate males must either occupy peripheral areas or fend for themselves as solitary bachelors. The dominant males lead the troop, prevent intragroup fighting, and protect the band against predators. In such social organizations, communication plays an important role, mostly by way of vocalizations and facial expressions. A study of the Japanese ape, for instance, reported that the animals used as many as thirty different vocal sounds in communicating with one another.

The Great Apes

The eleven species of great apes living today fall into four major categories, including seven species of gibbons, two of chimpanzees, and one each of gorilla and orangutan. Generally the gibbons are placed in a separate family (the Hylobatidae) and the remainder in the Pongidae, but sometimes all are placed as a subfamily (Ponginae) in the human family, Hominidae, because they have so many traits in common with man.

One of the common characteristics is the narrow septum that separates the nostrils, while a second one is a shoulder structure that permits locomotion

A

B

Figure 19.4   *Two species of leaf-eating monkeys.* A. The handsome black and white colobus monkey (*Colobus polykomos*) of Africa and, B, the proboscis monkey (*Nasalis larvatus*) of Borneo are among the more striking of this group of Old World monkeys. (San Diego Zoo photographs; B, by Ron Garrison.)

through trees by brachiation, that is, by use of the fore limbs held over the head. Several types of brachiation are recognized, depending upon the extent to which the hind limbs or tail assist in the processes. In *true brachiation* the hind limbs are not employed except at rest or incidentally, whereas in *modified brachiation*, they are used to provide occasional or partial support to the body during locomotion. In addition, *semibrachiation* occurs in some monkeys; for example, proboscis and colobus monkeys of the Old World use the arms overhead continually with the hind limbs, and the New World spider, howler, and woolly monkeys brachiate in conjunction with the hind limbs and tail.

The several species of gibbons are the only true brachiators extant today. These are found throughout much of southeastern Asia, including Sumatra, Java, and Borneo (fig. 19.5, A). Because of their long arms and short legs, these animals are awkward on the ground, but in the trees they brachiate so expertly that, according to some reports, they can travel at the speed of a horse. The smallest of the great apes, the gibbons have a combined head and trunk length of only 600 mm and a total weight of only 9 kg. The hind legs are about as long as the head and trunk together, while the arms are one-third again as long. One species of gibbon, called the siamang, is somewhat heavier but no taller, weighing up to 14 kg; this species of Sumatra and the Malay Peninsula is especially remarkable for its long arms, which are one-half again as long as the legs.

The orangutan, confined to the islands of Sumatra and Borneo, ranks next to the gorilla in size, males often growing to a total height of 1.4 m and weighing more than 100 kg in the wild and nearly double that figure in captivity. These shy primates, while partly arboreal, spend the largest part of the day foraging on the ground for the roots, fruit, seeds, and bark that make up the major portion of their diet. To these may be added eggs, young birds, mussels, and other windfalls on occasion. On the ground the orang walks on all fours or bipedally; in the trees, it normally progresses quadrupedally, holding onto overhead branches with the hands and grasping the supporting limb tightly with the feet. When frightened, however, they brachiate with considerable agility, using the feet to a limited extent in conjunction with the hands. An unusual sexual dimorphism exists, as the males develop bulky layers of tissue around the face, which greatly increase the apparent size of the head (fig. 19.5, B). Usually the animals travel alone or in small family groups.

In contrast, the two species of chimpanzees (fig. 19.5, C) that inhabit Africa form bands containing as many as thirty individuals. These are unstable in composition, individuals joining and leaving a given group freely. No hierarchy of dominance is displayed, but older males display dominance reactions on an individual basis. Nevertheless, an extensive ability in communicating has been found to exist, especially through facial and vocal expressions. Moreover, they have been observed in the wild to use such tools as throwing sticks, clubs, and grass probes. Chimpanzees are somewhat larger than gibbons but considerably smaller than orangutans. In combined head and trunk length, males may attain around a meter and may weigh up to 46 kg. The arms extend below the knees when the animal is standing and have a spread of one-half again that of the height. Much of

A

B

Figure 19.5 *The major types of Great Apes.* A. The best brachiators but the smallest in size, the gibbons, including this gray species (*Hylobates molock*), are confined to southeastern Asia. B. The orangutan is a shy species, in spite of its large size; it lives in Sumatra and Borneo. C. In contrast, the chimpanzee (*Pan troglodytes*) is outgoing and easily trained. D. Both the preceding species and the gorilla are inhabitants of Africa. Albert, shown here, is a lowland form. (San Diego Zoo photographs; C and D by Ron Garrison.)

Figure 19.5—*Continued*

C

D

their time is spent in trees, only about a third of the day being devoted to activities on the ground, where they walk on all fours. However, bipedal locomotion is engaged in occasionally, especially in tall grass. In the trees, they travel by means of a highly modified type of brachiation, the arms being employed alone for short distances but usually the feet are used as much as possible. While their food consists principally of fruit, leaves, roots, and seeds, they add meat whenever possible, occasionally capturing and consuming mammals as large as small antelope.

Gorillas (fig. 19.5, D) are by far the largest of the great apes, males often attaining a height of 1.85 m and weights up to 180 kg in the wilds. Their arms are not quite so long in proportion as those of chimpanzees, so their full spread is less than half again as great as the total height. Generally speaking, gorillas are quiet and retiring and do not molest people unless annoyed or attacked. Most of their day is spent on the ground, where they walk with a stooped carriage, but frequently stand upright. They do climb trees, however, to obtain fruit or bird eggs, but have not been observed to employ brachiation. Their groups usually consist only of family members, typically including a dominant male, four adult females, and perhaps eight to ten young, but on rare occasions groups as large as 40 individuals have been observed. Communication between members is at least as well developed as it is in chimpanzees. Succulent vegetation, mostly branches of shrubs, is the mainstay of the diet, but leaves, berries, ferns, roots, and bark are also consumed.

MAN'S FOSSIL HISTORY

Before attempting to trace the fossil record of man's history, it must be realized that the account is notoriously incomplete. First the chance of any individual mammal becoming fossilized is only one in perhaps a billion, and then only thick bones like skulls and jaws, or hard parts like teeth are likely to be preserved. Second, early humankind lived in tropical lands, where rapid decay and the abundance of predatory and gnawing animals reduces the chance of fossilization still further. And third, arboreal or semi-arboreal creatures are even less likely to become preserved as fossils than are terrestrial ones. Thus it is extremely improbable that mankind's history can ever be restored in full detail. Nevertheless, a sufficient number of fossils have now come to hand that at least the outlines of his past are beginning to emerge.

Distinctive Human Features

Since, at the earliest stages in his history, man would have diverged only slightly from the great ape ancestral stock, it facilitates recognition of any hominid trend that may have occurred to compare the modern apes and man. Thus existing distinctions that might more readily be fossilized can be sorted out from those that would not. Obviously furry bodies, skin structure, ear shape, sweat gland distribution, and pigmentation belong in the latter category.

Upright body carriage, however, is accompanied by concomitant changes in skull and pelvis, parts that do fossilize readily. Among the forms living today, the carriage is reflected in the location of the foramen magnum, the opening through which the spinal cord emerges from the skull. This foramen is located strongly posteriorly in the apes, whereas that of mankind is found near the center of the base (fig. 19.6). In addition, the shape of the pelvic bone is indicative of the carriage. Nonhuman primates have an elongate, narrow pelvis in contrast to man's broad, or flared, shortened one (fig. 19.7, D).

In profile, the skulls reveal a number of other sharp differences. The modern apes have prominent supraorbital ridges, or tori, located above the eyesockets; moreover, a forehead is virtually absent, the cranial vault is low or flat, and there is a prominent muzzle (fig. 19.6). When such a muzzle is present, the face is said to be prognathous. On the other hand man has almost no ridges above the eyes, the forehead is vertical, the cranial vault is high, or rounded, and the face is vertical, a muzzle being absent. Because of this absence, man is considered to be orthognathous.

The size of the brain case, or the cranial capacity of the skull, offers an important distinction between modern man and the great apes. In mankind the

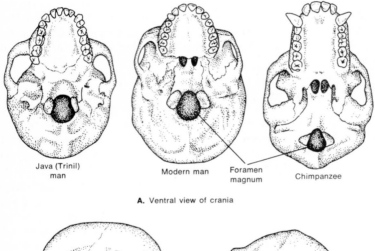

Java (Trinil) man   Modern man   Foramen magnum   Chimpanzee

A. Ventral view of crania

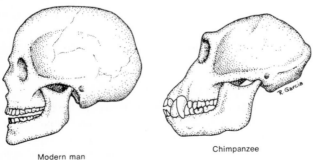

Modern man   Chimpanzee

B. Lateral view of skulls

Figure 19.6 *Comparisons of ape and human skulls.* (From Dillon, Lawrence S.; *Evolution,* 2nd ed., St. Louis, 1978, The C.V. Mosby Co.)

capacity ranges between 900 and 2,300 ml, with a mean of 1,350 ml. Contrastingly, that of the gorilla extends between 340 and 752 ml, with a mean of 506 ml, and that of a chimpanzee between 290 and 500 ml, the mean value being 375 ml. The body size of the individual, as well as intelligence, plays a role in cranial capacity. Small persons with relatively small cranial capacity may be as intelligent or even more so than a tall, heavily built one with a much larger cranial cavity.

The shape of the dental arch and certain features of the dentition are also sources of distinctions between human and nonhuman primates. Actually some of these features provide the most sharply defined differences between the two types. In all the great apes, the dental arch is essentially oblong, with parallel sides and rounded anterior, and the length far exceeds the width measured across the hind molars (fig. 19.7, B). Quite contrastingly in man the arch is broadly rounded, with the sides diverging posteriorly; furthermore, the width across the last molars distinctly exceeds the length (fig. 19.7, B). Another feature of ape dentition is the elongate canine mentioned earlier in connection with Old World monkey behavior, a feature that is accompanied by diastemata, behind the canines in the lower jaw and in front of them in the upper. Moreover, the ape lower jaw is strengthened anteriorly by a broad plate called the simian shelf, that is absent in the human structure. It should be noted, too, that the more posterior molars of apes are longer than wide, whereas the corresponding teeth in mankind are wider than long.

Early Human Fossils

The fossil record has in recent years become extended much further back into geological times than formerly expected, for a belief held sway for many decades that the whole of man's evolution took place during the million years that then were considered to comprise the Pleistocene. Now, that epoch has been established as having endured for two million years and the existence of man during the Miocene, more than ten million years earlier than that, has been thoroughly confirmed. Because of the nature of the fossils that have been found, it has even been proposed that the earliest stages in his departure from the ape line took place in the Oligocene at least 25 to 30 million years ago. Space limitations, however, do not permit the detailing of all the human types that now have been unearthed, so only a sample sufficient to supply the flavor of the record is presented here.

Miocene Fossil Remains

It should be continually held in mind that before the late 1960s the concept mentioned above that man had evolved completely in a million years pervaded the whole of anthropological thought, so that reports of finds of earlier dates were viewed with great skepticism or rejected entirely. Thus when a fragment of jaw was described from a Late Miocene deposit of India during the 1930s, it went virtually unnoticed for three decades. Only in the 1960s after that concept had been thoroughly discredited was renewed interest in this find displayed.

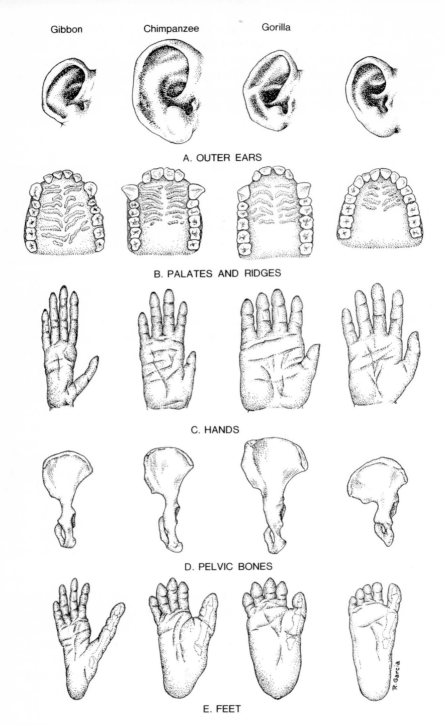

Gibbon   Chimpanzee   Gorilla

A. OUTER EARS

B. PALATES AND RIDGES

C. HANDS

D. PELVIC BONES

E. FEET

Figure 19.7 *Other differences between apes and mankind.* (From Dillon, Lawrence S.: *Evolution,* 2nd ed., St. Louis, 1978, The C.V. Mosby Co.)

This type, given the name *Ramapithecus brevirostris,* has been dated as 14,000,000 years old, that is, from near the boundary between the Pliocene and Miocene epochs (table 19.1). While consisting only of two fragments of the upper jaw, it clearly shows a number of distinctively human traits. The dental arch obviously is rounded and broader than it is long (fig. 19.8). Moreover, the canines are not elongate, no diastemata are present, and the molars are wider than long. Since such a shortened dental arch reflects an orthognathous type of face and the latter in turn is firmly associated with an upright carriage, it is evident that this earliest known hominid already possessed a number of distinctly human attributes. It is the existence of these traits in this early form that has given rise to the belief that man began is evolutionary line back in Oligocene times.

Pliocene Fossil Discoveries

Until the past decade or so, no fossil hominid specimens had been yielded by Pliocene deposits in Africa, but this condition is being rapidly corrected by recent and current explorations. Less than a dozen years ago, several human teeth and other fragments were found in Kenya, dating variously as between 3 and 10 million years of age, placing them in the mid to later portions of the Pliocene. Still more recently, however, much more complete remains have been uncovered.

One of the better examples of the humankind of this epoch is that known as the Hadar man (fig. 19.9). In eastern Ethiopia on the surface of the ground were found several fragments of femora, followed later by a well-preserved undistorted palate, containing a complete complement of teeth. Quite noticeable are such apelike features as the rather long canines and the diastemata. In contrast, however, the dental arch, although longer than wide, is not completely like that of the apes, for the sides diverge partially and then converge behind, giving a somewhat rounded configuration to the sides. Moreover, the molars are not longer than wide, but are equilateral. Thus Hadar man, more precisely referred to as AL200, had both hominid and apelike characteristics.

Equally interesting is the small number of types recovered from a site near Lake Rudolf, which also is in Ethiopia, but close to the border of northern Kenya. Here on and below the surface have been found a number of fossil types, the first of which is the East Rudolf man, which has been dated as being 2.61 million years old. With this nearly complete skull was associated some pebbles that clearly show signs of having been chipped and shaped by man. Thus it has required mankind at least 2,610,000 years to progress from the first use of such manufactured stone tools to his present state of technology.

More recently a series of primitive forms was discovered in this same area, including several well-preserved skulls of the type originally called *Zinjanthropus,* better described later. But such primitive types might well be expected at these relatively old deposits. What was quite unexpected was the type represented by the cranium given the designation ER1470 (fig. 19.10). Because of its rather rounded skull and low supraorbital ridges, this specimen has been placed in the genus *Homo* along with modern man. If this designation proves valid, the genus thus goes back into the geologic past for at least 2.9 million years.

Table 19.1 Geologic Time Scale of Human Evolution

Period	Epoch	Years ago	Representative Fossils
	Recent	0	Modern man (*Homo sapiens*)
		25,000	River Valley people (Homo sapiens)
Quaternary	Pleistocene (2 million years)	25,000	
		40,000	Broken Hill man
		45,000	Neanderthal man; Cro-Magnon; Tabun
		60,000	Shanidar Man IV
		350,000	Steinheim man
		490,000	*Homo habilis*
		500,000	Peking man; first known use of fire
		600,000	Trinil man
		1,500,000	Swartkrans man (Sk 48)
		1,700,000	*Zinjanthropus* (Olduvai Gorge); *Homo habilis*
		1,750,000	Taung man juvenile
		2,000,000	Sterkfontein Stw 53
Tertiary	Pliocene (11 million years)	2,000,000	
		2,610,000	East Rudolf man; the earliest known worked pebbles
		2,900,000	Hadar man; East Rudolf man 1470
		3,000,000	*Zinjanthropus* (East Rudolf)
		4,000,000	Kanpoi (Kenya) humerus
		7,000,000	Lukeino (Kenya) tooth
		10,000,000	Ngorora (Kenya) teeth
		13,000,000	
	Miocene (12 million years)	13,000,000	
		14,000,000	*Ramapithecus,* hominid from the Himalayas
		18,000,000	*Kenyapithecus,* apelike jaw, with some human traits
		19,000,000	*Proconsul* skull; ape, with some hominid features
		25,000,000	
	Oligocene	25,000,000	
			Possible origins of the human line?

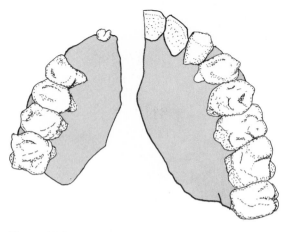

Figure 19.8   *A Miocene hominid, Ramapithecus.*

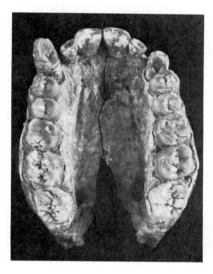

Figure 19.9   *Hadar man.* This palate (AL200) is from the Upper Pliocene of Ethiopia. (Photo courtesy of D.C. Johnson, Cleveland Museum of Natural History.)

Early Pleistocene Men

Hominids from the earliest portion of the Pleistocene (table 19.1) have been known since 1924, when several were found in South Africa. For many years, however, the fossils were the center of much controversy, as a prevailing belief at that time considered man to have arisen and evolved in Eurasia. Consequently, they were then often placed in a separate family or subfamily, between the great apes and the strictly human lines. Currently, they are accepted as one of several human types that diverged somewhat from the main branch of ascent.

Many of these South African men are of the type collectively referred to as australopithecines, sometimes considered to belong in the single genus *Australopithecus,* meaning "southern ape." As a group they share a number of

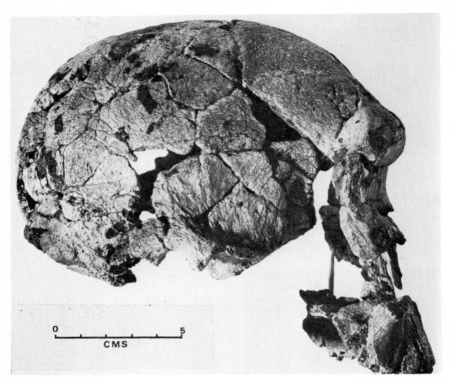

Figure 19.10 *A fossil hominid from East Rudolf.* This form has been tentatively assigned to the genus *Homo,* to which modern man also belongs. (Reproduced with permission of the National Museums of Kenya; copyright reserved.)

somewhat primitive and divergent traits, such as a low cranial vault and a prognathous face. Furthermore, the dentition is peculiar in consisting of small incisors, moderately short canines, and very large cheek teeth, that is, premolars and molars (fig. 19.13, B). Diastemata are lacking, as is also a simian shelf.

The very first specimen found was exposed by quarrying operations in a series of caves near Taung and was described under the name *Australopithecus africanus.* This fossil is a well-preserved skull of a juvenile, containing a cast of the brain (fig. 19.11); consequently, in spite of the absence of a large section of the cranium, it is possible to garner a fair idea of the head shape. Other noteworthy features are the lack of supraorbital ridges, the absence of a chin, and a prognathism that involves only that part of the face below the nose. According to the dentition, which consists entirely of milk teeth but with the first permanent molars beginning to emerge, the juvenile australopithecine would have been about six years of age. The skull, which has a cranial capacity of 440 ml, has been dated as from the period following the first Pleistocene glaciation, that is, about 1,750,000 years ago.

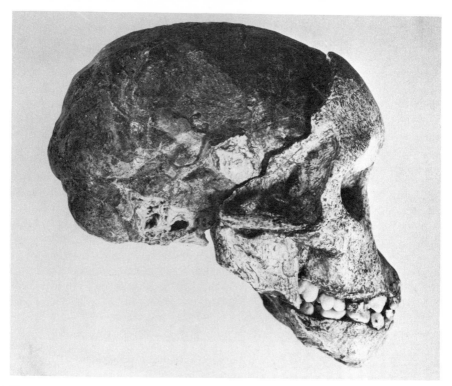

Figure 19.11 *The first hominid found in South Africa.* In this specimen of a child about 6 years of age, the prognathism involves only the lower portion of the face. (Photograph by Alun R. Hughes, used by kind permission of Prof. Phillip V. Tobias.)

Following the above mentioned discovery, a number of other sites in the same general area of South Africa have yielded valuable human remnants. Among these was a series of caves at Sterkfontein near Johannesburg. The earlier discoveries were largely of types obviously related to the Taung fossil, but dating from slightly younger deposits. As recently as 1976, however, more thorough exploration of the caves revealed a form referred to as Stw53, which is apparently from near the very base of the Pleistocene, that is, 2 million years ago. On a tentative basis, this has been classed in the genus *Homo,* and represents a species possibly related to *H. habilis,* to be discussed shortly.

The fossil from this area that clearly showed the most primitive features was one uncovered from a cave near Swartkrans. This, the best preserved of several different types of crania found here, is referred to as Sk48 and has many of the typical features of the australopithecines. However, the cranial roof is scarcely as elevated as it is in the two mentioned in the foregoing paragraphs, and, even more importantly, there is a distinct bony crest along the median line, recalling that found in gorillas except in being much reduced in size (fig. 19.12). The

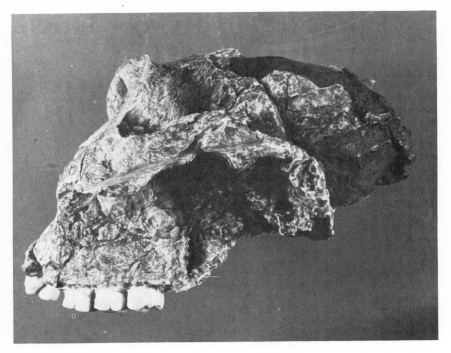

Figure 19.12 *SK48, the best preserved of the Swartkrans fossil hominids.* (Courtesy Dr. J.T. Robinson, University of Wisconsin.)

supraorbital ridges are pronounced, and the entire face is prognathous from below the eyes. The dental arch is somewhat rounded, but narrowed posteriorly as in the Hadar man (fig. 19.9), but no diastemata can be noted as in that earlier form.

During the 1960s and continuing to the present, areas in Tanzania and Kenya became the region of Africa most productive of fossils pertaining to mankind's history. Unlike those of South Africa, the specimens uncovered were not in caves but in a deep ravine known as Olduvai Gorge, located about 150 miles southwest of Nairobi. By far the most unusual of these was that described under the name of *Zinjanthropus boisei.* The skull, largely intact, apparently represented a young adult, because the third molars (wisdom teeth) had only recently erupted. The face is prognathous from below the eyes, not just below the nose, and is greatly elongated, especially in the region of the upper jaw (fig. 19.13, A). The cranium is but feebly elevated and has a capacity of only 530 ml; moreover, along the median line is a distinct crest, recalling that of the Swartkrans man, but is more pronounced. The dental arch is similar to the australopithecines in having small front and large cheek teeth, without diastemata and enlarged canines (fig. 19.13, B). Here, however, the molars are wider than long, not elongate as in the South African finds, and there is no tendency for the arch to narrow posteriorly. Using refined geologic techniques, this form was dated as being 1,750,000 years

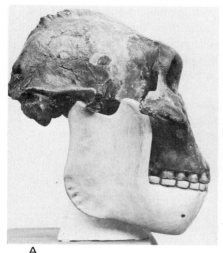
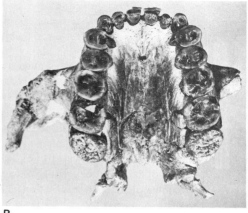

A   B

Figure 19.13 *The original hominid find at Olduvai Gorge.* A. The prognathism that involves the entire face and the crest on the top of the skull are especially noteworthy features. B. The dentition of this form is similar to that of the australopithecines in having small front and large cheek teeth. (Photographs by R. Klomfass; used by kind permission of Prof. Phillip V. Tobias.)

old. It should be noted that a number of nearly identical examples were later found at East Rudolf sites, so this particular species apparently persisted from at least 3 million to 1.75 million years ago.

One other type of approximately the same geologic age was found nearby in the same gorge, but this one had tooth characteristics like those of modern man. Accordingly described under the name *Homo habilis,* this type had a cranial capacity of 670 ml, and strong supraorbital ridges; a bone tool was found with the fossil, as well as some chipped stones. While the dental arch is longer than wide, diastemata are absent, the front teeth are not reduced in size as in the australopithecines and the premolars are noticeably smaller than the molars. However, the molars are longer than wide and a strong simian shelf is present. At higher levels in the gorge, similar remains have come to light and have been identified as being this same species. Since these have been dated as from deposits laid down 490,000 years ago, it is evident that this species, too, existed over a long span of time. Moreover, its original occurrence in the same beds as *Zinjanthropus* indicated that two species of men could coexist in the same region, a situation previously not believed by anthropologists to be tolerable.

Mid-Pleistocene Forms

In contrast to the confusing abundance of types found in early Pleistocene deposits, those of the middle portion of that epoch are rather sparse in numbers. Only four major finds have been made dating from this period, one of which, *Homo habilis,* has already received attention.

The first discovered fossils of this middle portion of the Pleistocene received perhaps more public attention than has any such discovery made since. This was the Java ape-man (*Pithecanthropus erectus*), described in the closing year of the Nineteenth Century from specimens taken in an ancient riverbed near Trinil, Java, and which subsequently were dated as approximately 500,000 years old. The cranium is notably flat, with strong supraorbital ridges, but is rather elongate, so that its capacity has been estimated at 900 ml (fig. 19.14). Unfortunately the first specimen was quite incomplete and lacked jaws; however, a second example found in the same region had the upper jaw intact. In this case, the teeth were large, with somewhat elongate canines and broad diastemata present. The dental arch was longer than wide, with the sides only slightly flaring.

Nearly thirty years later another type was uncovered in a large cavern at Choukoutien, 25 miles southwest of Peking, China. In the fallen debris of about 500,000 years of age, fourteen skulls were found plus a number of other skeletal parts in various stages of preservation. Originally described under the name *Sinanthropus pekinensis*, this form currently is considered to be a subspecies of the Trinil man. Although the supraorbital ridges are quite large, the cranial roof is sufficiently elevated that a forehead is in evidence (fig. 19.15). Accordingly, the cranial capacity approaches that of modern man, showing a range from 915 to 1225 ml. Moreover, the face is distinctly prognathous below the nose, and a chin is absent. The dental arch is rounded, but just about as wide as long; the teeth are not unlike those of modern man, diastemata being completely absent. In association with the skeletal remains were a number of crude bone tools, but much more importantly, ash heaps and pieces of charcoal were found, representing the first known use of fire by mankind.

Thus it appears that humankind spread through tropical Asia and then into the temperate orient before it penetrated into Europe, for the earliest finds made in this latter region date only to 350,000 years before the present. Among these, the

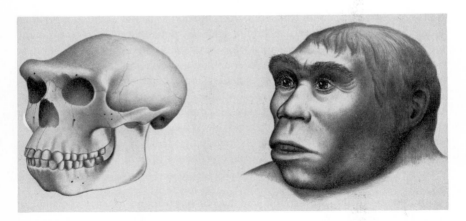

Figure 19.14 *The Java ape-man.* Here the skull is restored and an artist's concept of this form from Trinil, Java, is presented.

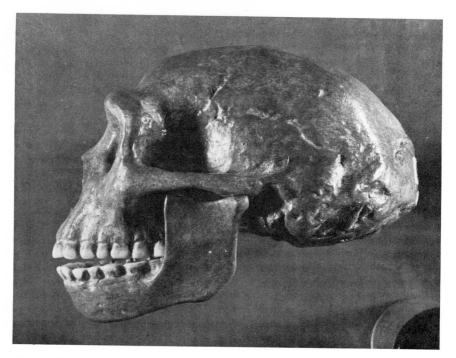

Figure 19.15 *The skull of the Peking hominid.* Cast of the best preserved skull of fourteen individuals found in the lower caves at Choukoutien near Peking. All the original material is believed to have been lost during World War II.

one of greatest importance is that dug from a gravel pit at Steinheim, 12 miles north of Stuttgart, Germany. Unfortunately, the facial portion was poorly preserved, but appears to have been distinctly prognathous and to have had strong supraorbital ridges (fig. 19.16). The cranial roof is well elevated, so that a capacity of 1175 ml has been reported. Unluckily, much of the upper and the entire lower jaw are missing, so that little can be said about the dentition.

Late Pleistocene Fossils

Relatively recent fossil specimens are far more numerous than are the older ones, as might be expected, for these would, of course, be closer to the surface than earlier ones. Since it is not possible in the limited space available to describe all that have been found, attention is confined to the more important and more complete examples.

Among these probably the most significant is the type known as the Neanderthal man, because this was the very first fossil hominid ever found. During 1856, quarrying operations in a cave in the Neanderthal Valley, Germany, exposed a cranium that caused considerable excitement in biological circles. Some viewed it as the remains of an ancient barbarian, others thought it had been

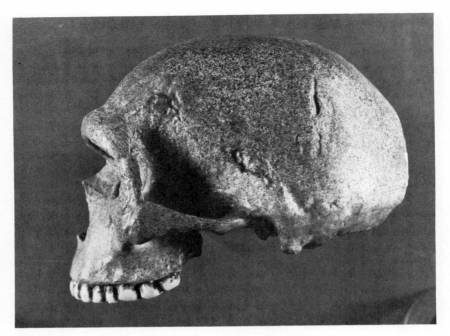

Figure 19.16 *The restored skull of the Steinheim hominid.*

diseased, and still others considered it to have been an imbecile. Only after Darwin's theory had been published and a scientist had examined the specimen was it recognized for what it really was, a distinct species of man, subsequently named *Homo neanderthalensis*. Some years later, a nearly complete skeleton of the same structure was encountered near La Chapelle-aux-Saints, France, that corroborated this conclusion thoroughly. The skull is large, having a capacity of 1620 ml, despite the sloping cranial roof. Supraorbital ridges are very prominent, the face is prognathous, and a chin is lacking. Because the extinct person during life had suffered severe osteoarthritis, the skeleton was misinterpreted and Neanderthal man has usually been shown as having a stooped carriage. Now the mistake has been corrected and his upright body, of stocky build, is fully recognized (fig. 19.17).

It is the current practice to classify any recent fossil form with low cranial roof and prognathous face as a Neanderthal man, so the original find is referred to as the classical type. Of the nonclassical varieties there exists quite an abundance, mostly found in a number of caverns in the Near East. Possibly the most interesting of these is that taken from a cave near Shanidar, Iraq, in deposits dated as 60,000 years old. This specimen, referred to as Shanidar IV, was found near the mouth of the cave at a depth of nearly 25 feet; these remains obviously had been carefully buried, suggesting that they belonged to a man of much importance. When analyzed, soil samples taken from around the body during excavation showed the presence of large quantities of flower pollen. Upon identifica-

Figure 19.17 *Neanderthal man at home.* The photograph is of a diorama made subsequent to the discovery, that, in life, the original fossil had suffered from osteoarthritis and that he had a fully upright carriage like that of modern man. (Courtesy, Field Museum of Natural History, Chicago.)

tion, the pollen was found to be from species still extant in the region around the cave. Because of the quantity present, it has been deduced that the flowers had been placed on and around the body at the time of burial; thus it has been suggested that the people of those days possessed some sort of religion.

Another find of great importance was made in the Cro-Magnon cave in France during construction of a railroad. Here, in a rock shelter that had become filled with soil, five adult skeletons and a number of infant bones were uncovered. These were arranged carefully, suggesting that they had been ritually buried. With them were associated tools of New Stone Age types, including some made of bone or antlers as well. Since the skulls had all the characteristics of modern man, they are considered as a separate subspecies of the species *Homo sapiens* (fig. 19.18). Surprisingly the cranial capacity was determined to be 1,590 ml, far above the mean of modern mankind. The forehead is high, supraorbital ridges are lacking, the face is orthognathous, and the chin is prominent. Thus the present species must be considered to have occupied much of western Europe for the past 45,000 years, and is probably responsible for the fine paintings in the caves of this area and Spain. In contrast, Neanderthal man seemed to have occurred farther eastward, especially from Switzerland and around the Mediterranean into the Near East.

The long, continual occupancy of western Europe by *Homo sapiens* appears to be corroborated by a series of recent discoveries made in river valley deposits dated as 25,000 years old. The several crania of this type, referred to as River Valley People, are alike in having typical *H. sapiens* features, including high

Figure 19.18 *A tent-village of Cro-Magnon people.* This subspecies of modern man was tall and had a very large cranial capacity. (Courtesy of the artist, Zdenek Burian, of Prague.)

foreheads, prominent chins, supraorbital ridges absent, and orthognathous faces. However, in contrast to Cro-Magnon, who probably exceeded 1.85 m (6 feet) in height, the average height of these people was closer to 1.60 m (5 feet, 2 inches). Deer seem to have played an especially important part in their diet, for many of the artifacts were made of antlers of the several species of deer extant in the region. For reasons that are not apparent, even such heavy-duty tools as axes and adzes were made of this material, rather than of the far more durable stone.

QUESTIONS FOR REVIEW AND THOUGHT

1. List the characteristics of the order Primata. Which seem to be adaptations for an arboreal existence? Which do not apply to mankind? To the prosimians?

2. Characterize the three types of prosimians described here. In what ways do certain New World forms resemble these prosimians? What traits suggest that the New World monkeys are further advanced than the latter?

3. Name the definitive primate characteristics found among the Old World monkeys. Differentiate between the two groups of monkeys that occur in Eurasia and Africa. Which species appears to be the most closely related to the great apes and man? In what ways?

4. Which of the great apes is most adapted for a terrestrial life? Which one is the most completely arboreal? How do the chimpanzee and orangutan differ from one another in habits? Examine figure 19.7 and determine in how many ways the gorilla is closer to man structurally than the chimpanzee. Then find traits, if any, in which the latter more closely resembles man than the gorilla does.

5. Make a list of structural traits that distinguish modern man from the great apes. Which of these could fossilize? Which are sharply defined differences and which are merely comparative?

6. How far back into time is there a clear-cut indication of man's existence? What is surprising about the Miocene fossil finds?

7. Enumerate the fossil types of hominids found in Pliocene deposits. Which most closely resembled modern man?

8. How long does it seem to have taken the hominid line to learn how to work stone into tools? How much longer than that to use fire? To fly? Specifically what technologies have enabled mankind to progress so rapidly during the last several thousand years?

9. Describe the several types of hominids found in Early Pleistocene deposits of Africa. Which are the most primitive in structure?

10. Which of the Mid-Pleistocene forms of Eurasia is the most primitive? What connection might there be between Peking man's being found in a cool temperate region and certain artifacts found associated with those fossil deposits?

11. Compare the Cro-Magnon and Neanderthal hominids structurally and geographically. Which one persisted to the present, if any? If Cro-Magnon is subspecifically distinct from modern man, how do you treat the River Valley People and what are the reasons for doing so?

SUGGESTIONS FOR FURTHER READING

Birdsell, J.B. 1975. *Human evolution.* 2nd edition. Chicago, Rand McNally College Publishing Co., p. 286–339.

Bourne, G.H., and M. Cohen. 1975. *The gentle giants.* New York, G.P. Putnam's Sons.

Coppens, Y., F.C. Howell, G.L. Isaac, and R.E.F. Leakey. 1976. *Earliest man and environments in the Lake Rudolf basin.* Chicago, University of Chicago Press.

Corvinus, G. 1975. Paleolithic remains at the Hadar in the Afar region. *Nature,* 256:468–470.

Erdbrink, D.P.B., C. Meiklejohn and J. Taxoma. 1978. River Valley People: Fossel human remains from river deposits near the Dutch-German border in the Rhine Valley, *Proc. K. Nederland. Akad. Wterns.,* C81:61–76.

Fallon, J.F., and B.K. Simandl. 1978. Evidence of a role of cell death in the disappearance of the embryonic human tail. *Amer. J. Anat.,* 152:111–130.

Hughes, A.R., and P.V. Tobias. 1977. A fossil skull probably of the genus *Homo* from Sterkfontein, Transvaal, *Nature* 265:310–312.

Johanson, D.C., and T.D. White. 1979. A systematic assessment of early African hominids. *Science,* 203:321–330.

King, M.C., and A.C. Wilson. 1975. Evolution at two levels in humans and chimpanzees. *Science,* 188:107–116.

Leakey, R.E.F. 1976. Hominids in Africa. *Amer. Sci.,* 64:174–178.

Leroi-Gourhan, A. 1975. The flowers found with Shanidar IV, a neander burial in Iraq. *Science,* 190:562–564.

McHenry, H.M. 1975. Fossils and the mosaic nature of human evolution. *Science* 190:425–431.

Mounin, G. 1976. Language, communication, chimpanzees. *Curr. Anthropol.,* 17:1–22.

Oxnard, C.E. 1975. The place of the australopithecines in human evolution: Grounds for doubt? *Nature,* 258:389–395.

Tattersall, I., and R.W. Suseman, eds. 1975. *Lemur biology.* New York, Plenum Press.

Vrba, E.S. 1975. Some evidence of chronology and paleoecology of Sterkfontein, Swartkrans, and Kromdraai from the fossil Bovidae. *Nature,* 254:301–304.

Washburn, S.L. 1978. The evolution of man. *Scient. Amer.,* 239(3):194–208.

Glossary

Abiogenesis. Origin of life from nonliving material, such as in the former belief that insects, frogs, and snakes arose from slime or muck.

Aboral. Opposite the mouth.

Acclimatize. To become habituated to an environment.

Adaptation. A structure, function, or habit fitted for a particular environment or activity.

Aestivate. To become inactive during the warm months.

Algology. The study of algae.

Allantois. One of the embryonic membranes of higher vertebrates; formed from the hindgut and primitively serves for respiration and excretion, in the higher mammals forms a major part of the placenta.

Amino acid. An organic acid bearing an ammonia (NH_2-) radical; specifically, those substances which are chemically united to form proteins.

Amnion. The innermost embryonic membrane, filled with watery fluid in which the embryo floats.

Amoebocyte. A cell which moves like an amoeboid, that is, by means of pseudopods; several types of vertebrate white blood cells are amoebocytes.

Amoeboid. An organism which resembles *Amoeba* in moving by means of cytoplasmic projections called pseudopods.

Amphibia. A vertebrate which has a complex life cycle, the eggs being deposited in water, where the larvae live for a while, whereas the adult typically is terrestrial. Examples include frogs, toads, caecilians, and salamanders.

Analogous. The condition of being similar in superficial features or in function but having a separate origin.

Apex. The tip, point, or top of a structure.

Apical. Pertaining to the apex; located at the apex.

Appendage. A movable projecting part of an animal body, having an active function, such as a leg, arm, or fin.

Aquatic. Living in water.

Arboreal. Living in trees.

Asexual. Vegetative reproduction; not involving the union of egg and sperm.

Astral ray. One of a number of microtubular rays surrounding the centriole during nuclear division in metazoans and brown seaweeds.

Asymetrical. Lacking a balanced type of bodily organization; no matter how the body is divided, mirror images are not produced.

Autotrophic. See Holophytic.

Basal body. A small body attached at the inner end of flagellum or flagella, usually between the centriole and nucleus; characteristic of certain complex protozoa and sponges.

Biflagellated. Bearing two flagella.

Bilateral symmetry. Bodily organization in which a plane passing through the long axis from the middle of the underside to the middle of the upper surface divides the body into mirror images, the right and left sides.

Biradial symmetry. A special type of body organization found in the comb-jellies (Ctenophora), which is basically a radial type but is made two-sided by the presence of a *pair* of tentacles, one on each side.

Blastocoel. The cavity usually present during the blastula stage of embryonic development.

Blastopore. The embryonic opening into the primitive gut in the gastrula and later stages of development.

Blastula. The so-called hollow ball stage of the embryo, following the solid, irregular sphere stage, the morula.

Blepharoplast. A body attached to the centriole in certain protozoa and the sponges; identical to basal body.

Body cavity. The cavity *between* the body wall of an animal and its internal organs; a cavity that contains the inner organs.

Bowman's capsule. The functional unit of higher vertebrate kidneys; a funnel-like structure enclosing a knot of capillaries that removes wastes from the blood stream.

Bud. A growth on an animal that produces a new individual or body part; a type of asexual reproduction.

Calcareous. Limy; containing or composed of calcium carbonate ($CaCO_3$).

Caudal. Pertaining to the posterior region.

Centriole. A self-producing body that secretes flagella, cilia, or spindle threads.

Cephalad. Toward the head.

Cephalic. Pertaining to the head.

Chitin. A complex containing amine sugars used in the exoskeleton of invertebrates, especially arthropods and tunicates; it is tough, pliable, and resistant to solvents and bacteria.

Chloroplast. The cell organelle containing chlorophyll that carries out photosynthesis.

Choanocyte. A funnel cell; one of the characteristic cells of the sponges, also found among certain protozoans.

Chromatin. The readily stained material of the nucleus that comprises the chromosomes.

Chromosome. An elongate rodlike body in the nucleus consisting of DNA and proteins in nearly equal proportions; carry the genetic traits of an organism.

Cilium (*cilia*, pl.). A bristlelike process of a cell, typically occuring in large numbers over the surface, frequently arranged in rows; actually a shortened flagellum.

Cirrus (*cirri*, pl.). A slender, often flexible structure or appendage.

Class. The major taxonomic category larger than an order but smaller than a phylum.

Cleavage. Those early stages in the development of the embryo when the zygote has just begun division.

Cloaca. In vertebrates, a tubular passage used in common by the digestive, reproductive, and excretory systems; in invertebrates, the terminal portion of the digestive tract.

Coccus. A spherical cell covered with a firm covering and devoid of any means of locomotion.

Coelom. The body cavity of advanced metazoans that is lined with a peritoneum; derived from mesoderm.

Coelomate. A metazoan that possesses a coelom.

Commensal. A symbiotic species that neither harms nor benefits the species with which it is intimately associated.

Commissure. A large nerve tract that provides intercommunication between major regions of the nervous system.

Convergent evolution. Similarity in form or structure between two unrelated organisms; usually involves separate acquisition of similar body shape or structural parts, as a whale resembling a fish in shape, having a tail, etc.

Cranium. That part of the skull that contains the brain; often used loosely to refer to the entire skull.

Crista (*cristae*, pl.). A double membranous partition traversing the interior of mitochondria.

Cyst. A small bladder, sac, or capsule; an inactive stage of protozoans and invertebrates, in which the organism is covered by a resistant protective coat.

Cytoplasm. That portion of a cell that lies between the plasma membrane and the nucleus (or DNA molecule in bacteria).

Dendroid. Branched, like a tree.

Devonian. A period of the Paleozoic era, which began about 405 million years ago and lasted for 60 million years.

Digenetic. Pertaining to a trematode that belongs to the order Digenea.

Diploblastic. Said of an embryo that develops from only two layers of cells instead of three as in triploblastic forms. The two layers are referred to as the entoderm and ectoderm.

Diploid. The usual condition of the cells of most animal-like forms, in which pairs of comparable chromosomes are present; one member of each pair is contributed by the sperm, the other by the egg; the $2n$ number of chromosomes.

DNA. Deoxyribonucleic acid; the nucleic acid found in chromosomes.

Dorsal. Toward or pertaining to the back or upper surface.

Ecology. The study of the relations of an organism or group of organisms to the environment.

Ectoderm. The outer layer of cells of an embryo.

Ectoparasite. A harmful symbiont that lives on the outside of the host.

Egestion. The process of ejecting food residues from the digestive tract.

Embryo. A young organism during the early stages of its development from the egg cell.

Embryogeny. The processes of development of the embryo.

Embryology. The study of the development of the embryo.

Endoparasite. A harmful symbiont that lives within the body of its host.

Endoskeleton. A supportive framework lying within the body of an organism.

Endosome. A rounded body of chromatin of certain protozoans, related to the nucleolus.

Endothermy. A warm-blooded condition.

Enterocoelomate. The condition in which the coelom is derived from the digestive tract in the embryo.

Eversible. Capable of being turned inside out.

Evolution. The processes by means of which new species and new types of organisms are believed to have come into existence.

Excretion. The discharge of the by-products of metabolism from an organism.

Exoskeleton. A supportive framework on the outside of the body, as in insects.

Family. A taxonomic category composed of one or more related genera; a unit of less importance than an order.

Filamentous. Threadlike.

Fission. The division of an organism into two or more equivalent parts by asexual means.

Flagellum (*flagella*, pl.). A long whiplike appendage of a cell, capable of being moved rapidly and employed in locomotion.

Flame bulb. A simple cellular type of excretory organ in which a single cell bears a tuft of flagella that propels the excreta into the excretory tubule.

Flimmer. Hairlike appendages on a flagellum.

Fluke. A type of parasitic flatworm.

Free-living. Not attached or parasitic; capable of independent living.

Gamete. A general term for a reproductive cell, either sperm or egg.

Ganglion. A body containing a group of nerve cell bodies or short nerves, acting as a center of nervous influence.

Gastrula. That stage of embryonic development following the bastula, containing three layers of cells and usually a primitive gut.

Gemmule. A reproductive body found among freshwater sponges.

Genome. The genetic material collectively of a cell or organism, whether the chromosomes, the DNA molecule as in bacteria and many viruses, or the RNA as in primitive viruses.

Genus. A group of related species or an isolate containing a single species with no close relatives.

Glomerulus. A knot of capillaries contained within the filtering unit (Bowman's capsule) of a vertebrate kidney.

Gonad. The organ that produces gametes; a general term for a gamete-forming organ, whether testis or ovary.

Gynandromorph. An individual that is unusual for the species in having both male and female parts or characteristics.

Habitat. The place or situation usually occupied by a given organism.

Haploid. The halved number of chromosomes formed by meiosis; the number of chromosomes found in normal eggs and sperm before fertilization.

Hemocoel. A modified body cavity used as part of the circulatory system, particularly characteristic of arthropods.

Hermaphroditic. The condition of containing both male and female reproductive systems, normal for the species, as in snails; contrasts with gynandromorph which is applied to abnormal individuals.

Holophytic. Having plantlike nutrition, that is, carrying out photosynthesis, as in *Euglena* and other protozoans.

Holozoic. Having animal-like nutritional habits, taking in particles of foodstuffs, whole organisms, and the like.

Homologous. Said of body parts which have had common ancestry.

Homoplastic. A term applied to two or more structures of similar appearance which have been acquired independently of one another.

Host. The species or organism that is parasitized.

Ingestion. The process of taking food into the digestive system.

Insemination. The process of introducing sperm into the female genital system.

Interzonal lines. Fibers which appear during nuclear division and extend between the daughter chromosomes after early anaphase.

Invertebrate. Any animal that lacks a vertebral column; includes protozoans, sponges, and all metazoans through the lancelets.

Juvenile. A young form which differs little from the adult.

Kala-azar. A usually fatal disease caused by the protozoan *Leishmannia donovani,* common in India and other tropical parts of Asia; characterized by enlargement of the spleen, hemorrhage, and emaciation.

Kingdom. The largest category in schemes of classification.

Lamella. A platelike layer, often thin or membranous.

Larva. An early active developmental stage that is strikingly different from the adult.

Leucocyte. A white (colorless) blood cell.

Lipase. An enzyme that breaks down fats and other lipids.

Lipids. Substances related to the fats.

Lumen. The cavity of a tubular organ, such as in the intestine, glands, ducts, and blood vessels.

Macronucleus. The larger type of nucleus in such taxa as the Ciliophora in which two size classes of nuclei are present; contrasts to micronucleus.

Medusoid. The jellyfishlike stage or body type in the cnidarians.

Meiosis. A type of nuclear division which results in the chromosome number being halved.

Mesenchyme. A loose sort of cellular aggregate, the cells of which are capable of producing specialized varieties and of developing into particular tissues or organs.

Mesoderm. The middle layer of cells in embryos, lying between the ectoderm and entoderm.

Mesoglea. The gelatinous layer between cell layers in cnidarians and ctenophores.

Mesonephros. A type of vertebrate kidney that filters both the blood and the coelomic fluid; characteristic of adult fish and amphibians.

Metamere. One of a series of repeated structural units of the body, as in the segments of earthworms.

Metamorphosis. The process of undergoing a marked change during development from a larval stage into the adult.

Metanephros. The type of vertebrate kidney that filters blood only; found in young and adult reptiles, birds, and mammals.

Micronucleus. The smaller type of nucleus in those organisms, which, like *Paramecium*, possess two size classes of nuclei; contrasts to macronucleus.

Mitochondrion (*mitochondria,* pl.). The cell part (organelle) located in the cytoplasm which carries out cell respiration.

Mitosis. Nuclear division in which the resulting (daughter) nuclei are identical in content to the original (mother) nucleus.

Monera. A name for a kingdom or other large taxon erected for those organisms which, like the bacteria, lack chromosomes and true nucleus.

Monoecious. Having both the male and female reproductive organs present in the same individual; equivalent to hermaphroditic.

Morphology. The study of the structure of an organism.

Mutualist. Any symbiont that benefits the species with which it is intimately associated as well as itself.

Mychota. A name sometimes employed for those organisms which lack a true nucleus and chromosomes; equivalent to Monera.

Nephridium (*nephridia,* pl.). A tubular excretory organ found in a number of invertebrate types.

Nitrogenous. Nitrogen-containing.

Nuclease. An enzyme which acts on nucleic acid.

Nucleic acid. A combination of many nucleotides joined in long strands.

Nucleotide. An organic substance consisting of a nitrogenous base, a pentose (5-carboned) sugar residue, and a phosphate radical.

Order. A major systematic category consisting of one or more families; larger than family but smaller than class.

Ordovician. The second period of the Paleozoic era of geologic history, following the Cambrian; began 500 million years ago and ended 75 million years later.

Organ. A part of an animal composed of several types of tissue that performs a specific function.

Organelle. A specialized structure within a cell.

Organism. Any living thing.

Orthognathous. Lacking a muzzle; having the lower part of the face aligned in a vertical plane with the forehead, as in modern man.

Paleontology. The study of fossil remains, typically of animal origins.

Paleozoic. The first great era of geologic history in which metazoan fossils are preserved; began with the Cambrian period about 600 million years ago and ended with the Permian nearly 400 million years later.

Palmella. A multinucleated cell with amoeboid characteristics.

Parallel evolution. Equivalent to convergent evolution. (*See also* Convergent evolution).

Parameter. A variable characteristic of the environment, such as temperature, light, etc.; any variable.

Paramylum (paramylon). A peculiar carbohydrate resembling starch.

Parasite. A symbiont that harms its host or lives at the latter's expense.

Parthenogenesis. Development of a new individual from an unfertilized egg, as in rotifers, plant lice, etc.

Pathogenic. Producing a disease.

Pellicle. A flexible coat on the cell surface, as in *Paramecium*.

Peritoneum. The thin membranous coat that lines a coelom, derived from mesoderm.

Phototrophic. Living by means of photosynthesis; equivalent to holophytic.

Phototropic. A response of an organism to light.

Phylum. A systematic category made up of one or more classes.

Pigment. Coloring matter.

Plankton. The minute organisms floating in water.

Planula. A flattened ciliated larva, devoid of a digestive cavity.

Plasma membrane. The membrane covering a cell; the cell membrane.

Plasmodium. A multinucleated amoeboid.

Polypoid. A stage or body type resembling *Hydra*.

Prognathous. Having a muzzle; that is, the lower part of the face in profile projects forward of the forehead.

Pronephros. A primitive type of kidney found among embryonic vertebrates that filters only the coelomic fluid; occurs also in larval and juvenile cyclostomes.

Protease. An enzyme that acts on proteins.

Protista (*Protoctista*). A taxon erected for those organisms that are unicellular.

Protobiont. A primitive or ancestral form of organism, which may have been acellular or lacked many of the metabolic processes found in the living things of today.

Protozoa. An active or holozoic unicellular organism.

Pseudocoel. A type of body cavity that is neither lined with peritoneum nor serves as a part of the circulatory system; a derivative of the blastocoel.

Pseudopod. A fleshy projection of a cell, usually temporary but permament in certain rhizopod amoeboids.

Radial symmetry. A type of body organization which is built on a circle. Essentially, radially symmetrical animals are cylindrical, discoidal, conical, or of other shapes involving a circle; sometimes the body may consist of similar parts arranged around a central axis, as in a starfish.

Respiration. The processes of breaking down carbohydrates in the presence of oxygen; breathing or ventilation.

RNA. Ribonucleic acid; a nucleic acid in which the pentose sugar is ribose.

Saprophyte. A plantlike organism, like the fungi, which absorbs organic foodstuffs from the environment.

Saprozoic. Said of an animal-like organism that absorbs dissolved organic matter from its surroundings.

Schizocoelomate. Having the coelom formed from a split in the mesodermal pockets during growth of the embryo.

Segment. One of a series of similar parts that comprise an appendage or body. *See also* Somite.

Sessile. Attached to the substrate, whether permanently or temporarily.

Silurian. A geologic period of the Paleozoic era, following the Ordovician. It lasted about 20 million years, beginning approximately 425 million years ago.

Solitary. Living alone, that is, not forming part of a colony.

Solenocyte. A cellular type of excretory organ, consisting of a cell having a single flagellum which pumps excreta into a fine tubule.

Somatic. Pertaining to the body; particularly applied to those cells or tissues which develop into the body and its parts, in contrast to the germ cells, which give rise to the gametes.

Somite. One of a series of similar body segments; a term used especially in embryology. Equivalent to metamere.

Species. One major variety of life, such as cat, lion, tiger, ocelot, or leopard, all of which examples are different species in the cat family.

Spicule. A hard skeletal element found in sponges.

Spindle fibers. Microtubular structures that extend between the chromosomes and the centrioles during nuclear division.

Substrate. The substance or surface on which an organism lives.

Symbiosis. An intimate association between two different species, such as parasite and host, commensals, and mutualists; occasionally used incorrectly as equivalent to mutualism.

Symmetry. A balanced plan of bodily organization.

Syncytium. A multinucleated living mass of protoplasm; a multinucleated cell, equivalent to plasmodium.

System. A group of organs which work together to perform one major bodily function, such as digestive system, reproductive system, etc.

Systematist. A person engaged in classifying, naming, and arranging species in an orderly and natural manner.

Taxon. Any particular systematic category which has received a name.

Theca. A firm coat covering an organism.

Tissue. A group of similar cells which are organized to work together in a certain capacity.

Tripartite. Consisting of three parts, lobes, etc.

Triploblastic. Derived from three different embryonic layers.

Trochophore. A type of larva, more or less pear-shaped or biconical, bearing a band (trochus) of cilia about its middle.

Unicellular. Consisting of a single cell; sometimes also applied to organisms which consist of a series of a single type of cell repeated many times.

Vacuole. A cavity or vesicle within a cell.

Vegetative. Reproducing by asexual means.

Veliger. A type of larva found among such mollusks as gastropods and pelecypods; it has a shell over its dorsal region and a swimming membrane anteriorly known as a velum.

Vertebrate. A chordate with a vertebral column.

Vesicle. A minute bladderlike container within a cell.

Xanthophyll. A type of yellowish pigment.

Zygote. A fertilized egg, resulting from union of a sperm and an egg.

Index

0 8 1 9